ALSO BY JOE BUFF, his **MILITARY W**
AWARD-WINNING and **MILITARY B**
of tactical nuclear war at sea!

The **Captain Jeffrey Fuller / USS Challenger** futuristic submarine war saga:

Deep Sound Channel
Thunder in the Deep
Crush Depth
Tidal Rip
Straits of Power
Seas of Crisis

All are available as E-BOOKS! Download the series today!

⁂

Praise for the Futuristic Submarine Novels of Joe Buff:

"A superb high-water mark in naval fiction!"
—MICHAEL DIMERCURIO, bestselling submarine novelist

"Superbly researched and well-written, Joe Buff's novels are the creme de la creme of submarine thrillers."
—STEPHEN COONTS, bestselling technothriller author

"Joe Buff takes the reader through a labyrinth of action and high adventure. A rare thriller, highly entertaining."
—CLIVE CUSSLER, bestselling maritime/undersea adventure writer

"If you want a hair-raising trip to the bottom of the ocean, Joe Buff's the guy to take you there."
—PATRICK ROBINSON, bestselling submarine novelist.

The Submarine Review **Had This to Say About Joe Buff's Writings:**

"Joe Buff gets it. *He understands the unique culture and values of the Submarine Force and the nuances of what it means to be a submariner.... Buff underscores the importance and effectiveness of today's U.S. Submarine Force in any possible global conflict, and highlights the technical excellence, outstanding training, bravery and teamwork of the crews that man these tremendous ships.... Buff's crisp comprehension of sonar science, of global oceanography, meteorology, and geography, and of 20th century history plus 21st century maritime theory provides an additional vivid background to the tapestry of his [novels and his] prolific non-fiction undersea warfare analysis and commentary!"*
—ROB WEBER, Commander, USN, in the quarterly professional journal *THE SUBMARINE REVIEW*, April 2007

Advance Praise by Professional Experts for *On 21st-Century Nuclear Deterrence*

"Joe Buff explains the complexities of nuclear deterrent strategy, past, present, and future, in a manner easily understandable by the interested lay person. He brings a refreshingly new, pragmatic viewpoint to an area of discussion that has long been delegated to the esoteric world of think tanks and great-nation statecraft. This work is worth reading, giving emphasis to the increased importance of the delicate interplay of nuclear deterrence in a multi-polar 21st century."

—GEORGE WALLACE, Commander, USN (Ret.), former CO of the LA-class nuclear submarine USS HOUSTON, & author of *OPERATION GOLDEN DAWN* & other submarine thrillers—including *FIRING POINT*, made into the major motion picture *HUNTER-KILLER*

"Conclusions drawn from outdated assumptions shouldn't be accepted as facts. America's decades-old Cold War assumptions about nuclear deterrence, not frequently reviewed, eventually hardened into dogma whose conclusions became somewhat questionable. Joe Buff has used a penetrating intellect and done some superb research to expose such outdated assumptions and then suggest credible, insightful updates to national nuclear posture and policy. Not everyone will agree with all Buff's new set of compelling recommendations—but to be credible themselves, dissenters will need to do some serious thinking and rethinking of their own."

—JAMES PATTON, JR., Captain, USN (Ret.), former CO of the Sturgeon-class nuclear submarine USS PARGO, & a frequent contributor to the US Naval Institute *PROCEEDINGS* and to the Naval Submarine League's *THE SUBMARINE REVIEW*. Captain Patton was the technical consultant to the making of Tom Clancy's *THE HUNT FOR RED OCTOBER* into a major motion picture

ON 21ST CENTURY NUCLEAR DETERRENCE:
RECOMMENDATIONS FOR AMERICA'S "NUCLEAR POSTURE AFTER NEXT"
VOLUME I

Best wishes,
Joe Buff

On 21st Century Nuclear Deterrence

Recommendations for America's "Nuclear Posture After Next"

VOLUME I

JOE BUFF, MS, FSA

Joe Buff, Inc.
"An Independent Defense Think Tank of One"
est. 1997

ISBN: 978-1-7363910-0-6

Published by Joe Buff, Inc.
readermail@joebuff.com

Cover art is a U.S. Navy image in the public domain

Cover and Interior page design and layout
by Stephen Tiano, Book Designer of Riverhead, NY
stiano@optonline.net

Indexing by Stacks Editing

Printed in the United States of America

Dedicated to sustaining long-term success of America's strong, diversified nuclear deterrence Triad as a reliable global preventive of nuclear blackmail, nuclear terrorism, and nuclear war

CONTENTS

FOREWORD

by Peter Huessy

Nuclear deterrence and nuclear modernization—the strategy of having the forces needed to stop bad guys from using nuclear weapons against the U.S., and the policy to keep such forces up to snuff–were central to the mission of the United States and its allies for the nearly half century of the Cold War and now the three decades of what is termed an era of great power competition. Joe Buff is a prolific writer on these subjects. His analysis is a welcome and much needed addition to the body of commentary on nuclear matters, including material produced by professional academics, the entertainment community, and U.S. government officials, both military and civilian. Like many political subjects, there is often a narrative that gets established from which conventional wisdom does not vary. In the nuclear business this involves the constant repetition that America's nuclear deterrent policy is outdated and dangerous; that its modernization efforts are vastly too expensive; and that the current program of record being proposed annually by the past two administrations and considered by Congress is causing an arms race and unnecessary tensions with our adversaries.

Joe Buff's book is a welcome antidote to these false narratives. Though lengthy, Buff takes the time to unwind the false narratives and then spends the time laying out the correct facts of the case. The need for clarity on nuclear matters is critical today. The entertainment industry keeps producing scare stories about nuclear conflict being imminent, because in a crisis it is assumed there is a high chance of the reckless and accidental launch of American land-based missiles triggered by a mistaken computer warning of a Russian missile attack. One episode of the NBC television drama *Madame Secretary* was devoted to this fairy tale, as was the documentary titled *The Bomb* that was shown repeatedly at the National Academy of Sciences this past year that portrayed endless nuclear explosions and a distorted commentary about the dangers of nuclear war, all aimed at portraying America's nuclear modernization efforts as unnecessary, dangerous, and too expensive. The dominant media in the United States also reflects the entertainment culture, as any nuclear modernization effort by the United States is immediately described as "leading to an arms race," while China and Russia and their nuclear modernization efforts–which are going forward at full throttle–receive a pass. The academic commentary is just as bad, as it echoes and reinforces the false narrative of the media and entertainment industry, with a push for eliminating all nuclear weapons ("Global Zero") or declaring U.S. policy should be "no first use" of nuclear weapons, or even unilaterally eliminating vast swaths of our own nuclear deterrent in the assumed faith that our enemies will magically reciprocate and get rid of their weapons too!

As Buff points out, the U.S. stopped building nuclear missiles, planes, and submarines in the 1990s, and it will be almost forty years from that time to the point where the U.S. will start putting into the field our first new and replacement bomber (2029), submarine (2032), or land-based missile (2030). We are doing so, as Buff makes clear, because our submarine hulls at 42 years old cannot continue to be at sea; our land-based missiles are now 50 years old, requiring costly maintenance, and will not meet future mission requirements; while all our current bombers will not in the future be able to penetrate enemy airspace and overcome sophisticated air defenses.

Furthermore, of considerable importance are three additional factors. Russia has adopted a policy of "escalate to win" or threatening the use of nuclear weapons early in a conflict. The unilateral disarmers in the U.S. take issue with such a description, but read carefully, the Russians consider being able to sustain aggression–such as invading the Baltics, not unlike their invasions of Ukraine, Moldova and Georgia–as critical to their survival as a nation. The idea that they would be the first to use nuclear weapons, but only after the U.S. was marching on Moscow, is patently absurd. Added to this Russian strategy is a massive, unprecedented modernization of Russia's nuclear forces, including strategic and theater systems, now somewhere between 85 to 100 percent complete, and not to be finished sometime in in the next decade as alleged by a recent arms control report. Second, with respect to China, the disarmament trifecta of the entertainment, academic, and political community continue to downplay the buildup of Chinese nuclear forces and the Chinese role in the proliferation of such weapons technology to Pakistan, North Korea, Iraq, Libya, and Iran.

Third, and critically important, is the additional fairy tale that the U.S. is opposed to or uninterested in arms control. Here Buff does a highly credible job explaining the limits of arms control, but more importantly how it has been the United States that has led the successful effort to reduce Soviet and now Russian nuclear weapons by multiple thousands, and that it has been Russia that walked away from the 1987 INF treaty eliminating thousands of SS-20 Soviet nuclear-armed missiles. It has been Russia that has built multiple new long-range nuclear missiles that it has also declared are not covered by existing arms control treaties such as the 2010 New START agreement.

Joe Buff deals with all of these issues in great detail. His material is a must read, as it is critically important that we undo the false narratives that dominate our nuclear discourse and stick to, as the famous TV show said, "Just the facts, ma'am."

* * *

PETER HUESSY is President and Founder (1981) of defense consulting firm GeoStrategic Analysis of Potomac, Maryland. He is also an Instructor at the United States Naval Academy, on U.S. Nuclear Deterrent Policy and Strategy. Over the years, Mr. Huessy has hosted more than one thousand seminars on Capitol Hill, about important aspects of national defense and strategic deterrence.

CHAPTER 1

INTRODUCTION
Deterrence is for Keeping Peace, Not Making War

Executive Summary: No "End of History"

Nuclear weapons are not a very welcome topic in most polite society. Yet it is only America's nuclear deterrence Triad—the highly-trained crews and high-tech weapons credibly backing the promise that we will retaliate for a nuclear attack with a proportionate nuclear counter-strike—which stands in the way of any heinous nuking by some foreign superpower dictator, rogue state madman, or black-hearted terrorist. Our nuclear arsenal also serves as very effective "bully repellent" against nuclear blackmail, intimidation, or coercion moves by today's various, aggressive and nuclear-armed geopolitical adversaries of freedom, large and small. And ever since the dawn of the Atomic Age in 1945, at "no extra charge," United States Strategic Command's diversified, dispersed, survivable nuclear forces have played a major role in preventing more big conventional wars like those 20th-century murderous slugfests—World War I and World War II.

Yet for a variety of reasons, having to do with adversary malign disinformation, domestic political opportunism, and over-optimistic American triumphalism, it became an article of faith to many good folks in the U.S. that the end of the Cold War in 1991 meant the demise of the relevance of nukes. The End of History—no more conflicts between different nations with different governmental, economic, and ideological systems—was proclaimed and widely celebrated; the Peace Dividend was savored by all lovers of freedom. A lot of political and financial capital was invested in these appealing (but self-deceptive) beliefs by various American pop-culture influencers.

Some of the peacemaking achievements were very real. The senseless, dangerous nuclear arms race of the 1970s and '80s, which had led to the U.S. and USSR together owning *some 70,000 strategic and tactical nuclear warheads*, was successfully reversed. The vast majority of those weapons were eventually dismantled. With much American financial aid and technical assistance, the many "loose nukes" kicking around the Former Soviet Union were secured under Moscow's control. But then this pragmatic, cost-cutting *nuke-count rightsizing drive* by both sides gained distorted momentum in America. It took on a life of its own, as a wish by some for the U.S. to *denuclearize completely*—a unilateral "race to the bottom."

Unfortunately, this almost manic euphoria did not last long: In 2000, former KGB operative Vladimir Putin came to power as President of Russia. He restarted a brutal war of oppression in Chechnya, went on to invade several newly independent countries in Russia's "Near Abroad," raised Hell in the Middle East (especially in Syria and Libya), and has been trying to seduce Turkey away from NATO. Mr. Putin has often made references in a threatening way to Russia's substantial, rapidly modernizing nuclear arsenal.

Meanwhile, China under President Xi Jinping has continued pursuing its aggressive geopolitical rise and technological advancement, which have proven to be expansionist and militarizing, not peaceful and benign as Beijing promised. China moved with impressive speed to field mobile ICBM launchers, nuclear-armed nuclear submarines, and modern strategic stealth bombers: the components of a robust, survivable deterrent-and-coercion force deployed on land, at sea, and in the air—a full-blown Chinese Nuclear Triad. Recently, China has threatened to greatly expand its nuclear arsenal, from some three hundred or so warheads ("minimum deterrence") currently, to instead match and rival the hydrogen-bomb inventories of Russia and America: 1,550 deployed strategic warheads each, with about the same number stockpiled as backup, under the almost-expired (as of year-end 2020) New START Treaty. If China actually does this, it would seriously disrupt today's hard-won, parity-based "strategic stability" between the other two superpowers. Worse, China refuses to even discuss participating in any nuclear arms-control negotiations with either the U.S. or the UN, while Beijing flirts openly with Russia about military cooperation.

At the same time, that American nuclear deterrence which had once so effectively—side-by-side with NATO and our other Allies—defended the Free World against an Evil Empire lurking behind the

Iron and Bamboo Curtains, instead suffered decades-long decline and neglect. This *diminishment* adversely impacted many aspects of our own strategic Triad infrastructure: It obsolesced the hardware needed for success of the vital defense-via-deterrence national mission; it limited the career tracks and hurt morale of the elite crews; it eroded the defense-contractor industrial base (businesses, factories, laboratories, highly skilled employees) needed to sustain the called-for weapon systems.

This trend of neglect also hurt the further advancement and updating of that *theoretical strategic-security framework* which had once been so vigorously studied among Cold War academics, think tankers, scientists and engineers, statesmen and stateswomen, and military personnel. As one Commanding Officer ("CO") of U.S. Strategic Command, Admiral Richard W. Mies, put it in writing almost ten years ago now (*Undersea Warfare*, Spring 2012), "We have raised a whole generation of war-fighters within DOD who have received virtually no professional education in the theories of deterrence, assurance, and dissuasion."

Only recently has this unfortunate trend, toward impairing and impeding these different dimensions of America's nuclear-deterrence physical infrastructure and intellectual capital, been reversed. That *badly-needed* reversal, as discussed in this book, is by no means today assured to continue—but *it must do so*, with that wise balance between *toughness* and *restraint* needed to keep the nuclear peace, and to see that American democracy prevails in this new era we all now live in, of Great Power Competition—of what really and truly amounts to a *Cold War II*.

Personal Journey of Risk-Mitigation and National-Defense Research and Writing

Why did I write this book? It is meant to serve three purposes: (1) as a non-technical, up to date guide to nuclear deterrence for *general readers* interested in and concerned about preserving nuclear peace in a nuclear-armed world, (2) as a current research report and relevant reference work for *professionals* involved in implementing national defense and nuclear deterrence, and (3) as a practical textbook for college, graduate school, and military *courses and seminars* on modern nuclear strategy. This book is also meant to inform—and hopefully to *reassure*—anyone who seeks a *comprehensive but readable way* to assess for themselves what 21st-century nuclear deterrence, counter-proliferation, and counterterrorism are really all about—a *way through the fog* of overly shrill admonitions by extreme-left and extreme-right propagandists alike. I hope this will help you be able to *sleep a bit better at night*, even as nuclear weapons—since the end of Cold War I—have been gradually spreading to more and more countries, while various sub-state/trans-state armed groups also keep trying to get some of them.

This book is the culmination of twenty-plus years of heavy reading, deep analysis, and critical (sometimes even *contrarian*) thought, exercised while writing six bestselling novels about future tactical nuclear war at sea, plus dozens of non-fiction articles, essays, and op-eds—and many hundreds of blog posts on Military.com, Facebook, and LinkedIn—about national defense. Along the way, the lateral-thinking ideas I presented were peer reviewed and critiqued by several practicing nuclear submarine and nuclear deterrence experts, whom I have come to know personally and whom I greatly respect. (Some of whom—those who did not request anonymity—I name and thank in the Acknowledgments section.) And over the years, my writings won a naval-fiction book award from the Military Writers Society of America, and five non-fiction annual literary awards from the Naval Submarine League.

Then, building on that effort, and drawing on my previous twenty-year career as an actuary—doing groundbreaking "quant" research in the financial services industry, on mathematical modeling and process enhancement for risk mitigation —I carried out, at a fundamental level, some rather thoroughgoing study of a very basic but complicated subject: Given that nuclear weapons have existed in human hands for a whole lifetime (so far), without being used in anger *even once* since Hiroshima and Nagasaki, while vocal efforts to ban all nuclear weapons worldwide have *really been getting nowhere* for just as long, then how can freedom-loving, peace-loving, forward-looking nations like America and our Allies around the world most effectively *zero-out* the odds that a nuclear war could in the future be started by some belligerent dictatorship large or small, by some fanatical terrorist group—or even just by accident?

(My work as an actuarial student, and then as a fully-qualified Fellow of the Society of Actuaries since 1980, also taught me a lot about applied organizational psychology; about the roles—good and bad—that tradition and history can play in any large and ongoing undertaking; and about the insidious dangers of groupthink, self-deception, and excessive political backbiting. This valuable side-education continued apace, and still does today, as I switched in 1997 to studying international affairs full time, while networking avidly with serving and retired military people from the U.S. and elsewhere.)

For the past six-plus years I repeatedly asked myself a challenging and fascinating question: How do sound, updated 21st-century policies, postures, and strategies to prevent any nuclear conflicts (ranging from a single low-yield A-bomb up to and including wholesale H-bomb Armageddon) either resemble, or differ from, the corresponding answers that were talked about extensively and implemented successfully back in the Cold War? The geopolitical lineup of adversary entities, including great powers, regional nuclear powers, nuclear wannabes, rogue states, and terrorist groups, has evolved considerably (and expanded alarmingly) in the generation since the Berlin Wall fell. So has the gamut of technologies, either deployed in the field or emerging in laboratories, that different players around the world can use to *deliver* nuclear attacks–or *instead* can use to *deter* such attacks to begin with, or *gain advance warning* of them, *defend* against them to a useful degree if necessary, and *mitigate* their horrific effects in the last resort.

The Value of Logical Rigor in the Nuclear Deterrence Policy and Funding Debate

I sought throughout this work to try to cast aside some of the primitive, even regressive psychological emotionalism that clearly has been playing a role in obscuring certain *essential truths* about America's ongoing, long-term need for strong, flexible, diversified and adaptable nuclear deterrence weaponry and supporting/enabling infrastructure. I wanted to help penetrate, with added clarity, that *obfuscating fog of adversarial argumentation* that seems to permeate the modern American political process, and which so wrongly prioritizes petty, dumbed-down instant gratification—and "winner take all" zero-sum gamesmanship—over inclusive, nuanced, collaborative problem solving.

With my training and professional experience as a pure and applied mathematician (Master of Science degree in algebraic topology from MIT, then self-study to pass the many tough exams to earn a Fellow of the Society of Actuaries), I sought to introduce a greater extent of what I thought of as "logical rigor." Rigorous reasoning and deduction—as opposed to disingenuous, intentionally manipulative rhetoric—must meet certain demanding criteria: It anticipates and successfully defends against counter-arguments; it embraces and is based on objective reality; and it does not ignore significant gaps, loopholes, and inherent contradictions within itself.

But beware. Only in pure mathematics is utter perfection genuinely attainable. In the sometimes controversy-laden, often bitterly competitive arena of statecraft and national defense, many obscuring factors come into play. Yet throughout this fray of ideas and personalities, "the perfect must not be the enemy of the good." So please ask yourself as you read on, Are the assembled perspectives and their justifications that I offer below, as the theoretical basis of a sound American doctrinal foundation for deflecting 21st century nuclear blackmail and preventing nuclear war, *good enough*? Are the lists of open questions, calling for more research and more policy debate in the U.S. and around the world, *thorough and results-oriented enough*? I urge readers to judge for themselves whether the material that follows below holds up to their own objective scrutiny.

As just one example, an interrelated quintuplet of specific Best Perspectives for *suggested improvements to American nuclear deterrence's multi-year planning/budgeting paradigms*—derived from lessons I learned in my long career working on varied *actuarial risk-management* projects—are given below in Appendix 1. Relying on such *pragmatic long-view* Best Perspectives in 1991+ might have (1) avoided some of the *bloody roller-coaster* seen in often-violent international affairs during the past generation's so-called "Peace Dividend," and (2) debunked a *persisting conundrum* over whether preventing a localized nuclear terrorist strike or an isolated nuclear weapon accident is more vital than preventing a general nuclear war. Such reliance on Best Perspectives, with its *stabilizing and clarifying policy discipline* over time, might have also *beneficially evened out* America's very necessary (and in fact very affordable) ongoing funding of our Nuclear Deterrence Triad's renewal and sustenance. This is now *an utterly urgent matter*, exactly *because* of the recent past's overly short-term thinking, overly prideful over-optimism, paranoia re the "wrong dangers," and resulting fiscal procrastination and policy neglect—a constant theme of this book.

Three Axioms at the Core of Effective Nuclear Deterrence Posture

As a disciplined system of logical inferences that is consistent and complete within itself, a good theory of effective 21st century nuclear deterrence, supporting strategic stability between *near-peer competing adversaries* and between *superpowers and rogue states*, can be built up from three "axioms." An *axiom* is a fundamental proposition so obviously true that it does not itself require proof by deduction, from other more-basic axioms and/or from provable-and-proven *theorems*.

These three axioms are: *First*, thousands of unspeakably destructive nuclear weapons do exist in the hands of a number of sovereign countries. *Second*, attempts to totally ban them worldwide will not be successful in the foreseeable future, due to a demonstrated *lack of willingness* to do so by many entities, and/or by a demonstrated *propensity to cheat* on nuclear arms-control treaties—or to *refuse to participate* altogether—by some entities. *Third*, because nukes can be miniaturized, deployed and hidden anywhere within any space-time domain that an adversary is able to access, and can then be dropped, flown, floated, rocketed, shipped, driven, orbited, man-carried, parachuted, or otherwise smuggled into any country on Earth—no matter how diligent and advanced that country's defenses—it is simply *not possible* to interdict with absolute certainty, and at a safe distance from one's Homeland or one's overseas bases or Allies, any concerted nuclear attack by a determined-enough, patient-enough adversary.

As a direct consequence of these axioms, as has already been determined by objective published research by many deep thinkers over the past seven-plus decades (see, for instance, the Bibliography section, below), effective prevention of nukings requires *"survivable deterrence."* Survivable deterrence can be defined as the credible threat, communicated clearly and unmistakably in advance so that it works on the decisions and actions of adversaries, (1) that any nuclear attack by them will be replied to with a retaliatory attack which, at the option of America's commander-in-chief, will use nuclear weapons to inflict upon the attacker damage that is in-kind, massive, and far exceeds any gain the attacker might possibly hope to obtain by their original nuclear attack upon American vital interests, and (2) that said retaliation can with certainty be delivered upon said adversary even *after* America might first suffer the severe damage inflicted by any nuclear surprise attack against us.

America and the USSR both achieved this status of survivable nuclear deterrence during the Cold War, via their dispersed fleets of increasingly stealthy, nuclear powered, nuclear armed ballistic missile submarines (SSBNs), supported, protected, supplemented, and backed up by geographically dispersed and technically diversified fleets of (1) ground-based intercontinental ballistic missiles (ICBMs), (2) dual-capable aircraft (DCAs) ranging from tactical fighter-bombers to long-range, heavy-lift strategic bombers, (3) air- and surface-ship- and submarine-launched cruise missiles (ALCMs and SLCMs) and (4) protective, escorting fast-attack submarines (SSNs).

Neglected Deterrence Assets, Forgotten Defense Imperatives

But the passage of time has meant that America's deterrence hardware, mostly built during the First Cold War, is fast wearing out, having served far beyond originally intended equipment-and-weaponry shelf lives. It is all now in desperate need of being replaced by up-to-date systems that are much more *safe, secure, reliable, effective*—and *cost much less* to maintain.

Worse, during this era of deterrence-budget parsimony and encroaching science-denial in the West, America's superpower adversaries Russia and China–our bitter rivals now in what some writers including myself call *Cold War II*–have not stinted on investing in their own nuclear weaponry and modernizing its supporting infrastructure. Moscow and Beijing have both been introducing new and numerous types of low-yield and high-yield warheads, mounted on various very-interception-resistant, stealthy delivery vehicles. They have both been aggressively pursuing next-generation military applications all across the vast new frontiers of artificial intelligence and machine-learning, quantum computing, maneuverable hypersonic platforms, and outer-space capabilities.

The short answer is for America and our allies to do what we've done since the start of the (First) Cold War around 1950, which in fact *all* the leading victorious powers of World War II—Russia and then the UK, France, and China—have *also* done once they were able to in the 1950s and 1960s. That is, deploy and sustain dispersed, diversified arsenals of nuclear weapons, safe and secure (*"survivable"*) against any enemy surprise attack, so that we each have in place *mutual nuclear deterrence*. But for this pragmatic condition of *strategic stability* to hold up, to America's benefit and the world's, the warheads in our own arsenal must be available in sufficient numbers so that, even after riding out the tremendous damage of any enemy surprise first strikes, the remaining assets can *with certainty* inflict (at our option, if necessary) enough retaliation on the adversary to not merely damage them as fitting punishment, but to in the extreme case even *threaten their regime's entire existence*. Only in this way can a necessarily strong U.S. nuclear deterrence Triad threaten an aggressor government with its own guaranteed demise, were it ever to be tempted to start a nuclear war—whether for selfish gain, or for misguided preemptive defense, or for any other real, imagined, or purported reason(s) or rationalization(s).

Nuclear deterrence as the foundation of America's defense policy has been a politically controversial topic since its inception in the late 1940s. In fact, even while WWII was still being fought, some of the Manhattan Project's brilliant weapon scientists feared the Hellish destructive power of the atomic bomb so much that they wished the very idea of it would be suppressed forever. But the genie could not be put back in the bottle. Instead, weapons experts resorted to nuclear deterrence: the threat, issued loudly and clearly in advance, of massive retaliation in case an enemy was ever the first to dare make war using nukes.

This fear of what nuclear weapons can do, even if just tested too often let alone ever used in anger in combat, is natural. It is a *vital human survival instinct*. Put starkly, even harshly, it is *exactly this fear* that is the source of the effectiveness of nuclear deterrence.

It is also vital for American voters to understand, now that nukes do exist aplenty around the world in the hands of both democracies and tyrannies, that they do not have to be detonated at all in order to be productively "used" *for beneficial peacekeeping purposes and good humanitarian effects*. They serve a quintuplet of needs that are *profoundly vital* on Planet Earth's always adversarial, often fragmented and brutal, high-tech geopolitical stage: (1) as a reliable deterrent against *nuclear war*, (2) as a dissuader to further *nuclear proliferation*, via reassuring non-nuclear allies, (3) as a dependable deterrent against another murderous, *big conventional world war* between great powers, (4) as a standing capability, to successfully defuse those coercive acts of intimidation known as *"nuclear blackmail,"* and (5) as a retaliatory option to deter against attacks by those *other weapons of mass destruction (WMDs)*, such as chemical and biological weapons, that America has foresworn but which some adversaries insidiously retain in their arsenals and/or which others *(including terrorist groups)* seek to obtain.

Anti-Triad "Info Wars"

Over the years and especially today, America's nuclear deterrence Triad arsenal, its funding and its vitality, have come under a verbal attack—*a war of words*—from two sources. One is *domestic and (mostly) sincere*, while one is *foreign and (mostly) disingenuous*.

The domestic source, which can be thought of collectively as the World-Denuclearization Movement, needs to be respected and valued. It should be embraced and worked with in those challenging areas where all rational human beings ought to agree: nuclear counter-terrorism, nuclear counter-proliferation, and nuclear arms control (prevention of senseless arms races). This Movement's goals are to preserve human life and human civilization, which are *admirable and vitally necessary*.

The foreign source, the amorphous body of malign-influence campaigners among various enemies of freedom, needs to be resisted to the utmost. It should be seen for what it is, a relentless troll-farm of nefarious disinformation with unquestionably hostile intent, and it must be debunked just as relentlessly. This faction's goals are to make Americans *fear our own deterrent Triad more than we fear foreign anti-democratic onslaught*, thus paralyzing us through divisiveness *even as adversaries cynically build up and modernize their own nuclear forces.*

This book is meant, in a small way, to help America and our allies sort out and defend our own true best interests, our genuine vital interests, in the face of this two-sided emotional assault from inside and outside our borders.

Value of "Thought Experiments"

Nuclear deterrence is an inherently abstract, theoretical subject simply because—given the topic here, nuclear war—the Empirical Scientific Method (the conducting of controlled experiments, using the real world itself as a laboratory) is precluded to all except sociopaths and other madmen. Fortunately for amassing sane and sound wisdom, and producing valuable practicum, nuclear deterrence is well suited to exploration in detail on paper and within human minds, in hypothetical case studies similar to what Albert Einstein called *"thought experiments."* A number of such thought-experiment deductions, expositions, and rigorous logical demonstrations are used throughout this book. (They will also be used in the additional Volumes to come, once the further mass of research notes and draft materials on my desk can be updated, peer reviewed, and then published.)

Book Organization, and Main Recommendations

This rest of this Volume 1 of *On 21st-Century Nuclear Deterrence* is organized in six chapters, supported by three non-technical but more specialized appendices. The work overall is further supported by a Bibliography of references, each of which I did study in their entirety. But I rarely include footnotes, as my volumes are meant to be practical and action-oriented, not too scholarly or overly academic. Instead, I follow the *convention of the professional literature on engineering*, wherein ideas and information common in that literature are *not footnoted*. As readers will have already seen, I use fairly extensive *italicizing* throughout, for numerous passages containing what I think are the key ideas and concepts, cautions and caveats, recommendations, and conclusions. These italics are meant as an aid to comprehension and memory. They also highlight those passages that you, gentle reader of the e-book edition, might yourself have wanted to highlight with a yellow marker pen, were you to be working through the hard-copy edition.

The *main recommendations* developed across the Chapters and Appendices of this Volume 1 now follow. These (long) paragraphs are being offered here in Chapter 1 as *mere summaries*. Readers who want to see more, or who have questions or concerns, can go on to peruse the sections involved (listed at the end of each summary paragraph here). Such a deeper dive will give you a better sense of the various details and nuances/subtleties, elaborations and explanations, and caveats and cautions all essential to proper, full explication—which couldn't all fit into the following overview/briefings:

- Some seemingly seductive popular narratives about U.S. Nuclear Posture either muddle together indiscriminately, *or* try to treat as wholly separate, the *distinct but closely interdependent* issues of (1) nuclear *deterrence* and (2) nuclear *warfighting.* Nuclear deterrence is meant to work effectively all the time, in advance of and to *prevent any nuclear wars.* Nuclear warfighting happens when deterrence fails, i.e., when one or both sides decide to *actually fight a nuclear war* even despite any mutual deterrence. What can be confusing sometimes to laymen is that even though concerted deterrence is undertaken with every desire and intention to *never* have to fight a nuclear battle, *nevertheless* both the proven ability and a well-thought-out plan for exactly such warfighting is *essential* in order for deterrence to most convincingly hold up under even the worst geopolitical pressures. Worse, some politicians and pundits believe that *many fewer* nuclear warheads are needed for *deterrence "only"* than for *"intentional" warfighting.* Using algebraic notation, where "n" is the number of nukes in an arsenal, we can label these two numbers n(d) for a deterrence arsenal and n(WF) for a warfighting arsenal. But this distinction as to "needed arsenal size," and the mathematical inequality that derives from it:

  $$n(D) \ll n(WF)$$

  are *both completely false.* (The notation << means "is much less than.") One of my most basic determinations, supported and justified throughout this book and subsequent Volumes, is that to be completely effective for nuclear deterrence under even the most dire circumstances—*which are precisely the circumstances that always matter most*—America's nuclear arsenal must at all times be *sizeable enough and survivable enough* to be able to inflict such massive damage on an enemy who might nuke us first that, *even after* we suffer devastating losses from *their first strike*, we are able by *our retaliatory second strike* to destroy their entire regime's very existence. This is to say, America's nuclear arsenal, properly *"rightsized"* for effective deterrence, is *exactly the same size* as our nuclear arsenal "rightsized" for any actual warfighting. Anything in the way of n(D) falling way short of n(WF) leaves *deadly loopholes*, where deterrence could *be ignored*, perhaps by an opportunistic-enough or desperate-enough adversary head of state, or by one willing to sacrifice some millions of their own citizens for big-enough geopolitical gains, or by a sociopathic-enough leader supported by a horde of sycophantic enablers. Therefore, mathematically, a *precise equality* always holds:

$$n(D) = n(WF)$$

This being the case, the distinction between deterrence and warfighting *is a specious one*: Nuclear war can never be "controlled"; attempts to "limit" nuclear war are highly likely to collapse into escalating global Armageddon; any nuclear combat, once started, cannot be "won" by anybody. (These conclusions are covered further in all subsequent book chapters.)

- The U.S.'s current strategic nuclear arsenal, with 1,550 "counted" deployed nuclear warheads and a comparable number stockpiled for backup—as allowed by the 2010 New START Treaty—is the *necessary and sufficient number* to effectively deter even the most belligerent and *non*-casualty-averse aggressors. (See Appendix 2 for a detailing of the *myriad military objectives* some adversary might hope to achieve by making different sorts of unprovoked nuclear first strikes of various magnitudes—*if* our deterrence has loopholes.) Our arsenal should *definitely not* be reduced any further, either to "keep up the momentum of arms reduction" just for its own sake, or in the misguided belief that a "minimal" deterrent (a small number of warheads) is somehow "safer" for anyone. Nor should our strategic warheads necessarily be greatly increased in numbers if adversaries do try to get into an *economically imperiling arms race* with us, of the sort that helped wreck the USSR. It is *much better* for America (and our nuclear-armed NATO Allies), in such a situation, to invest instead in *additional Columbia-class* (and other nations') SSBNs—to spread out our existing deterrent SLBM warheads across *more, separate hulls*. This would provide an even more robust, *better-dispersed survivable deterrent,* which we can build *much more affordably* that adversaries can build the 1000+ additional ICBMs needed to even begin to threaten one of our deployed-on-patrol deterrent subs via *wide-area anti-submarine saturation-barrage strategies.* (See Chapters 2 and 6 and Appendix 3 – which cover a simple calculation showing that a salvo of 1500 enemy H-bombs can in fact threaten to mission-kill an SSBN that has somehow been localized to within a few hundred nautical miles.)

- It is a *dangerous misnomer* to claim that nuclear terrorists can never be deterred; this *false claim* is sometimes combined with the *bugaboo* of a U.S. nuke eventually getting stolen by ISIS/al Qaeda, to urge total and immediate American denuclearization—as the only possible preventive of nuclear terrorism on our soil. But although some terrorists are indeed suicidal—either as expendable, rank-and-file "bomb carriers," or as part of a wider "death cult"—their *supporting and enabling* families and social contacts, surrounding civilian societies, and cultural/religious leadership are generally *not*; some of these less-radicalized-persons could be indirectly recruited to act as *"circuit breaker individuals"* who intervene enough to prevent the nuclear strike from actually taking place. Thus, terrorist groups in this larger sense could be amenable, after all, to the right sort of *nuclear-deterrence paradigms*: The long "kill chain" from, first, an extremist group's leadership thinking about trying to get their hands on some nukes, through, eventually, to a nuclear attack being delivered to its intended target, is subject to *interdiction-from-within*—to being broken via an appeal to the more reasonable people-links along that lengthy chain. To this end, the armed group's whole-of-community should be persuasively, pointedly, continually educated that even a single terrorist nuclear strike could easily trigger a *maelstrom of uncontrollably escalating nuclear "blowback" effects* that would surely, directly and indirectly, *endanger the survival* of their entire faith-based group, cultural tribe, and/or ethnic nation. For one thing, the group committing a nuclear attack against America might easily provoke some *"draconian"* nuclear-armed tyrannies, which do face Islamic extremism themselves (e.g., Russia and China) and whose regimes would naturally fear subsequent *copy-cat nuclear attacks* on their own vital interests, to *preemptively nuke* the terrorists' training lodgments and purported caliphate homelands. For another, such deterrence-education messaging by the U.S. and NATO should warn clearly that *ambiguity and error* in forensic attribution after a terrorist nuclear strike—amplified by the *damaging and deranging effects* on command and control of even one "limited" nuclear strike, plus the *international chaos, panic, rage, and paranoia* caused by *any* nuclear strike(s) *anywhere*—could easily ignite a general nuclear war between superpowers. This would lead quickly to a *global thermonuclear holocaust* of blast, fire, and radioactive devastation, followed inevitably by months- or years-long (1) planet-circling nuclear fallout, (2) the deep-freezing darkness of Nuclear Winter, and then (3) the killing hard-ultraviolet overexposures of Nuclear Summer—a "Three-Fold Geophysical Wipeout" that would cause a *total human extinction event.* No known, populously-adhered-to Deity or Deities could possibly be imagined *(by potential circuit-breaker individuals, at least)* to want Their fanatical follower(s) to *entirely wipe out every last one of Their own faithful followers forever,* and take everyone else on Earth with them. (See Chapter 3 for an extensive discussion of the practical ins and outs of this proposed nuclear-terrorist deterrence paradigm.)

- The step-by-step exposition of Chapter 3's suggested approach to enhanced nuclear deterrence of terrorists also introduces a *recommended paradigm* for guiding the choice of *how many adversary targets* to be hit, with *how many warheads of what yield(s),* in case any retaliatory second strike by the U.S. and/or NATO against a *sovereign state* ever does prove necessary—*if our nuclear deterrence ever does fail and that state nukes our and our Allies' vital interests.* (This paradigm is developed further in its own Chapter of upcoming Volume 2.) Demonstrably having such a clear-cut retaliation procedure in place is one *very important component* of overall, effective deterrence posture: If the U.S. Government is ever suspected (or alleged) to have no good pre-arranged plan for what *precisely* to do with our nuclear weapons, if some state-level adversary does make a nuclear first strike, then our deterrence could be weakened. Having a *simple, easily communicated,* non-classified (and publicly declared) baseline proportionate-retaliation plan—*rapidly and flexibly scalable under fire* to the enemy's own specific strike details—will definitively strengthen our nuclear deterrence posture. It will contribute usefully to any adversary being thoroughly convinced that no nuclear war they might someday be tempted to start could ever possibly be "winnable" by their side. The recommended paradigm is based on a very adult version of the children's game of *Tit-for-Tat*. This paradigm would help resolve *two conundrums* that are said to have plagued U.S. presidential administrations and Strategic Air Command planners for much of the long history of the First Cold War: (1) How can our counterstrikes possibly make intelligible, unambiguous yet nuanced "signals" to the adversary amid the utter disorganization resulting from nuclear warfare? (2) How can America gain hold of the psychological initiative during a nuclear conflict, demonstrate strength, savvy, and resolve—and get the adversary to back down first from the brink of utter extinction? Tit-for-Tat counterpunches in *direct equality* to how the enemy just punched at us; by *neither* escalating *nor* deescalating, relative to their nuclear strike(s), we put a very intimidating monkey on the enemy regime's back: "*You* started this deadly nuclear war, *we* are fully prepared to now fight it out, and it is up to *you* to decide whether to trigger a full-blown thermonuclear holocaust, or take the escalation-ladder *off ramp* to species survival." How would such a paradigm work? Rather than using *rigid pre-determined target lists,* America would base our (very) flexible response on nuking the *same number and type of targets, with the same yields of weapons, that the enemy used* when they made their first (or subsequent) strike(s). Tit-for-Tat would draw on crucial *asymmetric advantages* of America's free and open Way of Life, and our seasoned conflict-resolution practices, compared to the closed cultures and rigid mindsets of belligerent dictatorships. Declaring a Tit-for-Tat nuclear response paradigm, as part of our Nuclear Posture during peacetime, demonstrably assures the world that the U.S. *will* meet our paramount strategic goals, in the dire case that an adversary ever did start a nuclear war against us, of us never "abandoning" our Nuclear-Umbrella Allies, yet *always* trying to get all parties *off of* the nuke escalation ladder as quickly as possible—but *only on political terms favorable to America/NATO*. However—it is very important to include in our deterrence messaging to *both* Allies *and* adversaries—*no* paradigm used by *any* country can prevent *any* nuclear war, once it starts, from probably escalating out of control into planet-wide Armageddon; were such a war to ever break out, de-escalation and armistice negotiations would become *desperately urgent priorities for the entire international community*. Thus, ownership by *any state(s)* of nuclear weapons does impose pressing workable-peace-keeping responsibilities upon *all humanity*: "Mutual nuclear deterrence" assures *strategic stability*, whereas "total world nuclear disarmament" is *unattainable*, and "winnable nuclear warfighting" beliefs assure *mutual oblivion*. Tit-for-Tat as a U.S./NATO baseline counterstrike formula has the potential to assure that mutual deterrence-in-being remains as effective as humanly possible—while in the unlikely event that a robust, survivable nuclear deterrent ever does fail, our *precious democracy and freedom* will be *most ably defended* against the *onslaught of inhuman tyranny, encroaching enslavement, and likely genocide*. The reader might now well ask, What if a Tit-for-Tat nuclear war were to go on blow for blow, until both sides ran out of nukes, with who won and who lost being equivocal—so that the aggressor-state's pesky information warfare trolls could then claim "utter victory" over whatever was left of the world? Such an inconclusive final outcome is very unlikely to happen: A rule of thumb from the First Cold War was that any regime suffering 200ish H-bomb hits would be *obliterated*. A scientific discovery from 1970ish (led by famous astrophysicist Carl Sagan) was that a few thousand H-bomb detonations would cause a globe-encircling Nuclear Winter of deep freeze and endless darkness that would *wipe out civilization* and probably *extinct all Humanity*. Since New START allows two superpowers, each, *three or four thousand* separate H-bombs deployed or stockpiled, the U.S. and NATO following a Tit-for-Tat baseline strategy will most assuredly hold over the head of any authoritarian aggressor state a thoroughly daunting Sword of Damocles indeed. A declared, standing American defense posture of Tit-for-Tat conveys to any adversary who would start a nuclear war that they'll have to sooner or later either give up fighting, or die—and being forced to give up fighting in a nuclear war *that they started* would most certainly bring their entire regime to its knees before the avenging Sword of Democracy. Tit-for-Tat thus can offer to POTUS and STRATCOM (and also communicate to adversaries) a pre-arranged *"escalation breaker" baseline response paradigm*, to which, within each American counterstrike, and beside (1) the baseline "hit back equally" component, there could be (2) an additional "punitive component," whose scale/intensity (from zero to moderate to massive) would be custom fit to the scenario-specific circumstances of any actual future nuclear conflict. More to the point, this Tit-for-Tat total package helps prove for all to plainly see that *no* aggressor can win a nuclear war. Such is the essence of deterrence. (Chapter 3 and Appendix 1, especially Equation A1.1.)

- The *cultural mirror-imaging* that America is prone to can be very dangerous as an impediment to effective nuclear deterrence. Many people in the world *do not* think about important matters in at all the same way as we do. Deterrence is only effective if it works properly in *the minds of potential aggressors,* who may have values and goals, cherished beliefs, and cultural/institutional "operating codes" that are *very different* from those of Americans. This is particularly true when it comes to deriving facts and interpreting lessons regarding *"life going on"* after the massive casualties of (1) natural disasters such as the AIDS or Covid-19 pandemics and the Aceh tsunami, (2) the intentional nuclear attacks on Hiroshima and Nagasaki, and (3) accidental nuclear catastrophes such as Chernobyl and Fukushima. The observations that nuclear attacks did lead to *regime change* in Imperial Japan, and that a huge nuclear disaster was a major contributor to regime change in the Soviet Union, can lead aggressors to conclude that they could inflict similar regime change on the United States via nuclear war. Entities that are not casualty averse, who embrace reckless gambler mindsets, or who are feeling desperate and cornered from real or imagined domestic and/or foreign political threats, may be tempted to *"throw the dice"* by starting a nuclear war. To counter these possibilities, effective deterrence by America and our Allies requires our sustained commitment to comprehensive, assertive, but *custom-fit* educational efforts: We *must communicate*—using carefully crafted messaging that the different targeted foreign audiences will *each* themselves understand and take to heart—about the cataclysmic dangers to the entire infrastructure and population of *all* potential nuclear-war participants (attackers, victims, and neutrals alike, which means *everyone on the planet*). The essential goal here, just as in the case of trying to better deter nuclear terrorists, is to *appeal both stochastically and individually* to "circuit-breaker individuals" (influential good actors) who will, if ever needed, interdict actively enough to halt any attempt to make a first nuclear strike (or other massive WMD first strike), by any opportunist or sociopathic or other madman national commander-in-chief. (Chapters 3 and 4)

- Some simple equations, in mathematical notation using permutations and combinations theory, illustrate the tremendous importance of *arms control treaties and norms* for enforcing nuclear nonproliferation, as well as *comprehensive test ban treaties and norms* for banning nuclear test detonations. These equations have important *policy implications* for America and other countries: Any further *all-up testing* of nuclear weapons, even underground, would greatly increase the probability that one or more nukes will be used in anger, as an *act of war.* Recent *low-observable, very-low-yield tests* that do achieve nuclear-fission criticality, such as the U.S. alleges Russia and China are conducting, are highly problematic because they "pierce the nuclear veil," so they have the potential to *foment full-yield testing*—which would bring the world that much closer to the first nuclear first-use in combat in 75+ years. Worse, any increase in the number of countries who own nukes would lead to a *more-than-exponential growth* in the number of different ways in which a nuclear war could conceivably *get started,* and then *escalate and spread.* In short, any violation or non-renewal of *nuclear peacekeeping treaties and norms* significantly could raise the probability that the Human Race will annihilate itself. (Chapter 5)
- On the other hand, unfortunately, to reduce superpower nuclear arsenals to minimal levels on the way toward Global Zero would also be *dangerously destabilizing.* It would inevitably invite *cheating against such nuclear-weaponry elimination* among wannabe world dictators. Such excessive *nuclear-arsenal downsizing*—"wrongsizing"—would also be counterproductive by triggering *nuclear proliferation* among non-nuclear countries around the world that become worried about their national security—especially *current Nuclear Umbrella client-states* of any of the superpowers, who would feel "betrayed" by their purported Protector's disarming. This would all make nuclear attacks *much more likely* to occur, as (1) such strikes' (*and* their proportionate retaliatory counterstrikes') *perforce reduced scales* would make them *less existentially threatening (i.e., less deterring) to potential aggressors,* and as (2) nuke ownership spread willy-nilly to more, smaller states having much weaker (if any) nuke safe-custodial experience. Perhaps worst of all, achieving a true Global Zero would open the door

to the prolonged mass slaughter of a *21st-century conventional Big World War III*, accompanied in all probability by world-girdling, death-dealing wartime *famines* and badly-controlled, lethal *pandemics*. Such a conventional-weapons-based WWIII would also, inevitably, lead to a *mad rush of hypermodern Manhattan Projects* among all the major belligerents, in the end producing without a doubt (given the major high-explosive and incendiary combat and death that would *already* then be raging worldwide) *exactly the global thermonuclear holocaust* that Global Zero advocates think their approach would avoid. (Chapters 2 and 6)

- The very idea that America could make do with *only modern, precision-guided conventional weaponry* to deter or defeat aggression by adversaries who might use nuclear or other strategic weapons-of-mass-destruction (WMD) against us—especially were such aggression initiated by one or more *vast and populous* states such as Russia or China—is *dangerously specious.* Throughout modern history, conventional arsenals have often *failed catastrophically* to deter even *mere conventional aggression*, on many infamous occasions (WWI, WWII in Europe *and* in the Pacific, the Yom Kippur War, the Falklands War, and repeated ISIS and al Qaeda atrocities). If a nuclear-armed aggressor, that ever starts a mere conventional war against U.S./NATO and/or our other Allies and our vital interests, begins to fear that they are losing that war, then they are extremely likely to escalate to (at least) *tactical nuclear weapons*, and then (probably) to *thermonuclear weapons*, to stave off a humiliating final defeat. (It is exactly this mechanism that causes *mutual* nuclear deterrence to *also* deter big conventional wars between superpowers. But if the U.S. owned no nukes, this whole war-prevention mechanism wouldn't apply.) Nor should it ever be assumed that any actual nuclear attack will always be preceded by an "obvious international nuclear crisis," one that would give us some clear-cut advanced warning; adversaries will *always* use deceptions and distractions to hide their belligerent intent. It is therefore vital that America deploy a robust nuclear deterrent *from the outset, at all times.* What is more, *pride often goeth before the fall.* Complacency about one's "supreme conventional military power" is a sure-fire recipe for military disaster. Even worse, *generals (and admirals) are always preparing for the last war.* The scary fact is that America has *never* yet had to fight a Big Conventional War under 21st-century conditions of *hybrid and multi-domain conflict,* in which copious social-media psychological operations, strategic cyberweaponry assaults, concerted space war, and undermining "fake news" are *all* exploited by adversaries *simultaneous* with battling us in an all-out conventional onslaught, one that uses ingenious 21st-century *offset strategies* and innovative *asymmetric warfare.* Effective nuclear deterrence is the only way to assure that such a *Big Hybrid Multi-Domain Hot War,* conventional or nuclear, never breaks out to begin with. (All chapters)

- It might be wise, perhaps under UN auspices, to systematize some of the above ideas into a *global framework* that *supports ongoing nuclear peacekeeping* at the same time that it *damps down* two mutually contradictory but equally problematic world trends. The trends, both detrimental to strategic stability, are (1) international calls for *total world nuclear disarmament,* and (2) pressures among competing nuclear powers to *grow their nuclear warhead inventories* in a new arms race. Planetwide strategic stability is likely to be best sustained by an institutionalized program of *balance and compromise,* one that pragmatically recognizes the strongly held *differences* between vying countries' approaches to nuclear weapons, and then channels their rivalries in constructive ways: A few competing nuclear-armed states would serve as semi-permanent *mutual nuclear-deterrence sustainers,* while the remaining majority would serve as ongoing *nuclear-weapon abstainers.* This competition to excel at up-to-date, effective nuclear-deterrence theory could be *channeled and systematized* via periodic global conferences and contests that bring various countries' nuclear-deterrence experts together, to vie for *intellectual-product bragging rights,* and even for *prestigious new prizes* ala the Nobels, the Olympics, or—*perhaps most analogous given nuclear theory's mental gymnastics*—world chess championships. (Chapter 7)
- It could be helpful to *strategic stability* and also to *counterproliferation* to articulate an additional norm, namely that countries which cannot afford to build or buy/lease their own stealthy, highly survivable nuclear-deterrence submarines (nuclear-powered SSBNs or air-independent-propulsion SSBPs) should *avoid* acquiring nuclear weapons altogether, and instead arrange a *nuclear-umbrella protection agreement* with an existing nuclear-armed power. Part of this same normative requirement should be the Best Practice that SSBN fleets always be supported by very robust, jamming and spoofing proof

multi-channel Nuclear Command, Control, and Communications (NC3) infrastructure, plus on-board multi-spectral external environment monitoring, so that an undersea retaliatory strike is *always absolutely assured*—even against any attempt at a *preemptive "decapitating strike"* upon the defending country's National Command Authorities (NCA). (Appendix 3)

But One Volume Can't Address all the Relevant Questions and Conundrums

Modern (and future) nuclear-deterrence theory in general, and U.S. Strategic-Triad Best Policies, Best Perspectives, and Best Practices in particular, are vast topics. Professional opinions can differ vehemently. Everyone's grasp of exactly *what* needs to be achieved is continually changing. Exactly *how* the United States should most effectively—*and cost-effectively*—meet all these sometimes-conflicting needs, both as a *sovereign nation* and as a *responsible world leader*, is constantly evolving.

It will take several Volumes of *On 21st-Century Nuclear Deterrence* to cover all of my research and commentary, which are ongoing and will be for the foreseeable future. Currently, *at least four* Volumes in this non-fiction series are planned, to be released over the next several calendar years, God willing.

FYI, decent preliminary drafts of the principal Chapters and Appendices of each pending Volume, extending (as of this writing) up to about half-way through what will be Volume 3, do now exist on my desk. These are being edited for some professional peer-review comments, offered to me very kindly by several expert practitioners of different aspects of historical and current nuclear deterrence policy and its implementation. All those drafts will be peer reviewed more, and updated as needed, based on unfolding world geopolitical events and defense technological developments, in the months and years to come before each Volume's publication.

As just one example of subject-matter *barely touched on* here in Volume 1, but obviously of *great importance to positive outcomes* in our modern world—and intended for thorough coverage in Volume 4—is one particular, rapidly burgeoning cluster of operational concepts and actionable techniques clearly requisite for *successful global nuclear peace-keeping*. This *vital intellectual product* is now being very actively R&D-ed by U.S. Strategic Command and elsewhere within our Armed Forces, by various private-sector think tanks and defense contractors, and by academia, in the U.S. and in our NATO Allies—and presumably among our various adversaries as well. This interrelated cluster of *modernized strategizing, in the name of preventing nuclear blackmail and nuclear Armageddon alike*, involves what are being called Conventional-Nuclear Integration (Sub-/Pre-Nuclear Early Warning and Escalation Control), Adversary-Specific Deterrence Paradigms, Alliance/Coalition Management, Nuclear Counter-Proliferation, and Nuclear Counterterrorism. Each of these rapidly expanding topics certainly deserves, and will receive, its own chapter in Volume 4.

See My Writings in Joe Buff Inc.'s e-Newsletter, and on LinkedIn, Facebook, and Medium.com

For an *exclusive early-look* at further Volumes' conclusions and recommendations, regarding various "hot topics" of current nuclear-strategy thinking and planning, please consider subscribing to my free periodic e-Newsletter, *Interesting (Nuclear) Times*—or *"I(N)T"* for short. Preliminary drafts of upcoming Volumes' Chapters and Appendices are being circulated (to Subscribers *only*) as Research Reports in *I(N)T* e-issues. *I(N)T* started in March 2019; as of year-end 2020 it has been through twenty-one issues; existing Subscribers have been able to peruse tentative versions of the major portions of this Volume 1, as well as first-cut parts of upcoming Volume 2 and the so-far-written-up chapters of Volume 3. All *I(N)T* Subscribers automatically receive, upon first joining the confidential e-distribution list, all the back issues of *I(N)T* which include links to those previous Research Reports that are not yet close to being released via the trade-paperback and e-book formats of Volumes.

I(N)T is administered for Joe Buff Inc. by the major media company Constant Contact, Inc. To subscribe to *Interesting (Nuclear) Times*, simply e-mail me at readermail@joebuff.com.

You might also like to Follow me on LinkedIn.com, and/or Friend me on Facebook.com. (My username is joebuffsubs on both sites).

On LinkedIn you can see and comment on my "Daily War and Peace News Patrol." These posts, on LinkedIn.com's Home Feed, provide my own pithy, pragmatic three-line comments on each of several selected daily mainstream-media defense- and Cold War II-related news and op-eds/commentary items. The LinkedIn archive of my News Patrol posts is at: https://www.linkedin.com/in/joe-buff-38130853/detail/recent-activity/shares/

On Facebook, you might like to join the lively interactive discussion in my Group, "On 21st-Century Nuclear Deterrence," where I also blog about my life and work as a writer. Everyone is welcome to share their experiences, thoughts, ideas, questions, answers, and concerns there. The link to this Facebook Group is: https://www.facebook.com/groups/418535679472895

I very recently started posting defense-related articles and original/exclusive op-ed essays to Medium.com. Please do Follow me there, too, also at username joebuffsubs. A listing of what I've published so far on Medium.com is at https://joebuff.medium.com/

Conclusion

The above Best Policy, Best Perspective, and Best Practice imperatives are why I deduce that *American and Russian nuclear arsenals at the current New START Treaty levels help position Humanity in a beneficial Nuclear-War-Deterring "Goldilocks Zone"*—those current strategic warhead counts are *neither too large nor too small to be "comfortably" effective.* This Goldilocks Zone applies, at least for right now, beyond just the U.S. and Russia in isolation, because at present the *different strategic nuclear-arsenal sizes* of the five major Second World War victors (turned First Cold War and then Second Cold War adversaries) satisfy an *important equation of bloc strategic parity and stability*:

$$\text{US} + \text{France} + \text{UK} = \text{Russia} + \text{China} \quad \text{[Equation 1.1]}$$

This is one reason why it would be very valuable, nay essential to soon bring Beijing into the fold of nuclear arms-control negotiations between Washington and Moscow. Beijing has started saying publicly that it deserves and needs a strategic arsenal equal in size to the ones that both the U.S. and Russia now have. This would *more than quadruple* China's total, from about 350 nukes at year-end 2020 to the much higher New START Treaty's mandated 1,550 "strategic" (mostly H-bomb) nuclear warheads deployed (plus a similar number stockpiled) that are currently owned for each of DC and Moscow—and presumably China could then also decide to "keep up" with either or both "other superpowers" if the latter ever do get into an upward-spiraling arms race. No matter how you cut it, such a "three-player game" in H-bomb counts would be *highly destabilizing*: for strategic stability in particular, and for our entire planet's survival in general.

But whether or not New START is renewed with Russia alone, or can be extended to apply in some form to China as well—or is allowed to lapse as a geopolitical expedient—I hope that this book contributes to: (1) *perpetuating* the effectiveness of America's indispensable nuclear deterrence Triad at an *adequately robust* warhead-count and platform-diversity level, (2) *instigating* an American "Nuclear Posture After Next" that is in its own "just right" Goldilocks Zone of being neither too aggressive nor too squeamish, (3) *discouraging* ill-advised, destabilizing, further large reductions in strategic stockpiles (either unilateral or multilateral), while (4) *preventing* another dangerous and wasteful, upward-spiraling nuclear-warhead-count arms race.

The old, frightening First Cold War nuke arms race helped bankrupt the Soviet Union, causing its regime to implode and causing great suffering to her people. Neither the U.S., nor Russia nor China, should risk bankruptcy and implosion in this latest Era of Great Power Competition ("Cold War Two"). This is especially so since taking such military-economic competition too far, rerunning a frenzied warhead-building "Nuke Stockpile Supersizing Contest," would force the world out of its hard-won Goldilocks Zone and closer to the catastrophe-courting *Nuclear Holocaust Zone.* It should be quite clear exactly *who would lose* this time around (all Humanity)—and it is very unclear *who could be said to "win"* (nobody).

I want to repeat for emphasis that I tried to anchor all such conclusions in fact-based rational analysis, but these ideas cannot on their own approach perfection re what an *"ideal U.S. National Nuclear Posture Review Report (NNPRR) After Next"* should entail. (The test for perfection is simple, but endless: no nuclear combat *ever* ensues.) Each American presidential administration's Congressionally mandated, unclassified National Nuclear Posture Review Report is a *political construct,* and so for various practical reasons might vary from what would derive from sheer abstract "logical perfection." By giving my considered professional view, of what the *"ideal"* might conceivably look like during this complicated 21st century we all have to live in and deal with, I do hope to benefit the complex deliberations that lead to each pragmatic *"actual"* American Nuclear Posture. But make no mistake: The *wider the deviations* between ideal and actual, the *greater the risk* that each promulgated NNPRR might later fall down on the job. The single most essential thing for everyone in the world to bear in mind is that, for reasons the rest of this book and its sequels go into step by step, no one ever "wins" or "prevails" in a nuclear war. Once the mushroom clouds start rising in anger, it will be *exceedingly* difficult to stop before we're all dead. Nuclear combat cannot ever be counted on to even just stay contained enough to somehow be fought to a barely-survivable draw—which would itself be a terribly senseless and utterly tragic stalemate, one that would severely harm our species and damage our planet way beyond repair.

But to completely ban all nukes in the world is a forlorn hope, doomed to go the same way as Prohibition did a hundred years ago in America, despite that ill-advised "Noble Experiment's" own big wave (at first) of overly idealistic zeal. And just like that early-twentieth-century U.S.-wide alcohol ban, any modern worldwide nuke ban now would be *cheated on from the outset,* giving rise to *continual smuggling and organized-crime violence,* and would *eventually be abandoned.* Since the *genie of knowledge,* of how to make A-bombs and H-bombs, really can't ever be put back in the bottle, effective nuclear deterrence via a strong and diversified Triad is utterly indispensable.

Ultimately, in a democracy like America's, maintaining global nuclear peace depends on the voters and on their chosen leaders in Congress and in the White House. A better-informed national populace is certain to benefit everyone, worldwide.

So please read on, gentle reader, and do let me and your elected representatives know what you think.

CHAPTER 2

Why a Weakened Nuclear Triad (or Diad or Monad) Courts Disaster

A Math "Theorem": We're in a Nuclear Goldilocks Zone **Right Now**

Executive Summary: World Threats Show a Right-Sized U.S. Deterrence Triad is Crucial

21st-century Russia and China are both heavily-nuclear-armed, one-man-rule repressive dictatorships, with evident ambitions to become hegemonic global superpowers. Readers who doubt that both countries are *not* friends to world peace and freedom need only look at Beijing's and Moscow's aggressive militarized expansionism, their arrogant coercion and disingenuous suborning of neighbors, their egregious cyberespionage ops and human-intelligence intrusions, and their callous malign-influence disinformation/manipulation campaigns—all of which both countries continue to wage against vital American/Allied interests worldwide, even in the midst of the present Covid-19 pandemic. Such ruthless, conniving belligerence puts relentless pressure on the United States of America, which—whether We the People like it or not—has for over one hundred years now repeatedly been forced by external events to act as the free world's Arsenal of Democracy—for sheer self-preservation as much as for the greater good of humanity at large.

Further complicating America's (and NATO's) inescapable responsibility to defend our blessed Way of Life from adversaries large and small, are both *rogue states* and *sub-state/trans-state armed groups (terrorists, drug cartels, organized crime)*. Some of these amoral, violence-prone entities seek their own nuclear weapons; in future even more of them might do so; they would if they could use them without remorse, to exercise nuclear blackmail, and even to cause massive death and destruction by launching unprovoked nuclear attack(s). Foremost on this list of bad actors is, of course, North Korea, whose Kim Dynasty has outmaneuvered all international efforts at denuclearization—and now owns several dozen deliverable nukes. Not far behind North Korea is Iran, which continues, despite the outside world's best efforts, to stockpile refined uranium-235 for nuclear-bomb fuel; on New Year's Weekend 2021, Tehran announced they will now take this refinement up to 20%. Worse, terrorist groups such as Al Qaeda have since the 1990s been seeking their own nuclear devices—and they only need to succeed *once* at buying, stealing, or making a nuke, setting it off in a big city like New York or New Delhi, Tokyo, or Paris or Tel Aviv, to massacre millions of innocents.

This Chapter 2 is a concise but detailed explanation of why the U.S. really does need a fully modernized, adequately-sized, properly maintained—hence adequately *funded*—very diversified, very well-dispersed nuclear deterrent *Triad*, with some units based in the U.S. Homeland and some units stationed overseas and/or under the sea. Below, we will explain why the calls by some pundits and politicos to discontinue one or more legs of that Triad, supposedly to save some money, are in fact *extremely ill advised—especially* in light of the COVID-19 pandemic and the worldwide economic recession it is likely to cause; history shows that bad economic recessions lead to repressive over-nationalist onslaughts, which then do lead to world wars *if not properly deterred*.

America's nuclear arsenal, to be effective as a deterrent against any and all adversaries under any conceivable circumstances, needs to have *strategic warhead counts* very similar to those we have now, namely 1,550 H-bombs deployed and a similar number stockpiled, as are allowed the U.S. (and Russia too) under the 2010 New START Treaty. To *reduce* America's nuclear arsenal much further or to *over-concentrate* it within any single Triad leg, under *any* plausible geopolitical scenarios, would be a serious mistake, while to *increase* it by a lot—under *current* circumstances—would be both unnecessary and harmful. These conclusions are supported below with some simple mathematical modeling. Thus, as this author likes to say, America's present nuclear-arms and nuclear-capable delivery vehicle inventories are "right-sized": Our warhead count and force structure put us (along with the rest of NATO) in the sweet spot of a "just right" *Nuclear Goldilocks Zone.*

Our Triad's *purpose* ("tri" stands for its three indispensable legs: ICBMs, bombers with cruise missiles, and submarines with ballistic missiles), properly understood along a *different dimension* than its hardware *makeup*, is *also three-fold* across the dimension of keeping the peace. The Triad does *not* just exist to prevent nuclear war. It *also* protects us and our allies with necessary deterrence against devastating attack in a *much wider sense* as well. Specifically, this *broader, protective, effective deterrence* is declared in America's National Nuclear Posture Review Reports. It is important to appreciate that, on this particular point, the *same* thing is said by these periodically-updated key doctrinal publications as they were issued by *both* the Democratic Administration of POTUS Obama *and* the Republican Administration of POTUS Trump—*despite* these Administrations' rather disparate approaches to aspects of foreign relations. (This book is meant, in part, to give some possible inputs to the revisions and updates of the Biden Administration's version, and then especially to the subsequent "Nuclear Posture After Next.")

Here is how this "broader protective effective deterrence" is meant to work:

The National Nuclear Posture says that the United States may, at our option, if necessary, *also* retaliate with our nukes against certain *other* major acts of aggression besides a nuclear attack. These are ones for which we do *not* possess the adequate (or *any*) means for directly proportionate retaliation-in-kind—in many cases, because we adhere in good faith to various international treaties, conventions, and norms that *ban* them. This *"other heinous belligerent acts"* category itself consists of three different modes of attack:

- Attack with very-large-scale *(overwhelming, existentially threatening)*
  conventional-weapons (i.e., a *non-nuclear World War III*), or
- Attack with *other weapons of mass destruction* (WMDs, e.g., chemical, biological, or radiological-dispersal "dirty-bomb" weapons), or
- Attack with *strategic-level (i.e., very large scale, very damaging) cyberweapons* or *electromagnetic-pulse weapons* (EMPs), or *massive attacks on our vital space-based orbital platforms.*

All these forms of threatened nuclear retaliation against massive-enough attacks, in the modern world, are *critical preventive deterrence functions* of our diversified, dispersed, flexible and adaptable nuclear Triad.

Third and lastly, our Triad is just as important, if not—on a day-to-day basis—*even more important*, as a dissuader of nuclear (and other WMD) *blackmail, coercion, extortion, and intimidation.* Such ugly "peacetime," *cold war or hybrid war* tactics have long been part of the former Soviet Union's diplomatic-military culture. They have definitely continued under *de facto* dictator-for-life Vladimir Putin's rule in Russia, where covert manipulations of American voters' emotions and sentiments abound. The same very nasty tactics are manifest lately in strongman Xi Jinping's China, where bullying of neighbors and jockeying against American critical interests have become as commonplace as Beijing's expansionist thrusts throughout the South China Sea and beyond. The best way, in reality the *only* way, to say to some wannabe nucleararmed aggressor state, "Oh yeah? Kiss off, ya big bully," is to *conspicuously and committedly* field a robust, modern, comprehensive nuclear deterrence Triad—as *nuclear bully repellent-in-being.*

So, the U.S. and the human race actually get quite a lot in terms of *passive but effective global peacekeeping,* in return for America's ongoing investment in our nuclear deterrence Triad. This is especially true considering the *monumentally appalling cost,* in money and lives, that any actual *failure of weakened nuclear deterrence* might inflict on our species and our planet. Nuclear forces are in reality *particularly affordable,* because they can *leverage technology* rather than rely on *extensive troop manpower*—with the latter's *extremely expensive* career-long (and life-long) pay and dependents' allowances, huge meal and housing costs, family health care, and life insurance and pension benefit packages.

But wait, there's more (to this "too expensive" anti-nuclear bugaboo).

In fact, even though decades of neglect have raised the bill now for replacing all our obsolescent Cold War-era Triad hardware, the cost of doing so over the next thirty years runs at *only some 4%* of our total annual National Defense Budget. Put differently, when compared to the very significant costs/investments of America's indispensable social welfare programs, the annual cost of renewing and sustaining our nuclear Triad is *only about 7%* of the annual cost of *just one such program,* our (really essential) state and federal Medicaid (health care for low-income families) spending!

First, Keep Sight of an All-Important Distinction

Nuclear weapons can be used by any "state" (i.e., country) that owns them for two different, diametrically opposed purposes—which have *opposite* motivations and *opposite* legal/moral standing. When thinking and talking about nuclear weapons "uses" in actual warfare, it is very important to appreciate the profound impact here of whether your own country is the attacker or the defender, the aggressor or the victim.

Unprovoked nuclear attack: The actual dropping of your nuke or nukes on enemy targets *without them having first made a prior, truly massive attack*: that is, without any egregious and unprovoked attack of existential proportions first committed *against you (or your allies)* by the purported enemy you target with your nukes. This is the ultimate act of aggression. *The purpose* is to start a nuclear war and presumably (but delusively) fight it to "win." *The payoff* is purely selfish; winner takes all in military-political and geopolitical-economic gain; loser gets annihilated. (The wording of this definition, by my design, puts in this category of unjustified nuclear aggression any *supposedly preventive or pre-emptive* nuclear attack you might make. Justifying yourself sufficiently here—regarding the grave decision to be the one to initiate *piercing the nuclear veil*—is nigh on impossible, when intel of enemy intention to nuke you first is always suspect, and potent precision conventional weapons are available for preemptive purposes.)

Nuclear peacekeeping (deterrence), and peace-restoration (if deterrence ever fails): This is the ultimate act of legitimate self-defense. *The purpose* is to (1) deter, by threatening in advance to retaliate against the spectrum of nuclear/other WMD/cyber/EMP or conventional-existential assaults, via your own nukes, if necessary, *or otherwise* to (2) punitively end a nuclear war the other guy starts, on terms politically acceptable to you (rather than escalate to mutual doomsday, or roll over in abject surrender). *The payoff* is both selfish and benevolent; peace is kept or restored for your country, while freedom is defended for the benefit of all humanity.

Every National Nuclear Posture Review (or equivalent policy statements before NNPR reports began in the 1990s) that was issued by the U.S. since the dawn of the Atomic Age has made it clear that the sole purpose of America's nuclear arsenal is nuclear peacekeeping and peace-restoration, as defined here.

We *Are* Under Attack: How to Win the Information War

We Americans, and our friends, allies, and partners, need to proceed gingerly on the nuclear deterrence policy and funding front. We need to keep open minds and hearts, and ears. We need to join the wider debate about nuclear arms while displaying due respect (even compassion) for the varying opinions of all fellow peace-abiding citizens, while proceeding with decency and with civility. We also need open eyes. This is because misinformation about America's nuclear deterrent comes from two sources. One is domestic, and is certainly well meaning, even altruistic. The other is foreign, and is most certainly malevolent.

The domestic source of misinformation includes Hollywood's sometimes sensationalized and often misleading blockbuster-movie nuclear storytelling, and the sometimes overly emotional/utopian "Ban the Bomb" movement's messaging. These are done, in large part, to foist appealing messages on the movie-going and the voting publics, in order to *maximize entertainment industry revenues* and *exercise political influence* while "selling" the idea that immediate, one-sided nuclear disarmament by America is not just possible but is essential to human survival.

A prime example of the *foreign source* is Russia's (and before it, the USSR's) malign influence campaigning, to undermine American commitment to and confidence in our own nuclear deterrent Triad forces. This is done to weaken the Arsenal of Democracy, and thus remove a major impediment to repressive dictatorship running rampant across the world stage.

The former source of misinformation, the domestic one, is a double-edged sword. Making a good profit is key to free enterprise and the private-ownership system of capitalist democracy; exercising free speech is a fundamental right under the U.S. Constitution. These things lie at the very foundation of the precious American Way of Life, which we've fought to protect since 1776. And human survival is definitely of paramount importance, but as this book will explain in detail as we go, unilateral American nuclear disarmament is *not* the best available way to try to achieve this essential goal.

The latter types of source, using Russia as one example of a post-Cold War aggressor state, along with China, North Korea, and Iran as others, seek to *end* the American Way of Life. Such agencies of tyranny must be forcefully, proportionately resisted by every appropriate resource available to those who love peace with freedom.

Persisting Pop-Culture Myths Endanger Our Triad and with It Our National Security

A suite of *disinformatsia* tactics is the basic toolkit of the Russian Federation's Internet Resources Agency (IRA). The world has seen this recently in how Russia tries hard to interfere in Western (Free World) democratic elections. (And what a whiff of the old Cold War those turns-of-phrase are, "the West" and "the Free World"! *They're back.* They're appropriate and necessary again, because they're so characteristic and indicative of our times.)

Russia tries to "shape" (to use the military-diplomatic term for it), to *manipulate* our society's group psyche, to their regime's benefit. Russian influence-campaign operatives try to identify and exploit weak points and inaccuracies in America's knowledge and understanding of policy issues that can divide us, panic us—and ultimately, suborn and overwhelm us by non-violent means. More generally. America's near-peer and smaller competitors alike seek to act, and achieve their desired geopolitical effects, using methods that fall below the threshold of triggering a "kinetic" response from us—one that resorts to conventional armed retaliatory force. And they are very good at it. Russia, in particular, has centuries of practice at this strategy. Chinese and Iranian/Persian cultures predate America's by millennia; they are patient in ways American culture is not.

That is not to say that Russian, Chinese, or other malign-influence campaigns do not use a form of violence. In the dimension/domain of facts, logic, rationality, they are *bloodying* basic truths, *breaking* norms and taboos of accurate reasoning, *smashing* clarity of thought, *blowing up* objectivity, *bombing us* with disingenuous rhetoric, and *burning down* the once-unassailable edifices of unbiased history, science, and math.

Perhaps nowhere is this clearer that in Russia's prolonged efforts to seize the initiative in America's endless debate about the proper role, if any, for our nuclear arsenal as a guarantor of world peace and freedom from tyranny.

That debate goes back to 1945. Some of the Manhattan Project scientists wanted to "ban the bomb" forever, from the outset. Others wanted to press on, to gain a tool for ending World War II in the Pacific much more quickly and with less loss of life on both sides. Some of the latter Manhattan Project thinkers rightly foresaw that the Soviet Union, our indispensable ally against Hitler, would emerge as our major peer competitor once Hitler was defeated.

By 1950, the Cold War was on. As Henry Kissinger has said, from the beginning the Soviets tried to turn America's nukes into objects of fear, loathing, mistrust, and derision among our own citizens. Since the best lie is based on the truth, Moscow sought to convince our electorate and our leaders that our nuclear arsenal was "unusable," hence (supposedly) it was totally useless, hence we and the world would sleep much better without it. Moscow sought to trigger panic and paranoia at the very mention of the word "nuclear," turning it into a disruptive *dog whistle*, a *trigger phrase* within our national discourse. Yet with typical, cynical hypocrisy, and always serving their goal of offensive/defensive world domination, the Kremlin pressed relentlessly forward with its own thermonuclear triad development, its own hydrogen bombs and the various delivery platforms needed to detonate them on their chosen targets—in America.

Today, the U.S. collective consciousness is distorted, wracked, befuddled by various myths, misunderstandings, and misconceptions about what our nuclear Triad is for and how we would ever in real life, with the greatest reluctance, actually use it "in anger" (meaning in combat). Those duly-authorized uses, in the last extreme, are *solely* to retaliate against an enemy nuclear attack, or to save our national bacon by defending against some enemy's overwhelming, existence-threatening WMD (weapons of mass destruction) or conventional world-war-scale of attack.

The purpose of this book is to try to help restore some fair equilibrium to the ongoing Triad dialogue.

Harmful Myths about America's Nuclear Triad

What are some of these damaging falsehoods about our purely peacekeeping, protective, defensive triad?

Myth-cluster #1: That our Commander-in-Chief would *ever* follow extremely hazardous *launch-on-warning* hair trigger rules of engagement for retaliating against incoming enemy nuclear attack—including "attacks" that are *merely suspected, or maybe/possibly happening, or cyber-fakes, or complete false alarms*—unless and until (and this is the essential part that the misleaders always *leave out*) they are first *absolutely verified to be genuine nuclear attacks* using *the ground-truth of enemy nuke detonations on our Homeland's soil or on our other vital interests.* That POTUS allegedly believes that he/she has barely five minutes to "push the button" if the U.S. even just merely catches one unsubstantiated hint that such a surprise enemy nuclear attack *just might* be underway. That this highly misleading *non*-fact supposedly makes the world horrendously exposed to the species-extinction risk of a global nuclear holocaust that will come about at America's own hands, simply because our Triad exists at all.

Myth-cluster #2: That this (entirely made-up) five-minutes-long reaction time makes us and the world terribly vulnerable to an *accidental or inadvertent* nuclear war, caused by an early-warning false alarm or a front-line military blunder that can't be undone. That our silo-based ICBMs are such a "priceless treasure" that, even though they are very specifically intended as a (rather expensive but entirely necessary and effective) *expendable tripwire openly attracting any enemy first nuclear strike,* they would be so precious to the Pentagon that at the slightest scare they would be launched based on a panicky "use it or lose it" mentality. That our Triad, and with it all Humanity, are fatally vulnerable to bad-actor cyber-hacking, because this (alleged) compressed five-minute timeframe keeps us from blocking said cyber-attack, and identifying the false threat and the real culprits, before it's too late. (Purveyors of these particular nuclear bugaboos ignore the 75 years of Nuclear Age history so far, during which nuclear weapons, *rather carefully safeguarded indeed* by their various national custodians for obvious reasons, have *never once* gone off or been launched by accident, or been stolen or hijacked by either physical means or via cyber-intrusion. Such anti-Triad naysayers also ignore the fact that during this long history's various cold wars, regional/proxy hot wars, tactical and strategic nuclear crises, and even a superpower bankruptcy, inadvertent nuclear war was *entirely avoided,* via diligent use of *hot lines, absolute/rigid top-down controls over nuke release orders, plus suitable restraint and due caution* by all sides.)

Myth-cluster #3: That there is no distinction in morality and law between an entity that commits the *unprovoked use of nukes as an initial act of aggression,* and a country that commits a *second use in a proportional and discriminate retaliatory response,* even given the fact that said second strike is made specifically in order to (1) contain the aggressor, (2) forcefully punish that aggressor so as to strongly discourage any further such aggression or third-party copy cats, and (3) restore balance in the world order after such a psychotic first-use violation of basic humanity.

Myth-cluster #4: That to own an effective, robust, rightsized nuclear deterrence Triad, used as a purely defensive national asset, is indistinguishable from a willingness to engage in ongoing, recurring nuclear warfighting *by choice.*[1] That our deterrent Triad, as an indispensable tool for nuclear peacekeeping, and (in a worst case) nuclear peace restoration, is the *same thing* in purpose and method as a nuclear intentional-warfighting arsenal. That a properly-sized *strategic deterrence weapons system*—designed to ultimately save human lives—is the same thing as a bloated *nuclear warfighting weapons system*–designed to wage aggressive combat and thus risk species suicide. (As discussed below, they *are* the same *size,* but they are very much *not* the same in *intent* and *purpose.*)

Myth-cluster #5: That having a few low-yield, tactical, theater/battlefield nuclear weapons in America's arsenal somehow makes having *us* start a nuclear war a much more likely occurrence. That we can proportionally/discriminately, ethically/morally, legally, and entirely without fatal nuclear escalation toward Armageddon, respond to an enemy nuking of well under ten kilotons with one of our hydrogen bombs that yields almost a megaton; that this conundrum wouldn't in practice politically and morally handcuff us from making a nuclear retaliation *at all.* That it does not matter to us in the slightest that tactical nukes are *not* covered by the New START arms control treaty

1. https://www.linkedin.com/pulse/nuclear-deterrence-isnt-warfighting-joe-buff/

between the U.S. and Russia, nor is it an issue to us at all that Russia, in the European theater alone, has *ten times* the number of tactical nukes deployed as NATO does.

Myth-cluster #6: That the right way to keep our nuclear arsenal "safe" is to build in hardware features and storage procedures—such as large physical separation of the warheads from their delivery vehicles, and thorough de-alerting (stand downs) of their crews—so as to *by design* cause *lengthy delays* in any necessary, actual nuclear counter-strike employment—even or especially in a worst case scenario where such employment is imperative and *needs to be extremely prompt.*

The Current Threat Environment: Is Peacetime a Mere Interregnum to the Next Wartime?

The world continues to follow a cyclical "Kondratiev Wave," of years-long periods of peace and then of war both hot and cold. History has very much *not* ended: Even famous American political scientist Francis Fukuyama says he was wrong when he wrote a book about this back in 1992. Emerging, and according to post-Von Neumann/post-Hermann Kahn mathematical game theory, *dangerously unstable*[2] three-way nuclear superpower competition—between China, Russia, and the United States—demands an ongoing positive strategic-stability leadership role by America. We are *the* wealthy, populous, well-armed capitalist democracy able to protect *both* ourselves selfishly, and humanity and planet earth altruistically, from catastrophic nuclear war and creeping nuclear blackmail alike.[3]

I can't put it in more stark terms than that. It's simply because any attempt at global nuclear disarmament, even if all nuclear powers went along enthusiastically at first, would, from the current sound New START warhead-count levels, quickly reduce American and Russian

2. John von Neumann was the co-founder of mathematical Game Theory, focusing on strategy and tactics needed to "win" in sometimes-complicated contests between two opposing players; later game theorists showed that when three or more players vie at once, the results can be unpredictable, even chaotic—sometimes the *weakest* player comes out the winner, sometimes *everyone* loses. Herman Kahn was an early Cold War nuclear strategist and think-tank founder (the Hudson Institute) who popularized the notion of *"thinking the unthinkable"* about thermonuclear war, in order to best prepare for and deter it.

3. Despite the over-confrontational flavor of current domestic politics, Liberalism and Trumpism are *not* so very contradictory. E.g., America defended the post-WWII *Liberal* World Order when President Reagan, a noted *conservative Republican,* took a hard line approach to confronting the USSR; the result was the end of the First Cold War, which many defense analysts previously had believed would just go on forever; America's side was victorious.

arsenal sizes *below* effective mutual deterrence levels, *yet* leave everyone still heavily armed, *for years*, before every last nuke out of many *thousands* remaining in national inventories could finally go through the prolonged and complicated (and hugely expensive) process of safe dismantlement.[4] "Smallish" nuclear arsenals would enable nuclear wars that were vastly destructive and murderous, yet *not* existentially threatening enough to deter bloodthirsty, desperate, politically-cornered or psychopathic-gambler dictators from *starting and fighting them.*

Plus, some states will always *cheat*, as the Soviet Union did on the Biological Weapons Convention, Russia did on the Intermediate Nuclear Forces Treaty and the Open Skies Treaty, North Korea did on any number of treaties, agreements, and UN sanctions, and Iran allegedly did in violation of the P5+1's denuclearizing JCPOA agreement. The temptation to hold back and hide a few nukes, and then use them to intimidate and conquer the rest of the world once everyone else disarmed, would be impossible for power-mad potentates to resist.

The Whole Global-Zero Movement Does Do Some Very Valuable Work(!)

As discussed immediately above, the particular goal of complete worldwide denuclearization is unattainable for the foreseeable future at least, and quite possibly forever. As a consequence, America needs to be able to conceptualize our nuclear deterrence Triad as a *very long-term, essentially permanent, ongoing* responsibility and need, rather than as something horrible to be gotten rid of altogether, as soon as possible.

But, maybe, someday, Humanity's deadly aggressions and lethal enmities will be tamed enough to enable perpetual harmony. If some

4. The (literally) fatal flaw with the ultimate goal of zero nuclear weapons everywhere on Earth—even if we ignore the *intractable problem of bad actors cheating*—is that the only way to get there, now that nukes *do* exist aplenty in several countries, is by a *gradual* reduction in the total number extant—because it will take *years* and cost a *fortune* to safely and permanently dismantle the current huge inventories. We can think of that world total at any time "t" as a function f(t); in mathematical terms this is a *"continuous function,"* meaning it can only decline from thousands to zero in an incremental, i.e., *smooth* manner, at most a few at a time. Thus f(t)—and with it, the real world—must spend considerable time passing through a *very unstable "catastrophe zone,"* where enough nukes remain to (1) render *impossible* total planetwide Armageddon (so that deterrence threats become more and more *hollow*), but also (2) *allow* a devastating "medium sized" nuclear holocaust (because a nuclear war, to warmongers, then seems *survivable* and *winnable*). The stark result of this *f(t) continuity conundrum* would be to kill millions and millions of innocent people and leave the survivors struggling in a radioactive wasteland.

dedicated people don't keep trying for lasting World Peace, we'll never find out, and Mankind will have no hope of ever succeeding at this admirable goal.

In the meantime, some of the work of the Global Zero movement is laudable, immediately relevant, and *must* continue. This includes work on counterproliferation (avoiding the spread of nukes to more countries), counterterrorism (keeping all nukes out of terrorist hands) and arms control (preventing nuclear arms races). Another of the global denuclearization movement's *vital ongoing tasks* is to publicly and vigorously warn citizens and policy-makers alike against the *dangerous complacency* that is an endemic part of all long-running, successful human activities. This reminder should certainly include, in the 21st century, the importance of *eternal vigilance* during the responsible, safe, secure human custodianship of nuclear arms as peacekeeping mutual deterrents.

In the ongoing present world environment, nuclear deterrence has worked well enough to prevent *any* nuclear first-use in battle since 1945. But there have been a number of fatal military nuclear *accidents* in the U.S., the USSR/Russia, and elsewhere, which fortunately *all* fell short of the actual full-yield detonation of a nuke. These mishaps included Chernobyl (whose reactors made plutonium for weapons), the U.S. Army's nuclear reactor meltdown (Idaho Falls, 1961), the fuel explosion of an ICBM in its silo (Damascus, Arkansas, 1980), several sinkings of Soviet and Russian nuclear-armed submarines over the years due to reactor or weapon malfunctions (from *K-129* in 1960 to *Kursk* in 2000), and likewise several serious mishaps of U.S. Air Force strategic bombers (e.g., off Palomares, Spain, 1966). (America's tragic losses of the fast-attack subs USS Thresher and USS Scorpion with all hands, in the 1960s, were due to non-nuclear mishaps.)

Assurance of the constant, endless *safety and surety* of all nuclear weapons must never be taken for granted. Whatever good work the Pentagon and Department of Energy do in this pressing, world-on-their-shoulders Atlas-like burden/responsibility, certainly an independent organization beholden to the public, and not to the government or military, such as Global Zero and its companion groups, is an essential *de facto* member of the wider, inclusive nuclear deterrence establishment.

Nuclear weapons do exist in multiple countries—nine states at last count. This is a hard fact. Their invention, and subsequent proliferation, was a drastic discontinuity in the fundamentals of humanity-wide risk management responsibilities. From the beginning, most sovereign nuclear powers were unwilling to give up their nukes—serious proposals for centralized United Nations control of all nuclear arms, or instead for completely abolishing them, have gone *nowhere* for 75+ years. To put the cat of nuclear arms back in the bag of easier human survival is now, unfortunately, not possible in the real world. The evil genie, "I am Shiva, destroyer of worlds" (Robert Oppenheimer) cannot be pushed back in the bottle. This Shiva must, instead, be *pragmatically and diligently contained*—at not inconsiderable cost in taxpayer money and other resources.

It is a law of thermodynamics that *entropy* always increases; disorder in the universe only goes one way, *upward*. To reduce the disorder, external work must be performed. The laws of physics, the nature of our universe, dictate that fission and fusion weapons are possible, and the raw uranium and hydrogen needed for their fuel are plentiful. To reverse the consequent trend of rising chaos in the human system, aka the possibility and availability of nuclear arms to human beings, requires an application of *work from a source external to the whole system*—where the "system" is our whole Cosmos. To violate such overweening physical laws would need an *outside* input, which in this context would have to be the ultimate one, of theological magnitude: a miracle—literally, a benign Act of God.

Therefore, our full-blown triad *must* continue to exist and be large enough and diversified enough (with safety and surety enough) to work effectively for the foreseeable future, maybe for many human generations to come.

In the immediate term, to protect the current generation, it *must* include, but not be limited to, the entire planned dozen-plus Columbia-class submarines. U.S. government decision-makers and military commanders, and the rest of us, *must* stay immunized from the fatal error of *mirror-imaging*, of thinking that all adversaries see everything the same way we do. The key to unraveling and defeating enemy asymmetric warfare tactics in each domain and all domains is to grasp the truly profound differences that can exist in enemy emotions, perceptions, attitudes and thinking compared to ours. This is especially true in the arena of effective nuclear deterrence, where subtle, deeply submerged psychological factors can prove decisive. The pitfalls of cultural mirror imaging, and ways to avoid them, will be covered in detail in Chapter 4.

Now, We Switch from the Conceptual and Qualitative to the Analytical and Quantitative

The discussion below, for the remainder of this Chapter 2, relies on some basic arithmetic, and established facts of naval science. These are hard to deny or ignore, even amid today's malevolent foreign-government-sponsored information warfare trolling and our own domestic political divisiveness and incipient science-denial. The critical conclusion of this chapter will be as follows:

> All of America's three deterrent Triad legs, in adequate numbers of nuclear warheads and delivery platforms for each, are absolutely essential to the success of the whole, because the different legs interlock with, protect, and reinforce one another, as indispensable parts of one organic entity.

There's a Fatal Flaw in Minimal-Deterrence, Under-Resourcing Scenarios

The suggestion that America can safely get by with just a *very small number* of nuclear warheads and only a *single type* of delivery vehicle—*the "minimal" approach to deterrence*—goes back several decades. The concept, we will show, is a totally bad idea—but as an old saying goes, *"In Washington, DC, bad ideas never die."* For illustrative purposes, we will focus here on one particular, recently published approach to minimal deterrence. Our discussion of the flaws in this approach will help expose and explain *some very important general principles of military science* which are fundamental to the entire professional discipline of effective mutual nuclear deterrence. As with all professional disciplines, we will come to see how "someone not knowing how much they don't know" can, despite the best of intentions, easily lead to disaster.

Suppose the United States did—as a recent report by Princeton University and Global Zero[5], for instance, formally recommends—eliminate the ICBMs and almost all aircraft from our strategic triad, relying instead on what I think of as a "Mini-Monad": a greatly reduced number of the Columbia-class SSBN nuclear-deterrent subs, supplemented by just a handful of nuclear-capable aircraft. Those two august institutions, whose altruistic missions and prolific research outputs I greatly admire, assert—as a very serious policy recommendation—that a mere *five* SSBNs, with a token *forty* nuclear-capable bombers (rather than several hundred), are enough to keep America's and our Allies' global vital interests safe. This submarine-quintet-plus-some-airplanes would purportedly be adequately strong to reassure our own citizens, our Allies, and non-aligned states—thus aiding global nuclear nonproliferation. This minimal deterrent force would supposedly achieve said reassurance by reliably dissuading/persuading China, Russia, North

5. *The End of Nuclear Warfighting: Moving to a Deterrence-Only Posture—An Alternative U.S. Nuclear Posture Review*, Bruce G. Blair. Princeton University, September 2018, 109 pp., https://www.globalzero.org/wp-content/uploads/2018/09/anpr-180195-1736-1.pdf

Korea, nuclear terrorists, a nuclear-wannabe Iran, and possibly others in the future, into maintaining nuclear peace under even the most trying, stressful, desperate circumstances. *This is a very optimistic set of hidden assumptions, indeed!*

I seek to prove here using *rigorous logic*, with a touch of *mathematical risk theory*, plus *"actuarial contingent-timeline deconstruction methods"* thrown in (see the start of Appendix 1 for a definition), that such a very austere platform count is much too small to achieve its essential goals. With such a shrunken deterrent force, the handfuls of nuclear warheads that are installed together in each nosecone, but with independent targeting (MIRVing), on each of the sixteen ballistic missiles (SLBMs) in each of those mere five American Columbia-class deterrence submarines, would be *virtually all we owned that were based on survivable platforms*—and with *very limited* backup stockpiles held in storage. Period, full stop.

All submarines need to put into port periodically for lengthy periods of replenishment, maintenance and repair, not to mention crew rest, leave, and refresher training. (This is why our SSBNs each have *two* crews.) Furthermore, some of our SSBNs, at any one time, will be *busy traveling back and forth* between their forward deterrent-patrol areas and their rear-area home ports; these will be *out of position* for their missiles to have fully effective coverage of high-priority adversary strategic-deterrence targets. (This is because sub-launched ballistic missiles, to be able to fit inside the hull of a nuclear sub of practical "beam"—diameter—are too small to have the tremendous range of our bigger, silo-based ICBMs.) Thus, if our deterrence subs' patrols are to be spread evenly and steadily, both along the annual calendar *and* around the Earth's globe, then only about *one-quarter* of our entire owned SSBN fleet can be in effective-deterrence-position at sea *at any one time*. (And, a goodly portion of our overall strategic-deterrent sub fleet, covering the whole timeline and placed within effective SLBM range of all adversaries, absolutely does need to be at sea *all the time*.)

If the U.S. Navy only owned, say, five SSBNs, America could, as a steady, ongoing deterrent force, have on average *only one or maybe two at a time out where they needed to be*. As we shall demonstrate clearly below, only one or two SSBNs deployed, in a Mini-Monad with virtually no other nuclear weaponry in being, is the very epitome of a *"hollow force"*—a paper tiger that will let America down when we need it most. Worse, were America to give up our entire ICBM fleet and most of our strategic bomber fleet, as some disarmament zealots and over-stingy funding bean-counters have urged, we would free up the thousands of nuclear warheads owned now by Russia, so they could all be targeted *right at* that one deployed SSBN (in a nuclear anti-submarine wide-area barrage, as discussed below). Or, even worse, they could all be targeted right at America's most populous cities!

You Just *Can't* Surge the Whole Fleet All the Time; *Five* SSBNs Are *Not* Nearly Enough

This only-one-in-four-in-position ratio is true during *typical "peacetime" steady-state/ongoing SSBN deployment cycles*, as opposed to the *emergency surging* of all possible boats out to sea during a serious-enough *nuclear crisis* (which develops *gradually*, over a period of time, like the Cuban Missile Crisis did, giving us some warning). Beware, though, that—as all our adversaries surely understand—a "bolt from the blue" massive surprise-attack nuclear strike (a dreaded *"nuclear Pearl Harbor"*) would (by definition of "surprise") give us *no warning*.

We *must not* assume that the only conceivable adversarial nuclear-attack threats against us will be ones that we can see coming *clearly enough* and *far enough in advance* for Silent Service leadership to be able to successful mount a *very logistically complex surging* of even a too-small, minimal 5-vessel SSBN fleet! Our deterrence must be *perpetually* on guard against both *no-warning, "bolt from the blue" surprise attacks and out-in-public-but-very-sudden "insta-crises."*

If our in-position survivable deterrent is *not continuously and seamlessly both sufficiently numerous and adequately dispersed*—thus leaving our country with *severe protective loopholes*—then we are *inviting/encouraging* determined enemies to hit America devastatingly hard, precisely in those dangerous coverage gaps that are *inevitable* were we to adopt Princeton's/Global Zero's proposed 5-SSBN Mini-Monad.

Owning *only five* Columbias in commission, *instead of twelve-plus*, means there would be *very inadequate strategic dispersal* of America's deterrent forces[6]. One straightforward way of putting this goes back to Aesop's fables, from ancient Greece (circa 600 BCE): "Don't put all your eggs in one basket." In very compelling modern terms—as in something straight from the board game "Risk"—those subs would be too restricted in number, and thus restricted in their full global geographical coverage, to be able to hold under nuclear retaliatory-counterstrike

6. "Strategic Dispersal and SSBN(X) Count," Joe Buff, *The Submarine Review*, Naval Submarine League, Fall, 2013, p. 112. MIRVing uses Multiple Independent Reentry Vehicles to loft several separate warheads on one missile. SLBM means Submarine Launched Ballistic Missile.

threat, *simultaneously* as they need to, *all* of Russia's and China's very large, very far-flung strategic-assets inventories.

To repeat for emphasis, our strategic deterrent *must* be immediately available on station, in adequate and effective strength, *at all times*. We *must not* count on always having sufficient notice to mount the hoped-for submarine fleet surges that aim to tamp down the more evident/gradual nuclear crises—because *by no means all* nuclear crises will be of the more manageable type where we *do* have time to see them coming and get ready to prevent the worst.

This *unpleasant but inescapable fact* is because our adversaries watch our nuclear preparedness very closely, and they constantly practice *opportunistic, asymmetric warfare*, with clever *offset strategies* designed to try to counteract our strengths. If we were only able to effectively deter them during obvious nuclear crises, when we knew clearly and well in advance that we needed to strive to surge the bulk of our SSBN fleet of *only four or five boats*, then they would work extra hard to covertly set up a surprise attack, *lulling us* in the meantime with conditions that appear superficially *normal and benign*. The possibility of such an adverse scenario *definitively* negates the idea of owning only a minimal deterrent.

Strategic Antisubmarine Nuclear Area-Barrage Tactics Are in the Open Cold War I Literature

Consider the *nuclear area-barrage tactic* in "strategic" (i.e., nuclear combat) antisubmarine (ASW) warfare.[7] This is a "semi-focused bludgeon" approach: It attempts to preemptively mission-kill an adversary's stealthy SSBN fleet, hiding out in the deep blue sea on deterrent patrol, *before* they can launch their nuke-tipped SLBMs. This tactic could become *very appealing* to America's numerously-nuclear-armed Near-Peer Competitors (Russia and China), were the U.S. to be foolhardy enough to downsize our now-robust Triad to a Mini-Monad—as some DC pundits and politicos now seriously recommend.

For the barrage tactic to be at all practical, a very stringent condition must be satisfied: The enemy needs some vague hints or clues, or detection whiffs, that give their nuclear forces a rough idea of where one or more (or *all*) of our SSBNs on patrol are lurking at a given moment. The fewer SSBNs we own altogether, the fewer the enemy would need to somehow successfully target, to take them all out. The

7. *Anti-Submarine Warfare and Superpower Strategic Stability*, Donald C. Daniel, University of Illinois Press, 1986, 222 pp.

fewer they need to target, the more of their ICBM warheads in inventory they could aim at each sub, so the *larger* the area around each sub they could saturate and thoroughly sanitize—and thus the less information they would need to have about just where our on-station subs are.

The flip side of this basic math is that the fewer the SSBNs the U.S. Navy has in commission, the fewer can be on station at any given moment, on deterrence patrol—as opposed to being laid up for dry-dock maintenance, or busy going from home port to out somewhere that is within range of the strategic enemy targets they are tasked to threaten.

In short, fewer U.S. Navy SSBNs in being—with no fixed-silo ICBMs needing to also be taken out, and too few bombers sitting at exposed, vulnerable air bases—means many more Russian and/or Chinese nuclear warheads could be expended to try to simultaneously mission-kill our *entire at-sea deterrent,* in hopes of Moscow and Beijing freeing themselves from any fears of our retaliation for them nuking us. Too few SSBNs, and *no* ICBMs and *only a handful* of strategic bombers, would mean that what is now (with a *dozen-plus SSBNs, plus about five hundred ICBMs and hundreds of bombers*) the supremely survivable sea-based leg of our *diversified, dispersed* nuclear-deterrence *Triad,* would have instead *shrunk* and been *isolated* to the point that an at-times *single lonely on-station SSBN, as America's entire nuclear deterrent,* would no longer be nearly survivable enough.

What Could Happen if a Thousand H-Bombs Were Freed Up to Target One Isolated SSBN?

A *one-megaton warhead* (not atypical of those on Russian ICBMs), going off underwater, yields a *mission-kill radius* (i.e., the targeted sub is too damaged to fire any SLBMs) of around *ten nautical miles,* depending on environmental factors.[8] The kill radius is greatest when the warhead is set off at *considerable depth* within a *very deep ocean area.* U.S. Navy SSBNs tend to hide in such places, so that they can *preemptively detect any approaching potential threats* from very considerable distances away, and then *react as appropriate* (counterattack, or much more likely, evade at ultraquiet). They make such detections using their passive (listening-only) sonar towed arrays, which can be dangled down to exploit such benthic (deep ocean) battle arenas' *deep sound channels*—the

8. Literature readings, confirmed by private conversation with CAPT James H. Patton, Jr., USN(Ret.).

same natural phenomena by which whales sing to each other over *thousands of miles.*

The U.S. Navy works very hard on *operational security* (secrecy of deployment plans) and *submarine stealth* (low/no observability); this is part of why each of the new Columbia-class subs is so expensive. But *intelligence leaks* and *espionage coups* certainly can and sometimes do occur—witness for instance the infamous *Walker spy ring* and the deadly *Aldrich Ames spy case,* not to mention the U.S./UK *"Ultra"* cracking of the Nazis' Enigma code during World War II. Worse, some purely coincidental detection of an SSBN via a *chance encounter,* or a *miraculous enemy breakthrough in submarine detection technology,* might compromise one SSBN's location enough to permit an effective nuclear-barrage area-attack against it—*if* reducing our Triad to a Mini-Monad makes such a profligate use of H-bombs against one submerged submarine be feasible.

Against these very real risks, *there is great safety for our Triad, and for our Country, in fielding diverse weapons in big numbers*: a dozen (or more) Columbia-class SSBNs in inventory permits *four* to be continuously at sea at any one time, and the odds of *all four* ever being compromised at the same time, by a very clever and/or very lucky enemy, is *astronomically low.* If nuclear tensions were ever to rise to *serious crisis levels,* while America owned a full dozen-plus Ohios (now) or Columbias (in the 2030s), we would be able to mount a very formidable SSBN "surge" indeed, adding *significantly greater overall survivability* for our survivable second strike, via significantly greater numbers of SSBNs at sea! (In a *surge, every single one* of our SSBNs is rushed out of port immediately—if necessary, with some of her crews, her supplies, and even her captain left behind.)

So, what exactly is the *ASW nuclear barrage tactic*? It seeks—for every one of the limited number of deterrent subs (in a very parsimonious future scenario, *just one*) that the U.S. might actually have in position on patrol station—to *wreck all those subs' abilities to launch any SLBMs* in a retaliatory second strike. Were the Princeton/Global Zero recommendation to ever be implemented, America's Mini-Monad's one lonely on-station SSBN, once mission-crippled—*if* her "people tank" hadn't been lethally ruptured *and* some propulsion power could be regained—would face a long, grueling, and perilous voyage back to base for repairs—while probably being extra-noisy (extra-detectable, i.e. very vulnerable) because of combat damage, *and* while all of relevant U.S. home ports and dry docks would surely have been nuked to smithereens in the same hypothetical enemy surprise attack.

There are *many practical difficulties* to ever actually implementing a strategic ASW barrage—assuming, that is, that some belligerent nuclear-superpower adversary were ever reckless enough to try to knock out the hypothetical, future American Mini-Monad's only deployed nuclear-launching undersea platform in a surprise nuclear attack. One *particularly immense difficulty* would be the adversary somehow managing to *definitively localize* that ultra-stealthy SSBN, out at sea somewhere; *guessing wrong, or missing* a mission-kill (by peppering an area of ocean with H-bombs without seriously damaging that SSBN) would leave her capable of inflicting *massive retaliatory damage* on the aggressor, via any Ohio's or Columbia's dozens upon dozens of accurate, high-yield nuclear warheads.

But, as just mentioned above about Walker and Ultra, to accomplish such a *decapitating counterforce first-strike,* by localizing her enough to compromise that one deployed vessel's mission-worthy survivability, is *not entirely impossible*—if America's overall defensive Triad is too small, ala a 4-or-5-SSBNs, 0-ICBMs, few-bombers Mini-Monad. *Such not-entirely-impossible things are exactly the possibilities we have to prevent at all costs, when the stakes literally include survival of all life on our home planet.*

To try to achieve this SSBN mission kill—which would need to "get" *every single one* of the SSBNs the U.S. Navy does have out at sea, to avoid being counter-nuked to "the other side of oblivion" by the *surviving* subs (were we to have enough of them, backed by 500 ICBMs)—the attacker would need to use every clue they can possibly get about approximately *where* each submerged USN SSBN might be. Then they would have to *saturate* those broad areas of the ocean with a *very large number of their ICBMs* and other nuclear-armed ballistic missiles, and/or nuclear-armed cruise missiles, hypersonic gliders, aircraft-delivered gravity bombs, drone nuclear torpedoes—and even improvised nuclear depth charges dropped from conveniently located spy trawlers and disguised, pseudo-civilian "Q-ships."

One of the *key points* to having *several* SSBNs at sea plus *hundreds* of ICBM silos and *dozens* of air bases on land is simply the following *inescapable fact of arithmetic*: the more land-based nuclear-weapon targets we own, plus the more at-sea SSBNs we deploy, then the thinner the enemy must spread their nuclear arsenal among all those hundreds and hundreds of must-kill platforms, in any surprise attack that sad adversary ever hopes to survive. An adequately numerous, well dispersed, technically diversified U.S. Strategic Command Triad makes it *simply impossible* for any conceivable adversary to think that they could kill *all our nukes* in a successful preemptive strike, even one using *all their nukes.* What makes this "math theorem" true, what makes our

SSBNs so survivable individually, and such potent force multipliers as a fleet, is that *every single one* of our submerged SSBNs would require an adversary to use *a thousand H-bombs* to have even a snowball's chance in Hell of achieving a mission kill on that one sub![9]

(Note that one way in which, during any actual nuclear shooting conflict, an SSBN *would* reveal its location, while *remaining* a very-high-value nuclear-armed strategic target, would be if she were to make a *very conspicuous datum* by being utilized to launch a *limited* retaliatory strike, of *only one or a few* SLBMs, rather than all 16—the upcoming Columbia class—or all 24—the obsolescing Ohio class—of her missiles. If she still had other SLBMs aboard, as yet unexpended, and even if she fled the scene of launch submerged at flank speed, she would become localized to within a tight radius, while being a very worthwhile target indeed for an enemy ASW area-barrage counter-counterstrike! This is just *one more reason* why America needs a *diversified and dispersed full Triad*: We *must* have the option to launch small, limited, *very prompt* nuclear counter-strikes using silo-based ICBMs, to protect our high-value SSBNs by preserving their complete stealth as long as possible during any nuclear war. A limited counter-strike by one or more USAF strategic bombers could take *hours* for the long-range standoff air-launched cruise missiles to hit their targets deep in enemy territory—much too long a reaction time in some wartime scenarios, compared to the *thirty minutes or less* for either an ICBM or an in-position SSBN's SLBM to detonate at its aim point.)

Recap: Only a *Full* U.S. Triad Presents Our Adversaries with an *Unsolvable* Targeting Problem

An enemy's strategic target localization problem, which he/she *must* solve to have a prayer of succeeding against the U.S. with an ASW area barrage, is impractically intractable *if and only if* our Triad satisfies certain conditions: We've got to own a large enough total fleet of SSBNs so that even when keeping to a peacetime *non-surging* deployment schedule, we *always* have an adequate number of SSBNs in position at sea. The U.S. Navy has determined through careful analysis and modeling that this adequacy "magic number" is *four*—which is possible

---

9. 1,500 1-megaton warheads each with a 10 nautical mile (nm) mission-kill radius = 1,500 × Pi × 10^2 mission-kill area = 471,000 nm^2 mission-kill area. Adjacent, non-overlapping coverage by these circles is 471,000 nm^2, within smallest all-enclosing square whose area is 1,500 × 20 × 20 = 600,000 nm. Kill probability (P_K) in this square is 417,000 / 600,000 = 78.5%. Square's dimensions are square root of 600,000 = 775 nm on a side.

only with a total fleet of twelve in commission—to allow for (1) thorough *worldwide coverage* of very-spread-out adversary essential deterrence-target lists, with (2) a *margin for unknown contingencies* such as mechanical failures or crew pandemics, along with (3) *essential ship maintenance downtime* and (4) *the days each ship needs to transit* from homeport to deterrence-patrol position. In addition, it is *mandatory* for us to own an adequate, diverse set of other deployed "bodyguard" land-based Triad legs, including *literally hundreds* of widely-dispersed, silo-based ICBMs.

Beware indeed, enjoyers of nuclear peace and American freedoms, if you downsize your Triad by much at all from current levels! As simple models discussed in Chapter 6 will demonstrate quantitatively, taking this downsizing past current (and already very *budget-conscious*) levels will quickly reach a dreadful "tipping point": The effectiveness of America's nuclear deterrent-in-being to deter nuclear attack, and therefore also to dissuade nuclear blackmail, would *collapse into ineffectuality*.

To achieve the sought-after ASW barrage effectiveness goal for themselves, America's and NATO's adversaries must satisfy certain rather stringent conditions, which *only* adequate sizing and diversification of our Triad can *render it impossible* for our enemies to achieve: The adversaries must have enough nuclear weaponry available (because they don't need to commit it elsewhere, such as against America's current *500+ separate land-based ICBMs and command bunkers, plus our dozens of spread-out airbases and airports usable as strategic-bomber fields*) for them to mount a massive-enough ASW saturation barrage of a wide-enough area of the ocean. They must also, somehow, get a general idea where our patrolling SSBNs are. In a worst case, especially if only one American SSBN were available at sea at the time, such information might be betrayed by concerted espionage, or by a chance detection of the sub to be targeted, or by lucky surmise or sheer guesswork on the part of the enemy.

The fewer SSBNs we have, and *the fewer the other nuclear platforms to support them* directly and indirectly, the more of *their* warheads the enemy can allocate to crippling (not necessarily sinking) every on-station American (and NATO) nuclear-deterrent sub. Were we to ever have too few subs, and almost no other U.S. nuclear forces in being, then the figure for enemy-warheads-available-per-friendly-SSBN becomes huge, *almost 1000 to 1, or even more, in the current New START treaty warhead-count-limit environment*. As we will see below, such a huge nuclear volley can sanitize a sizable part of the ocean.

As detailed in footnote 9, a hypothetical enemy ASW barrage of 1,500 delivery vehicles each with a 1 megaton warhead (or a smaller number of

MIRVed vehicles, i.e., with more warheads on each) can "sanitize" a square of the sea measuring almost 800 nautical miles on a side. IF and ONLY IF an American SSBN happens to be lurking in exactly that spot amid the almost infinitely vast world oceans, the barrage will achieve a mission-kill success probability of 80%.

This kill probability, in the (currently) exceedingly unlikely event that it could ever actually be realized, is *much too high.* Having *four* SSBNs on patrol, forcing the enemy to divide their available nukes among several disparate SSBN targets, cuts this theoretical probability-of-deterrence-failure to 20%, but even that, in this idealized and unfathomably unlikely scenario, is *still too high.*

What cuts the kill probability the rest of the way down to a *truly negligible risk for America,* currently, is *also, simultaneously,* having in being (1) our 500ish widely-separated, hardened, underground land-based ICBMs, and (2) several dozen hardened command bunkers, plus (3) our numerous air bases and airports able to accommodate heavy bombers, which—for an enemy to be confident of destroying them all—must *each* be targeted with 2 or 3 nuclear warheads. Our many easily-dispersed and quickly-launched nuclear-capable bombers add even further to the impossibility of an enemy ever solving this targeting conundrum.

This explains how the different legs of our Triad *work together* to protect and reinforce each other. In essence, all of our hundreds of land-based nuclear-deterrent assets serve as "indispensable bodyguards, flypaper, *and* life insurance" for our sea-based nuclear deterrent assets, as well as being vital deterrence sentinels in their own right.

Crucial fact: At current worldwide nuclear arsenal levels, no adversaries can mount any effective ASW nuclear barrages against any American (and/or NATO) SSBNs since to do so would leave our land-based deterrent forces largely unmolested and able to deliver the devastating retaliatory second strike that said enemy tried to prevent by attacking our SSBNs in the first place.

In Any New Nuclear Arms Race, Build a Few More SSBNs, *Not* Lots More H-Bombs and ICBMs

What if an adversary *started an arms race* to build many more H-bomb tipped ICBMs, in an attempt to threaten both our land-based *and* our sea-based Triad legs along with our various other important national assets? As discussed further in Chapter 6, the U.S. should *not* respond by us simply acquiring and deploying more nuclear warheads and/or more ICBMs ourselves, although we would always hold the *option to do so*; in fact, *if* our Submarine Industrial Base ever became strapped for construction capacity, the best practical approach (and perhaps the most equitable among competing defense contractors struggling with COVID-19 effects and/or other economic downturns) might be for the U.S. to build *some* more hydrogen-bomb warheads, and *a variety* of delivery vehicles: *some* more ICBMs, *some* more strategic bombers, and *some* more SSBNs. (This approach would in effect *scale up* the different Triad legs *proportionally*, sustaining balance overall.)

But to avoid either *triggering* an arms race ourselves, or *joining in* one started by adversaries, a powerful baseline combined *arsenal-size-damping* and *enemy-containment* strategy for America—in the event of any new nuclear-warheads-count upward-spiraling acquisition contest between superpowers—could be this: The U.S. should focus on building more Columbia-class SSBNs, *to have more on patrol at any one time*; we should *spread our existing inventories*, of New START-level strategic warheads and of SLBM delivery vehicles, *dispersing them better* among this *larger* submarine fleet, by leaving a few missile tubes *empty* of weaponry on each sub. (Those tubes might instead, for instance, hold more non-perishable meal supplies, to *allow longer patrols* without either food rationing *or* the need to break stealth for reprovisioning.)

One additional Columbia sub built for our fleet, once serial production of this new sub class is already underway, costs *less than a fourth as much* as the hundreds of Russian MIRVed ICBMs, nuclear warheads, and hardened basing silos needed to threaten our one extra sub with an ASW area barrage—even assuming the enemy can somehow localize a *big* handful of our deterrent subs *all at the same time. If* Russia or anyone else ever tried to beat us in a nuclear arms race of *this* nature, they would *spend themselves into bankruptcy*, with self-induced regime change, *just as happened to the USSR.*

Note that this suggested SSBN-building arms-race containment strategy, if ever necessary, would be consistent with U.S. Strategic Command's current approach of gradually increasing the proportion, of all our deployed nuclear warheads, that are based on our SSBNs. This proportion is gradually being increased from a current 50% to a long-term goal of 70%. There are *two important benefits* to this: *First*, the more of our warheads are based at sea instead of on land, the less *our Homeland and our civilian population* would be subject so closely to the *terrible collateral damage* (nuclear blast and heat, radioactive fallout) from any enemy "counter-force" nuclear strikes against our ICBM fields and our strategic bomber airfields.

Second, placing even more of our deterrent warheads on our SSBNs would play to one of America's *greatest strengths* in the arena of weapons technologies: Our nuclear submarine construction know-how is the best in the world. While both Russia and China are making significant advances in this very challenging realm themselves, so that we must never grow complacent, America can benefit its own national security, as well as the *noble cause* of preserving world nuclear peace, by exploiting our *great comparative advantage* in building and safely, *very* skillfully operating *the finest nuclear subs in the world.*

But Triad force-structure *balance and diversification* remain vital: It would be a major mistake to move 100% of our nuclear-deterrence warheads onto an enlarged SSBN fleet. While they would be maximally survivable in the smaller sense, our resulting deterrent Monad would become vulnerable to *unforeseen Columbia-class-wide technical problems*, and (as discussed above) going to a Monad would "put all our eggs in one basket" relative to an *unforeseen advance in adversary anti-submarine technology.*

Furthermore, eliminating our widely geographically dispersed land—based nuclear forces *altogether* would mean *two very bad things*: (1) without many U.S. ICBMs which an enemy *cannot* ignore so that they *must* target them all, adversaries would be free to either *launch ASW area barrages* against our SSBNs or, worse, *nuke our cities*, and (2) without the (very mobile, recallable) strategic bomber leg of our Triad, the U.S. would lose the capacity for *clear, incremental (gradual) nuclear-deterrence signaling* to adversaries. (We will return to the topic of the bomber leg of the Triad soon, below.)

We Must Preclude ASW Area Barrages, Long Before a Desperate Enemy Resorts to Them

Strategic (nuclear) ASW area-barrage shenanigans would *play pure Hell* on our planet's environment, as well as on all oceanic commercial shipping traffic, coastal real estate values, and the beach resort industry—friendly, enemy, and neutral alike. The effects of massive drifting fallout clouds, and deadly radioactive contamination of edible seafood stocks, on worldwide public health would of course be *devastating.*

But at least nuclear ASW barrages avoid the planet-killing *nuclear winter* caused by persistent stratospheric soot-dust-aerosol clouds; for nukes set off on the open ocean the lofted debris will mostly be just steam, which would quickly condense and fall back to Earth as (very radioactive) rain.

The oceanic ASW barrage tactic similarly sidesteps the problem of *warhead fratricide*—interference between too many nukes used too close together in time and space, caused by one detonation's lofted debris damaging more incoming warheads: Fusing for *undersea* blasts, which yield hull-shattering concussions over wide submerged (and surface) areas, *don't* produce the massive amounts of rock-solid debris that are hurled far up into the atmosphere by nuclear blasts on land.

Thus, in the *immediate nuclear-warfighting* sense (i.e., ignoring the dire longer-term consequences), barrage tactics *do* have some *technical advantages* that could make them *overly attractive* for adversaries who have no regard for human life.

The barrage tactic does profligately drain the attacker's nuclear warhead holdings. But the enemy's backup MIRVed missile *stockpiles*, i.e., their non-deployed weaponry held in reserve, would be available for a *second-wave area barrage* against any of our SSBNs that somehow survived the first wave. This *mopping up* of on-patrol and in-transit subs might be achieved much sooner than our few surviving in-port Columbia-class subs (if any did survive) could surge to reach their forward deterrence/retaliation launch areas.

The threat of effective enemy ASW area barrages is very real, but any actual enemy implementation would *only* become possible if America's Triad were stripped of (1) *its current overall numerical strength* and (2) its *trefoil force-structure diversity*. Sustaining *both* essential attributes of our strategic deterrence forces—the large-enough number of weapons *and* the large-enough number of Triad legs—is clearly *absolutely vital.*

The tremendous benefit of having a sufficiently diversified Triad, with a sufficient number of the Columbia-class subs in the sea-based leg, is to force any aspirations by a belligerent aggressor, for their side to "win" or "prevail" in a nuclear war, into the category of "a snowball's chance in Hell," *a forlorn hope forever.*

The Advent of ASW Drones *Definitely Does Not* "Doom America's Doomsday Subs"

Nor does the advent of swarms of ASW drones in the world's navies really spell "the doom of doomsday subs." There are many *decisive tactical advantages* that a large, manned, nuclear powered SSBN—protected by seabed, submerged, surface, airborne, and spaceborne sensors and weapons, including those carried on the SSBN herself *and* on escorting fast-attack SSNs—enjoys over a drone-swarm's slower, dumber, poorly-coordinated robotic hordes. (This topic is covered more thoroughly in Appendix 3, along with other important aspects of SSBN deterrent-patrol "metaphysics.")

It's Time to Employ a "Helical Learning" Process, for Best Clarity in this Discussion

Not to pick on the Princeton/Global Zero disarmament study again, but it does provide an *excellent foil* against which to *unravel and explicate* many important principles of modern nuclear deterrence theory and practice. If the discussion below seems a tad repetitious, it is because following a *helical learning structure* is a good way to gradually weave together and add depth to the numerous *contrasting yet interlocking* aspects of the nuclear-deterrence arts and sciences, which (bear in mind) have been the subject of study and development by some of Mankind's best minds for an entire human lifetime now.

There Are Fatal Flaws in Having Too Few Nuclear-Capable Aircraft

The Princeton/Global Zero study's recommendation that the U.S. can make do with a mere forty strategic bombers, given the drastic realities of the modern hypersonic (Mach 5 to 25) world—is in practice fatally flawed. When adversaries deploy both conventional and nuclear missiles that travel so fast and can maneuver to avoid our defensive interceptor counter-fire, the *"escape time"* of every squadron on the tarmac—the time it takes from *early warning* to scramble them for takeoff loaded with second-strike nukes, and get them up into the sky and *safely away*—is reduced to at most three-hundred *seconds. A too-small nuclear-capable bomber force* would be ineffectual in a large nuclear (or even conventional) ambush, since *every last one* of so few planes could easily be accurately targeted, caught on the ground, and knocked out.

Our actual current nuclear-capable air fleet, of several hundred *heavy bombers and smaller fighter-bombers,* also does now have such tightly-constrained escape time, but *this by no means* makes those *very numerous* combat planes overly vulnerable let alone "useless" as a holistic deterrence leg—any more than it means that America's chief executive (POTUS) has only a "five-minute window" to order a retaliatory second strike back at a nuclear-attacking enemy—these bogus allegations are *completely fictitious bugaboos.*

Viewed as one *overall component* within the U.S. Air Force, a strategic bomber fleet can still be quite survivable; but this is only true if we have a *large enough number of widely separated* air bases, each *with a large enough number* of deployed B-52s, B-2s, and next-generation super-stealthy replacements (the B-21 Raider bomber). At least *some* of them would be able to be (1) dispersed to many "secondary" staging runways, such as those at larger civilian airports all across the U.S. Homeland, or even (2) put in the air at the first sign of nuclear trouble. (The U.S. does not currently maintain round-the-clock, airborne nuclear-armed bomber patrols "just in case," like we did in the First Cold War, but these *could easily be re-instituted* in case of a nuclear crisis that gives us some advance warning.)

Why is there such safety in large-enough numbers?

Being well spread apart, all around the U.S. and overseas, makes it exceedingly difficult for an enemy to take out all our bomber bases at exactly the same time as all our hundreds of ICBMs. The Earth's vast and complex geography helps us greatly as a defender here. This is because of the *varying flight times* needed by any very large number of enemy nukes to hit us: Each one would be fired, with very evident (detectable by satellite) launch signatures, from disparate points (with different distances to travel to target) inside enemy territory or from international waters and airspace. The very first *confirmed nuke detonations* would be *unmistakable tripwires* for our total national strategic response—somewhat *after* the very first detected launch signatures gave us *invaluable early warning.*

So, please remember two things, gentle reader: The ultimate survivability of America's deterrent triad *as a totality* hinges decisively, conclusively on having enough of our superbly designed, built, crewed, and commanded Ohio- and/or Columbia-class SSBNs, *and* our 500 ICBMs in hardened silos with their command centers, *plus* our well-dispersed strategic bomber fleet. Effective nuclear deterrence is very much *a game of numbers. And* as discussed more just below here—reflecting the extensive professional literature of nuclear deterrence going all the way back to the 1950s—our strategic bombers have *certain other essential advantages* as one critical leg of our Triad.

A Too-Small Nuclear-Capable Aircraft Fleet Can't "Penetrate" an Adversary's Cognitive Psyche

A *too-small bomber fleet,* however, would fail to add nearly enough *cognition of existence-threatening downside risk,* within any reckless, foolhardy, and not-very-casualty-averse adversary's military-geopolitical gain/loss calculations, for that too-small bomber fleet to help deter the adversary from making a surprise nuclear first strike. And knowing this—they'd just have to read American political and aerospace news—the adversary wouldn't be put off from *nuclear blackmail during nuclear peacetime* (which could include the all-important *nuclear twilight zone of active proxy or regional conventional* war), either. America being able to respond ("signal") in *gradually rising increments* while staying *well short* of a (catastrophic) actual preemptive first-use by us—in the case of a *serious enough nuclear extortion attempt (or nuclear crisis)* started by an adversary—is a *vitally important function* that our USAF strategic bombers are *perfect for*.

Only an *Adequately Big* Nuke-Capable Aircraft Feet Can Send Messaging "Signals" Safely in a Nuke Crisis

Nuclear-capable or *dual use* aircraft (DCAs) are indispensable deterrence and dissuasion tools. Alerting them, and visibly uploading nukes to them on the runway, can be a nicely nuanced and quite conspicuous way to *signal* rather unambiguously to an adversary about America's and NATO's *displeasure* and our *determination*. The DCAs' flight paths, from takeoff to final attack run, can take *hours* to unfold, with several intermediate waypoints that would be obvious on an adversary's radar warning systems. The DCAs—strategic bombers and tactical fighter-bombers—can be used to *gradually escalate our crisis messaging*, while staying *well short* of an unprovoked nuclear first use (by us). The DCAs are *recallable* at any time. Despite the overdramatized scare tactics by the writers of that famous novel and movie *Failsafe*, actual USAF DCA aircrews would never release their nukes without a *thoroughly-authenticated* positive final launch-confirmation order from U.S. National Command Authorities.

(The importance of our and our NATO Allies' own *strategic early warning systems* cannot be overstated. These include constellations of *surveillance satellites*, increasingly hardened and stealthy, that harness advanced *multi-spectral sensors*. They also include a diverse and widespread menagerie of powerful *ground-based radars*.)

U.S. Air Force Nuclear-Capable Aircraft Crews Are Very Brave People Indeed!

Being a USAF aircrew member in a nuclear crisis or nuclear war is no picnic! In a worse case, if the enemy commits a surprise first use, our strategic air bases would all be top priorities on their targeting list. Those of our bomber crews who do get up and away from the horrific nukings of their primary and/or secondary-dispersal bases, in a mission-capable condition (which requires much more than just a barely-flyable condition), would then face an additional *aviator's Hell on Earth:* A withering gauntlet of well-prepared enemy anti-aircraft defenses (such as Russia's next-generation Su-57 stealth fighter and her state-of-the-art anti-aircraft missile systems S-400 and S-500), extending over an air-penetration route toward and within enemy territory of possibly *thousands of miles,* before ever getting in nuclear gravity-bomb range of their strategic targets. This, by the way, is why the USAF's *next-generation nuclear-penetration stealth bombers,* the B-21s, equipped with *long-range, low-observable nuclear-capable cruise missiles,* the LRSOs, are so very important to successful deterrence and defense.

Why Adequate Triad Numbers Matter So Very Much

If we ever tried to rely on a too-small undersea nuclear-counterstrike force alone (the Mini-Monad idea), America's deterrent would have been rendered un-survivable by our own failure to grasp how effective nuclear deterrence does or doesn't really work, and by our national defense-budget parsimony. Once a Mini-Monad were all-too-easily neutralized by *enemy action* (or just by the bad-luck *mechanical breakdown* of our one or two on-station SSBNs), the U.S. could be blackmailed into major geopolitical concessions by only a few more deployed nukes left in the hands of a dastardly Yes-First-Use enemy. Our populous cities, spared nukings up to then, could be *held hostage from afar* against any further U.S. resistance to tyranny. We might even be disarmed and occupied, with a forced wholesale regime change, much as the U.S. and our allies did to Nazi Germany and Imperial Japan when our side won World War II.

New START currently limits Russia and the U.S. to 1,550 "deployed" strategic nuclear warheads each—these are ready for quick employment if ever necessary. More nukes are "stockpiled" (stored) as backup by each side—these would take longer to bring on-line. This number is way down from the total of some 70,000 nukes owned, between Moscow and Washington, a few decades ago.

Disarmament has indeed been *quite important,* to minimizing possible nuclear accidents, and to more generally help save human lives, taxpayer money, and Earth's natural environment. The Disarmament Movement has been *productive, meaningful, and very wise—up to now.* But *rightsizing,* as opposed to undersizing, superpower nuclear arsenals is very important to ongoing (and face it folks, permanently required) mutual deterrence and global nonproliferation efforts.

Suppose the U.S. does keep its land-based ICBM force at the current roughly 550 (non-MIRVed) nuclear missiles deployed and command bunkers manned. An enemy would need a full 1,100 of its own warheads—used *all at once* somehow yet with *no* advance clues given that this impending nuke Pearl Harbor was on the way—just to have the proverbial snowball's chance in Hell of reliably wiping out our dispersed, hardened underground silos while our ICBMs are all still inside. Here I'm using the Cold War-era rule of thumb that *two* warheads are needed to reliably kill one dispersed and hardened underground target.

A well-informed source tells me that the more ICBMs Russia wants to fire at America in a simultaneous, surprise launching, the harder (i.e., impossible) such *needed simultaneity* would be for them to pull off. This is because of *persistent limitations* of their missile and communication technologies, as well as the *impossible challenges* of so many missile flight paths having to transit so many varying intercontinental and transcontinental distances—yet *all* with the *exact same* launch times *and* detonation times. (Any of the inevitable "stragglers," i.e. "late arrivals," in such an all-out nuclear attack by Russia or whoever, would leave some of America's land-based nuclear forces *intact*—yet with *very ample and completely unambiguous launch-under-attack warning*—for long enough that they would be able to deliver an *unstoppable and devastating nuclear counter-strike.*)

Recap: One Vital, Hidden Role of the USAF's ICBMs Is as "Bodyguard" for the USN's SSBNs

Our ICBMs are the *least invulnerable* leg of the Triad—it's clear to our technically-capable adversaries exactly where they are, and they're unable to move—but they have powerful nuclear warheads, and they can legitimately be MARVed. "MARVing" makes each warhead *even more likely to get through once successfully launched,* by giving it *jinking capabilities* plus *penetration aids* such as decoys. MARVing is different from MIRVing, which is installing *multiple* warheads on *one* missile. America does *not* MIRV its land-based ICBMs. This is because it is *strategically destabilizing* to offer adversaries such a rich and overly threatening, thus tempting, concentrated single target that might all-too-easily *justify nuclear preemption*: why so threatening and tempting? Land-based MIRVs give their owner a *nasty force-multiplier advantage,* in that *one* MIRVed ICBM launch by them can take out *up to ten or even twenty* enemy ICBMs still in their silos. (Russia *does* MIRV some of their ICBMs: This fits in with their grand strategy of nuclear intimidation, and it rather arrogantly imposes upon America's "nuclear forbearance.")

Just one decisive value of our ICBMs to America is that any enemy seeking to get away with a devastating surprise first strike simply *must* take them all out at the start, or suffer truly terrible consequences. This ICBM-fleet role as bodyguards-from-the-sidelines (sometimes also described as "strategic flypaper"), providing *essential "blocking and tackling"* for our SSBNs—as discussed already above—seems largely *invisible, unsung and under-appreciated* by much of the American public (and by some in Congress, too)—*but this protective role is very, very real.* It is therefore eminently worth emphasizing (and *re*emphasizing) here, in writing, for the permanent record.

Plus, our silos are very difficult indeed to put out of action. Each is built from nearly *one-thousand tons* of reinforced concrete. Each ICBM is very well shock hardened, and their housing mechanisms (huge springs, hydraulic buffers) within the silo itself provide additional layers of protection. They are dug very deep into terrain whose geology gives them a serious chance to beat any incoming nuclear blast. To hit one fatally from strategic distances would require such *pinpoint targeting accuracy* by an enemy that *no one* could achieve the *mandatory direct hits* needed over a very large number of near-simultaneous counterforce strikes.

The U.S. (and NATO) nuclear-deterrence Triad enterprise is truly an inseparable, joint ("purple") endeavor!

This Is an Arms Race that Moscow Would Lose Badly—Again

Any enemy seeking to seriously threaten our whole diversified and numerous current Triad would have to up their nuclear weapons inventory back toward the crazy, stratospheric levels of old. They can be dissuaded both *financially and strategically* from doing so: If they tried, it would end badly indeed for them, the same way as the Soviet Union tried it and failed badly. Far better to *stick to the current strategic arms limitation norms,* and renew New START or at least continue obeying its limits after it lapses.

But the bad guys out there can also listen to General George Patton: "When in doubt, attack." They can try to compete, to intimidate, to disrupt us, by beginning a new nuclear arms race. *We cannot stop them from trying, but we can remind them of the lessons of their own unfortunate history. And we can take the basic policy-strategy precautions to make quite sure that in such an arms race, the harm to us is minimal.*

In any such new arms race, the adversary would need to sustain a *phenomenal* H-bomb and ICBM construction rate, to ever be able to *even begin* to materially endanger any of our adequately-sized SSBN fleet. To achieve such massive up-arming would not be instantaneous, either; to safely manufacture thousands of warheads and missiles would take years if not decades, giving the U.S. and NATO ample time to decide how best to react, and then to implement our chosen reaction counter-strategy.

And if Russia or China tried instead to gain some strategic advantage by building more nuclear submarines instead of ICBMs themselves (SSBNs, SSGNs, and/or SSNs), America's *powerful undersea-warfare technological and tactical superiority* would simply *bankrupt the adversary in a different way*—while making a Russia or a China *lose* the next so-called Silent War contest under the sea, *again just like the USSR lost big last time.*

I have started to think of the super-stealthy Columbia-class subs as "The Untouchables"—they're almost infinitely more so with our current ICBM and DCA forces backing them up. (See below for more on the vital importance of our SSNs and SSGNs to defending our SSBNs.)

To paraphrase General Patton again, the U.S. Air Force runs a *great defense* for our SSBNs (just one among the USAF's *many* vital contributions to national security) by running a powerful potential nuclear *offense.* If any nuclear bad actor out there ever even *thinks* about going too far in nuclear attack or nuclear blackmail, the USAF will come at them hard and fast. They will hit them simultaneously "high and low" through Earth's atmosphere—with bombers—and via the vacuum of space—with ICBMs—to deliver a devastating vengeance of truly Biblical proportions. *This is the very essence of effective nuclear deterrence.*

It should be getting clear now how very much our effective nuclear deterrence—the *bulwark* of American security and the *guarantor* of world nuclear peace—must be understood as a *holistic fabric,* woven into the entirety of America's economy, governance, and military. With all due respect for our hard-working CPAs and budgeting czars, our strategic deterrent cannot and *must not* be adulterated, parsed, and dismembered in some misguided process of "bean counting," let alone of misinformed "nuclear risk reduction." The "true fact" is that to acquire the hardware needed for our planned next-generation deterrent will add *only about* 4% to the annual U.S. defense budget. This money *needs to be spent* simply because our aged and obsolescing First Cold War-era deterrent hardware is fast wearing out, now being pushed too far past its "use-by date"; the idea that we can continue to *just get by* with these piles of decrepit near-rattle-traps—because total nuclear disarmament and a golden age of world peace are supposedly just around the corner—is a very dangerous myth, nay, a *truly insane delusion.*

Here's another true fact: Much of that supposedly already-bloated total annual Pentagon budget now goes to fund *pay and benefits* for active-duty people, veterans, and their dependent family members; it goes to fund salaries and combat pay, reenlistment incentives, housing and dependents allowances, schools and cafeterias, military and

Veterans Administration hospitals, other health care costs, retirement pensions, and the like, *not* nuclear bombs. And all the money paid to defense contractors, for all the different nuclear-deterrence weapons systems we need, does something else very good for America's citizenry, *especially* in this time of the Covid-19 Economic Crisis: *It creates jobs.*

To Repeat (Again) for *Reemphasis*: Adequate ICBM Count Is a Powerful SSBN Force Protector

In re of understanding some of the downside implications (just as examples) of parts of the Princeton/Global Zero report, it is rather important to recognize something: At present, fully two-thirds of Russia's deployed New START-level strategic arsenal is locked up by the priceless "nuclear shortstops" of our ICBM force. Suppose America does indeed retire and scrap all our ICBMs, anyway, along with all our cruise/glider missiles and most aircraft-delivered nukes. And suppose we do indeed have only five SSBNs, not just deployed on station at any one time, but in active service *at all.*

We need to *think through, very carefully*, the full implications of such a major policy move—and this is where the conceivable scenarios and possible outcomes get scary. At least, so far, on both sides of America's deterrence-vice-disarmament strategy/policy/budget debate, it's all been just an eye-opening *"thought experiment"*—an academic, intellectual exercise, not a real-world actuality.

In many ways, ever since the First Cold War began, and also after it ended, both this domestic, political debate about nuclear defense—and the concomitant international battles and campaigns of *nuclear geopolitical jousting and saber rattling with foreign adversaries*—have for the most part (barring various deadly nuclear accidents and near-death nuclear crises) been "fought" by just this type of Albert Einstein-like, exploratory and revelatory—but physically rather safe—thought experiments. Yet these ones here and now regarding the possible fate of our Triad, and with it our Democracy, are *not* abstract, purely studious, entirely academic inquiries like those beloved by astrophysicists.

Theoretical scientific inquiry is a *harmless parlor game* played on blackboards in university classrooms and faculty lounges; researcher errors made on campus are embarrassing, but the worst is the mistakes-on-paper must be retracted in peer-reviewed scholarly journals.

Compare this to what's at stake with nuclear deterrence: Nuclear deterrence is a *life-or-death blood sport,* one that calls for comprehensive national-level resources, and for the dedicated efforts of *thousands* of people all singing from the same policy/strategy hymn book (which in this context is America's latest Nuclear Posture Review). Wrong notes hit by *this* chorus and orchestra can bring on a *total thermonuclear holocaust.*

Anyone who doubts this fact need just think of the Cuban Missile Crisis. At a time when deterrence theory and practice, and the implementation technologies, were much less developed on both sides of the Iron Curtain, humanity came so close to the brink of thermonuclear World War Three that it's frightening to this day. This is exactly what can happen, *again,* if sound thought-experiments get botched and wise policy gets neglected; what can blow up isn't just some physics laboratory, it's the entire world!

With this caveat and proviso, let us now pursue further the grim scenario about an America with only five SSBNs, and little else, in a Mini-Monad.

Some Principles of Naval Science Really Matter Here

For any size of SSBN fleet, in order for *ongoing* (steady-state, *not* surge) survivable/undersea-based nuclear deterrence of adversaries to be sustainable, at any one time about one-third of the subs *must* be sidelined in port for essential maintenance, repairs, upgrades, reprovisioning, and such. In today's world of ultra-intrusive ISR (intelligence, surveillance, and reconnaissance), HUMINT (human intelligence, i.e., spies), and cyber espionage (computer hacking), those in-port "boats" are *sitting ducks* for an enemy first-use surprise nuclear strike. Of course, in case of an international nuclear crisis building up over days or weeks, the U.S. Navy could and would rush them out of Navy-owned or contractor dry-docks or away from their homeport piers, reloaded with weapons and provisions and surged to reinforce our far-flung on-station undersea deterrence (even if some non-essential on-board systems don't work right).

But a well-planned and executed surprise bolt-from-the-blue nuclear strike is *not* the same thing as an evident, escalating international crisis. By design, the enemy would try to give us *no warning,* presumably *avoiding* any crises or tensions in order to lull us. Nor should the chance of such a bolt from the blue be derided. Adversaries will exploit our weaknesses, ruthlessly and opportunistically, as per Sun Tzu. They are *dedicated professionals,* as talented and hardworking as we are, and it's their *job.* Minimizing in our minds and in our political rhetoric the chance of "a nuclear Pearl Harbor" could create *exactly* such a fatal opening. In guaranteeing nuclear peace, one should *never say "never."* Sheer bureaucratic inertia, over-prideful complacency, "unprepared mindsets and failures of imagination" (the 9/11 Commission Report), or preparing for "the last war" instead of *the next one*, these all get people killed.

Another third of the SSBN fleet at any one time has to be underway, heading toward or away from their forward patrol areas far from base but *not* on-station yet, *out of range* of their assigned strategic targets. Given the *vast extent of enemy geographically dispersed high-value military assets* that our deterrent forces need to hold at risk planet-wide, and the *not-infinite maximum range of each of our SLBMs*, these in-transit subs could be out of position for an effective retaliatory strike for many days, even weeks, after a war starts. This is especially so when our subs are forced by hostilities to *always move at ultraquiet speed*.

Only one-third of the total SSBN fleet might thus be in immediate striking range of assigned deterrent targets at any one time. This will generally be the case whenever the threat environment is perceived by us as one where ongoing, sustainable, regular crew-and-ship deployment rotations are appropriate, rather than crisis/emergency short-term surging.

Now, in some not-inconceivable future nuclear warfare scenarios, America's hypothetical retaliatory second-strike would *not* need to be delivered immediately: "Revenge is (sometimes) a dish best served cold."

But in other, rather conceivable scenarios, we *would* need to be able to deliver our retaliatory strike right away; such adversary nuclear first-strike scenarios would *not* be able to be effectively deterred by a Mini-Monad. One example is the situation where we would need to launch a very urgent counterforce strike, a so-called *"blunting counterattack"* intended to diminish the enemy's remaining nuclear arsenal, for intra-war own-side *damage limitation*. If one or more of our at-sea SSBNs needed days (or even just *hours*) to get close enough for a viable counterstrike, it would in this scenario come *too late*.

Arithmetic-Deniers Are Either *Conmen or Madmen*, or *Both*

One-third of five equals 1.67. The proposed Mini-Monad's fleet of just five SSBNs would give America *only one* Columbia actually on station the majority of the time! We would have *absolutely no* ICBM force as distracting, protective "linebackers" for that sub. We would have very few Air Force bombers reinforcing our *nonexistent* ICBMs. In such a proposed very austere weapons-acquisition scenario, a determined enemy could concentrate almost its entire New START-level deployed arsenal of 1,550 warheads against *just one (or at most two)* deployed U.S. SSBNs. If that enemy were somehow able to mobilize its *stockpiled weapons* covertly, without alerting us in advance, that 1,550 could easily, at the very start of a nuclear war, be *doubled.*

You don't need more than a rough idea where our one or two subs might be in order to try to hit them, when such a massive individualized nuclear ASW barrage is available. How rough an idea? Is this argument just pedantic sophistry?

No, it's hard, pragmatic arithmetic.

A simple calculation[9] shows that a barrage of 1,500 warheads, each of one megaton yield, could threaten a square of ocean almost *eight hundred nautical miles on a side* with a mission kill probability of almost *eighty percent.* That is one whopping, non-trivial body of water. If at least one of our SSBNs is in that *kill box,* the odds are *4 out of 5* it will be decisively knocked out. This risk, as I think most U.S. defense professionals would agree, is *completely unacceptable.*

Imagine, then, that some desperate, power-mad or politically-cornered gambler/sociopath enemy superpower head-of-state decides, opportunistically and maybe delusionally, that he or she should roll the dice on neutralizing our *very lonely one or two Columbia subs* out there all alone defending freedom, while he/she also expends a *small handful of nukes* to preemptively knock out *all* of our few B-21s at their airbases and all of our in-port SSBNs. America's whole nuclear deterrent, too diminished by our own foolhardiness, could in such a Mini-Monad scenario be this easily *turned off, neutralized, wiped out.* (Any at-sea SSBNs that survive this onslaught in mission-capable condition might be *way* out of position to enter the fight.)

Sociopaths throughout history have been willing, even eager, to sacrifice *millions of their own citizens* for their personal aggrandizement. (Look at Napoleon, Kaiser Wilhelm, Hitler, Stalin, Saddam, Milosevic, Idi Amin, and Pol Pot.) *So what* if a bunch of radioactive steam wafts ashore from mid-ocean? *So what* if a handful of U.S./NATO nukes do manage to somehow get through to the well-protected dictator's Fatherland/Motherland? That tyrant's prize from a nuclear ambush, with a projected eighty percent success rate, would be *lifetime job security as ruler of the world.*

Two Models Say We're at a *Good* "Bend in the Hockey Stick"; Don't Go Higher *or* Lower

As part of my ongoing research on 21st century nuclear deterrence, I've developed two unrelated, simple models for calculating the critical value, *How many nukes are really "enough" for America (on a stable, semi-permanent basis), but neither "too many" nor "too few?"*

The first of these two models is a *bottom-up approach*, which suggests that New START's cap on strategic nuclear warheads is close to the sweet spot of what is necessary and sufficient. (This model produced as its "right answer" *1,800 deployed warheads*, distributed across a diversified Triad—this is *similar to the actual number* of American warheads under New START because the model and the treaty "count" them a bit differently.) And no, I did not cook the assumptions to "back into" the New START level as the answer I wanted to get. I set the assumptions objectively and realistically, and only then performed the calculation, just once—and it came out the way it came out.

This model is explained in Chapter 6. Readers need not jump ahead unless they are curious, as the main portion of this book, in the intervening chapters, doesn't draw on any of these technical modeling details.

My other model is a *top-down approach*. See footnote 9 on page 61 for a simple description of this model. Like the first model, and as already explained above in this Chapter, it also implies that shrinking our nuclear Triad by very much from current New START-compliant levels would be a *serious impediment to maintaining strategic nuclear stability with Russia and China.*

Don't Cut Deterrent Arsenals More, But *Do* Fight to Keep Them from Growing Again

What these twinned models are telling us is that the long, and (thank God) ultimately successful multilateral effort to get global warhead counts down from the suicidal overkill levels of the 1970s has served its purpose. *It served that purpose very well.* But it has now reached what should be articulated clearly as its *ultimate goal and stopping point.* The urgent arms control goal, now and prospectively, should be to *keep those counts from heading back skyward.* Drastic overpopulation of American and Russian nuke arsenals wouldn't just be economically and environmentally destructive.

As Princeton and Global Zero aptly warn, this would give *terrorists* more nukes to try to *steal*, were weapon safeguard lockdowns allowed to lapse. This would also produce more nukes that could go off *by accident*, were safety-oriented hardware features and personnel procedures ever to be neglected. It makes no sense to expose Humanity to more of these two risks *unnecessarily*, just like (see Appendix 1 re *comparing mathematical expectations of loss, not just probabilities of occurrence*) it makes no sense to panic over those (*secondary*) dangers now: Reducing strategic arsenals further would quickly bring the world to a point where *general nuclear war would not be deterred,* because a *smaller* threatened, survivable counter-strike could no longer surely end the adversary regime's existence. (See the third paragraph down in this subsection.)

Worse, a drastic up-spike in available warhead counts would wreck the very fabric of effective mutual superpower deterrence: It would *enable* those now-impossible effective strategic ASW barrages. Such enablement, once realized, would tempt (or panic) both sides into a deadly, paranoid race to *open fire first,* which is the very essence of *crisis instability.* Next stop: nuclear holocaust. By the time the nuclear winter cleared around our dying home planet, it wouldn't matter who had fired first!

And yet, to go any further into superpower strategic nuclear *dis*armament, either unilaterally (by just the U.S.) or bilaterally (by both the U.S. and Russia) would be counterproductive, too. To use that bugaboo of the First Cold War's academic literature on nuclear deterrence, it would, just like the case of having too many nukes, be *destabilizing.* In practical, laymen terms, this means it would encourage the very nuclear attacks that deterrence is meant to prevent.

This is because effective nuclear deterrence is heavily dependent on having the *guaranteed absolutely-worst-case option* (if ever deemed both necessary and legally/morally justified) to inflict *catastrophically massive damage* on an adversary who nukes us first, come what may. We and the bad guys *both* need to be 100.0% confident that hundreds of America's retaliatory nukes could hit enemy strategic targets in our (proportionate) second-strike, in spite of an utterly devastating enemy surprise first-strike, and even despite superb future enemy defenses of their own—i.e., despite Moscow or Peking (or both) fielding their own Reagan-esque Star Wars and their own large-scale Ballistic Missile Shields some day. *Without* such potentially-devastating, survivable mutual deterrence forces deployed in strength, plus stockpiled backups assured to survive any First Nuclear World War (for *future use* deterring a Nuke War II), a nuclear attack is a lot more likely to occur.

This is *really ugly stuff* to have to think about, but it is precisely this *stark realization,* of the *fearsome consequences* of any adversary's nuclear first-use, which is the *foundation and bedrock* of successful mutual nuclear deterrence and worldwide strategic stability!

Minimal deterrence will not cut it. When faced with only a *"small" punitive retaliatory strike as the only counter-strike possible,* a belligerent dictatorship may too easily seduce itself into a dastardly nuclear first-use. Some *really bad people* who are really out there, e.g., sociopaths surrounded by a "bubble" of blindly sycophantic yes-men, may be willing to sacrifice a few of their own cities with a few millions of their own people. (It is a historical fact that *Mao Zedong* and *Fidel Castro* both thought this way.) If their country boasts dozens of cities and hundreds of millions of people, this sacrifice might seem inconsequential, compared to *kingship* over all Humanity, *destruction* of America, and the *adoration* (in their own minds) of future history—which *they'll* get to write, assuming they themselves survive.

The absolute requirement of effective nuclear deterrence is that America and NATO be able to inflict a retaliatory second strike of truly existential scale on any nuclear-attacking enemy superpower, even after that enemy (1) does their very worst to eliminate our entire nuclear Triad in their surprise first strike, and then (2) does their very best to intercept our diminished second strike.

The View From 60,000 Feet is the Same from "Over There" as from Right Here

This calculus of life and death works in *exactly the same way* from Russia's and China's defensive perspectives, too. They need to be 100.0% confident, and they need to know that we are also 100.0% confident, that if some hypothetical, belligerent-enough future American regime were to ever scheme to launch a "nuclear Pearl Harbor" *on them* (more *a propos*, a "nuclear Port Arthur" per the Russo-Japanese War, or a "nuclear Nanjing" per the Second Sino-Japanese War), *we* would still be absolutely creamed by *their* surviving nukes.

Parenthetically, this touches on the international controversy over the small-scale U.S. missile-shield system currently (as of mid-2020) being developed and deployed. This shield is designed to be limited in capacity, to protect us *only* against a *modest number* of ICBMs, which might come our way from the likes of North Korea or Iran. But an important collateral benefit is that such a shield would *also* protect America and our allies from *nuclear blackmail and coercion* by a superpower adversary who threatens to, or actually does launch a *very limited* nuclear strike in our direction (***the following paragraph, like some others further into the book, is indented for greater emphasis***):

> An effective limited-capacity Ballistic Missile Defense (BMD) shield very importantly beefs up America's deterrent-in-being as a nuclear *bully repellent.* As one for-instance, it prevents any delusion that a "large" adversary can threaten to (or actually) inflict on us a "pin-prick nuking"—as if there could ever be such a thing—using *only one or a few*

ICBMs. Such a BMD-in-being clearly prevents an enemy from trying to strike at us *"below the threshold"* of some hypothetical future reticent/anti-nuclear POTUS's willingness to retaliate in kind (that is, with *our* nukes). As a second for-instance, a good BMD also prevents the scenario where a hypothetical future very-belligerent, non-casualty-averse enemy sees potent geopolitical advantage in breaking the nuclear peace via making a "small" nuclear strike at us, while *accepting* the limited damage from our proportionate nuclear counterstrike; such a move would be like forcing an exchange of queens in a chess match, to achieve a superior position on the game board.It does happen in chess. It *could* happen with nukes.

I suspect these two different thought-experiment scenarios help explain why America's peer competitors do *not* like our burgeoning missile shield one bit. Both scenarios also touch on an important way in which the mutual-deterrence interplay between us and our peer competitors is *not* symmetric. The probability is low that the U.S. would ever succumb to a takeover by a nuke-happy demigod demagogue; we are *not* in the business of threatening innocent people with small nukings for coercion. Vladimir Putin, in contrast, has several times lately issued not-so-veiled threats to other nations regarding his ample nuclear-arms inventory. And if China continues on its current path of intensified international bullying *and* nuclear-arsenal growth, then Xi Jinping will sooner or later start doing the same. This is precisely why having a good BMD, as *a force-protector and thus force-multiplier* for our Triad, is so essential to America and our Allies successfully keeping the global nuclear peace.

As then-Commander of U.S. Strategic Command, Admiral Cecil D. Haney, put it very clearly (at an Atlantic Council's Brent Scowcroft Center on International Security conference in early 2015, as reported in DOD News), America's early-warning sensors *and* our BMD systems are *critical elements of our deterrent's overall infrastructure.*

For Deterrence, Unstoppable Is Good

The question of whether more R&D—and deployment—should be pursued re making deterrent retaliatory second-strike nukes in large enough numbers *even more unstoppable* is worth mentioning at this point. Suffice it to say that, at least in theory, new weapon systems such as *MARVing* and *hypersonic delivery platforms do* strengthen the assurance of nuclear peace which effective, survivable strategic deterrence can bring.

We Also Simply *Must* Be Able to Win the Big-Picture Sub-On-Sub Fight

There is *another front* to technical R&D, and robust hardware deployment, that is *also* essential to America's ongoing role as a keeper of global nuclear peace. Just like force-protecting and force-multiplying BMD development, this other front very much does merit and require the committed services of some of our country's best and brightest scientists and engineers. This is the front, the dimension, already referred to above, of *undersea superiority*, of *underwater battlespace dominance*, of *sea control from beneath the sea*.

The U.S. Navy's Submarine Force is divided into three types of sub. Besides the nuclear-deterrent SSBNs, there are also the Virginia-class (and earlier) SSNs, and the Modified Ohio-class SSGNs—which will soon start to be replaced by Virginias equipped with an extra, extended-hull Payload Module.

(The modified Ohio-class SSGNs concentrate on having very large magazines of cruise missiles (over 100), and very large compliments of Navy SEALs and other Special Ops commandos (up to 100) with their heavy equipment—including dry deck shelters and/or minisubs. The SSGNs' primary focus has been *"influencing events on land"* (ala famous American sea-power theorist Captain A. T. Mahan, a contemporary of Teddy Roosevelt whose writings inspired 1907's Great White Fleet). This power-projection influence has been achieved via conventional Tomahawk missile strikes and clandestine SEAL operations. The extended-hull Virginias will each have an 85-foot-long extra hull section housing four large-diameter vertical launch tubes, each of which can hold seven Tomahawks—which in the new Maritime Tomahawk variant, will have a *significant long-range anti-ship capability*. The added Virginia Payload Module variants will *replace the high capacity* lost when the Ohio-class SSGNs need to be retired fairly soon due to old age and pressure-hull metal fatigue.)

The SSNs, known as "fast-attacks," serve many high-value purposes, complete many indispensable missions; they are the Silent Service's powerful, stealthy *jacks of all trades*. In nuclear deterrence, the SSN role is quite essential. They *very ably protect our SSBNs*, sanitizing their patrol areas of enemy threats to the SSBNs, if necessary even *"making a datum"* (firing weapons) while our SSBNs remain undetected, *"hiding with pride."* This is because SSNs can move fast, have powerful active (pinging) *and* passive (listening) sonars and fire-control systems, and boast big torpedo and cruise-missile magazines. They can hunt for, find, and sink enemy subs and surface ships that are trying to threaten our SSBNs. And threaten our SSBNs is definitely something that Russia's own excellent Submarine Force will continue trying to do. This was made evident via some exciting First Cold War fiction such as *The Hunt for Red October*, and the equally exciting (but more real) non-fiction of bestsellers such as *Blind Man's Bluff* (Sontag and Drew) and *The Silent War* (Craven). One of the first signs that the Second Cold War with Russia was definitely *on* was the significant increase in Russian submarine operations against American vital interests in the last few years.

A strong, numerous, well maintained and always ready force of the world's best designed, built, equipped, commanded, crewed, and maintained SSNs is in a very genuine sense the *"fourth leg of America's deterrence Triad."* We shortchange this essential leg at our national peril, and at the peril of global freedom and world peace. (The continuing relevance of a robust Silent Service to nuclear deterrence and nuclear peacekeeping is elaborated upon below, in Appendix 3.)

Our Current Nuclear Warhead Count Is (as Martha Stewart would say) "a Good Thing"

In summary, America should *hold with what we got* on the warhead-count front in the giant poker game and chess game of superpower cold-war nuclear deterrence. As a campaign slogan or bumper sticker might put it, think "Hold at 1,550!" The mathematical justification for this slogan is presented in detail below, in Chapter 6.

Whether by luck or pluck, whether by the prescience and professionalism of the disarmament negotiators, or by Divine Providence or Fate or Karma or Kismet or Destiny or just sheer random chance—or because of the benevolent guardianship of super-intelligent alien astronauts, if you're into Erich von Daniken—we've arrived at the right answer right now: New START or very close to it. This is, perhaps, *in spite of* the world's various arms control efforts as much as because of them. We have reached a *detent*, a stopping point, the proverbial "bend in the hockey stick." To continue the same course of action or inaction (disarmament *or* rearmament) will bring upon us all some very grave consequences indeed.

We do not need to get into any new arms races, any more than we need to further disarm. *And neither does Russia.* If Moscow does build up its nuke arsenal much beyond New START levels, in some misguided attempt to frighten our citizenry and intimidate us, they would be wasting their own finite money supply, depleting their internal political capital, despoiling their natural environment, and even sacrificing Russian lives. So long as America going forward has our dozen-or-more Columbia-class SSBNs, rotating through untouchable deterrence patrols and protected by our rightsized Virginia-class SSN/SSGN fleet, we should sit tight—hold, in the language of Texas Hold' Em. Definitely *don't* see 'em and/or raise 'em, any more than we would throw in the cards and fold. Our ace in the hole is that if our peer-competitor adversaries start to spend enough to build enough additional nuclear forces to ever wipe out the land-based legs of our Triad *and* threaten our boomers via ASW barrage or SSN combat, we then—and *only* then—commence rapid construction of *even more* SSBNs (and SSNs), with the ever-present option to also add some loaded ICBM silos and more B-21 strategic bombers to the weaponry mix. And the point of view represented by this *arms-race response plan,* the strategy characterization and nomenclature that applies, the *Best Perspective* we should take on this, is one of *defense, not offense.* It is most certainly not *"nuclear warfighting"* on our part—despite what the domestic naysayers and the foreign disinformation trolls alike might falsely claim.

Enjoy Life in Today's "Just Right" Nuclear-Deterrence Goldilocks Zone!

We are at what math people call *a point of inflection,* a *local minimum,* in the curve that plots the number of warheads in U.S. and Russian nuclear deterrence arsenals versus the risk of a nuclear war. For all the hard years of the disarmament movement's efforts up to now, that risk has gone *down.* But to go any lower now, it would start to go back *up.*

Another way of putting this key finding is that humanity, regarding the superpower deterrence environment, is now in what astronomers and exobiologists call a Goldilocks Zone: In a planetary system orbiting some alien sun, the Goldilocks Zone is the distance from the star at which the water on a planet's surface is *neither* all ice *nor* all steam. At least some of it is in liquid form. Such a planet is *neither too close* (like Mercury) to *nor too far* (like Neptune) from its star, so that it is *"just right"* to support life as we know it.

Something else is worth noting. The way in which our Triad legs developed historically seems somewhat *decoupled* from the crucial role they actually play *together* now, in *implicit mutual cooperation and cross-support,* despite the long-standing inter-Service political rivalries about resourcing and sustaining each of the Triad legs. These legs all form an inseparable, interlocking system of *force multipliers* for extra-potent *force protection* of the *seamless, survivable entirety.* This is especially true as to how the ICBM fleet and the DCA fleet work for the SSBNs' benefit.

The three legs originated out of classic inter-Service competition: Sailors, Flyers, and Air Force missileers all wanted *a piece of the action, and of the defense budget,* in order to master and wield the awesome new thermonuclear weapons and their various sexy delivery platforms. Management theorists refer to these *mutually antagonistic organizational subgroups* as stovepipes, or houses, or even, yes, silos. (*Interagency stovepiping,* in the realms of intelligence sharing and counterterror preparedness, is what left the U.S. a *sitting duck* for al Qaeda's 9/11/01 attacks on our Homeland.) Stovepiping is also a familiar problem in the private sector, and the effects on a corporation as a whole are seldom very beneficial. And yet, *here we are,* resting nicely just like Goldilocks, in the middle of a comfortable, "just right" Goldilocks Zone, in a world that *can never realistically be made to forget how to build hydrogen bombs.*

Is this, perhaps, at least in part, why the progressive reducing of superpower arsenal strategic warhead counts *stopped* with the inception of New START? Is this part of why *resistance has hardened* to further nuke-count cuts in both the American and Russian governments in recent years? I have not seen this particular issue discussed much in the open literature, but I could easily have missed something. The literature is vast and reading time is short.

Has some sort of wise, humanity-saving understanding been reached, behind the scenes, between the military and statecraft minions in Moscow and in Washington, DC?

I am no sort of conspiracy theorist, but historical conspiracies are *real.* Look at Hitler's secret preparations for Operation Barbarossa, his massive surprise attack against Stalin's Soviet Union. The two countries had just signed a major friendship pact. And look at Dr. A. Q. Kahn's now-infamous covert international nuclear underground black market. Never before or since has one man done so much to wreck world efforts in nuclear non-proliferation, counter-terrorism, and the maintenance of nuclear peace. He did it all for ego and for greed.

Still, speculative fiction isn't just good plain fun. It can be a *powerful analytic and learning tool.* Studying the possible hidden humanist forces that can shape history is an informative and worthwhile endeavor.

Alternate-history storytelling has come to be recognized as a valuable investigative technique. Plumbing the *"what-ifs" of worst-case scenarios* in disaster planning is also of value. (Too often in real life, the worst-case scenario becomes *the* scenario. Osama bin Laden did not expect the Twin Towers to collapse. Hundred-year storms have become an almost annual occurrence.) The purpose of such outside-the-box investigations is, in a disciplined way, to *raise possibilities, not make predictions;* it's all about Red Teaming against staid expectations and unprepared minds. Is Humanity the unknowing beneficiary of some secret guardian cabal or fraternity, like the Rosicrucians or Masons, like Opus Dei or even the supposedly extinct Knights Templar, working across the superpower-adversary divide to maintain strategic stability in this Thermonuclear Age? Obviously, I'm having some fun here, but the math is indisputable: the current Goldilocks Zone of nuclear deterrence is real.

Conclusion: Keep Our Entire Triad. Keep it Effective. It's Right-Sized Right Now

We run the grave risk of enabling a nuclear war if we ever mistakenly do pursue *the worst possible sort of false economy*. In any thermonuclear combat that could *all too easily start with a nuclear Pearl Harbor*, were America's robust Triad to be cut to a Mini-Monad—our stabilizing global leadership-influence utterly prostrated by precisely said surprise nuclear assault—*billions could die*. The survivors would be forced to endure true Hell on Earth: *at first, dark and shivering nuclear winter; later, hard-UV-searing nuclear summer; always, starving (due to worldwide famine), agony-filled (due to lack of medics for the wounded), radiation-poisoned foreign oppression.*

No, chopping America's Triad down to a Mini-Monad, eliminating our ICBMs and cutting the Columbia-class subs and any new strategic bombers to a literal handful, would be most unwise. The above discussion has sought to give a logical *reduction ad absurdum*, a QED, to decisively reject such a proposal. Today's international environment is *grim*: Relations with Russia are decidedly unfriendly, nuclear arms control and nonproliferation are under threat globally, nuclear-wannabe terrorists are out there seeking nukes every day, American nuclear forces and their nuclear command-and-control infrastructure *badly* need renewing, and fast up-arming China has never yet signed a strategic arms limitation treaty—while Beijing hawks have started to talk openly about growing their now fairly small H-bomb arsenal to rival in numbers ours and Moscow's.

CHAPTER 3

Are Nuclear Terrorists and Madmen Deterrable? *There's More We Can Be Doing*

Executive Summary: How to Deter Nuclear Terrorists Has Been a Vexed Question

It is widely recognized among defense strategists that nuclear-armed terrorists, nuke-owning rogue state leaders, and madmen with access to nukes, can share traits that make these three (sometimes overlapping) classes of "bad actors" *especially difficult to deter* from making one or more nuclear attacks against their various real or imagined enemies—which, too often, include U.S. and Allied vital interests. In certain *radicalized separatist* cases, such as Chechnya's Muslims versus Russia, or Xinjiang's Uyghurs versus China, the terrorist groups might even some day *try to buy a "loose nuke," or steal one, and then target America's superpower adversaries.*

Many regional nuclear powers—the UK, France, Israel, India, and Pakistan—have *also* been the targets of deadly terrorist attacks—conventional ones so far, using guns, knives, chemical explosives, poison gas, or moving motor vehicles, since up to now those are the only weapons the terrorists could gain access to. But a country does not need to own nuclear weapons for it to become a *conduit* for trade in illicit nuclear materials, or to have its peaceful nuclear technology *diverted* into acts of terror, or even to possibly be *targeted* for one or more terrorist nukings. Countering nuclear terrorism is pressing business for everyone, worldwide.

Ominously, according to declassified Western intelligence reports, a few terrorist groups have been trying to get nukes and/or other WMDs (including radiological or "dirty" bombs) at least since the mid-1990s. The conspicuous *terrorist abstinence (or at least, absence)* up to now from that awful final act in the chain—a nuclear detonation—suggests something good: That national-level nuclear-weapon *lockdown* measures (materials safeguards, counter-theft, counter-proliferation) and international nuclear *counter-terrorism* efforts (counter-smuggling, counter-recruiting, counter-financing) are bearing valuable fruit. But over time, the bad actors are surely getting smarter at evading authorities and at gaining access to nuke ingredients and expertise, so the forces of nuclear peacekeeping had better keep getting smarter, too.

This includes *more proactive focus on deterring nuclear terrorism within national nuclear postures.* To say, "Nuclear terrorists can't be deterred," touches on some essential truths that cannot be ignored, yet to leave things simply at that would "leave way too much on the playing field"—potentially courting catastrophe.

Let us deconstruct the apparent nuclear-terrorists' *enabling community mindset,* then look at some possible risk-mitigation action steps that *just might* help the good guys to deter them:

> One *complex of traits* shared by terrorists, madmen, and rogue-state leaders alike, which presents difficulties re effectively deterring *any* of them, lies in the *mental and moral realm*:
>
> *Terrorists* can crave indiscriminate, unlimited death and destruction while often, at least at the rank-and-file levels, being suicidal. *Rogue state leaders* compulsively transgress moral codes and behavioral norms, sharing some murderous goals with terrorists, but usually crave their own survival and aggrandizement, rather than being suicidal by choice. In certain cases, *authoritarian superpowers*—USSR/Russia, or China—or *regional nuclear powers* (e.g., Pakistan) or nuclear-armed *rogue states* (e.g., North Korea, or wannabe Iran) have all in the past and might in the future wield terrorists (ISIS, al Qaeda, the Taliban, Hezbollah, etc.) as *proxy combatants,* giving them *conventional* arms. Eventually, this trend might potentially worsen to the point of *intentionally supplying* to their terrorist partners one or more *nuclear* weapons, with which to make attacks against their *shared perceived enemies*—especially against the U.S. and/or the State of Israel.

These *multitudinous modern interrelationships and interdependencies* make nuclear peacekeeping an extremely challenging profession, calling, and vocation for the warriors who benefit from proper training, field experience, and inspired leadership. Further complicating all such issues, modern psychology and economics both tell us, is that *"rationality" in human decisions and choices is not an absolute*; rational or irrational behavior is almost always a *relative* thing, founded in personal *subjectivities* and interpersonal *ambiguities*. And outwardly irrational behavior can be *intentionally faked*, as part of a subterfuge or a bluff or a dare.

Clearly, one of the "nontraditional" nuclear-deterrence responsibilities of the 21st century is for *all* state-level owners of nukes to continue making absolutely sure that *none* ever fall into the hands of bad actors. (America's *Nunn-Lugar Cooperative Threat Reduction Program* after the First Cold War, helping secure potential "loose nukes" in the Former Soviet Union, is a successful model for further such global efforts.)

Furthermore, someone with terrorist sympathies or allegiances, beliefs, or mental makeup—or someone who thinks they "can do business" with terrorists—might in some circumstances infiltrate legitimate politics to become head of a sovereign state: *a hybrid type of bad actor*. Nuclear-armed *madmen*, who can also overlap with terrorist-group heads and rogue-state potentates, but are driven by *bad personality disorders ("insanity") rather than by geopolitical purposefulness*, can have similar cravings for power and death/destruction—with or without having a strong personal death wish. Madmen can be (or can eventually, progressively become) so mentally unstable that they lose all sense of consequences of the actions they take; they can *start out* seemingly rational but *end up* seemingly (or actually) suicidal.

In all these cases, the potential aggressor's mind might be incapable of any self-contemplation, real comprehension, empathy for strangers, or caring at all, regarding themselves and/or their in-group's members suffering massive retaliatory obliteration in case the leader does choose to execute a nuclear strike. Alternatively, they might believe that *subterfuges* such as (1) using deniable proxies, or (2) making vehement protestations of innocence, or (3) "framing" some other entity as the culprit, or (4) somehow sabotaging adversary nuclear-attribution forensics, or even (5) becoming an incognito international fugitive, will let them *evade* retaliation altogether. (This complex of issues is quite distinct from a *populous bloc of sovereign states*, by conscious and deliberate, calculating intent, taking huge casualties to achieve total, permanent global victory over a hated adversary—the way both Mao Zedong and Fidel Castro at one time urged Nikita Khrushchev to nuke the capitalist West. This *rather frightening historical fact* should serve as a harsh reminder, for all time, that even state-on-state nuclear deterrence must never suffer from neglect or complacency.)

The fundamental psychological mechanisms of nuclear deterrence, i.e., (1) *comprehending* the threat of massive retaliation, and in consequence (2) *refraining* from nuclear (or other WMD) attacks, will *malfunction* in the case of any bad actor with *cognitive failure* over grasping and caring about consequences—or who has *excessive faith* in reckless evasive tactics.

> The *other complex of traits*, peculiar to trying to deter terrorist and madman (but not rogue-state) bad actors, is *geopolitical diffuseness and geographical invisibility*. Unlike all aggressor *independent states*, whether large or small, terrorists and sub-state/trans-state madmen in contrast lack a specific, internationally recognized sovereign homeland territory which defending states can subject to a retaliatory nuclear counter-strike threat/promise, in order to deter them in advance.

But useful things *can* be done by defenders to uphold nuclear deterrence and sustain WMD peace, even in the face of these troubling terrorist psychological and geographical trait complexes. *One key* is recognizing, and then exploiting through *forceful public messaging*, the involvement of *many individuals* in the internal planning and implementation loops within *any* entity trying to commit a successful nuclear or other strategic WMD strike—*including any terrorist group*. It is quite possible (but must never be taken for granted) that some of these individuals will have the *prior remorse, due to clear cognition,* and *also the ability to act on that remorse,* sufficient to prevent the nuke or big WMD strike from actually taking place—*especially* if they are *warned (educated) in advance, in the starkest terms, about said strike triggering a likely human-extinction blowback event, and then they are appealed to compellingly, by believable social-peer voices, to actualize their remorse and* intercede to "short circuit" the strike. (For purposes of this discussion, we will call such people "circuit-breaker individuals.")

The ultimate choice of action(s) will lie with the offenders—the terrorists and any state sponsors—and will depend on the military and political goals of the groups' leaders at that time. But anti-terrorism-, anti-proliferation-focused states, such as America, also have choices to make re their own actions. These defenders' choices include important ones that come on the timeline *well before* any terrorist nuclear attack can occur—and sometimes, even before a bad-actor nuke strike can first be seriously considered.

What sort of *anti-nuclear-/anti-WMD-strike stark-warning messaging* is called for, to reach out to such potential *circuit-breaker individuals* within the bad-actor group and its wider enabling community?

Well, the essence of nuclear deterrence is, *before* any nuclear attack, to threaten punishment to the entire attacking team that will be so severe, painful, devastating that any benefits to *any* of them in making the attack will be *more than completely offset* by the penalties guaranteed to follow said attack. To deter *state sponsors* of nuclear terrorism with the threat of state-level nuclear retaliation, as America currently does, is a good way to discourage states from helping proxy terrorists get their hands on nukes—*but it is not enough.*

The terrorists *themselves,* at *all* levels of leaders, followers, suppliers/enablers, and even dependents (blood relatives, extended family), must be made to understand clearly that they will see *all* their most cherished goals completely denied in perpetuity, *all* their most prized possessions (including life itself) taken away forever, and their *very souls* damned to Hell (of whatever religion) in this life *and* in the afterlife.

The key to achieving this is to spread far and wide, by every messaging technique and technology available (detailed later in this chapter), *a fundamental truth that always applies* when nuclear weapons are in play: Due to the untold damaging and deranging physical effects of nukes, and the panicked, enraged, and paranoid emotional malignancies that any first-use is guaranteed to provoke *worldwide*—what First Cold War analysts called the *"Intra-War Nuclear Unsafe-User Principle"*—*any* nuclear attack *anywhere,* fed by a breaking-news and social-media frenzy of a magnitude *never before seen in history,* could very easily lead to rapid and uncontrollable escalation to planetwide Armageddon. In this *genuine, total nuclear holocaust,* the deadly long-lived radioactive fallout, freezing nuclear winter, and then broiling nuclear summer (what I call *"the Three-Fold Geophysical Wipeout"*) will obey *no* borders or boundaries, will respect *no* sanctuaries, and *will exempt no one whatsoever on Planet Earth.*

What conceivable Deity or Deities would ever want their followers to obliterate the entire human race for all time—including *every single one* of that Deity's most pious devotees and *every one of their descendants forever*? What hideously tormenting, eternal Biblical or Quranic (or other) Hell must await the bad actors who perpetrate such a willful, arrogant act of cosmic nihilism? The first sentence of the Book of Genesis—a time "in the beginning" when there was *not one mortal creature alive* on this planet—would become, as well, a grim prophesy of just such a nuclear aftermath: "The Earth was without form and empty, and there was darkness on the face of the waters. ..." This appalling imagery stands a *good chance to get through* to even the most fanatical extremist whole-of-community.

So, there are indeed things we in peace-loving democracies can do, to more forcefully deter the dangerous, contemporary nuclear-terrorism threat—moral and ethical and legal things. These things are founded in scientific fact. They exploit (laudably non-lethal) education/communication measures that have proved workable in various conventional conflict zones: mass-propaganda leaflet drops, intrusive cellphone calls to adversary influencers, preachy Hollywood movies and dramatic TV shows (with subtitles, or dubbed, as appropriate), plus the full gamut of current and emerging Internet-based and artificial-intelligence/machine-learning social media techniques. (These latter, computer-assisted methods can be engineered to penetrate into a targeted community both individually *and* "stochastically"—the latter relies on mass exposure to score exploitable random "hits.")

But there is *an additional thing* that ruthless-enough superpower dictatorships and beleaguered-enough regional nuclear powers alike might sooner or later resort to, within their declared/public nuclear postures, or just in their highly classified nuclear action plans—or even entirely unplanned, "on the spot," *after* a terrorist nuking somewhere, anywhere does in fact ever occur. This *"draconian deterrence"* option would be *decidedly less moral/ethical, and less legal under international law* than non-violent educational messaging to terrorists. Said draconian option would seem rather hard for the U.S. to prohibit worldwide—so we dare not ignore its possible uptake by our adversaries.

This not-entirely-inconceivable additional tactic would involve targeting *terrorist support and training areas* with a deterring threat/promise regarding *direct nuclear retaliation, or even nuclear preemption.* This approach might be deemed by certain authoritarian regimes to be especially useful, *and useable,* against (1) *separatist regions within the state's own homeland,* and/or (2) those locales that terrorist groups themselves have declared to be *modern Caliphates* (nominally making them be "sovereign states"). Thus, at least in the abstract, draconian deterrence policies fall along a *spectrum of severity.*

In the most severe conceivable case of hypothetical *"ultra-draconian deterrence,"* the hardline defender's threatened (and/or *actual*) nuclear retribution might even go as far as to *also* nuke (3) any rogue states that have in the past ever sponsored *mere conventional terrorism* against the ultra-draconian-deterrence-adopting state, if it does ever suffer a terrorist nuclear strike. Such misconduct would amount to ultra-draconian nuclear deterrence indeed—and since it cannot be entirely precluded somewhere, somewhen, going forward, it needs to be considered now, in this chapter.

How can America, recognizing both the challenges of deterring nuclear terrorists and the importance of doing so as thoroughly as possible, best exploit some *compelling facts* from physical and behavioral sciences? How can we and our Allies also reasonably draw upon this hypothesized possibility of *"draconian deterrence"* by certain (rather unamerican) third parties? Can such powerful "info/influence ammunition" provide for more effective nuclear peacekeeping that everyone can live with during the day, and sleep better with at night?

Lateral thinking—*the power of "and"*—plays an important role in developing the suggested, prospective Best Perspectives and Best Practices offered in this chapter for deterring future nuclear terrorism.

(Accordingly, just as elsewhere in this book, the discussion below braids together several continuing threads, unraveling each thread part way and then circling back to say more, in what educators call *helical learning*. What might seem at first as repetitious is here done by design; each "repetition" introduces more detail, addresses wider concerns, draws further connections, and adds to the actionable clarity. The point to bear in mind, gentle reader, is that *effective* nuclear deterrence—the only kind that matters, since it's the only kind that works—is a matter of *sweating the nuances*: Media "click bait" one-liners, and dumbed-down sensationalized "bumper sticker" slogans, do not cut it.)

Do Nuclear Terrorists Need (at Least Indirect) Nuclear Threats to Be Effectively Deterred?

The Obama Administration's unclassified National Nuclear Posture Review Report (2010) stated the ambitious goal of seeking to *reduce* America's reliance on its specifically *nuclear* deterrence capabilities as a major pillar supporting our and our Allies' national security. According to this Posture, the threatened use of our considerable conventional force *capability* (power of each of our weapons) and *capacity* (total number of our weapons), when used for retaliation, was deemed sufficient to be fully effective in most cases, *even* if the adversary—whether terrorist or state-level—were to use nukes or other WMDs against us.

There are *two basic things wrong* with this position, which has not been followed in the subsequent, superseding Trump Administration's National Nuclear Posture Review Report (2018). But first, "let me make one thing perfectly clear," as POTUS Richard Nixon used to say: POTUS Trump's nuclear posture—though it has been criticized by political opponents, disarmament advocates, and our adversaries alike as "too aggressive"—does not once mention the idea of what this book calls "draconian" deterrence. That whole concept is something I am introducing here *solely for objective discussion and contingency-planning purposes.* In other words, our national nuclear posture, as of the time of this writing in early 2021, does *not* say that America would ever use a nuclear counter-strike against a terrorist group that makes a nuclear (or strategic-level WMD) attack on us and our Allies. (*States* who give the terrorists such weapons are another matter.)

But as the gradual exposition in this chapter will show, our *"Nuclear Posture After Next"* text might, even so, appropriately and beneficially draw on *indirect forms* of a terrorist nuclear first-strike's *own almost-inevitable/unavoidable aftermath-consequences,* in order to in effect mimic—for deterrence messaging-education purposes *only*—an American nuclear retaliatory strike's effects—*without us ever intending to or ever actually making such a strike.* Why bother with this admittedly convoluted extra posture verbiage—which would, at a minimum, cost time and money for policy debate, drafting changes, and internal promulgation? The answer is this: Such a perfectly honest (and perfectly legal/moral) big-picture cautionary *posture plus-up* could usefully strengthen our future deterrence against sub-state/trans-state armed groups—whether their nuclear ambitions were aided by state-level bad actors who use the terrorists as proxies, or (especially) if the terrorists were somehow able to obtain a working nuke without such aid, *on their own.*

One drawback of the Obama Administration's Nuclear Posture, in my humble opinion, is this: Up to now, throughout military history of the most recent 100+ years, *conventional* deterrence has proven *not* particularly effective against either (1) large, state-level powers (which have a great deal to lose if defeated) *or* (2) smaller states or non-state organizations (which might have less to lose or more to gain when they gamble), just regarding the comparatively straightforward task of deterring mere *conventional* aggression:

> Belligerents of all sizes have in the past felt quite unconstrained by conventional deterrence alone; they often started *conventional* world wars and smaller conflicts—some *before* the invention of nukes, and some *even afterward.* Japan was not deterred by U.S. military power in 1941. Germany was not deterred either, *prior* to the dawn of the Nuclear Era, from starting two world wars against the combined conventional might of the US, UK/Commonwealth, France, and Russia/Soviet Union. Nor were Egypt and Syria deterred from attacking *nuclear-armed* Israel in the 1973 Yom Kippur War.

History has shown time and again that the risk (or even likelihood) of loss in conventional warfare is *not* an effective deterrent: Losing WWI did *not* deter Germany from trying again in WWII. Losing was seen by both Syria and Egypt as a *real form of winning* on the world diplomatic stage in '73. Non-nuclear Argentina was *not* deterred from starting the Falklands War in 1981, by the nuclear-armed UK's superior military power.

The *other drawback* with hoping to use only the threat of conventional retaliation to deter terrorists from making a nuclear attack is that, worldwide, terrorists have *already* been subjected to concerted conventional punishment *for decades*. They have *not* flinched from their continuing acts of indiscriminate mass murder and destruction. They continue to make coordinated conventional attacks and kill up to *hundreds* of innocent people at a time, from Europe to Africa to Asia. They still present a constant threat to the U.S. Homeland and to U.S. and Allied security interests abroad. And they still are trying to get their hands on nukes.

What Deterrence Needs to Do in Order to Work—Or Else It *Isn't* Working

In 2018, as then Commander, Strategic Command, U.S. Air Force General John Hyten, said (see "Strategic Deterrence," a talk posted on YouTube.com, 14 November 2018)—quoting early First Cold War nuclear deterrence theorists Herman Kahn (*On Thermonuclear War*, Hudson Institute, 1960) and Thomas C. Schelling (*The Strategy of Conflict*, Kindle Edition, 1981)—a deterrence threat against any form of attack, conventional or nuclear, must do three things to be effective:

1. It must make clear to the potential attackers that any and all the goals of them making the attack will definitely not be achieved.
2. It must make clear to the potential attackers that they will be punished for making the attack, significantly beyond just the denial of all their goals.
3. It must promise that if adversaries do not attack U.S. and Allied vital interests, then we will not attack them either.

General Hyten was recently promoted to Vice Chairman of the Pentagon's Joint Chiefs of Staff, with an even broader perspective on national security challenges. The U.S. Navy's Admiral Charles Richard, a former Commander, US Submarine Force, succeeded him at Strategic Command and as of this writing in early 2021 is the incumbent CO there. In an interview on Omaha, NE's Station KETV's "Chronicle" feature—see https://www.ketv.com/article/chronicle-sitting-down-with-us-stratcoms-newest-head-of-command/33104870#—Admiral Richard said that his command is at work on updating nuclear deterrence "theory and concepts" for the changed conditions of the post-Post Cold War world—a process which this book and its subsequent volumes are meant to help. In a 30 July 2020 interview in *Air Force Magazine*, ADM Richard said further that in the new era of hybrid warfare and rapidly modernizing adversary nuclear forces, "what the U.S. does strategically is influenced by what it does conventionally. ... The idea that there is a ladder here, I think is flawed. It is nonlinear. There are discontinuities, and there are points, where a competitor's decision calculus may flip very rapidly on you."

It is worth noting here that America's *conventional-deterrence actions against conventional terrorism*—if our actions can be cast (or recast) in the terms of deterrence —over the past two decades (2001–present) have had *mixed* results. Termed "overseas contingency operations" (by President Obama), formerly known as the Global War on Terror (under President George W. Bush), this prolonged offensive started as Operation Enduring Freedom against the Taliban and al Qaeda in Afghanistan, then added Operation Iraqi Freedom, and then spread elsewhere. It has included various covert/clandestine special operations, overt troop buildups and drawdowns, with more and more heavy equipment being sent in, including but not limited to significant airpower, at different points during the two decades since the 9/11/01 attacks. Most recently, President Trump called these continuing conflicts "Forever Wars"—too apt because the enemy, the terrorists, seem willing and able to hold out *forever* against our conventional forces, while repeatedly sallying forth to make very deadly offensive strikes against our troops and innocent civilians worldwide.

What Should We Do About Nuclear-Wannabe Terrorist Groups?

The traditional military approach, to any enemy who is holding out against our current application of conventional force, is to *escalate* that force, but not if it means the U.S./NATO Alliance introduces the use of nuclear weapons *first*. It becomes (in theory) simpler to see what we should do to if an enemy were the first to cross that ultimate redline—at least, *if* the enemy is a *sovereign state*, having a *clearly-demarcated* land area and *clearly-designated* government infrastructure. In this particular type of situation, what we do is relatively straightforward (to *say*, though certainly not to *do*): We declare publicly now that we would *in future* retaliate to any nuclear (or other strategic WMD) first-strike with a nuclear counterstrike.

But what if the entity is a *terrorist group*—with *no* clearly demarcated sovereign territory and *no* publicly revealed top leadership—which (instead) makes a practice of dispersing itself, blending in, and *hiding* among innocents in a number of countries whose governments play host *quite unwittingly/unwillingly*?

How in the case of such a terrorist group could nuclear deterrence ever be enforced, when any retaliatory nuclear second-strike would be the same thing as initiating a nuclear *first-strike* against several *innocent states and their civilian populations*?

To gain clarity, preserve morality, and propose a palatable action plan, it will be helpful to first review some basic military principles.

We introduce this next part of Chapter 3 by summarizing the *conundrum in question* here: If retaliating *in kind* (i.e., with our own nukes) against a terrorist nuclear strike would involve such *drastic expansion* ("escalation") of the conflict, utterly violating morality and international law, while to retaliate against a terrorist nuclear strike with mere *conventional* forces ("de-escalation") would be *ineffective*—telegraphing weakness, implying de facto surrender, and/or inviting additional copy-cat and me-too terrorist (even state level) strikes—how can America find a way to deter terrorists that is *both* legal/moral *and* would be effective?

The key is to examine in detail the complex military topic of *escalation ladders*, then the simple children's game of *Tit-for-Tat*, and then draw a real-world analogy using the abstract math of *Venn diagrams*.

Escalation Ladders Can Be Elevators Down to Hell, Not Stairways to Heaven

This brings us (and the terrorists, too) to the topic of *escalation ladders*, something else that then COMSTRATCOM (senior-most uniformed combatant-commander of America's nuclear forces), four-star General Hyten, mentioned in his public talks.

An *escalation ladder* is a linear scheme for ranking military operations that use increasing resources to try to inflict increasingly violent loss on the enemy, in order to force a truce, negotiated armistice, or unconditional surrender. Escalation can involve the number of warriors engaged, how heavily they are armed, how widespread an area they attack, whether invading ground troops are sent in to follow up on naval blockades and airpower bombardments, whether other countries come into the fighting (as allies and/or as enemies), and so on.

A very fundamental, three-step escalation ladder would be (1) *conventional operations* (high explosives and other chemical-energy/kinetic-energy weapons), then (2) *tactical nuclear operations* (shorter range, lower-yield, fission-powered "atomic" weapons), then (3) *strategic nuclear operations* (longer range, higher-yield, fusion-powered "thermonuclear" weapons). Herman Kahn examined nuclear escalation ladders in considerable nuanced detail in *On Thermonuclear War*. He presented for discussion a ladder with some *three-dozen* different gradations of violence between mere verbal threats on the bottom rung and total thermonuclear Armageddon on the top. (I offer a different sort of cataloguing of adversary unprovoked nuclear first-use options, in Appendix 2 below; it overviews the veritable legion of specific, focused military objectives which an enemy might attempt to achieve via nuclear strikes that are "nuanced," not "spasmodic.")

Using the general ladder perspective, we can see that any defender responding to an attacker's latest military move always has *three basic choices*: (1) stay on the *same* step (rung) on the escalation ladder as the attacker is on, or (2) move *up* one or more steps, or (3) move *down* one or more steps. It is a *foundational doctrine* of America's National Defense Strategy for our armed forces to always sustain *escalation dominance*. This means being able to escalate *further and faster*, beyond any attack or escalation by any enemy, and making sure all potential enemies *know* in advance of our ability. Escalation dominance is the best way to be able to establish and enforce deterrence—*or* to defend and retaliate proportionately, with a *flexible response*, if deterrence ever fails. This holds true equally well for *both* conventional *and* nuclear (and other strategic-level WMD) warfare.

We note that it would be *entirely consistent* with such U.S. doctrine if STRATCOM were to have available a *scheme for messaging* re "nuclear escalation dominance" *against terrorist groups*—provided, of course, that such a valuable deterrence tool were *entirely legal and moral*.

Nuclear Tit-For-Tat: A Simple Way to Try to Control Escalation, *If* Deterrence Ever Fails

As General Hyten has stated publicly, in the case of a nuclear conflict the absolute priority should be getting *off* the escalation ladder to the extent we have any choice, not escalating further. This is because the ultimate "destination" of nuclear escalation always equals global thermonuclear holocaust—human extinction. In the case of armed conflict between America and another nuclear superpower, this *getting-off process*, under acceptable political settlement terms, would be absolutely imperative—such powers own enough strategic firepower to obliterate each other several times over, and trigger a full-on *Three-Fold Geophysical Wipeout* (see below) all across our planet. (It is precisely the compelling fact that this "getting off" is *not* assured, because of the uncontrollable chaos of nuclear war, that makes nuclear deterrence be *so very persuasive* a peacekeeping tool. Truly, trying to deescalate once a nuclear war were to ever break out would be a *totally desperate, totally last-ditch* attempt to save human civilization, *with no guarantee of any success.*)

One possible response option, in any such appalling actual nuclear-combat situation, beyond concerted diplomatic conflict-resolution efforts as appropriate, could include retaliating against the enemy's nuclear attack in *closely matching exact proportion*, using against the enemy the *same number and yield* of nuclear warheads, "dropped" in the *same way* (i.e., air burst, surface impact, undersea, ground penetrator) against the *same number and types* of targets, *as that nuclear enemy used (so far) against our side.* This plays pure *Tit-for-Tat* against their heinous acts of aggression. Tit-for-Tat is *neither* an egregious heightening of intensity (escalation), *nor* a decline toward abject surrender (de-escalation). Rather than trying to "signal" either excessive strength (winner-take-all *counterpunching?*) or regressive moderation (dismissed as *weakness?*), it puts the onus of ceasing fire *squarely on the shoulders of the enemy who started it all.*

It is relatively easy to explain such doctrine *in advance* to one and all, both foreign and domestic. It is simple for our strategic deterrent forces to train for, and in the worst case, with the proper equipment and NC3 infrastructure, straightforward for them to implement. It amounts to subscribing to *neither* the First Cold War view "better dead than Red," nor its reverse, "better Red than dead," and declares straightforwardly our leadership position that America stands for the modern geopolitical equivalent of "neither Red *nor* dead." It is one area within the overall arena of nuclear defense where specificity, not ambiguity, seems beneficial to maximizing effective deterrence. It can be seen as having seized the psychological initiative in any nuclear conflict *before* said conflict has even begun. For friend and foe alike to adopt the same posture amounts to a definite "both win" situation for nuclear peace, as *neither side* if caught in an intensifying nuclear crisis would start to shoot nukes at the other side first.

We will next explore relevant aspects of a formal Tit-for-Tat strategy as a possible *state-level* nuclear deterrence-and-defense/retaliation paradigm, in part because it seems like a solid enhancement to America's National Nuclear Posture regarding sovereign-state adversaries: It is simple to understand, easy to explain, resolves any counterproductive ambiguities in *exactly* how the U.S. would respond to adversaries *if* our nuclear deterrence ever did fail, and evaluation via some thought experiments suggest it would serve well the goal of urgent-yet-unyielding nuclear peace-restoration.

But furthermore—and importantly for Chapter 3's terrorist focus—while America does not *need* to explicitly adopt Tit-for-Tat *against states* in order to be able to sustain useful nuclear deterrence *against terrorists*, nevertheless starting from the former as a logical baseline will provide *pedagogically-elegant (simple, concise) clarity and rigor* that will *naturally ground and guide* developing a workable extension to terrorist groups. In general, first deconstructing (dissecting) America's well established and clearly understood approach to deterring states, will then inform this chapter's as-parallel-as-possible adjunct recommendation for deterring terrorists.

It should be noted that Tit-for-Tat is meant here, and is best used in nuclear posture development, as a clarifying, systematizing *baseline* that could help in calibrating America's actual nuclear-counterstrike intensity. I.e., when viewed as a paradigm to be incorporated in our nuclear posture, Tit-for-Tat is *only a starting point*. As will discussed in more detail in Appendix 1, any actual counterstrike would need to be *calibrated carefully* to the circumstances of the *particular military-geopolitical scenario* in which our nuclear deterrence ever does actually fail: Any *actual counterstrike* can be conceptualized as including both a strict Tit-for-Tat "strategic-balance restoration component," and an additional country-specific and custom fit "punitive component" (which might be zero, or modest, or massive, depending).

Some Definitions and Prerequisites for Implementing Nuclear Tit-For-Tat—Against States *Only*

First, a clarification of terminology is in order:

By *"in kind"* retaliation we simply mean striking back with nuclear weapons against the enemy's unprovoked first-use of nuclear weapons (or other strategic-level WMDs), as opposed to with just our conventional weapons.

That any retaliation be *"proportionate"* is a requirement of the International Laws of War; the right to *defend one's self proportionately* in the face of an enemy aggressor's attack is embodied in the United Nations Charter. Proportionality means that the types and quantity of weapons used, and targets attacked and damage inflicted, in one's retaliation bear a *reasonably proportionate relationship* to those of the enemy's act of aggression itself. Proportionality is a somewhat vague, approximate notion, one perhaps best characterized by saying "a fair-minded observer would know when they see it, or don't see it." For instance, retaliating to an attack by main battle tanks which are firing conventional armor-piercing rounds, by using your own tanks and anti-tank guns also firing AP rounds, would be proportionate; retaliating by dropping nuclear weapons on those enemy tanks, or by fire-bombing the enemy's civilian schools and hospitals, would definitely *not* be.

Proportionality *per se* is a broad, at times somewhat vague, and (intentionally) militarily flexible concept. It allows for a moderate amount of escalation or de-escalation, including a further punitive component *in addition* to a component for "evening the score." Proportionality also does allow varying the time, place, and precise mode of retaliation to serve the defender's rightful tactical and strategic purposes and goals—such as to seize and exploit the initiative.

Tit-for-Tat is a *particular form of proportionate retaliation* chosen out of the much broader set of generally proportionate retaliations always possible. Tit-for-tat involves *as close to an exact mirroring as is practicable* in "doing to the enemy precisely what he/she just did to you."

The challenges of and prerequisites for implementing the suggested Tit-for-Tat tactic in America's National Nuclear Posture are:

- National Command Authorities and Strategic Command need accurate capabilities for (1) real-time assessment of nuclear battle damage that *our side inflicts on the enemy*, along with (2) hardened, survivable, responsive capabilities to assess and report the weapon yields and damage achieved by warheads which *the enemy sets off against our side.*
- Guidance manuals and procedures need to be developed during peacetime, and their use practiced and war-gamed extensively, regarding how to quickly and accurately select specific, actual target sets among enemy assets appropriate for tit-for-tat retaliation, given the specific, actual friendly (American and Allied) target sets that the enemy conceivably might nuke. This preparedness needs to be driven by mock reporting exercises that stretch and stress the damage-reporting system mentioned in the previous bullet point.
- American nuclear weapons need to be able to very rapidly and reliably have their guidance and targeting parameters set (or reset), by authorized personnel only, to the appropriate Tit-for-Tat strike coordinates, even during an ongoing nuclear conflict. This requires a very robust NC3 infrastructure and very robust aim-resetting capability. *If* America were ever forced by a deteriorating geopolitical situation to abandon

current Open Ocean Targeting (in which weapons are intentionally aimed at empty ocean spots, for safety), then our 450 ICBMs might be individually pre-targeted across a "medley" of potential targets that would, in advance, span a representative "menu" of different Tit-for-Tat second-strike possibilities. This might put less pressure on personnel and systems were a nuclear war to ever break out, by adopting during peacetime a version of warfighting readiness that would need less intra-war retargeting.

Though there would be these infrastructure *costs* (expenses) to adopting strict Tit-for-Tat, for personnel training and for communications, battle damage assessment, and targeting-reset hardware and software, the *direct benefits* would be significant: Deterrence of adversaries, and assurance of Allies, could both be strengthened to a useful degree, because a simple, viable paradigm would be in place to try to control any nuclear escalation during wartime *without abandoning* the basic principle of nuclear retaliation in kind. *Ancillary benefits* could be twofold: (1) Domestic opponents of U.S. Triad renewal might be *validly reassured/placated* that STRATCOM does have a well-thought-out way to responsibly strive to stop any nuclear combat from ever escalating all the way to species extinction, while (2) *nuclear-armed adversaries* might be *validly cautioned* that any escalation-management paradigm is *never guaranteed* to succeed, so if those adversaries ever do start a nuclear war it could very well lead to their own absolute and utter obliteration. (If all this mental rigmarole starts to give you a headache, dear reader, please remember that abandoning America's Triad-renewal instead, in the face of today's multiple heavily-nuclear-armed adversaries, would sooner or later give you and the whole world much, *much* worse headaches indeed!)

With nuclear Tit-for-Tat, America would be taking a very high "high road" approach to *restraint* in our nuclear retaliation and peace restoration strategies, thus setting a fine example for evaluation and possible adoption by our nuclear-armed NATO Allies, and even influencing our non-suicidal adversaries—including (very importantly) any reticent *"circuit-breaker individuals"* among terrorist- and madman-led entities.

Focused Messaging Methods and Content Are Essential, and Differ for States and for Terrorists

In addition to the delivery vehicles and warheads in America's and our NATO Allies' nuclear arsenals, we need an additional, different sort of arsenal of purpose-built and custom-fit "weapons." This "arsenal" is almost as important as our nukes, for effectively deterring adversary states and sub-state/trans-state terrorist groups—and for successfully restoring peace while defending our vital interests, if deterrence ever fails. This "other arsenal" must comprise a comprehensive toolkit of messaging techniques, and message content, optimized to serve several indispensable purposes:

- *Nuclear deterrence of adversaries:* Conveying our National Nuclear Posture to adversaries (peer-competitor superpowers, regional nuclear powers, rogue states, nuclear terrorists) during peacetime, and very forcefully reminding them, during geopolitical crises, of the dire consequences of any nuclear aggression.
- *Tit-for-Tat:* Messaging to adversaries which explains with confidence our specific retaliation paradigm during nuclear peacetime, and emphasizes with equal confidence our commitment to continue delivering on that threat *during any nuclear war.*
- *Nuclear peace-restoration:* Achieving, on politically acceptable terms, a cease-fire and armistice in case a nuclear war ever does break out, via use of negotiating and conflict-resolution techniques, communicated (via "hot lines" and other emergency interlocution methods) to adversary heads-of-state and their envoys.
- *Assurance of nuclear-umbrella Allies:* Supporting America's non-proliferation, alliance solidarity, and coalition management goals, via credibly persuasive messaging (different from that used with adversaries) to convince our Allies that "we definitely do have their backs"—that America will assuredly deliver on our promise to retaliate against any aggressors, on behalf of the whole-of-Alliance, using our nukes, if any of our nuclear-umbrella Allies are ever attacked using nukes or strategic-level WMDs
- *Instigation of reticent "circuit-breaker individuals" behind enemy lines:* Recruiting influencers within a nuclear adversary's society who can *proactively intervene* within a rogue, madman, or terrorist leadership structure to prevent a nuclear strike or *defuse* a nuclear crisis.

For deterrence in general and the Tit-for-Tat nuclear-response paradigm in particular, the *(1) audiences, (2) methods, and (3) content* differ between sovereign-state adversaries and terrorist groups. This is simply because of the different characteristics of these two types of adversaries. Each major class of adversary subdivides into several distinct personnel subcategories: *leaders, top subordinates, rank-and-file followers, quasi-combatants (family-member enablers, indirect supporters, passive sympathizers) and non-combatants (uninvolved dependents, miscellaneous innocent civilians).*

These subsets all differ as to their wants and needs, levels of initiative and volition, and political status. Just within one adversary, individuals will vary greatly as to their levels of government authority and direct or indirect involvement in nuclear decisions and actions, socio-economic situations, geostrategic placement and goals, moral/ethical stances, ideological/theological drivers, levels of political and scientific sophistication, general education levels attained, and levels of access to various communication technologies (ranging from "Arab Street" word-of-mouth gossip to state-of-the-art satellite phones).

For all these reasons, both the *methods* of communication (e.g., via "Hot Line," propaganda leaflet drops, *muezzin* loud-speaker announcements or *imam* sermons, etc.) and the *content* of the individual and collective communications (literacy and reading-grade level, emotional versus scientific appeal, what spokesperson delivers it, etc.) will differ by more than just whether the audience(s) are within a sovereign state or within a terrorist group. Both method and content will need to vary across the *two distinct dimensions* of (1) *whom* within the adversary is being messaged to, and (2) *how* to best achieve influence within each different sort of "whom."

As explained earlier, we will next, perforce, *first* cover further Tit-for-Tat against state-level adversaries, *then* modify and extend its consistent quasi-analog as most appropriate and fitting for terrorists. In fact, comparing and contrasting various relevant chracteristics of sovereign states as opposed to sub-state/trans-state armed groups (terrorists) will be important to the analyses throughout the rest of this chapter.

How Tit-For-Tat Exploits America's Unique Warfighting and Peacemaking Strengths

Tit-for-Tat, as a baseline deterrence/retaliation paradigm against *state-level* adversaries (but *not* against terrorists), in America's "nuclear posture after next," would make maximum use of *certain genuine asymmetric advantages* that the U.S. and our NATO (and other) Allies have over any belligerent dictatorship that does start a nuclear war. These advantages are to be found in (1) our nations' time-honored, battle-proven, bed-rock freedom-loving and humanitarian ethos, compared to the questionable ideologies of repressive, warmongering tyrants, and in (2) our side's ability to message compellingly regarding precisely this drastic/ dramatic contrast, to potentially *reticent* (or at least, *educable*) influencers and decision-makers who might act as *intervening-interdicting "circuit-breaker individuals"* within America's adversaries that might ever seek to execute a nuclear first-strike.

These latter, repressive and bellicose types of states and their personality-cult strongman leaders—the likes of a Vladimir Putin or Kim Jong Un (current) or a Saddam Hussein or Muammar Gaddafi (recent past)—amount to geopolitical "bullies" who, as do all bullies, try to bluff their way along through a superficial display of "brittle bravado." These countries' heads and their policies are generally very selfish and brutally punitive, overemphasizing oppressive control of their entire societies; they lack any strong, positive moral values (beyond cobbled-together extremist ideologies) and don't possess the truly inspiring, self-effacing leadership abilities that could keep their people solidly grounded, mission-centered, and unfalteringly courageous during overwhelming thermonuclear stresses. As such, in any hypothetical future First Nuclear War, these regimes can probably (though not 100%) be counted on to respond to continuing, firm U.S./Allied resistance with a form of unstatesmanlike "self-preserving cut-and-run instinct": Faced with our predetermined-yet-responsive Tit-for-Tat declared Nuclear Posture, and then our patient, right-back-in-your-face Tit-for-Tat actual counter-strikes to their bombardments, such dictators are likely to buckle and cave-in first, to save themself and their aspiring blood-line dynasty (i.e., immediate family) from further massive devastation and imminent death. Such a tyrant would have a lot less to lose in a nuclear war by bailing when the going gets tough than would the U.S.: We stand firm as the ultimate (and last-resort) guardian of human freedom, fighting for something *much greater than ourselves*, namely to preserve (and share) our precious, free Way of Life—and we would face de facto enslavement by the tyrant and their secret police if ever defeated.

Our high idealism is a *much stronger motivation* of durable loyalty and commitment than are a dictator's hate and avarice. Democracy is *much more merciful and generous* to defeated or surrendered enemies than is any authoritarian dictatorship. World War II's and then the First Cold War's ebb-and-flow of conquests and capitulations both show this very vividly. Such added asymmetries would also likely cause dictatorships to "give in" first in a nuclear war, while trying to preserve their lives, some wealth, and some dignity. Rather than making further nuclear-combat strikes, which they know we would just continue reciprocating for in exact Tit-for-Tat kind—*ad infinitum* if they forced us to—they would seek a cease-fire and peace treaty, especially if we seemed receptive to such overtures.

The above analysis helps expose how America's *durable self-image as a humanist force for good and the Arsenal of Democracy* is *very foundational* to our successful nuclear deterrence posture. It is worth noting, in *stark contrast*, that the two deceased dictators referenced above, Saddam Hussein and Muammar Gaddafi, both *deserted* their leadership posts and *fled* for their lives during *conventional* war or civil war, only to be hunted down and hanged or shot by vengeful fellow countrymen.

Another key to Tit-for-Tat functioning well as a prompt nuclear-peace restorative would be America crafting, along with the adversary's negotiators at the time, a peace treaty that is *not* like the Unconditional Surrender Doctrine of past major wars, but rather which seeks to quickly stop the nuking via such *diplomatic tools* as waivers of regime change, grants to leaders of extended-family amnesties in opulent exile, and offers of rebuilding assistance (as in the post-WWII Marshall Plan). These could be significant bargaining chips in the nuclear peace negotiations, wherein America's traditional appetite for harsh and pervasive punishment of defeated war criminals (as in the WWII Nuremberg Tribunals) has to take a back seat to *saving human civilization.*

(Actual regime-change in an adversary that moves to start a nuclear conflict, while clearly desirable, nay *necessary*, to punish the culprit and prevent subsequent copycats, would have to—and could—wait until *after* nuclear hostilities were safely ended and the original *casus belli* adjudicated and dissipated. The regime-change goal might even be achieved with a minimum of direct U.S. involvement: After the multiple disruptions that nuclear brinksmanship or worse would wreak on an entire aggressor's society, decisive *internal* drivers of regime change might grow ascendant. These could include rising domestic political rivals of the dictator, and/or widespread, cathartic disillusionment with and detestation of the dictator—especially when amplified by strained recovery from the grim aftermath of any actual nuclear exchanges.)

Returning to the idea of instigating "circuit-breaker individuals" behind enemy lines, under the above circumstances, enemy "follower" (rank-and-file) individuals would have an obviously much better chance to survive the nuclear war (which their side already started or intends to soon start) by *defecting or deserting* to the good guys, or by otherwise *resisting* until cooler heads prevail, compared to staying loyal to the tyrant. This stark choice would be well understood by worldly wise senior and some midlevel enemy combatants, despite (or even *because of*) a tantruming dictator's bloodcurdling promises of the death penalty for abandoning their posts. (An overwrought bully's raging tantrums would clearly convey to many direct witnesses his/her inherent weakness and vulnerability.)

Potential *circuit-breaker individuals* among the tyrant's subordinates, positioned within his/her nuclear establishment—where they could best pull off *covert or overt intervention* against the first (or next) nuclear strike taking place—would likely be among the adversary society's most educated, geopolitically savvy, technically sophisticated, and emotionally mature and perceptive individuals. They would probably also be amply endowed with electronic devices able to access the Internet and/or other elements of the international communications grid; they would be well able to understand U.S./NATO science-based *messaging* about the ultimately Hellish catastrophe which that nuclear first-strike, or continuing nuclear combat, would bring down upon them, their loved ones, their nation, and the whole world community.

It would certainly be challenging for such messaging to penetrate the *commnications fog of nuclear war* (enemy jamming and censorship, enemy's Internet-quarantining "off switches," electromagnetic pulse damage), but the U.S. is reputed to possess extremely effective offensive cyberwarfare capabilities. Plus, once a nuclear war broke out, we would have nothing to lose and everything to gain by *making the attempt* at both individualized and stochastic recruiting of such "circuit-breaker, Earth-saving good folks."

Unlike in some past *conventional* conflicts, where U.S. messaging content might not have been especially effective (such as the Vietnam War), in the vastly different case of an impending adversary nuclear first strike or actual nuclear war, the operant contrast would *not* be between an (allegedly) imperialist, profiteering, distant-meddler America and a (purportedly) liberating, revolutionary, deserving homegrown regime. It would amount to a *simple, utterly stark contrast* between either continuing (or restoring) nuclear peace, or enduring agonizing nuclear annihilation. Compared to the debatable question of whether the U.S. is or is not "the Ugly American incarnate," i.e., an exploitive neo-colonial empire (as Hanoi could allege during Vietnam), the issue of nuclear life-or-death would be undeniable and inarguable.

Tit-for-Tat against states thus provides a highly specific, structured nuclear-retaliation paradigm that implicitly and explicitly *draws on and exploits the major divide*—in cultures, values, attitudes, governance, motivations, and prior histories—between states that are democracies and states that are tyrannies—between the forces of light and life, and the forces of darkness and death. It can *potently leverage this divide* via properly crafted messaging content, conveyed during normal nuclear peacetime and during dangerous nuclear crises—and even during nuclear combat—which could be plausible and convincing enough *across any divide.*

Tit-for-Tat keeps *"the monkey of apocalypse"* squarely on the nuclear-aggressor's back, where it belongs. In short, it avoids the risk of appearing to telegraph weakness from America/NATO making a *less powerful* counterstrike, and at the same time avoids the risk of contributing further to complete Armageddon from us making a *more powerful* counterstrike. It can erect the *"Golden Bridge"* that Sun Tzu said should always be kept open to one's enemies in battle, to let them back down, save face, withdraw, and make peace.

Actionable Ways in which Terrorist Groups *Do* Resemble Sovereign States

The above discussion was intended to dissect "the world of state-level nuclear deterrence," and expose some aspects of its *operational sinews* in such a manner that we can now begin trying to extend such deterrence processes and phenomena to terrorists and other armed groups. The one major difference, the *major constraint,* that must apply to this extension—at least for American/NATO policy—is that (of course) we would *never* intentionally retaliate directly against a widely-dispersed terrorist group, acting on its own (i.e., without some state regime's direct connivance), by hitting back at its members, locations, and/or assets with our nukes.

Yet exactly such retaliation lies at the *very epicenter* of nuclear deterrence as America *does* now apply it to states: Nuking back is the *one specific action* we would take in case an adversary *state* ever did nuke us first. During nuclear peacetime, our nuclear arsenal-in-being supports precisely such a drastic threat; this promise to counterstrike using our Triad is the *prime mover* underlying America's whole National Nuclear Posture (encompassing also strategic-level enemy attacks by *other* WMDs). Again, we ask the crucial question, what more can we do to deter nuclear terrorists?

Let us pick apart this problem thoroughly, and address its components one by one:

> If we switch gears to looking at the *similarities* between them, terrorist groups and adversarial states manifest comparable, underlying "demographic recipes," which are in fact *always* highly relevant to achieving nuclear deterrence:

Fundamentally, both any adversarial state (e.g., Russia, North Korea) and any terrorist group (e.g., ISIS, al Qaeda), whether or not they own or want to own nukes, comprise a widespread collection of human beings who share a strong sense of belonging and a unifying identity, and who as part of their common sense of purpose strive for certain geopolitical goals, which sometimes-to-often include doing American and Allied vital-interests great harm. As such, their members were each brought up from infancy (by parents, other relatives, and/or orphanages or madrasas) to have individual values and motivations (possibly anti-American and pro-militancy) that they might, or might not, now willingly subordinate to a combative, militaristic ideology; they possess free will that they might, or might not, now willingly surrender before the whim of a radical leadership. Each member has at least *some* degree of loving attachment (and/or dysfunctional resentment) to parents, siblings, children, and/or ex- and current romantic partners; each member has at least *some* degree of either a self-preservation instinct, or a drive (perhaps through brainwashing) to sacrifice their life violently for the aggrandizement of their group. Even dedicated terrorists do belong to the *human species*, and as such their bodies (including their *brains*) and their *minds* (which are housed in their brains) obey certain *"physiological laws of behavioral cause and effect."*

Consequently, each terrorist who is (1) *old enough* to participate *directly* in acts of nuclear aggression (*not* just as a decoy or shield) and is (2) *educated enough* to contribute significantly to any such complex nuclear-attack operation (not just as a "mule" or laborer) *will have a somewhat-predictable mind.* Inside this mind *it is sometimes (certainly not always) possible* for America to *ignite a battle of choice* between (1) existing group indoctrination-propaganda-radicalization in favor of making a nuclear strike, thus achieving group goals in the narrowest sense but also risking entire-group annihilation, and (2) restraint-reticence-moderation in favor of preserving nuclear peace and insuring their group's continuing existence. Igniting this inner battle, and then having aspect (2), "restraint," win out—to aid effective nuclear deterrence, by empowering "circuit-breaker individuals" to try to resist completing said strike—depends very much on *effective messaging.*

Note that such a nuclear-deterrence goal is *significantly more limited in scope, extent—and difficulty*—that trying to convince a terrorist to completely give up *conventional* anti-American violence, let alone "rally" (to borrow the Vietnam War term), i.e., "convert" (defect) to *support* U.S./Allied interests; this more limited goal might thus be *significantly more attainable.*

Practical Ways to Message about Nuclear Deterrence to Terrorist Groups and Their Helpers

We laid out earlier in this chapter how America's successful deterrence of *states* requires "two types of nuclear arsenals": *nuclear-retaliation warheads plus delivery vehicles,* and *nuclear-deterrence messaging methods plus content.* This entire Chapter 3 is dedicated to explicating an *effective substitute* for American nuclear counterstrikes, an *acceptable alternative,* that could be exploited instead to *help deter nuclear terrorists.* Since communicating is nonlethal per se, a messaging arsenal that can be directed at potential nuclear terrorists does *not* present a democracy with serious moral/ethical or legal problems—especially when the message content is *truthfully based on scientific facts.* Effective messaging about nuclear deterrence to members of terrorist groups *does* present some *big* implementation challenges. However, workable solutions are by no means impossible.

Messaging methods: Terrorist group members can be found living, training, and operating almost everywhere, from dense urban environments in First World countries, to isolated and sparsely settled Third World areas amid arid desert or lush jungle terrains. Clearly, any single communications technique will not be able to reach all of them; a broad gamut of messaging techniques, varying from the old-fashioned to the highest tech, needs to be harnessed. As anticipated in earlier Chapter 3 sections, methods *at the lower end of the technology scale* can utilize the everyday socializing phenomena of rural tribal villages and urban ethnic neighborhoods alike, such as the rapid and very influential grapevine known colloquially (at least to Western analysts) as "the Arab Street."

Most human beings, everywhere, tend to be curious to hear and pass on local gossip, and are garrulous about each other's opinions, viewpoints, and ideas. Many folks love to discuss and debate world news, local politics, and everything in between. Even those only allowed to interact during strictly supervised study of fanatical group ideology/theology are still human beings. They will at times be swayed by their own human nature to find ways to exchange "disallowed" thoughts. World War II prisoner-of-war camp "Great Escapes," for instance, provide multi-cultural examples of mankind's ingenuity at acting out *rebellion* and planning *resistance,* even or *especially* under the harshest thumb of hostile authorities. Teenage boys *anywhere,* whether WWII POWs or extremist madras acolytes ("inmates"?), experience *floods of hormones,* and developmental emotional pressures, that can fuel aggressive skepticism and rebelliousness—quite possibly by *just enough* to benefit nuclear-counterterror deterrence influencing campaigns.

While it is important to avoid simplistic stereotyping, many wannabe nuclear terrorist groups do happen to be Islamic fundamentalists. Muslim areas around the world, especially those in Third World countries, make continual use—as already noted—of what some Western analysts call "the Arab Street." This is an amorphous but pervasive person-to-person oral network for quickly disseminating news and information throughout the gathering places and byways of many largely Islamic communities. (Of course, many Muslims are not ethnic Arabs.) Furthermore, the minaret loudspeakers (or very loud voices) used by muezzin to call the Faithful to prayer could, in pressing enough situations, and *primed with the right sort of nuclear-peacekeeping content* (see below), be used by mosques to send "civil defense" messages to a whole neighborhood. These possible messaging pathways might be reinforced, when appropriate, by mullahs and imams during sermons and teaching sessions. They might choose to do this once they themselves can be convinced about nuclear deterrence, via more targeted messaging to such authority figures from worried American coreligionists (who perhaps can best bridge cultural, technical-understanding, and language gaps).

In addition, even the most impoverished, infrastructure-deprived areas almost always have at least a few people who own TVs, laptops, or cell phones, and have ways to plug in or recharge them (gasoline-powered portable generators, solar cells, or vehicle cigarette-lighter outlets), which they will either rent out to others for their use, or share for communal enjoyment. Improvised temporary rabbit-ears antennas, or DVDs and thumb drives snuck in and passed around clandestinely, can substitute for cable or satellite access. If terrorist leaders try to forbid or confiscate such devices, or block pro-American Web sites, it would only *heighten their appeal* to some reticent or rebellious followers—especially post-pubescent males, given this demographic's nearly irresistible craving for Internet porn. (CIA and NSA counterterror cyber- and psy-ops could exploit this craving to boost deterrence effectiveness.)

Thus, it might be difficult to find a terrorist group that is entirely cut off from *all* Western nuclear peacekeeping/deterrence messaging.

At the higher end of the technology scale, it seems especially likely that terrorist-group members entrusted with aspects of executing a nuclear strike will be equipped with cell phones and other devices with which to communicate with each other, and with which to maintain *vital situational awareness* while traveling through intermediate waypoints and then toward their final target. American experts charged with messaging about nuclear restraint can exploit such devices in several ways: making targeted cell-phone calls to the terrorists (as was done by the U.S. against Saddam's lieutenants), use of targeted social media for positive (pro-deterrence) influencing, and issuing press releases that can be taken up on targeted communities' locally trusted news venues (lubricated by CIA payments to receptive reporters and their sources?).

The more "senior" within a terrorist group's hierarchy someone is, the more likely they are (of necessity?) to be continually "plugged in" to Internet content and the cellular airwaves in general—including American news-and-opinion media. But even rank-and-file terrorist family members and passive supporters are more and more likely to have good Internet access nowadays: the launching by several competing commercial space enterprises of "mega-constellations" of satellites, designed to give 24/7 communications access anywhere on Earth—combined with increasingly widespread ownership of personal devices, driven by the rising availability of such constellations—means that as time goes by, any current "technology barriers" for messaging to nuclear-wannabe terrorists will likely diminish.

Since terrorists are not likely to be able to obtain all-up working nukes without the help of *"rogue" nuclear scientists, illicit arms brokers, and/or organized crime bosses,* such individuals are also important points of leverage for nuclear-counterterror deterrence messaging—and for reinforcing such messaging to the terrorists with whom they do business. Even if such outside-the-law mercenaries do share extremist terrorist ideologies, or are just sympathetic "fellow travelers," or become radicalized over time through skillful "recruitment" by terrorist operatives, they will be relatively sophisticated, educated persons, able to *properly comprehend* deterrence messaging and in *ample possession* of devices for good Internet connectivity.

It should be noted that up to now such "collaborating mercenary/outlaw experts" *have* been involved in a number of cases of trafficking nuclear materials to terrorists, but this has been successfully confined by international counterterrorism efforts to either minimal amounts of *dirty-bomb* materials, or *complete hoaxes* such as "red mercury" or "osmium." It is quite possible that the simple reason "rogue scientists" have *not* yet provided terrorists any working nukes—or even significant amounts of component materials—and *never will,* is because, while they want and need to take earnings from terrorist coffers, they are *already acutely aware on their own* of what any Three-Fold Geophysical Wipeout can easily do to them, very personally: No amount of money from terrorists could make up for becoming *radioactive ash,* or for them taking a quick trip into the stratosphere *one superheated-plasma ion at a time.* (This rather vivid imagery leads us right into the next messaging topic.)

Messaging content: Various techniques and approaches frequently used by civilian public-relations professionals could be valuable starting-points for developing content for nuclear counterterror. The specific context here is a drastically military one: Terrorists need to be convincingly educated that they are likely to suffer terrible "nuclear blowback" consequences to them and their entire communities, if they ever do make a nuclear attack.

Terrorist leaders are known to use constant indoctrination, conditioning saturation and sensory deprivation, social/cultural isolation, fear of punishment or shunning, group hysteria, and peer pressure among their toolkit for keeping followers toeing the line of extremist ideology. Nevertheless, defense/deterrence authorities in the U.S. and our Allies can exploit a well-documented aspect of human behavioral responses, to the advantage of nuclear peacekeeping: Once someone is exposed to information or imagery (even a ridiculous false rumor, obvious fake news, or outrageous political cartoon), which puts the *seed of doubt* in their mind about something, it is *very difficult* for them to ever completely expunge that seed; the doubt will linger, fester, and might come to influence their subsequent *making of choices* regarding the topic in question. Imagine *how much more effective* this seed-planting campaign can be when the topic is *genuinely beneficial* nuclear deterrence, and the content is driven by *honest, factual, proven science.*

Education of terrorism-prone populations about nuclear-blowback dangers is probably best done incrementally, during nuclear peacetime, by a menu of themes which range from *entertaining, appealing background* in the natural-science basics of nuclear and other planet-wide risks, through to *very directly telling* the terrorists the extremely good reasons they should always "Just say no" to making a nuclear strike. Background content for heightened awareness of Earth/climate sciences in general, and nuclear dangers in particular, could include fictional movies such as *Failsafe, The Day After Tomorrow,* and *Dr. Strangelove,* and non-fiction documentaries such as *Cosmos* and *An Inconvenient Truth,* all with local-language dubbing (subtitles can be unpalatable, and they presume good literacy), all streamed free-of-charge on the Internet and on targeted local broadcast TV channels.

One aspect of nuclear-deterrence messaging content to terrorists could involve "turning a (*very distasteful, murderous*) lemon into (*less toxic*) lemonade." This would involve pragmatic *"diversion feeding,"* i.e., engendering suggestions of *much-less-lethal* (though still devoutly to be avoided) ways in which terrorists might exploit the situation if they ever really did somehow come to possess one or working nuclear weapons, *other than* to set them off against "enemy" targets. (The goal here would be to get the terrorists to stick to making *only conventional* violent attacks, thus maintaining stasis as to the historical/current lack of any actual terrorist nuclear detonations.) These "*non*-mushroom-cloud" forms of nuclear terrorism could involve: (1) using the nuke(s) to *sustain the group's own nuclear deterrence posture*, perhaps to protect a declared Caliphate area from bombing or invasion, (2) using their nukes for *nuclear blackmail* (intimidation, coercion), in which the threat to detonate them is used to extract concessions from enemies, but they are *not* actually ever set off, and/or (3) *selling them* to the U.S. (or another state), to raise cash to fund further conventional-only terrorist activities. Note that (1) and (2) are not mutually exclusive; as with states, a nuclear-armed terrorist group might deter and intimidate *at the same time*; (1) and (2) do offer terrorists a rather Machiavellian tradeoff between *one-time* mega-murder, and *ongoing "enjoyment"* of their nuke as an asset-in-being. Also note that (1) and (2) would *buy time* for U.S. and Allied authorities to either take back the nuke-in-being, or convince the terrorists to adopt diversion-feeding recipe item (3).

Some *nuclear-underground weapon scientists (rogue nuclear physicists)*, as mentioned above, already are working as—perhaps inadvertent—hybrid sorts of "circuit-breaker individuals" whenever they ply a *different* sort of diversion feeding: getting paid for low-value or even hoax nuclear materials. With prodding by the right sort of focused messaging and inducements, they might usefully reinforce diverting their terrorist customers away from making actual nuke attacks: The rogue doctorates might subtly join in helping convince the extremists to *deter, blackmail, or sell, but not detonate*. This prodding process could be lubricated by covert CIA payments to the "mercenary PhDs" in question, exploiting their existing greed, and building on their own self-preservation motives discussed above.

Messaging communication facilitators "on the ground" could also be found among more neutral, more law-abiding individuals, whose duties and callings bring them into areas frequented by terrorist populations. These good people are available in many disadvantaged or impoverished regions, rural or urban, where they already have beneficial interactions with locals. In rural areas these include aid workers such as Doctors Without Borders, Red Cross and Red Crescent, Peace Corps, Habitat for Humanity, the World Health Organization (WHO), or other non-governmental organizations (NGOs) or government agencies (such as the State Department's USAID), that provide food, medical, and infrastructure aid to the needy.

In more urbanized areas, where incognito terrorists or radicalizing young people sometimes live, train, and operate, various welfare, child services, youth/cultural center, and first-responder employees and volunteers will have frequent, casual/social conversational contact with community members over a typical week, month, or year. All these people, beyond their primary assistance functions, are technically sophisticated enough, and have the ears of those they assist often enough, to be important *"force multipliers"* for nuclear counterterror—if first asked to help by nuclear-deterrence experts, to act in the interests of the people they assist. Nuclear counterterror is certainly a *humanitarian cause* which should *not* antagonize these "neutrals," nor compromise their primary aid missions.

In general, the ultimate goal of deterrence-messaging content is to get amenable individuals within the terrorist group, or those supporting it, to reconsider their commitment to the group as far as going through with executing a nuclear strike. This is best achieved by combining subtle, seductive *suborning* with unsubtle, explicit *bludgeoning.* Either way, terrorists should be asked to think long and hard about whether their ideologies really justify them seriously risking *wiping out all humanity* just to *revenge some historical grudges.*

Cult-member deprogramming methods, of the sort used to renormalize impressionable young people who are rescued from a fringe-group's clutches, might be a particularly fruitful area for adaptation by deterrence practitioners. This could be drawn on when developing counterterror message content that *"deprograms by long distance"*—just enough to stop nukings. After all, cult leaders tend to resemble terrorist leaders in some key ways: Both are charismatic, manipulative, exploitive, they espouse extremist ideas, seek recruits among the emotionally vulnerable or socially disaffected to then sequester and brainwash, and some expect their followers to sacrifice everything, even their lives.

We have now overviewed the "other deterrence arsenal," the sorts of barrier-piercing, hurdle-jumping deterrence messaging *methods* that could deliver compelling and persuasive content in order to more comprehensively support U.S./NATO (and other national and international) nuclear-counterterror efforts. We return next to fleshing out the main, load bearing "platform plank" of this suggested communication "political campaign": *what that messaging should say.*

How Could Tit-for-Tat Be Extended to Terrorists by Democracies—*and by Dictatorships?*

In planning for the *disastrous downside scenario*—of American or Allied vital interests ever actually suffering a fission- or fusion-bomb attack by terrorists—the baseline Tit-for-Tat deterrence/retaliation paradigm pertaining to *states*, suggested earlier, should be *deconstructed* carefully, and then *extended with modifications as appropriate* to the nuclear counterterror deterrence mission. This extension needs to be tightly formulated, and then espoused internationally, *well in advance of any such downside scenario taking place.*

There are several good reasons why the U.S. urgently needs a *well-explained deterrence posture* in place to forcefully dissuade something even as "small" as "just" a single sub-kiloton improvised A-bomb terrorist strike. These reasons include:

- To take the official position that "nuclear terrorists cannot be deterred" openly *invites* terrorists to try to make a nuclear attack, since this implies that we would have no way to retaliate except by using conventional weapons—an already familiar sort of retaliation they can expect to absorb, survive as a group, and bounce back from readily.
- Terrorist leaders may have *additional* "homegrown" nuclear warheads being held backfor further attacks—for reasons/purposes such as waiting to see the full effects of their first strike, and/or lulling their victims into a sense of relief that "it could have been much worse" before hitting them again with something indeed much worse (an H-bomb), and/or sowing panic which they let spreas before they sow even more panic.
- The terrorists might yet (if not already), as *proxies*, be supplied with efficiently-weaponized (smaller, lighter, yet higher-yielding) "national" nukes, by a covertly-acting state-level adversary of the U.S., one that has a very numerous nuke inventory at its disposal and which was favorably impressed by the terrorists' initial nuclear-strike success and wishes to see more of the same.
- If the attackers are not very visibly and decisively punished, and swiftly, then subsequent copy-cat attacks (by the *same* terrorist group *and/or additional* groups) would only be further encouraged, inspired by the original success as well as egged on by intra-group and inter-group "*me-too* and *one-upmanship*" rivalries and jealousies.
- Any successful terrorist nuclear strike, due to the *Intra-War Nuclear Unsafe-User Principle*—plus other *pre-existing geopolitical hair-trigger enmities, rivalries, and jealousies,* not to mention any *conventional armed conflicts then raging*—might trigger, all too easily, wider inadvertent and/or opportunistic involvement

by further nuclear-armed states, leading to uncontrollable nuclear spasm war.

Thus we can say, at least for purposes of discussion, that what America needs (*if* it can be found to exist) is a *morally and legally appropriate "deterrence/response/deterrence" posture paradigm for nuclear counterterror*, given that (just as with nuclear attacks by states) there are *three distinct phases* to the entire future world timeline. These extend *from well before until well after* any first ever terrorist nuclear strike: (1) *effectively deterring* all terrorists during nuclear peacetime, (2) *responding* appropriately and promptly in case of any terrorist nuclear attacks, and then (3) *restoring effective nuclear deterrence of terrorists (and of states, including those that might use terrorists as proxies)* immediately after the first-ever terrorist nuclear attack has been made.

Finding and adopting such a nuclear counter-terror posture is critical, because it is their perceptions of any weak or nonexistent deterrence that makes bad actors think that nuclear weapons are useable by them in strikes against us and our Allies. Effective (very strong and very convincing) deterrence is what prevents bad-actor first-ever nuclear strikes.

Bear in mind that a terrorist group that does make a nuclear attack has itself chosen to proceed *much farther up* the escalation ladder, compared to all other terrorist attacks so far, which have relied "only" on the *conventional* high-explosive/incendiary and kinetic/potential-energy of hijacked airliner crashes and building collapses, bullets and bombs and knives, or motor-vehicle rundowns.

I personally find it hard to believe that the entire younger generation of jihadists (or other violent extremists), and further potential radicalizing recruits, will view having themselves and their homes and families be (1) raided yet again *domestically* by local police and national counterterror forces, or (2) shot at yet more *overseas* by pro-government militias, or (3) *bombed* yet more by coalition warplanes with conventional munitions, or even (4) *invaded* yet again by American-led multinational ground forces, as sufficiently daunting for them to not use nuclear weapons against us—if they and their leaders do ever somehow come into the possession of one or more nukes.

Many jihadists and their recruits, and violent separatists, and some far-right domestic terrorists live in areas already subject since before they were born to considerable *conventional* armed strife—including in some "domestic" cases a mix of street gang, drug cartel, and/or law enforcement violence. Individuals, and families and communities, do learn to adapt—as they did in Europe, Russia, China, and

Japan during World War II, and as Israelis have been forced to adapt since the Jewish State's independence in 1948 (if not before). People become inured to the constant destruction and death, whether terror or counterterror, and even come to expect it; in the worst cases of violent psychological pathology, they come to be *addicted to it* and even crave *wreaking more* of it. When the counts of their own dead in counter-terror strikes are limited *by our intent*—as is the case with conventional munitions used by democracies who typically do try to *avoid collateral damage*—then bad actors can even view their own deaths in battle as a *glorious release* from dreary worldly cares—and, for radicalized Muslims, as the *sure path* to heavenly Paradise.

The case I have been trying to make throughout this chapter is this: Anyone seeking the most reliable deterrence of nuclear terrorism has to first *very carefully consider* what types of weapons could, should or shouldn't, and might or would—in case of an actual terrorist nuclear attack ever taking place—be used to retaliate by any affected (or further threatened by copy-cats) sovereign state(s). This amounts to asking where America should go on the escalation ladder, and where other countries might themselves choose or feel forced to go. *Potential actions* by beleaguered, nay existentially threatened regional nuclear powers (such as India and Israel), and especially by revenge-crazed, callous nuclear dictatorships (such as China and Russia), have to be taken fully into account in this discussion.

It must be remembered, too, that *ideas, knowledge, and—above all—understandable warnings, backed up by hard facts about overstressed-human behaviors, organizational unreliability, chaotic foreign relations, high-energy nuclear physics, and atmospheric-circulation mechanics* definitely need to join the list of "weapons" to be considered, in the "messaging arsenal" that every nuclear power needs to deploy. It is likewise essential to cast the *widest possible net* for compiling, evaluating, and prioritizing potential U.S. response-options—and their consequences—while staying within the letter of international law, and adhering to proper American moral and ethical norms.

In the case of the attacker being a *sovereign* state, this chapter proposes a baseline answer to the nuclear-combat escalation-ladder question, which will be discussed further in this series' Volume 2: play Tit-for-Tat, i.e., *always respond on the same step* of the ladder that the attacker just moved to, where "respond" means to closely mimic the attack-victim's own nuclear weapons use(s) and "same" is measured down to the finest available details. This very specific paradigm seems to be *entirely consistent* with every U.S. Nuclear Posture ever promulgated, and it would appear to give America the best chance of forcing a *prompt* armistice on political terms *favorable* for the good guys. It also, simultaneously, harnesses the clear and present danger of any nuclear war uncontrollably escalating unto Armageddon, in order to put *insurmountable pressure* on the adversary to come urgently to the negotiating table. (The glaring/blaring fact that *nothing is completely guaranteed* to stop said catastrophic escalation is what adds shark-like teeth to America's peacetime nuclear-deterrence threat and promise, to begin with.)

But what about *terrorist* nuclear attackers? How do we play Tit-for-Tat with a *terrorist group* that nukes us? What can and should it *really mean* for America to "stay on the same rung" of the escalation ladder as terrorists who are the first to *go nuclear*?

In the *most morally troubling and most extremely reprehensible option* available to America, but only in theory, that *same* type of weapon (nuclear) could be worked into our particular retaliation threat-and-promise posture, for use even against terrorists hiding from retribution among innocent civilian populations within previously-uninvolved countries. Responding to nukes with nukes is after all, without doubt, the indispensable, theoretically sound, ethically justified, and logically rigorous core of effective deterrent posture against *attacking sovereign states.*

To be clear, and as will be made even more clear below, I am *definitely not* recommending that America follow this highly immoral, utterly illegal path of us nuking back any and all nuclear terrorists, wherever they lurk as they live and train and then flee to cower and hide. I am recommending only that we (1) *be aware* of the wider implications, as listed above, of not doing so, and then (2) evaluate carefully a *suggested alternative,* one that might merit inclusion among Nuclear Deterrence Best Practices by it being, quite possibly, *as effective as nuking back at the nuclear terrorists*—while it *also* takes the *highest high road* to righteous morality, international legality, and impeccable humanitarian values.

As an *added bonus,* this suggested alternative would be *quite free* from the problem of America ever being *self-deterred,* because it relies *solely* on natural forces and geopolitical behaviors over which America would have no control.

The *further, self-correcting and self-reinforcing beauty* of this suggested terrorist deterrence paradigm is as follows: Even if, in the worst case, it somehow does *not* succeed in either *effectively deterring before the fact* or indirectly *thoroughly punishing after the fact* any terrorist group which actually *does* make such a hypothetical *first-ever* nuclear strike, such (temporary) failures would only *vastly increase the probability* that the whole nuclear-armed world would *subsequently* be put on such hair-trigger hyper-alertness that states would almost certainly, both intentionally *and* inadvertently, deal out the harshest imaginable nuclear retribution in the case of *any further* terrorist nuclear strikes whatsoever—but again, definitely *without* the U.S. needing to intentionally target the terrorists with our nukes.

A Morally Acceptable Yet Perhaps Effective Nuclear-Counterterror Deterrence Paradigm

We will now develop further the *consistent but moral/legal quasi-analog* to effective nuclear deterrence's Tit-for-Tat state-on-state retaliation paradigm, an analog which could be adopted and declared in order to more effectively deter terrorist nukings. It makes use of a clear-eyed statement of the unpleasant wider realities of *any* nuclear combat on Planet Earth, in order to engineer a *de facto* retaliatory threat/promise of *a thermonuclear-consequences Doomsday*. This not-itself-lethal "info war" threat/promise, clearly and forcefully declared in National Nuclear Posture and incorporated in messaging to bad actors, is one which ought to help effectively motivate *any* self-interested terrorists to *always* confine their further attacks throughout the world to conventional weapons *only*. Yet this paradigm, to repeat (again) for (more) emphasis, *does not ever involve the U.S./NATO Alliance using any nuclear weapons that we ourselves intentionally aim directly at the terrorists.*

The point will be established—both for defenders who must deter and for terrorists who must be deterred—that despite this (totally appropriate) humanitarian and moral stricture on the retaliatory behavior of the good guys, nevertheless objective and rational cause-and-effect analysis demonstrates logically that the *inevitable, wider physiological/psychological, geopolitical, and geophysical effects and aftereffects of a terrorist nuclear attack* will very likely lead to mimicking what would happen if a democracy *did* actually making a nuclear counterstrike: The initial terrorist nuke attack itself would very likely trigger inadvertent and uncontrollable, wholesale Armageddon that completely extincts *all* human cultures and *all* religious faiths on Planet Earth.

It is this *mimicking* that makes this approach be an *inherent analog* of the usual state-on-state nuclear deterrence methodology. In the latter, the defender's threat/promise is made that the nuclear aggressor will be punished by the defending state's nuclear counterstrike aimed directly back at him/her. In this suggested, widened, counterterror-optimized Best Practice posture, which also does promulgate a threat/promise of sorts to terrorists, this class of aggressors would *also* be punishable by nuclear fire, which they instigated themselves via their own nuke attack. But in their case, that punishment would "proceed from the general to the specific," as follows: *Globe-wide* nuclear devastation, resulting from their own nuclear first-strike, would inevitably include them *wherever* they tried to hide.

A *consistent logical quasi-analogy* applies here because (1) with state-on-state Tit-for-Tat, direct retaliation is promptly targeted at the perpetrator, while wider Armageddon likely then *follows*, whereas (2) with democratic-state-against-terrorist deterrence, indiscriminate Armageddon is indirectly triggered by the perpetrator group's own nuke attack *first*, and those widespread effects *then* envelop that entire terrorist group along with the rest of Humanity.

In the *mathematical language of Venn diagrams*, this analogy works like so: Imagine a large circle representing All Humanity, and within it a small circle representing The Nuclear Aggressor. With state-on-state nuclear combat, if the Aggressor does execute a first strike, then retaliation occurs *first* against the small circle, and then Unsafe User and Three-Fold Wipeout effects spread to "get" the whole larger circle. But in the case of a terrorist strike against the U.S./NATO, the terrorists hide somewhere within the large circle; their attack "gets" the large circle via uncontrollable-escalation effects; the nuclear holocaust "gets" them since their lair (the small circle) will be situated *somewhere* within that large circle; any *draconian-deterrence retaliation* (see below) will just add to the devastation heaped on their heads. (Draconian counterstrikes can easily touch off *horizontal escalation*—dragging in more states—which then feeds on itself.)

How useful this suggested methodology might be, to be part of and reinforce a *wider* nuclear deterrence posture that could apply to *any* bad actor—whether aggressor state *or* sub-state/trans-state terrorist group—depends on *how likely* an initial terrorist nuclear strike actually is (and is perceived to be) to trigger uncontrolled escalation unto Armageddon. That likelihood, that *mathematical probability*, does *not* need to be an absolutely certain 100% in order to be a valuable adjunct to existing deterrence posture. During the First Cold War, the saying was prevalent among strategists that "to *assure a skittish ally*, who might otherwise build their own nuclear arsenal, America's deterrence threat needs to seem to them be a solid 90% credible, but to *deter a bellicose adversary*, just 10% chance they'd be completely wiped out by nuke blowback is plenty enough."

Would 10% probability of triggering all-pervasive Armageddon be "enough" to deter a bloodthirsty terrorist group, who obtains a working nuke, from actually striking with it (as opposed to, say, *deterring others* with it or *blackmailing* with it, or even *ransoming* it back to finance further *conventional* attacks)? Maybe yes, maybe no. But the prior question that we *should* be asking, rather than trying to read terrorist minds, is this one: Roughly what is the probability that such a hypothetical terrorist nuclear strike would trigger a global holocaust? My own gut feel, given my almost religious respect for Murphy's Law, Chaos Theory, Complex-Systems Reliability Theory, and the Law of Unintended Consequences, is that this answer is *"somewhere around 50%."* My gut also says that a risk of such a magnitude, properly conveyed to the world terrorist "community," while not guaranteed to be "high enough to *always* deter" would definitely be "high enough for the added effort of adopting this deterrence posture enhancement to be *well worth* the results it could bring to world nuclear peacekeeping."

Speaking of *assuring allies,* to plug current nuclear deterrence's "terrorism gap" when developing America's National Nuclear Posture-After-Next would also help achieve our ongoing *nuclear counter-proliferation goals.* It would do this by taking away, from use by any Allies skeptical of America's overall Nuclear Umbrella extended-deterrence promise's reliability, the particular (and currently, *truthful*) complaint that our posture now allows a big loophole re terrorist nukings. To officially and visibly *plug this loophole* would squelch any agitation within foreign governments and societies—by domestic political-opposition parties, hawkish policy-influencers, or fearmongering populist rabblerousers—that these Allies ought to "go their own way" and get their own nukes.

Think about the Unthinkable, Then Get Terrorists to Think Hard and *Unthink* the Unthinkable

Just one of the good reasons that democracies must think about this grim topic with the utmost thoroughness is this: Autocratic dictatorships–states that do not value freedom, morality, international law, and human rights as we do–are also subject to the direct and indirect threats of nuclear terrorism, in part via their own internal Muslim-separatist movements. So, they will also be thinking about these same deterrence conundrums very carefully, in the framework of their own rather different "value-sets."

To review, morally acceptable ways are indeed available to "threaten" nuclear terrorists with the effects of nuclear "retaliation" that most emphatically do *not* rely on a democracy having to use nuclear weapons aimed directly back at those terrorists. Two of these ways are:

1. warning about the "blowback effects" of immediate, local and very intense nuclear fallout, soon followed by possible/probable uncontrolled nuclear escalation to Armageddon

(*the Intra-War Nuclear Unsafe-User Principle*), with subsequent, long-lived worldwide nuclear fallout, *then* global nuclear winter, and *then* global nuclear summer ("the Three-Fold Geophysical Wipeout"), and
2. warning about the very real danger that a superpower dictatorship, or an existentially beleaguered regional nuclear power, whether a democracy or a dictatorship, will take matters into its own hands, adopt what I call *"Draconian Deterrence,"* and retaliate (or preempt) using nukes aimed directly at the terrorists.

These warnings can be strengthened further by disabusing terrorists that national-level nuclear deterrence Triads would remain, even under ongoing nuclear-combat conditions, solely as utterly reliable, restrained, predictable, controllable instruments of entirely justified, proportionate nuclear retaliation. Terrorists, and their whole wider societies of supporters, helpers, enablers, funders, and dependents, need to be made acutely aware that once nukes do ever start going off "in anger" anywhere, *all* nations' nuclear weaponry will be dangerously unsettled by the *simultaneous* impacts of Murphy's Law, Chaos Theory, Complex-Systems (Un)Reliability Theory, the Law of Unintended Consequences, and (most of all) the Intra-War Nuclear Unsafe User Principle. Once any form of nuclear warfare breaks out, *no* human being can predict what will happen next—except to say that it will probably be unspeakably murderous to all life on Earth. No Deity, whether Jehovah, Allah, Vishnu, or Anyone(s) Else, can be counted on to miraculously counteract this *staggering rise in planetwide subatomic-particle entropy (disorder of cosmic proportions)*. Rising entropy is a fundamental property of our universe that said Deity Themself created.

Terrorists Can Use Tactics Not Available to Nation-States

By dispersing and hiding among civilian populations, terrorists in effect use innocent people as camouflage and human shields. While this is illegal under international law, the tactic prevents the U.S. from retaliating against a terrorists' (or non-state madman's) nuclear attack with a nuclear counterattack—which is exactly what we *would* do if the attacker were another state (country).

At a minimum, the human-shield/hiding tactic can cause *delay*, allowing perpetrator *escape*, as retaliating authorities are forced to *slowly and carefully* analyze their response-options. They would first need hard-to-gather real-world, real-time data for unassailable situational awareness re two pressing matters: (1) immediate disaster rescue/recovery measures and evacuee succor, plus longer-term reconstruction aid, and (2) *decisive forensic attribution* of the nuclear attack to a specific originating state or sub-state/trans-state armed group.

Meanwhile, *controversy* would rage among those same authorities: *Precisely how severe* were the death and destruction from the nuking(s) you just suffered? *Whom* do you hit with nuclear retaliation, *where*, in a way that is adequately discriminating (against innocent civilian casualties) and proportionate (not overly excessive)? *How* do you retaliate without inadvertently escalating—by dragging in peer-competitor nuclear superpowers, and/or (smaller) regional nuclear powers, and/or by inflicting (1) long-lived radioactive fallout, (2) malfunctioning/misguided "live" warheads, and/or just (3) destructive spent missile stages, on previously-uninvolved third parties? How can you and the rest of the surviving world possibly mitigate the effects of planetwide nuclear winter and nuclear summer, to save the human species from becoming *completely extinct*? (Simulations show that this would take a century or two, as a badly diminished global population, struggling for survival in a devastated natural environment and with an enfeebled gene pool, shrank to zero over the next few generations.)

Such *predictable bureaucratic-authority delay and controversy* would buy time for non-suicidal terrorist masterminds who directed the attack to disperse, blend in with innocent local populations, and go to ground invisibly—for years, or forever. The *nuclear terrorism cancer will spread*, if the "original tumor" is not excised and cauterized thoroughly and visibly—assuming it hasn't already triggered and locked in a planetwide human extinction event.

Dictatorships Can Use Tactics Not Available to Democracies—But This Can *Help* Democracies

Bear in mind that unless *stringent measures* are taken in the immediate aftermath of a terrorist nuclear strike—assuming civilization does somehow weather it, maybe via a *UN-arranged "global nuclear-arsenal lockdown/hold-your-fire" that holds up 100%*—then the first successful strike might very well not be the last. (Unfortunately, *paranoid suspicions* that a terrorist nuclear strike *simply had to have been* covertly enabled by an *adversary state*, using *a proxy sub-state/trans-state group*, would create such a *casus belli* that global thermonuclear war seems more likely than preserving state-level nuclear peace via any such utopian "lockdown/hold-fire" counter-escalation pact.)

It does seem likely that any carrying out of a first-ever terrorist nuclear strike, that does somehow *not* trigger wider nuclear escalation, would so *totally alert and motivate* the (un)civilized world to implement desperate measures to *strengthen their nuclear deterrence postures* that the *second* such strike, if it ever does occur, *will* also be the *last*—one way or another. In particular, the probability will surely skyrocket that nuclear-armed dictatorships (Russia, China, North Korea?), or chronically existentially-threatened regional powers (Israel, India, Pakistan?) will selfishly adopt full-on draconian deterrence—including even making subsequent counterterror nuclear *preemptive strikes*—*after* the world's first-ever terrorist nuking—and then for sure would retaliate with nukes to the second.

Just one factor driving this likely "up-alerting" and "up-draconianing" would be that of *divisive national selfish self-preservation*, as follows: If a successful terrorist nuclear strike were ever to come as a tactical surprise (which seems highly likely), the severe systemic shock of it would impugn all states' nuclear-security Indications and Warnings intelligence processes, to the point that each would have little choice but to "circle their nuclear wagons" in a most draconian way. With *nuclear restraint* at that point so badly challenged, and *"nuclear hawks"* so enabled, even the U.S. and NATO (UK, France) and other democracies (India, Israel) might then be drawn into adopting the draconian approach themselves out of *sheer emotional, political, and national-security necessity*. This particular, hypothetical but not-inconceivable international scenario (a "thought experiment") is so unstable, it should motivate lovers of nuclear peace everywhere to *absolutely maximize their deterrence effectiveness against nuclear-terrorist groups*—and to do so sooner rather than later.

Alas, this *invitation to maximize*, which seems impossible to get away from, does openly invite repressive regimes to adopt draconian deterrence *now* versus nuclear terrorists. Note that for such authoritarian states to do so would *not* in any way weaken U.S./NATO deterrence posture against those same sovereign (authoritarian, i.e., *adversary*) states—which is *the entire compass/scope of U.S. posture* currently. The actual, incremental (i.e., added/heightened) danger right here is that dictatorships going draconian *might* channel any nuclear terrorists into attacking only U.S. and Allied vital interests, *rather than* those of China and Russia. This in and of itself is clearly undesirable for the U.S. and NATO! But this very same danger-heightening phenomenon *could* also *strengthen* a key (de facto, implicit) American counter-nuclear-terror goal: properly wielded fact-based messaging, about draconian dictatorship postures, could help convince *all* wannabe nuclear terrorists to continue confining their violent attacks, *anywhere against anyone*, to conventional weapons *only*.

What America needs to do is twofold:

1. *Directly optimize/maximize* morally acceptable ways for us to deter terrorists, by fomenting educational communication about the Intra-War Unsafe Nuclear User Principle and the Three-Fold Geophysical Wipeout, i.e., about the Armageddon hair trigger terrorists could easily set off by them making one nuking.
2. *Indirectly leverage off of* dictatorships' potential or actual draconian postures, which could easily lead to direct retaliatory or even preemptive nuclear strikes on terrorists, by us referring to those draconian possibilities (as detailed below) in our counterterror-education campaigning.

Since nuclear-armed superpower dictatorships and smaller rogue states alike might well think of going draconian on their own—if they haven't in secret already —it behooves the U.S. and our Allies to "take charge and move out" on items (1) and (2) here.

Remember Osama bin Laden, and Think about Modern Caliphates

Speaking of terrorist leaders going into hiding to escape retribution, bear in mind that Osama bin Laden hid successfully for *ten years* after 9/11/01, with covert support from factions in Pakistan, which is a nuclear power. The whole time, al Qaeda expanded its geographic reach, furthered its global financing network, diversified its weaponry, disrupted free societies, and took thousands more lives.

On the other hand, when a Muslim terrorist group declares a broad land area to be part of its sovereign caliphate, as ISIS tried to do in Syria, it is claiming to have *become a state*. It is no longer hiding in the shadows. It has given the world, or at a minimum given states which do follow draconian nuclear-deterrence postures, an area they can target for a retaliatory nuclear attack—or maybe for a preemptive (i.e., immediately *preceding*), or conceivably even preventive (i.e., *earlier* than preemptive) nuclear "spoiling" *pre-attack* counterstrike on said caliphate.

It is not clear whether either terrorists, or terrorist-deterrer sovereign states, have thought through the full implications of this New

Caliphate *sea change.* This remains a pressing issue because, even if any particular claimed modern caliphate is not particularly persistent-in-being in practice, the *lingering wider implications* of any terrorist group having ever in modern times made such a sovereign territorial claim gives a putative justification (i.e., an enabling excuse), to a sufficiently ruthless or desperate nuclear-armed authoritarian state, for a premeditated act of draconian retaliation.

While some folks within democracies might well smirk or even rejoice were such a prevention, preemption, or retaliation "heavy lifting" to ever actually be perpetrated against nuclear terrorists by a nuclear-armed dictatorship, bear in mind that this whole scenario would amount to a *terrible double-whammy* against civilized world order and world nuclear peace: A nuclear *exchange* would have actually taken place, the nuclear taboo thoroughly violated in a way that would court Armageddon—and nukes would have been used by both sides in absolutely heinous mega-slaughter of innocent civilians.

Why It Is Useful to Analyze Draconian (and Later Below, Even *Ultra*-Draconian) Deterrence

Having introduced draconian deterrence above for discussion purposes, we now analyze it, and then later below we push it as far as it can go to ultra-draconian deterrence, for these reasons:

- While it is *very* inappropriate for the U.S. and our Allies as democracies to ever adopt it, some other types of states someday might do so: repressive superpower dictatorships, rogue states, and chronically existentially-beleaguered regional powers. Were any other state to do so, nuclear terrorists might be "channeled" to be more likely to make their attack(s) only against U.S. and Allied vital interests, rather than those of the draconian/ultra-draconian state(s).
- But since any in practice draconian state might choose to itself retaliate against a nuclear-terrorist group that attacks *U.S.* interests—out of opportunistic "solidarity" with us and to prevent copy-cat nukings anywhere (including against that state)—this book's raising draconian issues could, if anything, *on net strengthen* America's nuclear-counterterror deterrence.
- The mere hint at the possibility that *any* states *might* ever adopt a draconian deterrence policy against nuclear terrorists, and might then implement such a policy via a retaliatory

strike *in response* to any actual nuclear terrorist attack, provides useful and morally/legally acceptable "ammo" *now* to democracies' counterterror educational messaging campaigns.

There is certainly *much more* to trying to deter terrorists from making nuclear attacks—via educating them about the *very real* risks to their entire populace, culture, and faith—than just making reference to the potential for draconian retaliation. As will be explained shortly, the Three-Fold Geophysical Wipeout, for instance, is an *entirely separate, additional issue* with *considerable counterterror potential,* as is the Strong Form of Strategic Ambiguity.

What Are the Dimensions of Draconian Nuclear Deterrence/Retaliation Postures?

On close enough examination, retaliation policies within state's nuclear-deterrence postures reside on a spectrum, actually a *multi-dimensional spectrum.* This is true in general, whether the discussion is about deterring sovereign states, or about deterring terrorist groups. Democracies and tyrannies are likely in practice, if not also in publicly declared posture, to fall at *opposite ends* of this spectrum.

This issue isn't just theoretical, especially regarding the subject of this Chapter 3, which of course focuses on deterring terrorists, although it also uses some observations about deterring sovereign states as foundational background:

> As noted earlier, Russia faces Islamic extremism in separatist Chechnya and the unstable Caucasus region; China faces it with the Uyghurs in Xinjiang, who are existentially threatened by Beijing's genocidal repression; both these Eurasian superpowers have suffered conventional terrorist attacks by these and other groups on their soil.
>
> In mid 2020, the "frozen conflict" between predominantly-Christian Armenia and predominantly-Muslim Azerbaijan—on the Caucasus isthmus within Russia's "Near Abroad"—flared up: Armed-drone attacks threatened an active Armenian nuclear power plant with an old Soviet design as dangerous as the four at Chernobyl. Nearby Islamic anti-Moscow terrorist factions, if not swiftly educated re the imminent dangers to their own side, might yet be tempted into triggering "another Chernobyl" to get back at Russia.

One dimension or parameter of any state's retaliation policy—regardless of *whom* it is aimed at—concerns *evidence of guilt,* i.e., *how much proof* that state's government requires regarding who was responsible for a nuclear attack, before taking the severe retaliatory action of a nuclear counter-strike. A lot or a little proof? Beyond any shadow of a doubt; or just beyond reasonable doubt; or merely based on suspicions, surmises, some circumstantial clues, or some mere pre-existing grievance which is a *convenient excuse* for a massive counterblow—or even just an irresistible craving for *revenge against somebody, anybody, and fast?*

Another dimension is the one which lays out what sort of entities are *ever considered at all "eligible"* for a retaliatory nuclear counter-strike—i.e., *whom* it might ever be aimed at. This is tantamount to charting how *casualty-averse* re unaffiliated civilian deaths, and how cognizant of the attacker entity's *sovereign-state status* (or lack thereof), the victim state's government is, whenever it decides whether to strike back at a nuclear strike via using its own nukes. Is a declared New Caliphate, within a larger "failed state," or within a "failing state" wracked by civil war (Syria, Libya?), so eligible? Is an isolated, desert training camp in a *small but stable state*, but one with *no nuclear umbrella protection*, so eligible? How about such a camp in a *larger unaligned state*, or even in just a *separatist-leaning* province of some adversary, with which a big nuclear dictatorship has bad enough *pre-existing "beef"*? And what if the separatist region is part of the vengeful dictatorship's *own homeland?*

How far can these hair-splitting "eligibility" (counter-strike *allowed*) criteria be taken, in the name of effective deterrence or even *nuclear preemption*, by sociopathic despots who feel no legal or moral restraints?

In mathematical terms, these two parameters together define a broad two-dimensional draconian nuclear-posture *Cartesian coordinate space*. The United States and our Allies would (and should) never choose to dabble beyond the *null point*. By null point I mean the lower left corner of the graph, at origin coordinate {0,0} which signifies {*require conclusive proof, must be recognized sovereign state*} as the only situations for which nuclear retaliation is ever allowed. Authoritarian states, such as the current regimes in Russia and China, in contrast, might choose to place themselves far to the upper right, their postures charted instead by the coordinates {*weak proof is sufficient, any terrorist concentration is eligible*}. Authoritarian regimes could make this decision either in advance of any terrorist nukings, by analysis and design, or in the first hours *after* a terrorist nuclear attack is made against them. In the latter event, they would be driven by an emotional craving for vicious revenge, plus heavy domestic pressures to retain political control—by being seen to be doing *something* drastic, shocking, and utterly bloodthirsty, like the strongmen that they are or that they wish to be seen as.

DEFINITION: A *draconian counterterror nuclear-deterrence state* means one that *either* (1) based on a preponderance of soft/cursory forensic analysis, or surmise, suspicions, and geopolitical opportunism, but *not* any objective domestic or international judicial inquiry's recognized very high standards of proof, chooses in practice to make a nuclear retaliatory counter-strike against the purportedly responsible party(ies) after first being nuke-attacked by that party(ies), *or* (2) does so *despite* the counter-strike perforce being targeted into territory of any sovereign state, by aiming it directly at a self-declared separatist entity such as a splinter province or self-declared caliphate, or even just at a terrorist group's "hometown" base-of-operations, training area, and/or region of origin wherever located; *or that does some of both (1) and (2).*

The rest of this chapter, since it pertains specifically to enhanced deterrence of nuclear terrorists, will focus on dimension (2).

Can Terrorists Be Educated re Nuclear Combat Perils? If So, How?

Can and should terrorists be *educated against the deadly radioactive perils* that any nuclear attack they make themselves would immediately and/or eventually pose to them and all their followers and co-religionists? Are they now perhaps *too* fixated on the damage they could cause to their supposed enemies, and *not cognizant enough* of what nuclear blowback damage they would inevitably, as a consequence, bring down on *themselves*?

A draconian-enough deterrence posture followed by any state(s) along Dimension 2 of the 2-D Cartesian coordinate spectrum, i.e., one that does lead to a nuclear counter-strike against the terrorists, could cause the mass of that terrorist group's population, and *all* their religious authorities, texts, and holy sites, to be *directly* vaporized, even *before* the massive fallout and nuclear winter and then nuclear summer could hit them. Factional dreams of a new caliphate would die forever. In fact, as mentioned above, the claim and/or actual establishment of a caliphate significantly transforms a diffuse sub-state/trans-state terrorist group into a state territory *of sorts*. As a purported state, it could easily be said that the caliphate is just as legally/morally eligible for nuclear retaliation as is any other state that commits a nuclear attack. Have the terrorists themselves figured this out? If not, how can they be taught to understand this?

Three Ever-Present Sources of Danger to Nuclear Terrorists

Regardless of the always-equivocal (morally repugnant?) issue of draconian deterrence and retaliation, grave nuclear harm to the terrorists themselves could occur from one or more of *Three Ever-Present Sources of Danger*:

1. from their own nuclear strike's very widespread lethal and toxic effects,
2. from nuclear retaliation against them by a draconian nuclear-deterrence state (or states)—including ones that do not have any draconian policy *before* the strike occurs, but are instigated by that strike to immediately adopt such a policy and even make a prompt, "retroactive" retaliatory and/or further-preemptive nuclear counter-strike,
3. from the wider effects of an unlimited nuclear war between third-party states that the initial terrorist strike triggers via *inadvertent escalation*. This "force of nature" derives from the Intra-War Unsafe Nuclear-User Principle combined with the Three-Fold Geophysical Wipeout.

Source (1) here deserves elaboration: Heat, blast, and especially fallout from even a single nuclear weapon, set off at some distance, can still cause significant casualties, plus lasting contamination of soil and water, among the attacking group. And since terrorists are not always the most careful or disciplined of warriors, a terrorist group that obtains a working nuke might set it off prematurely, *on their own turf*, by accident, or out of impatience or truculence, or in panic if faced with imminent interdiction by enemy security forces.

There is significant overlap in this *suggested trefoil anti-terrorism education syllabus*, between Sources (2) and (3): Draconian retaliation might turn out to be *just one small part* of a horrific, progressively expanding *global spasm war* that gets touched off by the terrorists' initial, single nuclear detonation. Spasm war—in which many or all nuclear-armed powers shoot off many or all of their nukes at one another, either by intent or through total loss of control of their over-excited, battle-damaged nuclear forces—is a *Dr. Strangelove*-style ending to the world.

A democracy will find it quite morally acceptable (even *necessary*) to educate everyone worldwide regarding a single nuclear terrorist attack quite possibly igniting an uncontrollable wider threat of nuclear-war human extinction—Source (3), also known as Armageddon, aka a thermonuclear holocaust. A ruthless dictatorship could/should go much further, obviously, with additional "curriculum" re their draconian measures of direct nuclear retaliation against the terrorists' population centers-of-gravity—Source (2). Democracies can further their own nuclear-counterterror deterrence goals by mentioning, thus *riding on*, dictatorships inflicting Source (2).

In any case, some terrorist deaths would be immediate, while others would be slow and agonizing. Caliphate territory would be contaminated by lethal radiation for decades, or generations.

This warning might be enough to deter any terrorist nuking, most strongly so for one involving potential targets situated within an authoritarian sphere of influence which takes the draconian path—e.g., Russian or Chinese homeland territory and their foreign vital interests. But any nuclear deterrence effectiveness would gain useful preventive traction with terrorist decision-makers (which is where it is needed) *only if* such nuclear dangers *to them personally*, i.e., the trefoil dangers labeled Sources (1) through (3), are forced to the forefront of the terrorist leaders' own and their followers' minds. This is where the necessary *deterrence-messaging arsenal*, mentioned already, comes directly into play.

The Twisted Ethics of Dictatorships "Going Draconian"

The ethical problems of draconian deterrence re terrorists only come into important practical effect if a terrorist nuclear strike does first take place, and then a draconian deterring state does make a retaliatory nuclear strike; short of such a drastic outcome, draconian policy would be merely a policy on paper.

Draconian deterrence concepts will cause even less moral trouble to tyrant superpower leaders who do carry them out *in the future*, if those leaders do first use effective ways to bring potential nuclear terrorists up to speed on 21st century nuclear deterrence *in the present*—including *the idea of the draconian spectrum*. Then the claim might be made that any wannabe nuclear terrorists have been *duly warned*, and so *they deserve what they get*.

Terrorist Groups Could Go Draconian, Too, with Several Major Implications for States

For completeness, we should mention that terrorist groups, or more generally *any* sub-state/trans-state armed groups, which come into possession of one or more nukes, could in theory—just like states—use them for deterrence against nuclear attack *based on a draconian posture*: These violent, lawless entities certainly do not respect human life and human rights any more than would "normal" (and presumably now *only hypothetical*) draconian-deterrence state dictatorships. What is more, any non-state armed groups that do not now covet specific regions as their modern caliphates, or as other *exclusive spheres of influence or operating areas,* certainly might come to do so in the future.

Let us think of our home planet on the most fundamental terms: Any *spheroid's surface* can be conceptualized as an uncountably-infinite collection of 0-dimensional points that together comprise a two-dimensional manifold embedded in three-space. In particular, every point on Planet Earth has a unique two-dimensional longitude and latitude coordinate, fixed once a "North Pole" and a "longitude 0" point (e.g., Greenwich, UK) are specified. Sub-regions on the planet are designated as either various *sovereign countries* ("states") including their *territorial waters* (if not land-locked), or as global-commons oceans ("international waters") that none own and all can use. (*"Sovereignty"* means that a state has supreme and independent power; no other state or organization can *make* it do something or not do something except by *armed force.*)

In the 21st century, every point of dry land on earth is internationally recognized as being part of at least one sovereign state—there are no more "undiscovered" territories waiting to be "claimed in the name of the monarch" by some latter-day colonialist explorer. Problems arise, though, whenever more than one state *claims the same point of land as their own.*

Sometimes the disputed area is a contiguous (in mathematical topology terms, "path-connected") land region that falls along the border between two adjoining states. Sometimes it is an entire small island, reef, rock, or shoal at sea, usually lying outside any state's twelve-mile territorial limit but within *overlapping* two-hundred-mile exclusive economic zones. (The UN's 1982 *Convention on the Law of the Sea* specifies clear criteria for resolving ownership of overlapping EEZs, but some states refuse to agree with these boundaries.)

Land-border disputes that have been the subject of one or more wars since World War II include those between India and Pakistan over Jammu-and-Kashmir, between China and Russia over part of the Amur River, between China and India over parts of Ladakh in the Himalayas (which flared up recently), and an ongoing one (as of early 2021) between Ukraine and Russia over Crimea and Donbas. *Disputes over island ownership* are epitomized by the Falklands War between Argentina and the UK, by the Kuril Islands dispute between Russia and Japan, and by ongoing tensions between China and several neighbors over points in the Sea of Japan and the South China Sea. In some of these cases, one of the states, generally the winner, *owned nuclear weapons* at the time of the crisis—and/or the other was *motivated to obtain nukes* because they lost.

What makes any *sub-state/trans-state armed group using nukes for deterrence* be, potentially, *strategically destabilizing* is this: Such an odd, now-only-hypothetical geopolitical phenomenon would inevitably draw in the state(s) (called here the "host state(s)") that officially own those area(s) which were to be claimed by the armed group as being "protected" from nuclear attack by that armed group's nuke(s). One or more of several things could happen, none of them good: Any state which the group attacks with nukes, that makes a *draconian retaliation* back *against said group*, has ipso facto just made a nuclear first-strike *against the host state(s) at the same time*. If that host state or states (1) owns nukes, or (2) is or can soon become part of a Nuclear Umbrella treaty with a nuclear power, or (3) subsequently acquires nukes and has a long memory about the nuclear retaliation on its soil, then a state-on-state nuclear war will likely result either quickly or slowly.

Thus, *as with states, any* nuclear deterrence (and *especially* draconian nuclear deterrence) by a sub-state/trans-state armed group can contribute to *horizontal escalation* of any nuclear conflict—*contributing to Armageddon* if any entity nukes that armed group, either in a preemptive first strike or in a retaliatory second strike. Equally destabilizing, *if* states wish to avoid such terrorist-triggered escalation, then a terrorist group residing within a nuclear-armed host state (perhaps one that gets its nuke or nukes *via a proxy granting or by stealing them* from said host state) has *gained sanctuary from nuclear retaliation*. (For instance, nuclear-armed Pakistan does play host state, willingly or unwillingly, to some Islamist terrorist groups. Some defense analysts are concerned that nuclear-armed North Korea, or nuclear-wannabe Iran—both of which are known to sponsor conventional terrorist proxies—might give or sell nukes to such groups.)

As noted earlier, America's current National Nuclear Posture specifies that we would retaliate with nukes against any state that *gives* nukes to terrorist proxies that they use to attack our vital interests—not specified but implicit in this position is "*whether or not* the state also 'hosts' those proxies." In the language of this chapter section, the U.S. would *definitely* choose retaliation against the nuke-giving host state, rather than respect it granting "sanctuary" to the terrorists. In effect, we warn off all potential such bad actors, by declaring in advance that we would consider a state sponsor of nuclear terrorism and the proxy terrorist group so sponsored as *one entity*, and we would act as if we deemed the *sponsoring state* to also be the proxy group's *host state* (as it well might be). In this convoluted sense, using the language of this chapter, America does now de facto follow a *limited form of "draconian-like" deterrence.* But this is a good thing. To repeat for emphasis, the imminent danger of any first nuclear attack escalating uncontrollably to Armageddon is what gives our nuclear deterrence posture and messaging their real "bite."

If, instead of taking nuclear revenge itself, a state that was nuke-attacked by the non-state armed group does seek retaliatory nuclear revenge, but—showing admirable restraint—it asks the *nuclear-armed host state itself* to act as the perpetrators' nuclear punisher, a very strange situation indeed could arise. If the host state refused to "nuke itself," it could be accused of "intentionally harboring *nuclear fugitives,*" or even of "enabling nuclear proxies *after the fact.*" It might then get nuked by the offended victim state—*outside* the internal geographic region specifically claimed by the non-state armed group as its own controlled turf.

If, on the other hand, the hosting state *did* agree to detonate a nuke "in anger" on its own soil, to retaliate against the terrorists *and* mollify the victim state, this could be an effective way to keep the necessary nuclear retaliation against the nuclear terrorists "limited" in scale, *preventing Armageddon.* (This approximates the fictional American president's gambit in the ending of *Failsafe.*)

It would seem that a state that hosted terrorists *unwillingly, inadvertently,* might be more willing to nuke itself to "end the matter decisively," than might a state that hosted and sponsored the terrorists by *intentional design.* But this might not be the case, which would also seem to give one more good reason for terrorists to *never* strike with nukes, *especially* with ones they might be given by a hosting state-sponsor: There is a clear and present danger that, after they do make a nuclear strike, *harsh reality* will set in on their sponsor/host, the imminence of Armageddon will suddenly get *very real,* and they will *be betrayed and be nuked* by that *same* host/sponsor state. After all, "there is no honor among thieves"—nor between terrorists and their state sponsors!

(An "innocent," *unwilling/non-sponsoring host* might nuke the terrorists to *share in justified retribution* along with the original victim state—while, pragmatically, forcefully eliminating an internal terrorism problem. A "guilty," *willing host/sponsoring state* might do this, too, to back up their untruthful protestations of innocence to the victim state and the world—while getting away with *indirectly (via terrorists) nuking an adversary state* and then ruthlessly "killing off the witnesses (the terrorists)." A lot would depend on *where* the terrorist personnel and their operational assets were concentrated. An isolated rural area, such as some terrorists use inside Pakistan along the border with Afghanistan, might cause the *least self-damage* to the state that nukes itself. Terrorists might prefer such an area for *operational security*—military secrecy—while preparing their nuclear strike. A double-dealing sponsoring state, that in advance intends to nuke the terrorist concentration after they nuke someone else, would want to sequester them in just such *an "expendable" area*, as well.)

It is perhaps fortunate that most areas that have been or might become candidates for modern caliphates, or less "official" basing/training locales, lie within regions of the world that, while they are subject to much conventional armed conflict, have largely been excluded from membership in the "Nuclear Club" (those states that do now own nukes). Ratified *nuclear-free zones*, such as those covering Africa, Latin America, and Oceania, help to reduce any draconian retaliation's inherent spasm-nuclear-war risk, but at the same time they suggest places where nuclear terrorists might seek to more safely base their people. International organized-crime "mafias" and contraband-smuggling cartels sometimes operate within states that *do* own nuclear arsenals—including the U.S. and Russia. And several Muslim states across the Middle East's very active *conventional* conflict zone—Libya, Syria, Iraq, and Iran—at one time had efforts underway to gain nuclear weapons, which some of them might now still be pursuing, or which they might in future revive. (The late Dr. A. Q. Khan's *nuclear-centrifuge black market* helped gestate some of these programs.)

While seemingly far-fetched at present, it is not entirely out of the realm of possibility that at some point in the future, *more than one caliphate*, locked in bitter age-old enmities with each other, might come into existence, might get nuclear weapons, and might adopt nuclear-deterrence postures against their "enemy" state powers (the U.S., Israel, India, Russia, China?) plus draconian deterrence *against each other*. (The thought-experiment scenario in which Sunni and Shi'a caliphates fight a nuclear war with each other is touched on again below, and also in Appendix 2.)

In a seriously-dysphoric speculative future, in which some major nuclear powers become suddenly "Balkanized" (splintered apart—like the USSR or Yugoslavia) or they collapse into failed or failing states, *more than one* sub-state/trans-state armed group around the world might acquire nukes, and then use them to (1) blackmail (*coerce*) law enforcement into impotence, to (2) blackmail (*extort*) wealthy entities for "nuclear protection money," to (3) *deter* attacks on their feudal turf—by states and/or by one another—or even to (4) *fight nuclear wars.*

Note that when the Soviet Union collapsed in 1991, the U.S. invested heavily (the Nunn-Lugar Act) in helping Moscow secure all its nuclear weapons stored in ("separatist") *former* Soviet republics—including Ukraine. This *urgent counterproliferation effort* succeeded, but the same thing *might not succeed* the next time a sovereign state breaks apart. Possession is nine-tenths of the law, and those coming to possess of some of the "loose nukes" might be non-state entities who won't *just hand them over* to a recognized government.

Such hyper-imaginative scenario testing (as in *actuarial contingent timeline deconstruction,* per Appendix 1) illustrates the vital importance of *all* nuclear-armed states maintaining at *all* times—even amid the worst strains on national economies, human society, and world order—*genuinely impenetrable, theft-proof* nuclear arsenals equipped only with *tamper-proof, ultra-secure* weapon designs—along with *very concerted, genuinely cooperative global efforts* to message against, and otherwise counter, both nuclear proliferation and nuclear terrorism.

While planning for dystopia perhaps deserves low priority among the many pressing responsibilities of American (and other states') diplomats, policy planners, and deterrence-Triad commanders, this chapter section does reinforce the basic point of this entire book: *When it comes to the theory of nuclear-war prevention, more thorough analysis is better and safer analysis, because forewarned is forearmed.*

The admittedly Byzantine investigation here has established an additional useful point: It highlights the selfish utility to non-state armed groups of them *holding onto ("diverting")* any nukes they get *instead of (away from)* detonating them in an attack, exploiting them rather as ongoing deterrents-in-being (plus blackmailing tools) against both sovereign states *and* any emerging/competitor non-state nuclear-armed entities. (The first sub-state/trans-state armed group to successfully get nukes will, alas, likely open the floodgates for rivals and imitators.) A non-state group that obtains *more than one nuke* might *attack* with one while holding the rest for *deterrence and blackmail*—this would be the *most nightmarish* of these different nightmare scenarios.

To recap further, this section's detailed exploration also helped eke out the *significant risk of draconian nuclear retaliation by a terrorist group's own state sponsor and/or their (maybe different) state host(s),* for any terrorist group that is given nukes by—or steals them from—such states and then uses them for megadeath. (In other words, *sanctuary is illusive.*) This pithy observation, by reinforcing the Three Sources of Danger to Nuclear Terrorists, *helps strengthen both counterproliferation (preventing them acquiring nukes) and effective deterrence/diversion (preventing them attacking with nukes).*

Nuclear Counterterror Messaging Is a Godly, Humanitarian Imperative for All Faiths

Various education/warning methodologies to try to reach nuclear terrorists certainly do exist, Internet-based, "pulpit-based," and otherwise. These are much more than merely selfish "fake news" and "malign info-war" psychological operations ("psy ops") and manipulative-propaganda techniques. Some of this messaging will be *especially appealing* to anyone already cherishing anti-violence, humanitarian, pro-human-rights and spiritual values: Since any single nuclear attack can all too easily ignite complete nuclear Armageddon for our whole planet, there are strong, "real news" *truth-based* reasons right there for good people of *any* (or even no) religious persuasions to help nuclear terrorists see reason.

The investment of time and money in an effective worldwide deterrence-education campaign, *especially* when boosted by the "politically/militarily neutral" pastoral and missionary resources of various (pro-peace) religious institutions around the world, has more than just self-preservation benefits; it has *life-preserving benefits* to all human beings, *including even the terrorists themselves.*

Eastern and Western theologians and preachers/evangelizers have very good reasons to help carry this genuinely interfaith messaging throughout their ministries on every continent. They are well positioned to do so: They mingle continually with locals throughout the communities they're embedded in, when they render aid and proselytize their denomination's religious beliefs; terrorists similarly mingle, as they too worship, network, recruit, and train; nuclear counterterror efforts, i.e., pro-deterrence "buzz," from the mouths of the one group will inevitably diffuse and percolate to the ears of the other.

Many clergy *will be educated enough and receptive enough to be coached and scripted* to drop *gentle hints*, use *indirection*, to help terrorists *figure out for themselves* that total nuclear abstinence is best for them and their cause; one way to address this topic naturally with local listeners, while not raising too many hackles with any terrorists and their helpers-sympathizers-dependents in the audience, is to couch this messaging as spreading the word about (and on behalf of) *the world nuclear-disarmament movement.*

While this book has tried to argue that such disarmament, though noble, is impractical in today's adversarial Cold War II world—it would itself heighten serious *minimal deterrence failure* and *cheating* risks to strategic stability—nevertheless, the Global Zero movement provides a *consistent and benign carrier signal* that nuclear counterterror messaging can ride on. Ultimately, terrorism can best be diminished worldwide by a combination of forceful suppression, transformation from illegitimate violence to legitimate political participation, and both-win negotiations to resolve various conflicts, enmities, and beefs. Of course, *no* terrorism is best, but until that far off day arrives—if it ever does—keeping terror and counterterror *limited* to conventional violence *only* is an essential intermediate step. Clergy can play an indispensable role helping conduct the pervasive conversation that needs to go on about nuclear counterterror counterproliferation. Religious organizations (except technically for the sovereign Vatican State), after all, are *"sub-state/ trans-state" entities* themselves, like terrorist movements, only at opposite ends of the "lover or fighter spectrum."

Making a nuclear attack that could well lead to the complete extinction of the human species—including the terrorists, their fellow fighters and all their families, their spiritual leaders, and all other followers of any version-denomination-sect of their religion or of any other religion—can't make much sense to *any* imaginable Higher Power or Deity, to *any* God or (for polytheists) Gods. The utter destruction of *all* the world's holy sites, holy books, and holy relics would even mean that no future sentient beings, whether Earth-evolved or even alien interstellar archeologists, could—*for all eternity*—ever rediscover Islam's precepts (or any other human faith's), to be thusly inspired to proselytize across their part of the galaxy, gain converts (as did Muhammad), and render renewed devotion to Allah—or any other earthly God(s). In particular, any Muslims responsible for such Earth-wide murder and destruction would surely condemn themselves to the eternal, blazing fires of *Jahannam* (Islamic Hell)—not *Jannah* (Paradise) with its (controversial, perhaps allegorical) 72 virgins (*"houris"*) for each jihadist martyr. The nuclear terrorists will have committed the ultimate, unforgivable sin, in Arabic called *shirk*—playing God.

To amplify what was already touched on in an earlier Chapter 3 section about nuclear counterterror messaging, clergy and lay preachers *of all religious faiths everywhere* can help, and ought to want to help, to educate their flocks and the general public against terrorist nukings.

An Essential Distinction: Conventional Wartime Self-Sacrifice Can Benefit a Society

Conventional suicide bombers do sacrifice themselves, but it is (in their own minds) to *benefit* their co-religionists and their families, who as a group *survive* the attack. One historical example, from a non-Islamic culture, is the Japanese *Kamikaze* pilot (and *Kaiten* human torpedo) phenomenon of World War II. These young men willingly gave their lives, not to destroy the human race, but to *protect* Japan, the Emperor (who was a deity to them), and their families. Another historical example, again from a different culture (a diverse one that does include Muslims), can be seen in the many American troops who earned posthumous Medals of Honor over our long, proud military history. They made the supreme sacrifice for *very positive* reasons, to protect their unit buddies, their families, their country, and the cause of freedom.

But if everyone in a warrior's group or their whole species dies, nobody benefits at all.

When it comes to even a violent, disordered terrorist mind, state nuclear-peacekeeping authorities can and should reach out directly and through *helpful neutral intermediaries* (missionaries, aid workers, etc.), both to identifiable terrorist sympathizers *individually*, and to covert bad actors "embedded" in a community *stochastically*. Those helpful intermediaries can induce a valuable "multiplier effect": As extra human links, in America's communications chain into terrorist minds, they can amplify and reinforce making said terrorists aware of the *extreme extincting-potential* of their groups making nuclear attacks.

The unmistakable, gigantic contrast between *assured group survival* after making a chemical-energy/kinetic-energy bombing, vice *high risk of species extinction* after a fission- or fusion-energy bombing, ought to establish an very obvious *difference in kind* re nukes compared to conventional weapons. The difference is certainly both stark and striking. It stands a good chance to influence *someone* in any given terrorist's circle of leaders, *confreres*, subordinates, direct helpers/sympathizers, dependents/relatives, and any close personal friends, to *do something preventive*, if/when they get wind that their affiliated terrorist group is seeking to cook up nuclear devastation.

The difference-in-kind will be crystal clear to many—*if* the U.S. and NATO use good messaging, to penetrate through the "clutter and noise" of typical terrorist community mental states. That clarity could help motivate *someone* in any given nuclear terrorist's closest social circles to help successfully influence or interdict them in favor of nuclear restraint. While the probability of this "intervention" working in the real world, in a high-stress operational context, is certainly not 100%, it will be high enough above 0%, enough of the time, to deserve evaluation and implementation by national nuclear-counterterror forces.

Nuclear Counter-terror Efforts Are Expensive; Nuclear Counter-terror Efforts Are Bargains

This leads to two rhetorical questions. Can a *public education program* about nuclear deterrence, whether run from a democracy or a dictatorship, or both, be effectively targeted at the eyes, ears, and minds of potential nuclear terrorists? What *direct action* (forceful interdiction) counter-terrorism measures are essential to continue preventing any terrorist group from ever getting any nukes? I suggest the answer to the first question is: Yes, if done thoroughly, and without us falling into a trap of self-referential *cultural mirror-imaging*. (Cultural mirror-imaging will be the subject of Chapter 4.)

The answer to the second question is: *Preventing any terrorists from ever getting nukes to begin with is always the critical key.* Cooperative international intelligence, and military, border patrol and customs, and law enforcement efforts—many of them highly classified for obvious reasons—so far appear to have been 100% successful. But if terrorists ever do get nukes somehow, then this book's suggested American "Plan B" agenda, of instigating diversion-feeding choices (i.e., away from an actual nuke attack), will require stringent action, *not* self-satisfied passivity. If ever *nuclear blackmailers* do break cover with credible threats and demands, *utmost efforts, prepared for and trained for in advance*, must and *will* be carried out to apprehend them and safely repossess their purloined nuke(s). Intelligence operatives from different agencies, law-enforcement officers of every jurisdiction, armed-forces special ops troops wherever deployed, customs inspectors and border-control officers, and concerned citizens who "see something and say something," all have vital roles to play in the interdiction, diversion, and recovery of any loose nukes in terrorist hands. Nuclear counter-terrorism must continue to be a whole-of-government, wholeof-community, and whole-of-world urgent effort.

All such heightened effort can be a *significant added expense* to national defense and homeland security budgets. However, the magnitude of that expense is *surely dwarfed* by either (and certainly by both) of *two other expenses* that nuclear weapon-owning states face, one by choice born of necessity, the other involuntarily through any neglect that enables catastrophe.

The first of these expenses is the already-considerable price-tag for maintaining, and periodically modernizing, America's whole nuclear-deterrence weapons Triad and nuclear command, control, and communication (NC3) establishment, along with existing nuclear counter-terrorism and counter-proliferation activities—including deterrence-messaging development and implementation.

The other would be much larger still: the truly incalculable, all-in, eventual cumulative expense of suffering a terrorist nuclear strike, let alone an all-out nuclear war triggered by that strike. As President Theodore Roosevelt said, at a time when dreadnoughts were mankind's most powerful weapon systems, "Battleships are cheaper than battles."

Effectively deterring nuclear attack is much cheaper than suffering it.

Social-Networking-Based Counter-terror Education Efforts Already Do Exist

Truth-based/fact-based educational indoctrination of the bad guys by the good guys would add an *additional* layer to the current, indispensable, extensive and layered preventives and defenses already in place to keep terrorists and nukes *well separated at all times.* As anticipated above, this indoctrination could be accomplished via targeted messaging on the very same social networking websites and cellphone apps, and Dark Web sites, that the terrorist organizations themselves use to communicate, and to recruit new members. Examples, two of which are summarized now, are in the unclassified literature.

It was recently reported that the U.S. Government is using such social network based, emotional information to deter conventional Islamist-jihad fighter recruiting. In one example of this influence-video product, a family is shown gathering for dinner with one place empty at the table. As a voice-over narrates, the mother, broken-hearted, severely misses a son who went off to fight for jihad in Syria. Imagine how much more impactful this imagery would be to deter a terrorist *nuclear attack*, were it to show a blinding flash and rising mushroom cloud outside this family's dining room window, and then they all get vaporized, as the initial terrorist nuking on some distant target quickly spreads uncontrollably to global thermonuclear war.

Google LLC recently announced a proactive Internet-based approach to deterring wannabe jihadist fighter recruits, developed by Google's Jigsaw think-tank division. This uses a "redirect method," which watches for Google searches done on keywords used by such budding terrorists, then exploits Google's existing advertising architecture to display materials than counteract ISIS and al Qaeda online manipulation and brainwashing-radicalizing content. These ads can include segments, offered by YouTube LLC, interviewing former extremists who have changed sides, along with candid videos, smuggled out of Islamic State-controlled areas, showing the caliphate's internal paranoid brutality, and its severe domestic mis-governance and leadership dysfunction.

It ought not to be difficult to add to these ads some materials about the danger of a single Islamist nuclear strike leading to spasm thermonuclear war, global radioactive fallout, freezing nuclear winter, sizzling nuclear summer, and the resulting extinction of all humanity including all Islam. This nuclear-peacekeeping content could be triggered by Internet searches on such keywords as "Jihad," "suicide attack," "nuclear bomb," "implosion lenses," "uranium centrifuges," and "plutonium."

To Deter or Not to Deter—There Can Be No Real Question

So there does seem to be such a thing as states deterring nuclear terrorists, if not with 100% guaranteed good results, then at least for a useful part of the time. This is at once separate from, and an essential part of, more mainstream nuclear counterterrorism efforts, in which layered international defenses are used to *forcefully, physically* prevent any terrorists from getting a coveted nuke to begin with.

As the U.S./NATO and our other allies make their latest policy "pivot," to confront and contain Russian and Chinese expansionism, it is vitally important that we not drop the ball on countering nuclear terrorism. Surely the terrorists will be watching us like hungry jackals, waiting for their opening to swoop in for a kill—*unless* we can make them see that they would also, quite likely, be killing all their own hopes and dreams, their whole tribes and families, and their entire Faith and any rewards in their version of Kingdom Come.

Terrorists Are Maybe All Mad by Definition; with a State Government's Staff, Not So Much

When it comes to "madmen" as meant colloquially in English-speaking countries, the above-discussed direct and indirect nuclear-deterrence counterterror messaging techniques need not make the distinction between who is or is not "mad" within terrorist groups. Perhaps *anyone* who orders and/or makes terrorist suicide attacks, whether conventional or nuclear, "has got to be crazy." But as clinical psychologists know, madness is a *question of degree*; some terrorist minds might be able to comprehend deterrence messaging enough to act usefully in support of nuclear peace.

To summarize this chapter so far, sub-state/trans-state armed groups seek to be diffuse and stealthy; their members work covertly to evade being identified, by fading into local streetscapes; their communication and financing pathways, some traditional/ancient and some hyper-modern, are by design opaque to outsiders. Thus, deterrence messaging needs to be directed at *communities at large*—so as to reach those would-be terror-enablers who can be reached at all, primarily via stochastic recruiting methodologies. There can be two distinct but related goals here. The *first messaging goal* is to elicit any percipient *circuit-breaker individuals* "hiding in the woodwork" to *act just enough to de-enable* any nuclear strike, and by so doing keep the nuclear peace. Next, by *"diversion feeding"* we mean a terrorist group that does somehow get hold of a nuke choosing to use it not for actual attack but for its own deterrence, or to coerce enemies, or to sell back to a state, so as to gain political concessions from adversaries and/or raise funds for further conventional terrorism. *The second messaging goal* is to reinforce any terrorist group with a nuke making the "somewhat better" choice in favor of holding or selling it, rather than the "much worse" choice of detonating it in a strike.

Now we need to confront the problem of what to do about *genuine madmen at the head of nuclear-armed sovereign states.* All nations' president and/or prime- and other top ministers and senior military commanders' identities tend to be *rather conspicuous* to outside observers (except sometimes for secret-intelligence czars). State nuclear infrastructures—barring on-again-off-again conflicts with the likes of Saddam's Iraq, the Kims' North Korea, and Khamenei's Iran—are subject to UN International Atomic Energy Agency *inspections and safeguards.* Though some head-of-state bad actors have temporarily been able to conceal their nuclear-weapons programs, *organization charts and personnel lists* are for the most part accessible by foreign intelligence agencies, if not by the public media.

By *state-level madmen,* we mean persons, *who are normally permitted access* to their country's nukes as "authorized personnel," who have become so deranged that the compelling logic of nuclear deterrence just does not work on their severely disordered minds. As with terrorists, we will find on close enough examination that there are indeed, at least some of the time, opportunities for intervention or interdiction of the madman (or madwoman) by *nearby or subordinate circuit-breaker individuals,* within their administration and chain of command and/or within their families and social circles. In addition, "diversion feeding" ala terrorist groups could be advocated by these individuals to their mad leaders, literally diverting their insane impulses into conventional aggression—not ideal, but vastly better than nuclear war.

It is to these hopefully not-so-mad individuals that nuclear-deterrence messaging needs to be directed.

Whether or Not a "New Hitler" Could Recur, the Original Hitler Can Teach Us a Lot

Historical analysis of the nation-state madman Adolf Hitler indicates that the Nazis made serious attempts to develop an atom bomb, as well as a two-stage ballistic missile (the A-10 rocket) that could have hit New York City or Washington, DC from Germany. Hitler surely would have used this strategic weapon system if his had been the first state to obtain it. But by the time it became clear to all that Nazi Germany was going down for final defeat, Hitler's twisted mind had snapped to the point he was acting out *frustration aggression*. (This is a psychological term for turning against his/her own followers in brutalizing rage, because they have failed to achieve a megalomaniac leader's grandiose goals.) At that point in his *Gotterdammerung* final act, the threat of nuclear retaliation in kind by the U.S., had this actually been available to us in early 1945 (i.e., the Manhattan project ready, and declassified, months sooner), would probably *not* have been effective in deterring Hitler. For Germany itself to be "deservedly annihilated" because it had lost the decisive "war for survival between the Aryan master race and the *untermenschen*" was a sick part of Hitler's delusional ideology.

The real point, to be discussed further below, is that on several important occasions, Hitler's more insane orders were *disobeyed* by his senior military commanders, preventing even more widespread death and destruction than did occur under his truly mad reign.

Dealing with State-Level Nuclear Madmen

Having suggested ways to strengthen deterrence of nuclear terrorists, we now extend the discussion to the *"state-level nuclear madman"* problem. By a state-level madman (or madwoman) we mean, specifically, someone within a state's senior civilian leadership or military chain of command who is so mentally deranged that nuclear deterrence has no effect on their mind, and who *either* (1) themself *has the authority* to order launching a nuclear strike, *or* (2) *has ongoing legal access* to the state's nuclear warheads and their delivery vehicles, as part of their job, and who attempts, *without* the necessary and proper orders from above, to *grab sufficient improper control* of one or more of weapons to make an unauthorized nuclear strike.

(Stringent, layered security precautions to stop *illegal intruders*—domestic or foreign terrorists, other criminals, or madmen *not* part of a state's government or nuclear establishment—who try to force their way or sneak their way into nuclear arsenals, are another matter altogether, *outside the scope of this book but touched on in the open literature.*)

The second situation, Madman Case (2), of lower-ranking weapons workers, is the more straightforward deterrence/interdiction situation, for which effective preventives have been in place for decades, steadily enhanced as procedures and technologies improve. As part of any nuclear power's responsible custodianship over its nuclear arsenal, numerous features are built into the relevant processes and equipment. Launching any nuclear strike must pass a number of exceedingly stringent hurdles—as for that matter, periodically, must each staff member to continue being employed in and around said nuclear arsenal.

One of these hurdles is the requirement, verified both by always-skeptical professionals and by tamper-proof electromechanical devices, for a very counterfeit-proof valid launch order, coming from that government's head-of-state or commander-in-chief (who in some countries are not the same person); this leader sometimes (as in the USSR/Russia model) must also have the formal concurrence of *two other* very senior civilian ministers and/or military commanders, each equipped with their own special authorization devices—the *"triumvirate model."*

Another such hurdle is the built-in necessity that *at least two rigorously pre-certified, closely monitored, and carefully supervised persons,* each equipped with counterfeit-proof keys, triggers, or other physical proofs of legitimacy, must all be *physically present* at the local consoles (in ICBM silos or aboard SSBNs or strategic or tactical bombers) that control final release of any individual nukes. These persons must all concur *willingly and simultaneously* as to said final release. The *provision of firearms* to these persons, as well as to highly trained guards throughout nuclear-arsenal facilities, *prevent any launch technician(s) from succumbing to duress* by another technician or any intruder. *Nefarious schemes* to extort or dupe weapons crews into launching improperly, such as kidnapping and threatening their loved ones, or using elaborate "Mission Impossible" subterfuges to similar effect, are defeated in advance by crews being *carefully indoctrinated* that all-encompassing horrors such as the Three-Fold Geophysical Wipeout almost certainly await any unjustified, unauthorized first-strike launch—just as they would any other first-use, whether state-level or terrorist.

Madman Case (1), of national leaders who lose their minds, requires more discussion here. It applies to a madman/madwoman whose state government's laws and regulations—either *before* he/she became mad or while failing to recognize that he/she *had* become mad—officially empowered them with sole (or partial, in the triumvirate model) authority to *initiate an order* to make a nuclear first strike. (If the strike, based on that state's current nuclear posture, is a *justified retaliatory strike* against an adversary's nuclear or strategic-WMD *first strike*, it does not matter nearly so much that the leader is mad and needs to be relieved of duties. In this second-strike situation, the greater problem would be mental derangement that might cause the leader to *refuse* to launch nukes when they ought to launch them.)

Since any state's sole-person or triumvirate nuclear-command top leadership does officially-legitimately "own" authority over first-strike nuclear-weapon launches by the state, any very sudden launch order they do transmit downward will be properly seen by the weapons operating crews as having been triggered by some good geopolitical justification unknown to the rank and file—such as an *urgent preemptive strike*—rather than it being possibly caused by leader madness. *The Russian-style triumvirate* model provides an additional layer of protection against a madness-launch catastrophe: It only takes one of the two other senior authorizing officials to sense said madness for them to delay actually transmitting a launch order to crews, while appropriate steps are taken to address the leader-madness issue. However, this has *two weaknesses*: One is that an insane leader might be able to disguise his/her madness, or get the other triumvirate members to go along with the launch order anyway—perhaps neutralizing their *veto power* via dissembling, trickery, and/or intimidation. The other weakness is the possibility that *all three members* of a triumvirate have gone insane together, in what clinical psychologists might label a *folie a trois.* (Local killing sprees by civilian *folie-a-deux* couples are well known to criminologists, and are a favorite theme of TV true-crime forensic documentaries such as *Forensic Files* and *Body of Evidence.*)

Fortunately for nuclear peacekeeping in today's times, which can seem like a "Mad, Mad, Mad, Mad World," even a sovereign state's single low-yield nuclear weapon used to make *any* first-strike very much involves a *team effort,* of activities that perforce unfold gradually over time. Some not-mad individuals close to a madman within the state's nuclear-attack chain of command—and some immediate family members of that madman, often in a position to sense the disturbed person's moods very keenly—might exhibit a spectrum of willingness (or *lack* thereof) to go along with—or intervene effectively *against*—the ultimate heinous act of committing a not-properly-justified first-strike nuclear attack.

While deployed front-line launch crews are carefully trained to always obey any order that passes all verification tests, *those nearer the top of government* such as cabinet ministers, four-star admirals and generals, and direct successors to the head-of-state job (such as a vice premier or vice president) are—if not mad themselves—all positioned in *two very relevant ways*: (1) due to their access to the leader, they are well situated for continual, *critical observation of his/her behavior* and thus of his/her mental state, and (2) they are well supplied with *top-secret intelligence and geopolitical threat assessments* to judge for themselves whether a first-strike just then is truly justified—or not. And such senior persons, as a rule, are *not* sequestered from their immediate families, as *are* the launch crews deployed in missile silos, in deterrent submarines, or on airbases; those senior people *will* be able to interact with their own close relatives, who might reinforce their qualms beneficially during a serious enough leader mental-health crisis, thus acting to help prevent any unjustified first-strike launch order.

Education on the severe blowback risks to themselves, their loved ones, and humanity at large of just one unprovoked-first-strike madman/madwoman nuclear weapon launch, when that education is broadcast (stochastically and/or individually, as appropriate) to *all* relevant world audiences, could be especially effective with any hesitant "weakest link" in the personnel chain of any such utterly inappropriate strike execution. That weakest-link person (or persons), somewhere (anywhere) in the chain, might be situated (on the spot, locally) to perhaps influence and enlist other, like-minded (hesitant) staff. They can be further motivated were U.S./NATO to *step up* the deterrence-education campaign whenever their intelligence agencies get wind that a foreign national leader seems to be "going crazy." This can reinforce the weakest link's own deeply troubled evaluation, of leadership's state of mind vis a vis any actual geopolitical threats that do or don't justify nuclear preemption. That person(s) can then serve as a decisive *circuit-breaker individual(s)*, in the event that one or more of the following do indeed occur: (1) an attack is *planned* by a state's (a) madman sole leader or (b) overly compliant triumvirate or even (c) *folie a trois*, then (2) one or more nuclear-delivery platforms are brought up to highest alert for an unprovoked first strike, and (3) an actual first-strike launch is *ordered*.

Since the upper hierarchy within a nuclear-armed state are fairly likely to be sophisticated, worldly people capable of an at-least-passable understanding of Earth sciences and nuclear-weapon effects and after-effects, this suggested approach of American/NATO deterrence messaging "recruiting, empowering, and exploiting" circuit-breaker individuals could in practice be *even more effective* against state-level madmen/madwomen that it might be against sub-state/trans-state bad actors.

Tactics for Circuit Breaking Can Range from "Suicide Missions" to "Stuxnet III"

Circuit-breaker tactical options for these "resistance operatives," with useful preventive effect, can vary from *temporary ones* (to buy time for more effective intervention) to *permanent ones* (eliminating the mad leader and/or the nukes). Tactics can also vary on a "behavioral" spectrum all the way from acts of *polite "civil disobedience"* to acts of *overt interpersonal uses of force*; the latter especially would require *great courage* and possibly the *willingness to risk death*. The non-violent tactics could include (at least for *better-run countries*) such steps as (1) *arguing* very forcefully against the strike, (2) *insisting* on delay until leadership mindset can be professionally evaluated, (3) *refusing* to pass along the launch order as a blatantly illegal order, or, in an extreme case, (4) *relieving* the leader(s) of duty by consensus of their direct subordinates, and perhaps, with the concurrence of their family and their designated successors, even (5) *confining* them to a mental institution.

In the case of *Third World rogue states*, which (almost by definition) tend to lack effective governance institutions and strong military-ethics norms, more forceful interdictions might be necessary: (1) *deposing* the leader in a bloodless coup, or *killing* them in a bloody one, (2) *damaging or hiding* the nuclear devices beyond repair/retrieval, (3) *warning* targeted authorities of the impending attack with information on how to interdict it, or even (4) *stealing* the nuclear device(s) and *defecting* with it/them to the targeted authorities or to the latter's local allies. These forms of forceful, even violent resistance are very similar to those available to any circuit-break individuals within terrorist groups.

Since highly-placed persons in the madman's or madwoman's regime will have some professional experience at pitching ideas and planning operations, they are likely—even when circumstances require them to move quickly—to first try using a relatively discrete means of influencing the leader against the nuking, with more strident means held in reserve as their Plan B. They might intervene while working solo, or might first attempt to engender collaborators, carefully testing whether others share their own growing concerns about the leader's increasingly erratic conduct—such as his/her alarmingly manic and depressive mood-swing cycles, hours-long obsessive-compulsive tirades, magical omnipotent denial of obvious realities, and other symptoms of dangerous derangement.

An intermediate form of resistance, *especially appealing* for individuals who are senior enough to be able to make covert contact with U.S.

or Allied intelligence services, would be to urgently offer to serve as the *clandestine, on-site human agent* to introduce into their own state's strategic-weapon computer systems a *crippling cyberweapon*. Such a tactic might be particularly appealing as being effective at *self-preservation*, by permanently concealing the circuit-breaker individual's identity from their vengeful mad leader and his/her brutal secret-police apparatus. (The lack of a successful attack's mushroom cloud on the news would immediately tip off the leader that something had gone wrong, triggering a witch-hunt for culprits to be tortured and executed. Fortunately for the recruiting of circuit-breaker individuals, some mechanical failure in the weapon itself can also explain why it never went off.)

Some news-media reporting about the Stuxnet virus attack against Iran's uranium centrifuges suggest that there was just this sort of inside help. The series of fires and explosions at Iranian nuclear-related facilities during 2020, which the media has dubbed "Stuxnet II," might also be due to such a human-carried, infiltrated cyberweapon. An inside job by a concerned circuit-breaker individual, who sneaks in a keychain drive with a *"Stuxnet III"* virus, can defeat the air gapping by which strategic systems are isolated from external, remote computer-hacking intrusions.

Fortunately, Obtaining Nukes and Setting Them Off Is Much More Than a One-Person Job

There are huge long-term financial, STEM, industrial, and raw-material challenges involved in manufacturing nuclear weapons *from scratch*, starting from raw uranium ore. Any nuclear-wannabe terrorist group might therefore, instead of this route (or in addition to it), try to somehow obtain one or more *already-built* nuclear warheads, along with their activation codes and pre-arming keys; to date, all functional nuclear warheads known to have ever existed have been built by states, not non-state groups; for reasons as idealistic as the terms of the Nuclear Nonproliferation Treaty and as pragmatic as self-preservation against Armageddon, no nuke has ever yet been known to have passed from a state to a non-state group.

Either route to a working nuke requires special capabilities that would have to be *granted by, or bought from, or stolen from* within the nuclear establishments—or unemployed former staff—of one or more states that have such establishments. To state the obvious, an actual, assembled and functional nuke could only come from a state with at least a small, "starter" nuclear arsenal.

But some necessary skills and items might be obtainable from *Nuclear Supplier States*, which are states internationally recognized and certified as technically supporting the *global civilian nuclear power and nuclear medicine industries.* Not all such states have any nuclear weapons programs, but the dual-use nature of some *peaceful* nuclear technology can be covertly diverted into weapons development. *Some* bomb-making necessities could be gotten from *any* state that does have such industries, and/or has indigenous *pure-science nuclear research facilities,* even if (or especially if) they are *not* certified members of the Nuclear Supplier Program—which has stringent safeguards against unauthorized diversion into weapons work.

Unfortunate prior history, exemplified by the *underground nuclear-proliferation network* led by Dr. A. Q. Khan for many years until 2004, shows that both nuclear expertise and some bomb-precursor nuclear materials *can* be accessed nefariously and then smuggled across borders, *if* individuals suffering from the right combination of greed, corruption, and treasonous tendencies can be identified and exploited by internationally-ranging, rogue state "nuke comparison shoppers."

In pursuing a workable route to the Bomb, terrorists might resort to outright thievery. But beyond states just suffering as victims of such nuclear thievery, *voluntary help* to a terrorist group might be provided either with the *knowing connivance of a state's national leadership,* or without it but rendered instead by *an illicit underground subgroup* (maybe as small as one person) within the state or states.

In addition, a terrorist group can attempt to send one or more qualified members for advanced university education in nuclear physics and nuclear engineering.

Just as do the terrorists, any "deep state" helpers would need to choose between the two paths to a working warhead: build, or buy/steal/be given. Alternative to trafficking a turnkey working bomb, complete with arming codes, is to instead deal in the fissile material and other specialized items needed to build a bomb, along with detailed guidance in how to assemble it. But in reality, in the latter case, great technical expertise and engineering know-how, and state-of-the-art machining skills and extremely precise equipment are also required.

It is in many ways much quicker and simpler to traffic in a working bomb, but obtaining one *by force,* out of a state's highly secure nuclear arsenal, is no easy task. Attempting this path to a terrorist nuclear strike would cause an *extremely loud warning signal.* Instant and violent state *counteractions* will likely result in the arrest and/or killing of raiders attempting the arsenal pilferage, followed closely by the "rolling up" of their whole network. While more discrete and thus more able to obviate such violent direct-action countermeasures, assembling a functional warhead from all the necessary bomb components including *an entire critical mass of weapons-grade fissile material* is also a much more complex and slow undertaking, which requires various expert human resources way beyond just "a bunch of terrorist raiders with guns."

So far, according to what is known publicly, and based on the conspicuous lack of any terrorist nuclear strikes, both of the routes to getting nukes have proven too difficult for any terrorist group to reach the "end zone." But partial progress on the build-your-own path has been made by several Muslim-dominated rogue state regimes (in Iraq, Libya, Iran, Syria), as is well documented in the news media. And the obtain-a-built-nuke path, *when the state that owns it cooperates,* avoids the pitfalls of trying to break into their closely guarded nuclear arsenal to steal one.

National leadership authorities that are known to sometimes intentionally support (conventional) terrorism, *to help accomplish their own belligerent geopolitical goals,* include those of Iran and North Korea. *Illicit subgroups* acting (at least partly) against the wishes of national authorities include the Russian and Eastern European so-called Mafias. A subgroup acting with *some* alleged state connivance, until its unmasking by foreign authorities, again, is exemplified (as above referenced) by Pakistan's international nuclear black-marketing ring led by the late Dr. A. Q. Khan—which began by importing items for Pakistan's own nuclear weapons program, but then turned around and started *exporting* such items to wannabe rogue states.

Any state that does chose to directly support nuclear terrorism-by-proxy has the option to either *give* or *sell* one or more nukes to their "preferred" sub-state/trans-state armed group. Analysts quoted anonymously in the media have said that the "going rate" for such a nuke is $100 million, but such quotes never mention whether weapon yield might be a pricing factor. Which group the state chooses to support, and how generously they do so, would depend on tangible and intangible factors, such as: Does the state (North Korea is often mentioned in this context) need to raise *"foreign exchange"* desperately enough? Does the state have previous experience of sponsoring *conventional* terrorism by the same group, with pleasing results in violent bloodshed which it wishes to *seriously/dangerously escalate?*

To repeat for emphasis (and belabor the obvious), in order to prevent terrorists ever committing a nuclear attack, it is essential rather than only trying to *deter* them, to in addition—as is of course being done now stringently around the world—*prevent them* from obtaining any working nukes to begin with. And the above discussion tries to explain that the fastest, surest way for them to obtain any working nukes is to be *given them* by a nuclear-armed state-sponsor. Thus, a very important part of nuclear counterterrorism is *effectively deterring states from giving nukes to terrorists.*

For exactly this reason America's nuclear posture declares that, if there is ever incontrovertible proof that a nuclear-weapons state *gave a nuke* to terrorists who then used it in an attack against our vital interests at home or abroad, we would *not hesitate* to retaliate with a nuclear counterstrike *against that offending/enabling state.* This alone, however, does little if anything to dissuade the nuclear terrorist group *itself.* It *also* might not say and do enough to deter a *clandestine "deep state" faction* within a state's government, a faction that *covertly* funnels nuclear arms or materials to terrorists while believing that they themselves can *evade* nuclear retaliation.

So preventing nuclear terrorism, via interdiction of nuke-tech trafficking and via deterrence of non-state wannabe- and actually-nuclear-armed groups, goes hand in hand with deterring superpower dictatorships and rogue states from ever supporting nuclear terrorists. To do *any* of these critical national defense functions well, it is necessary to do all of them well.

Ultimately, as discussed shortly, the *"strong form of strategic ambiguity"* comes into play here. It is a powerful *"cosmic inflator"* of the Three Sources of Danger (mentioned earlier) *to any terrorist nuclear attacker and to any terrorist-attack enabler/helper state or persons.* The next stretch of this chapter establishes how such strong-form strategic ambiguity arises, and how it provides a rather powerful disincentive to nuclear-attack aggression of all kinds—*especially* by terrorists and madmen.

Just as with more familiar forms of nuclear deterrence, strong-form's cognitive prerequisites among an adversary group's decision-makers, for effectiveness as a deterrent, are two-fold: *being reasonably rational in general,* and *being adequately informed about strong-form strategic ambiguity.* As this chapter has already anticipated, these prerequisites can be met by motivating well-placed circuit-breaker individuals, via defender states like America using the right sorts of messaging methods and content.

Tyrants' Ultra-Draconian Retaliation for Nuclear-Terrorist *Enablers* Could Become "a Thing"

A superpower dictatorship or nuclear-armed rogue state, in the *most extremely amoral and belligerent scenario of all,* might decide to *absolutely, maximally* step up efforts for deterrence of nuclear terrorist attacks against that state—by going as far as what we will call *"ultra-draconian" posture.* (Imagine a totally ruthless and paranoid sociopath, already very bloodstained from repressive internal purges and external conventional war—like a latter-day Josef Stalin. How would he/she retaliate to a terrorist nuclear attack?)

This reprehensible but not *entirely* inconceivable, *truly ultra-draconian* stance would comprise a policy that encompasses, *not just* nuclear retaliation against any sovereign state whose national government sponsors a terrorist nuking against them, and *not just* the *draconian* nuclear retaliation against the declared caliphate, separatist province, or other *primary locus(es)* of the terrorist group that committed said nuking, but *lots more besides*: nuclear retaliation against *virtually any party* that aided and abetted the terrorist nuking *before or after the fact.*

DEFINITION: *Ultra-draconian nuclear deterrence* means a posture that includes draconian deterrence, *plus also* the threat/promise of nuclear retaliation against: (1) any *other* states (besides the terrorist-proxy-sponsoring state itself) that, *before the attack,* also—willingly or unwillingly—harbor (house, accommodate) or otherwise help members of the non-state group that then commits the nuclear attack, *plus* (2) the primary foci of any *other* non-state groups that *merely assist, equip, finance, or otherwise help* the non-state group that actually conducts the nuclear attack, *plus* (3) any *additional* states that simply serve—willingly or unwillingly—*as hiding places or sanctuaries after the fact* for the terrorist nuke strike's direct perpetrators and indirect enablers-accomplices.

(In the rest of this section, we will focus on ultra-draconian deterrence/retaliation criteria along the dimension of *eligibility to be hit by a nuclear counter-strike.* Later in Chapter 3 we will widen things, touching on ultra-draconian criteria for *how much if any proof of guilt is needed for an entity to be counter-struck.*)

Such extreme "out there" positioning on the Cartesian coordinate chart of draconian-ness could include a declaratory policy that if a nuclear attack by terrorists was enabled, at least partially, by (1) a particular organized-crime group, (2) a rogue-scientist nuke development gang, (3) a nuclear-materials smuggling network, or (4) a separatist political faction, any of which are harbored within a particular state (or across multiple states), whether *knowingly or unknowingly* on the part of those national governments, then that *state itself* (or those multiple states themselves) will (or at least might) be subjected to a nuclear retaliatory strike.

Such severe policy could be contemplated, even adopted eventually, by any dictatorships that have *already embarked* on a "regular" draconian nuclear deterrence path. Presumably, any retaliatory strikes under such all-inclusive ultra-policy would be aimed at areas of concentration of the accused facilitator non-state group(s), *if* such areas can be specifically localized within particular states. If not, other eligible targets as the "next best thing" might include that state's or states' nuclear forces (if any), its/their military bases in general, political-control assets, industrial complexes—and even its/their capital city(ies), whether or not terrorist perpetrators ever congregated there, with or without the state's/states' connivance.

In short, ultra-draconian deterrence seeks to deter any terrorist nuclear strikes via completely inclusive, "catch all" (literally) eligibility criteria: The threat/promise is made to nuke back *any and every* state and non-state group that played any role, willingly or unwilling, in enabling or carrying out the attack, and/or that later on harbors the persons who conducted the attack, as well as any significant population concentrations of the non-state groups whose members were involved.

A (morally and legally questionable) *"practical advantage"* of such ultra-draconian posture is that the retaliating state need not bother even *trying* to first determine if a state's alleged offense of "harboring" was willing or unwilling, and whether the state nuke used in the terrorist attack was stolen from, or voluntarily given or sold by, the alleged state of origin of the nuke. These issues are particularly relevant since the nuclear-terrorist attack itself might obliterate much forensic evidence that could guide such determinations.

Ultra-draconian posture prescribes the *most merciless imaginable nuclear retaliation* against any states and non-state groups that sponsor, enable, or otherwise participate in any aspect of a terrorist nuclear attack—perhaps even those which have their own nuclear weapons with which to counter-counter-strike and *escalate the widening conflict even further*. As such, it is the nuclear-deterrence threat/promise most likely to (1) force *all* sovereign states to pay maximal attention to preventing/interdicting *all* nuclear-wannabe terrorist groups *and* their state-level enablers, and (2) discourage nuclear terrorism all the time everywhere, but also to (3) *trigger horizontal escalation unto Armageddon*. In the latter context, it is also in execution the threat/promise most likely to suffer from self-deterrence in the moment, or at least to suffer from "cherry picking" those retaliation targets least able to make further nuclear strikes.

Just as with "regular" draconian policy, ultra-draconian deterrence and retaliation—for now simply an *extremely extreme thought experiment*—seems more likely to be adopted, if ever at all, in the fulminating aftermath of a first-ever terrorist nuclear strike. But extremely extreme thought experiments can be the most informative of them all for purposes of developing practical, usable Best Practices for nuclear peacekeeping in democracies. So please read on.

"Strategic Ambiguity" Can Motivate Circuit-Breaker Individuals in Madman States and Terrorist Groups

"Strategic ambiguity" means a state's government taking the stance of *not disclosing some details* of how it plans to respond to different sorts of nuclear crises, blackmail attempts, and actual enemy nuclear (and other strategic WMD or overwhelming conventional) attacks. Dr. Henry Kissinger espoused the U.S. taking this approach, since it can add to the valuable *"fear factor"* underpinning effective nuclear deterrence. Ambiguity lets an adversary's imagination run wild, with morbid nightmares of what America *might* do if that enemy ever dared to nuke us. Israel, for instance, pursues notable strategic ambiguity regarding their nuclear posture, not even officially confirming whether or not they possess any nuclear weapons. Every state uses strategic ambiguity to some degree; since national nuclear postures are written documents of necessarily finite length, it is not practical for them to lay out *every* intended response in *every* potential scenario.

For better or for worse, an implicit or background—but powerful—deterrence *reinforcer* is available to any nuclear-armed state government. It has good effect at all times, and without added expense to implement—because this reinforcer is operative tacitly, "in the ether." The beneficial reinforcer is the unavoidable fact of *strategic ambiguity* of a particular sort, which we will label for clarity here *strong-form strategic ambiguity*.

This "strong-form" prefix distinguishes it from something else, that we will label the *weak-form of strategic ambiguity*. Here are definitions of both:

DEFINITION: *Weak-form strategic ambiguity* (what Dr. Kissinger specifically advocated) occurs whenever a state *intentionally withholds* publicly specifying part of its nuclear posture, to try to foster *pacifying* doubts and *paralyzing* uncertainties in any potential attacking enemy's risk/reward calculations.

DEFINITION: *Strong-form strategic ambiguity* puts a name to the unavoidable, pervasive fact that *no one anywhere can be completely sure what anyone (including themselves) will actually do* once nuclear weapons start being set off in anger—no matter what anybody's public nuclear postures and classified action plans might specify.

Strong-form strategic ambiguity results in part from what First Cold War nuclear strategists called the *Intra-War Unsafe Nuclear User Principle* (for short, "the Unsafe User Principle"). Recall that this says that once nuclear explosions start happening during a nuclear war, *such extensive chaos, rage, paranoia, and panic* will occur among *all* nations, along with *so much physical damage* to states that are involved in the war, that all neat and well-organized, pre-war nuclear-weapons controls and restraints, safety features, limitation plans, and targeting accuracy will *quite possibly* collapse into an *uncontrolled orgy* of widespread nuclear annihilation. The overwhelming impact of this frightening statement, that *benefits* effective deterrence via the fear factor, lies in the fact that even the exact meaning of "quite possibly" is *ambiguous and unknowable*—but the probability and *the mathematical expectation of loss* involved (see Appendix 1) are sufficiently large, given the cataclysmic consequences to everyone alive, *to be decisively daunting for anyone sane and sophisticated enough to comprehend this.*

Note in general that we can make a *very deterring* statement about probability inequalities: Since any specified event is guaranteed to either happen or not happen, let us call the probabilities of these opposite eventualities, whatever the "event" might be, P(E) and P(not E). In mathematical notation, $P(E) + P(\text{not } E) = 1$. If we can then say "event E is more likely to happen than not," i.e. that $P(E) > P(\text{not } E)$, what this dictates arithmetically is that $P(E) > 50\%$. Thus, whenever the Unsafe User Principle is "more likely than not" to trigger catastrophic escalation of a nuclear attack, what we are saying is that the odds of Armageddon resulting are *higher than fifty-fifty.*

Attaching an exact probability to whether the Unsafe User Principle comes into effect in any particular scenario is probably impossible, but that is not the point. For purposes of deterring an adversary from making an unprovoked nuclear first strike, such *existential-level uncertainties* can indeed be *decisively daunting to any rational actor*—at least some of the time, enough to be well worth bringing to the attention of all such adversaries. This perhaps helps explain why, ever since at least two states owned working nuclear weapons, starting in 1949, *no* entities have yet made any nuclear attacks. But wait, there's more.

As noted earlier, some leading First Cold War defense analysts in the U.S. and NATO (while debunking the bugaboo that the risk of self-deterrence would defang all Western Triads) considered that having odds, of a state-level nuclear attacker actually being retaliated against with a nuclear counterstrike, of a minimum of *ten percent* would be enough to effectively deter any rational state government from making an unprovoked nuclear first strike. Compared to this, the greater-than-50% odds of the Unsafe User Principle's terrible effects kicking in due to an unprovoked nuclear first strike committed by *any* entity—including a terrorist group or a sane *or* madman state—might very well be a whopping *five times or more as large as the minimum needed to deter a rational state actor.*

Let us look at strategic ambiguity from the point of view of a leader, whether state or terrorist, contemplating ordering a nuclear first strike. Not the least of the *intimidating deep uncertainties* behind *"strong form"* strategic ambiguity, about the enemy's, your own, and every other nuclear power's actions once the nuking starts, are (1) the conflict-wide effects of the ensuing KIA, WIA, and MIA casualties among senior decision-makers and nuclear weapons-systems crews; (2) crippling or deranging combat damage to their platforms and systems from nuke blasts, unbearable shock waves and earthquakes, deeply-penetrating ultra-hard radiation bursts, intense heat and all-consuming fires, and pervasive EMPs; (3) breakdowns in nuclear command, control, and communication (NC3) links and nodes; (4) simultaneous cyberwarfare attacks; (5) sabotage attacks by sleeper cells of *Spetznaz*-style enemy suicide commandoes using briefcase and backpack nukes; (6) rampant exhaustion, fear, grief, anger, panic, and hysteria; and (7) other factors that can't even be imagined in advance.

Beyond a democracy recognizing, and *proactively educating terrorists,* that dictatorships—as detailed above—might intentionally, willfully resort to draconian or ultra-draconian deterrence, this *added factor* of strong-form strategic ambiguity arises *in the human-and-geopolitical environment itself,* as if by spontaneous generation, to bring into play what amounts to a de facto, implicit, unofficial, potentially-ultra-draconian deterrence posture against terrorist nuclear attacks *even for democracies.* How so? Simply because *any* terrorist nuking could "easily" (with P > 50%) lead to the entire terrorist group being enveloped and exterminated in the resulting global thermonuclear holocaust.

Strong-form strategic ambiguity, by the same mechanism, *also* provides a *powerful motivation* for potential circuit-breaker individuals to be sure to "do something" to halt a *"mad-leader nuking,"* in any *state* that is (or might come to be) led by a madman or madwoman.

A Hint of (Ultra) Draconian Policy Heightens Strategic Ambiguity, Aiding Effective Deterrence

While a too-broadly-punitive official nuclear posture might be seen as *overly draconian* for a human-rights-loving democracy, *a little bit of it,* selectively applied, could have beneficial effects, even for democracies.

Such an approach could motivate state sponsors of terrorism to, *with the utmost possible care*, refrain from allowing any terrorists to obtain from them or through them, even inadvertently, any nukes, or their components and bomb fuels. It could motivate states that suffer from internal criminal mafias, or possible underground nuclear-weapon black marketeers, to take more rigorous, and thus more effective, measures to interdict all such bad actors. It could discourage bad-actor/rogue states, that might be tempted to harbor, succor, enable, or exploit sub-state/trans-state armed groups as terrorist *proxies*, from ever doing so within (or even just near) the nuclear weapons arena of power politics, violent strife, coercion, and mega-death. And a little bit of draconian could effectively deter terrorist groups from wanting to ever escalate from conventional atrocities to nuclear attacks against democratic-state targets.

In the actual world of thinking, feeling human beings living in democracies, do any security-related *objectives* (i.e., desirable self-defense and peacekeeping *effects*) justify a doctrine of "(very) *hot* pursuit of perps and accomplices" that applies to terrorist nuclear attacks? By this I mean seeking to deter via threatening to retaliate, with the nuclear option, against *all* "indicted and convicted" *enablers/accomplices and other co-conspirators* as well as *direct perpetrators* of that terrorist attack? Maybe, in some *future* extreme circumstances that are hard to fully imagine today, American nuclear-security concerns will become severe enough that such an *all-inclusive retaliation doctrine* is necessary. In other words, might America herself need to become a draconian nuclear deterrence state at some point in the future, for reasons that cannot now be foreseen?

Ultimately, this question might be unanswerable, but the important point is that it does not *need* to be answered. Fortuitously, as it turns out, *inevitable, unavoidable, tacit strong-form strategic ambiguity*, over how *even a democracy* would react after suffering an actual nuclear terrorist atrocity, works *right now* in that democracy's favor as a *potent added deterring factor*, *without* the higher moral/ethical cost of an open draconian declaration, in advance, within current nuclear posture. This is simply because even a state that does *not* promulgate draconian deterrence in advance, today or soon, might in actual practice, *after* suffering an actual terrorist nuclear attack *someday*, become so deranged and disrupted by nuclear war as to *behave as if it is* exacting draconian nuclear retaliation on *all* the guilty parties. (This can also be viewed as a beneficial *specialized form* of the Intrawar Unsafe Nuclear User Principle.)

It must also be said, for completeness of this discussion, that it is not entirely inconceivable that one *immediate worst-case domestic political effect* of a terrorist nuclear attack on a democracy is to hypothetically cause that democracy to *deteriorate quickly into a fascist dictatorship*—

perhaps facilitated by a need to declare martial law after the nuking. If the democracy owns a sizable nuclear arsenal *before the attack*, such an altered regime—suddenly authoritarian, ultra-nationalist, nativist-populist—might use that arsenal for draconian retaliation *after the attack*. (The rapid deterioration of Germany's Weimar Republic into Hitler's Third Reich in early 1933 shows how a combination of economic and military shock and disaffection can foment such a drastic regime change.)

This entire general line of reasoning, about the unavoidable fact of strong-form strategic ambiguity leading to more than *un soupcon of draconian-ness "for free,"* demonstrates why it can be useful in a democratic state to surface and discuss the concept, and the ins-and-outs, of draconian deterrence.

Pushing the matter even further for logical thoroughness, this raises a philosophical or even theological conundrum: Is the *somewhat immoral* act of post-actual-terrorist-nuke-attack draconian nuclear retaliation ever justified, via "an eye for an eye" or "the ends justify the means" retribution principles, in order to punish (and prevent further acts of) *certainly substantially-more-immoral* first strike (or copy-cat) nuclear terrorism? Should (or *can*) the fact that the perpetrating group is *not* an actual, officially recognized sovereign state be any sort of deciding factor, given that American nuclear posture has always specified *nuclear* retaliation against states that make nuclear attacks, *qua* states?

This is something that terrorists can (and let's hope, *do*) agonize over endlessly. It would be almost infinitely better for them, and their beliefs and causes, for them to stick to *conventional* attacks ("diversion feeding"), which when such attacks do occur warrant conventional coalition counter-attacks. The challenge for peace-loving democracies, to repeat for emphasis, is to mount and sustain an effective campaign of communication and education about these issues, aimed at the terrorists and their wider community of families/relatives, friends/neighbors, and supporters/enablers/suppliers.

America Needs to Watch Out for What Russia and China Do

Even if the U.S. ever did take the drastic "old-school law and order" step within its nuclear posture, declaring draconian retaliation policy against terrorist nukings, presumably we would only do so because our national leadership felt forced to do so in the absolute last extreme. We would still require ironclad, incontrovertible *proof of guilt* of a specific terrorist-sponsoring state's and/or terrorist group's responsibility for a nuclear strike, before we made a nuclear counterstrike against any of them anywhere: America possesses probably the world's most capable nuclear-detonation forensic-attribution capabilities, plus other superb, relevant law-enforcement investigative skills and tools.

But an authoritarian/dictatorial nuclear power like Russia or China might very well, in their own declared nuclear postures, go "full draconian" along *both* Cartesian coordinate dimensions—including the *evidence* dimension, by acting on *weak* or uncertain evidentiary proof of guilt for the terrorist strike. What could *that* mean for the U.S., and what would we do then? Such repressive, tyrannical superpowers might even "go totally ultra-draconian," extending the extreme "ultra" form of draconian-ness *beyond* ("orthogonally to") the dimension of eligibility for a counterstrike, *also going far out to the right (i.e., with slack evidentiary standards) along the "proof of guilt" dimension.* Just as with the scope of who/what is "eligible" to be counter-nuked, *proof* of who "deserves" such counter-nuking falls on a spectrum:

> What if Russia or China lowered their burden-of-proof criteria for a nuclear retaliation to be not "beyond any shadow of a doubt," but rather the weaker "beyond any reasonable doubt?" What if they went to something weaker still, such as reliance on purely circumstantial evidence, or just hunches or grudges? What if they didn't even divulge their culpability/guilt criteria at all, maybe because the standards were ad hoc, or chaotic—or even involved intentionally lashing out at "miscellaneous" terrorist groups, using a nuking by a *different* group as a *convenient excuse to wipe out a pesky thorn in their side*?
>
> What if we factor in the real-world current-events fact that the dictatorships in question already have track records of repeatedly ignoring international law and human rights? And what about the highly volatile case of a three-or-more-player game in this context, where China, Russia, and maybe some other future autocratic nuclear-weapon state or states as well, all adopted such tactics, each for self-protection, and then *openly vied against each other* to be the *most* ultra-draconian of all? They might this way, as already hinted above, selfishly protect *themselves* against terrorist nukes, individually (and maybe also, at times, acting collectively), by intentionally motivating such terrorists to strike elsewhere instead—ultimately, *at America's expense.*

The spectacle of dictatorships competing for *"draconian deterrence-posture supremacy"* is something devoutly *not* to be wished. It is not a minor issue, since security of nuclear weapons storage sites has at times been *notoriously lax* outside the West, and one way terrorists could get nukes with which to attack is by stealing them.

While Pakistan, for instance, according to the U.S. non-profit watchdog Nuclear Threat Initiative's 2020 Index, recently improved its score for nuclear-arsenal security, the broader problem is the difficulty (impossibility?) of knowing *which* nuclear power (if any), and *when*, will *next* become a failing/failed state, like happened to the USSR. (Might it be North Korea? Pakistan?) The next Nunn-Lugar type of U.S. foreign aid program to prop up a weak state's nuke lockdown might not be as effective as the 1990s one was.

The easiest way for nuclear terrorists who do steal a nuke to "make a flaming datum" is to set it off *in place* where they first seize control of it (the failing state itself), not try to smuggle it across multiple international borders to some distant target (the U.S.). Stringent-enough draconian deterrence posture, however, could motivate the terrorists to make such a smuggling attempt—again, at American expense. But rather than "stick its own head in the sand" by suppressing the whole topic of draconian deterrence, the U.S. should take this as a clarion call to (1) further *strengthen and support* worldwide nuclear security, counterproliferation, and counterterror efforts, and (2) robustly *modernize and sustain* our own Deterrence Triad and Nuclear Posture capabilities and messaging, and our own nuclear arsenal's security infrastructure.

Draconian Posture Contests Could Become Their Own New Type of Deadly Arms Races

The competition to establish the more (most?) *draconian nuclear-deterrence posture*, on the grounds that it would be more (most?) selfishly protective, could turn into a peculiar form of "arms race" between several nuclear powers. They would in effect be fighting over the *most severely punitive territory* far out to the upper right in the {eligibility, evidence} two-dimensional Cartesian-coordinates posture space of the draconian deterrence spectrum.

While nuclear weapons aren't actually being set off in anger anywhere (yet), since this "arms race" concerns only declared *posture*, bear in mind that nukes weren't used in combat during the whole First Cold War nuclear arms race either, and that race nevertheless was seen by many as *frighteningly competitive*—and inherently unstable. However, in this policymaking context, ultra-draconian means just that: the willingness to use nukes to hit back against sub-state/trans-state bad actors, wherever they lurk after a nuclear attack, regardless of collateral damage and civilian deaths, *and* regardless of whether incontrovertible proof exists of their culpability. This adds *two more* grim dimensions to the context of "frightening."

Elaborations and Caveats re Draconian Deterrence, and re Nuke-Strike Attribution in General

The above formulation and exposition of what I am calling "draconian nuclear deterrence" are founded on certain perspectives that, in case they were not already clear to readers, are worth articulating now. Particularly *a propos* to draconian posture, but applying far beyond that hypothetical/specialized topic alone, to *deterrence theory in its widest sense*, are various ins-and-outs of *complete, timely nuclear forensics and intelligence for accurate attribution of any attacks to their perpetrators.* One might even say that accurate attribution is as essential a "fuel" of a state's effective deterrence, as are the deterrence-messaging methods and contents it uses, and the fissile-metal bomb fuels in its nuclear warheads. Some of these points apply to nuclear deterrence of *states* as well as of *terrorists*, and/or were already covered above but are being highlighted now for more clarity.

- It is a very important distinction, in American and Allied policymaking circles, as to the *basic attribution and retaliation issues* that would apply, depending on whether an unprovoked first-strike nuclear, other WMD, or other existential attack were to be made against our vital interests by (1) *another recognized, sovereign state,* as opposed to by (2) *a sub-state/trans-state terrorist group*, and whether that group (2.a) *does* or (2.b) *does not strike with the support of a state for which it acts as a proxy.*
- In the case of a *state* attacker, I am assuming that the U.S. and NATO would not retaliate with nuclear weapons prior to obtaining *incontrovertible attribution* of said attack to the perpetrator(s). This is because state-level nuclear attackers, and any nuclear-armed umbrella-ally states of theirs, will own *further* arsenals of nuclear weapons, and/or other WMDs, and/or could present existential threats comprised of massive *conventional* coalition armies. Given this fact, to mistakenly retaliate against the *wrong* nuclear-armed party would not only amount to a reprehensible, *unprovoked nuclear first-strike* on an innocent state. It would also cause *geographic escalation* to a wider, potentially holocaust-level global nuclear war—because that innocent state (with its umbrella protector) would probably make what they see as a *justified* retaliation against what to them would be *our* unprovoked *first* nuclear strike; they might angrily refuse to believe our seemingly-convenient claims of "an honest mistake." This in turn could well be the tinder for Armageddon. (Related to this issue, it can be seen that one

form of *"partial self-deterrence"* would be this sensible hesitation to make a nuclear counterstrike while lacking conclusive attribution. The importance detailed earlier of *not* being self-deterred from nuking back against the actual perpetrator state(s), lest the floodgates be opened for copy-cat first strikes and worse, ought to motivate *strong funding and policy support for nuclear forensics.*)

- It would inherently be somewhat less difficult to conclusively attribute an attack by a state to that state, than it would be to attribute an attack by a non-state group to that particular group. While different states might *blame one another falsely,* in order to attempt to *evade punishment* themselves, it would be hard to do this credibly and for long. Since a sovereign state's very extensive set of military and political-control assets and facilities "has nowhere to run, nowhere to hide," unlike terrorist individuals, there would be *much less time pressure* to retaliate (with any nuclear counterstrike) in the case of a state-level attacker. The rather irate international community would have access to *nuclear forensics exemplars,* using *material samples* available from the U.S. Department of Defense, Department of Energy, and the CIA, the highly regulated International Nuclear Suppliers Group, and the UN's IAEA. In contrast, multiple terrorist-group claims, *each group taking credit* to gain *aggrandizement* (while feeling *immune* to American/NATO non-draconian counter-nuking posture), seem much more likely to occur; states are *very unlikely* to falsely claim credit, given the retaliatory consequences against their rich, immobile set of "always eligible" targets for such a counterstrike.
- As to *"national-level" types of military platforms* used to deliver the nuke(s) set off in a first-strike attack: In the case of a nuclear attack delivered by one or more intercontinental, intermediate range, medium range, or short-range ballistic missiles (ICBMs, IRBMs, MRBMs, SRBMs), or military dual-capable aircraft (DCAs), American and Allied warning systems and other radars would provide forensic proof of point of origin. In the case of a nuclear weapon (missile, torpedo, or mine) launched from a nuclear-powered, diesel/air-independent-propulsion, or full-sized, ocean-transiting "straight diesel" submarine, the exact nationality of the sub might take some time to determine, but presumably it would be quickly clear—from the sub's operational abilities and

behaviors, and from its sonar signatures—that this was a *state-owned* asset—from one of a limited number of candidate states. If the state-of-ownership claims the sub had been "hijacked by terrorists," the same issue arises as if a state claims that their nuke-attacking military aircraft or missile silo was taken over by terrorists—who also "just happened" to get all the codes and keys needed to successfully make a nuking. *Such a convenient excuse, made after the fact of a nuking, is likely to not be believed.* (This valuably highlights, once again, the vital importance of nuclear-arsenal security against theft, and the even more vital importance of immediately interdicting any armed groups who make such a thieving/hijacking attempt. See *the next two bullet points below* for more on this topic.)

- In the case of a single or small number of *state-built nukes* covertly transported *by that state* via land, sea, and/or air on *civilian-type platforms* (motor vehicles, merchant ships, small aircraft, "narco sub" smuggling submersibles), two points can be made. *The first* is that forensic analysis of radioactive after-products would attribute the weapon(s) to its/their state of origin. *The second* is that a state with a large nuclear arsenal, one knowingly subject to advance covert forensic "exemplar" sampling (including environmental swabs) by covert American intelligence assets (and/or unclassified inspection and sampling demands by the UN's International Atomic Energy Agency—the IAEA), would not in the end achieve anything by mimicking the minimalist transport-and-attack tactics used by terrorists. The state would almost certainly have brought its armed forces to *a very high state of alert* (detectable by U.S. Indications and Warnings assets) *before* making the disguised attack, out of self-preservation. They might even have already been involved in a heightening international crisis, one that would point the nuclear-attack's blame-finger *plainly right back at them.*
- In the case of a state that makes a *terrorist-mimicking* attack and tries to blame it on a (named or unnamed) terrorist group having stolen from them the weapon(s) used, there are such high risks with this subterfuge that it is unlikely to ever be used. This is because—if the U.S. were ever attacked by a nuke or other WMD that the state of manufacture claims is stolen from them without their prior knowledge or help—America stands a very good chance to *not* believe these protestations.

The claims of innocence could easily seem too pat, especially given *the lack of any advance warning* from the state that the weapon had been stolen and was "in play" in terrorist hands. And if such a (misleading) warning were in fact given, the odds of the entire charade succeeding would be significantly diminished, *erasing its utility to begin with.* (Of course, in the case that any state does indeed ever suffer a *genuine theft of a working nuke*, it should warn the international community *immediately*, and should strive diligently and cooperatively for *interdiction* of the culprits and *recovery* of the weapon. Ditto for the theft of fissile metals and/or other items in quantities near *one critical mass*, which can be used to make nuclear bombs—about 10 pounds for plutonium,
40 for a uranium implosion bomb, 140 for a uranium gun bomb.)

- Some *works of fiction* have posited storylines where a *state military platform armed with nukes*, such as a strategic bomber or a missile submarine, is taken over by terrorists or rogues who then seek to make a nuclear attack. In these exciting and scary novels and films, the culprits are usually (but not always) foiled at the last minute by brave commandos and clever intelligence operatives. It should *in our real nonfiction world* be explicitly and transparently recognized by all state government officials everywhere that such extreme events *could* someday occur in real life, and *might not* have a happy ending. This emphasizes the paramount importance of sustaining all nuclear-armed states' facilities guarding and personnel screening security measures, along with all the other multitudinous aspects of *layered defenses* in place against nuclear terrorists and any other unauthorized access. The probability seems rather low that such a hijacking or mutiny and subsequent *terrorist or unauthorized* nuclear attack might ever succeed at passing itself off as an *authorized state-level first strike*, as a subterfuge for the culprits to avoid targeted retribution, or even for them to trick two nuclear-armed states into fighting a nuclear war; again, it would be *vital* for the *victim state* of such a terrorist hijacking or weapons-crew mutiny to *sound the international alarm immediately*; a cover-up due to wounded pride would, *literally*, blow up in that state's face. Furthermore, the fact that the U.S. does not follow draconian retaliation policies does *not* in any way preclude our use of *very highly skilled and superbly equipped elite Special Ops forces of all kinds* to interdict, apprehend, and punish the terrorists/ mutineers.

- In the case of a nuclear attack genuinely carried out by a *non-state group that was able to build and deliver their own working nuke* (i.e., without state-level proxy sponsorship), attribution in this particular situation might proceed as follows: First, analysis of all evidence, especially detailed assay of fresh radioactive isotope samples from near the blast(s), would show that no complete nuke with the known (or post-attack determinable) signature of any *state's* nuclear arsenal had been utilized. Second, further analysis of available evidence would give clues as to *the area of origin* of key bomb materials, such as *what raw ore(s) from which mines* were used to extract the natural-uranium starting point, *what breaker plants and whose centrifuges* were used to refine it to reactor- or weapons-grade uranium-235, *which reactor(s)* were used to irradiate uranium-238 to obtain plutonium-239, *what processing plant(s)* were used to purify the plutonium, *what labs* made the specialized conventional triggering explosives, *what sources* were used for any initiators and tampers, and so on. Any nuclear power that was *genuinely innocent* of the attack would cooperate with such investigations, to (1) avoid suspicion of culpability-via-proxy-support, to (2) help bring the perpetrators to justice, and to (3) help prevent more such attacks where they themselves might be the victim.
- It needs to be restated that there is, at least in theory, for any state that abhors draconian "evidence" policy, such a thing as *being self-deterred from counter-nuking by one's inability to attribute a nuclear attack surely enough to a specific enough perpetrating entity.* ("Failed-attribution self-deterrence.") In this case, the state suffering the attack might, as a *second-best choice,* carry out a "nuclear-weapon demonstration." This means detonating a nuke not against an enemy target, but on its own testing range or somewhere else that is globally conspicuous but does much less harm than any actual attack—such as far out in international waters, with extensive pre-arranged media coverage. That could serve as a *strong warning* to any entities thinking that they too could get away with nuking their adversaries. It could convey the messages that (1) more complete attribution capabilities *will be forthcoming,* (2) the earlier, unavenged

attack's perpetrators are *still being avidly hunted* and *will yet be punished*, conventionally or unconventionally, and (3) all further nukings *will be retaliated against* with a second nuclear strike. This issue, once more, emphasizes the vital importance when deterring *any and all nuclear adversaries*—whether they be state or non-state—*of sustaining sophisticated nuclear-forensics and other intelligence support for the best attribution capabilities humanly possible*—and of never being complacent on this front of nuclear detective work.

- In the context of a nuking with *very uncertain attribution but not none at all*, the victim state—whether "on the draconian spectrum" or not—might choose to make only a *conventional* counterstrike, as under the circumstances being less problematic and more appropriate than either nuking back *or* doing nothing.
- One particular scenario of *failed-attribution self-deterrence*, in which attribution in fact is unnecessary because *nuclear retaliation is de facto unnecessary*, is the case where the first of the Three Ever-Present Sources of Danger—*the nuclear detonation itself and its blast's immediate effects*—destroys the evidence of who conducted that terrorist nuclear attack—because it also obliterates a main concentration of the responsible terrorist-group's people and their activities. Note that this obliteration, which obviates the need for the victim state to retaliate, might also *permanently erase* any evidence as to which non-state group's members were the culprits. Such a nuclear attack might *go forever unattributed yet have been immediately punished*. Victim-state authorities could be left permanently wondering whether the perpetrators got clean away, or got vaporized. It seems likely in such a case that *conspiracy theorists* would then have a field day!
- A *possible loophole* in U.S. posture is what we would do in case one state uses another *state* as its nuclear-attack proxy, giving it a nuke or significant nuke development aid. Is it "eligible" on a draconian spectrum?

(The above considerations, taken as a whole, support formulating the complex and nuanced "draconian deterrence" discussion—with its various *vexing questions and current conundrums* about both "*eligibility* for retaliation" and "*evidence* of guilt"—as applying specifically to *terrorist* attacks, not state-level attacks.)

Just One Terrorist Nuclear Strike Would Commence a Terrifying New Era

A single successful terrorist nuclear attack, or a "small" nuclear attack by a rogue or madman nation-state, anywhere in the world, would *usher in an entirely new era* never before experienced by humankind: an era involving the actual detonation of one or more nuclear-attack *war shots,* during a time of *nuclear plenty* among *several* large state nuclear powers. (The distinction made here is versus World War II, wherein the U.S. was the only entity to own any A-bombs when it nuked Japan twice.) The *"nuclear veil"* will have been pierced for the first time since 1945, the *ultimate taboo* of making a nuclear strike would have been violated. These powerful norms, which for a lifetime (so far) have helped keep states from ever fighting a nuclear war, would be terribly weakened.

This awful future transformation would need to be counteracted and reversed, as quickly as humanly possible. The world would be very likely to see at least *some* states adopt nuclear deterrence policies that are *significantly more draconian than previously*—if only to try to put a full stop to any further terrorist (and other) nuclear strikes.

Democracies need to be aware of such future "posture-language arms race" risks, in order to have planning in place for how best to deal with them. This should be included in the (perhaps classified portions of) recurring, all-encompassing nuclear posture reviews. Doing so will have the concurrent benefit of amplifying/emphasizing the vital importance of all the various other measures preventing nuclear weapons ever falling into the hands of terrorists, and being set off by them.

As emphasized recently by current US COMSTRATCOM, Admiral Richard, it is important that such reviews occur in the wholistic (big picture) context of *all* of America's strategic defense needs, not just nuclear deterrence in "stovepiped" isolation. (These multi-domain warfighting and peacekeeping preparedness needs include space operations, information warfare, and cybersecurity.)

To Gain Leadership, True Madmen Are So Disorganized They Need (Some) Sane Subordinates

Any state-level rogue (a Kim Jong Un or an Ayatollah Ali Khamenei?) or madman or mad-woman leader (a future Hitler?) and their whole nuclear weapons "establishment" (personnel and infrastructure) are subject to some of the same deterrence/interdiction considerations as, on the one hand, terrorists with at-best rather improvised establishments, and, on the other hand, superpowers with very fully developed, highly disciplined, and redundant nuclear establishments.

During stable times of nuclear peace, every nation-state's nuclear weapons arsenal is likely to be at least nominally safeguarded against accidental or unauthorized use, in thoroughgoing, complicated ways. But all-too-human complacency, mismanagement, lax personnel procedures, and/or corruption pose serious risks to the safety, security, and reliability of that establishment. A number of *very responsible, highly trained* personnel will be needed to manage/enable and verify/validate the processes of constructing and protecting the weapon stocks, servicing and maintaining the weapon systems, issuing and conveying orders for nuclear alerts and actual strikes, preparing any nukes for actual use, uploading them to delivery platforms, and then delivering them, fused and armed, to their chosen targets. Heads of state and commanders in chief like to be seen as good leaders, and good leaders *delegate.*

This is bound to be true in dictatorships, whether large or small. Why so? Authoritarian regimes tend to be particularly paranoid against any internal and external opposition, including opposition that might sabotage or steal their all-powerful nuclear arms. In consequence of the resulting stringent guarding and handling considerations, even the most absolute dictator will be *dependent on the cooperation of a number of other people,* at different levels of senior and rank-and-file government and military personnel, to *actually carry out a nuclear attack* that he/she orders. This justifiably paranoid infrastructure caution, intended to preserve the dictator's power, can actually work to limit it.

If America's national nuclear deterrence posture continues in the future to be effectively communicated worldwide—as has certainly been the case up to now at the state-on-state level—then a few local people with *reasonably good human consciences* (against using nukes for unprovoked attack) will almost certainly, by random events or *by design,* or both, happen to be embedded in and around the belligerent adversary's nuclear offense decision-action loop. Such people will, under more ordinary circumstances such as a *conventional* aggressive attack on a neighbor (e.g., Saddam Hussein invading Iran and then Kuwait), remain loyal to the leader and his/her regime, at least so long as things go well. These people will *not* have trouble passing security screening to confirm their trustworthiness. But most if not all military professionals, plus many organized-crime gangsters and thugs, and even some extremist Muslims, *have inner personal codes of honor* that would rebel against nuking innocent civilians by the millions or billions—especially knowing such action could so easily bring on complete human extinction. This inclusion of latent human *"circuit breakers"* isn't necessarily true *all* of the time, but it is true a very valuable *some of the time.*

In the case of any heinously excessive and provocative act of nuclear aggression ordered by the *mad/rogue dictator*, one that is likely to have catastrophic "blowback" consequences for the dictator's own entire society, these people can act to refuse or ignore "just obeying orders" to launch the nuke, so that the nuke does not get launched. Supporting this is the legal precedent of the 1945–1946 Nuremberg Tribunals, which established that "I was only following orders" does not absolve someone of complicity in a war crime or crime against humanity—assuming they even survive said crime themselves. In the devastating, mass-extinction event of a nuclear attack, coupled to the Armageddon and nuclear winter and then nuclear summer very likely to follow, the *anguishing, torturing punishment* would be dished out, not by a human tribunal and its hangmen, but by the *righteous nuclear retaliation* from the states attacked coupled with the *inescapable forces of Mother Nature herself*: uncontrollable nuclear escalation, murderous nuclear fallout, un-survivable nuclear winter deep-freeze and killing darkness, and then (due to nuclear destruction of Earth's ozone layer) the lethal hard-ultraviolet exposures searing down on all life whenever the Sun does shine.

The key here for the good guys is to *systematically educate* all potential bad guys at all levels. Warn them that, if they ever attack first with nukes or other strategic WMDs, U.S. and NATO Triad forces will without fail mercilessly inflict punishment upon them that the attackers themselves caused, which they unquestionably deserve and cannot escape. Leave nothing to their imaginations, spell out in *awful blood-curdling detail* the hideously punitive blowback to befall leaders and followers equally along with their precious causes and all their loved ones and their cherished ideology—*if* they make the *ultimate* mistake of setting off an unprovoked, unjustified nuclear/strategic-WMD first strike. Closer in time to any nuclear-attack danger point (such as a heightened international crisis), appeal both stochastically (*en masse*, through Internet-based media) and individually (through U.S. and allied intelligence capabilities) to those with good conscience to act as the specifically-*not*-mad/*not*-rogue "circuit-breaker individuals" mentioned above, to prevent the nuclear attack. (U.S./NATO forces would not be vulnerable to enemy messaging, since it would not be us making the unprovoked first strike.)

Let's Look at Hitler's Germany Again

There is *encouraging historical evidence* that this resistance to orders to commit serious violations of the International Laws of War can indeed take place. This is true even in the *worst case* of a large state-level dictator madman—one who controls a *massive, sadistic secret police apparatus*—issuing murderous orders using *"merely" conventional weapons*, years into *actual, raging, major wartime*—when moral codes are likely to have already been *badly eroded*, and disloyal or hesitant subordinates already *ruthlessly weeded out*. Nazi Germany provides several examples:

1. Hitler's order to execute all captured Allied prisoners of war in North Africa who were Jewish was *ignored* by General Rommel and his Afrika Korps commanders.
2. The German Sixth Army did *not*, as ordered by Hitler, fight to the point of suicidal self-extinction at the end of the Battle of Stalingrad—General von Paulus surrendered his command to Soviet forces.
3. Paris was *not* destroyed by retreating German forces as Hitler had ordered in 1944.
4. The order by Hitler in early 1945 to introduce poison gas on the battlefield was *ignored*.
5. Final orders by Hitler for the mass self-destruction of German property and murder of the German people, because they had failed him, were *ignored* by his military commanders, who surrendered to the Allies after Hitler committed suicide.
6. There were *at least 42 historically documented cases* of (alas, unsuccessful) attempts on Hitler's life, because of his extremist policies, made by those who *actively resisted* the Nazi movement. In addition, a large number of persons throughout Germany, acting alone or in groups, in other ways *resisted* these extremist policies, either passively or actively.
7. For instance, many thousands of would-be victims of the Jewish Holocaust were successfully harbored and/or shepherded to safety abroad, by individuals who knowingly risked their own lives. These very real circuit-breaker individuals are now honored by the State of Israel as "the Righteous Among the Nations." As of 2019, *over twenty-five thousand* such Righteous persons were rigorously documented and named at Yad Vashem, Israel's Holocaust Memorial, for their repeated or substantial acts of defiance of the Nazi regime's genocide.

This all suggests that a good national nuclear deterrence policy for America should declare clearly and firmly that, in the case of a nuclear first strike ordered by a dictator known or strongly believed to be insane (however exactly defined by expert psychologists), the defending/retaliating state (i.e., the U.S.) will hold responsible and will treat as *valid military targets* the entire enemy military and political control apparatus, including all enemy nuclear weapons personnel and installations. This is very similar to the current U.S. nuclear deterrence posture against *any* state attacking with nukes—so it seems more a matter of *special emphasis* than of any new policymaking. But a more forceful articulation might be useful to strengthen such posture for successfully deterring even a madman—*by more emphatically deterring the many persons whose obedience that madman is dependent upon for actually going nuclear.*

Such a declared policy would discourage, in advance, any personnel in the adversary's nuclear-strike decision-and-action loop from imagining that the U.S. and our Allies would somehow hold them innocent because they were only following orders, *even or especially the orders of a lunatic.* In other words, the diagnosis of leader madness would be *no shield,* for loyal lieutenants, against *human MAD-ness.* Nor would it be any shield whatsoever against the inevitable forces of *thermodynamic entropy and Mother Nature herself* likely obliterating the attacking entity and *all* its enablers, through uncontrollable escalation and global nuclear winter and nuclear summer.

Terrorists Might or Might Not Be Madmen by Democracy's Standards

Deterring terrorists as madmen: It can be counterproductive to debate too much whether terrorist leadership and followership are madmen, or coldly rational on their own terms, or some of both. The truth, individual by individual, probably falls along a wide *spectrum* of mental makeup and motivational characteristics. This can work to the benefit of nuclear peacekeeping.

One complicating factor is that even a state that is led by a *de facto madman* supreme leader might wish to deter nuclear attacks made against it by *other madmen*—including but not limited to terrorists. Presumably, and hopefully, the supreme leader's rational subordinates would see to it that a "normal" program of deterrence posture declaration and education is administered coherently.

Specific mention should be made for one diagnosis of "madman," who is as skillful at passing to laymen as "normal," even "brilliant and charismatic," as he/she is at viciously minimizing the credibility of observers who note the madman's dangerous abnormalities.

Certain violent despots, at all levels from rebel groups to superpower states, have been or could be *sociopaths.* Their behavior is not so much the incoherent rantings voters associate with "lunacy," as a specific sort of character malformation or even a brain development deficit (mostly likely some of both). They have no conscience, no remorse, no empathy for the negative impact of their destructive cravings upon other human beings. At the same time, they can be captivatingly charming, highly socially and politically skilled, deeply ambitious, ruthlessly competitive, stupefyingly narcissistic, and *diabolically manipulative*. They are, quite possibly, the most dangerous type of "insane person-in-chief."

Fortunately, actual sociopaths in overall human society are rare (studies say about 1%), but empirical evidence suggests they tend to become concentrated as bosses and leaders (about 4%). This low percentage makes any big group of terrorists be somewhat heterogeneous, i.e., not entirely sociopathic, within their various deepest selves. But—unlike the sociopaths—the *hesitant or remorseful* manner in which *some* individual terrorists are known to have occasionally behaved in *conventional* attack situations suggests something *potentially useful*: In any group of terrorists, some at least might respond properly to nuclear deterrence.

This valuable hesitancy or remorse might be especially operant if—again, recognizing the severe legal and moral problems with any such policy in the U.S. and NATO—some *ruthless dictatorship's draconian retaliatory strike* would be anticipated to take place against them and "their people" and their most cherished assets if they allow a nuking to occur—where the "people" in "their people" might refer to the nuclear terrorists' home village, family, clan, sect, or tribe. It might be particularly useful, when democracies message about this risk, to emphasize that such a draconian dictatorship might very well be *led by a sociopath*—one who would certainly *not* hesitate to order a "justified" draconian retaliatory second nuclear strike.

Dictatorships don't think like democracies: This concept surely sounds horribly draconian to any democracy that shares basic values with the United States. But as hinted already, dictatorships subjected to the threat of terrorist nuclear attack do not always share basic values with the United States. Such a dictatorship's senior nuclear policy-making body might determine, to their greatly self-satisfying self-justification, that the most logically consistent projection or stretching of America's own nuclear deterrence policy—from how we *do* apply it to *adversary nation-states* that attack using nukes, to how the dictatorship *could* apply their own policy to *terrorist groups* that do so—should be *exactly* this type of draconian anti-terrorist posture phraseology.

After all, consider what a democracy is really saying when it pronounces that an adversary nuclear-weapon state's sovereign territory (including, in effect, its atmosphere and ground and subterranean environment), its political control assets (including ruling-party and secret-police headquarters with clerical and janitorial staff), and its military personnel and bases (which usually house civilian employees and civilian military dependents), are all *acceptable target-sets* for a countervailing nuclear retaliatory strike.

The dictatorship's policy board (such as a Moscow Politburo or a Beijing Central Military Committee) might easily convince itself that America is merely calling out as *valid targets* various things, and people, that could be seen as the *direct analogues* to a terrorist group's home territory and all its residents; to their operating, training, and living locales including structures, possessions, and weapons; and to the fighters themselves, plus their logistical and technical support "staff" and co-located dependents and employees.

Since any democracy's nuclear retaliatory strike, no matter how limited and how precise, is likely to cause collateral damage, including the deaths of (innocent) civilians and destruction of (civilian) property and infrastructure, a dictatorship can conclude (at least among its own ruthless policymaking body) that a certain amount of death of terrorist families (women, children, the elderly and infirm, and other relatives) and other innocent people near ground zero (clerks, secretaries, school teachers, doctors and nurses) is *acceptable*. They might even conclude that this is *necessary* for optimal deterrence of the nuclear terrorist threat. Through this line of reasoning, draconian deterrence would win *support and approval* amid even a *perfectly sane* dictatorship's power structure.

But can any terrorists be deterred this way? The answer might well be "Yes" just often enough to make such a draconian deterrence policy against nuclear terrorist groups be, conceivably, *effective enough* for a dictatorship to deem the modest effort/cost to enact, uphold, publicize, and enforce it *worth the effort*. And if the answer were "yes, often enough" for dictatorships, there would be *concurrent benefits* inuring even to democracies who shun draconian-ness: The dictatorships would *de facto* assume all the ethical/theological burden of draconian "heavy lifting," to make terrorists think twice before ever wanting to try to access the nuclear option.

The previously mentioned effects of the Three Sources of Danger's *escalatory thermodynamic entropy* and *Mother Nature's aftermath-wrath* would tend to beneficially *extend* to democracies a sort of "protective umbrella" derived from the draconian deterrence adopted by tyrannies. This is because *any* states adopting draconian deterrence significantly raises, toward 100.0%, the odds that *any* unprovoked nuclear attack will inevitably trigger *complete human extinction*.

Conventional terrorist groups have had defectors: For instance, in the case of some conventional suicide bombings ordered by Muslim terrorist groups, some group members have occasionally indeed "chickened out," for whatever reasons. They instead voluntarily *turned themselves in* to defender authorities, and/or occasionally even *changed sides* to speak out and act against their former terrorist cronies.

Dictatorships can compete for the draconian high (low?) ground: If any ruthlessly authoritarian state might adopt a draconian policy to deter nuclear terrorists, then more than one such state might do so. Once again, we encounter a dangerous *three-player game* in which nuclear weapons are on the table, a volatile game little contemplated in First Cold War deterrence theory.

For instance, as mentioned earlier, both Russia and China face their own clear and present dangers of anti-state terrorist actions, with Caucasus rebels and Uyghur separatists. *Both* these nuclear superpowers might adopt a draconian declaratory deterrence policy themselves. And they might do this for *two different reasons.* One is for blatant self-protection. The other is to also shift the danger, of being targeted by any terrorist nuclear strike, onto democratic countries (specifically the U.S./NATO, the third "player" in this Cold War II game), whom the two superpower dictatorships both see as geopolitical rivals and military competitors—and whom terrorists might see as more hesitant to retaliate against them using nukes. This adversarial "shifting of the danger" might then in fact increase the probability that some nuclear-wannabe terrorist group will focus all its energies against, and will make a nuclear attack against, the U.S. and our allies, not Russia or China. It is therefore incumbent on the "good guys" to forcefully educate *terrorists and tyrants* alike that draconian deterrence *anywhere* could raise the odds of nuclear extinction *everywhere.* Since the dictatorships seem likely to stand pat on any such draconian deterrence posture if once they adopt it, it then behooves the terrorists to avoid self-annihilation by confining their attacks to conventional weapons, or at least to only the "diversion feeding" uses of any nukes they ever do manage to obtain.

A good example of what makes three-player games so unpredictable and dangerous is that China and Russia could vie against each other for "draconian deterrence supremacy." As hinted earlier, each could compete publicly and/or privately to put their own declared posture *further upward and to the right* in the 2-D "Cartesian coordinate system" spectrum of draconian-ness. They could each strive to put the monkey of nuclear terrorism onto their authoritarian rival's back, as well as onto the Arsenal of Democracy's back. This would be especially problematic for American interests if the two other nuclear superpowers ever collaborated against the U.S.—as they sometimes threaten to do now, and as during the First Cold War they sometimes actually did do.

How Can the U.S. Counter Any Draconian Deterrence of Terrorists by Other States?

Perhaps the above particularly unpleasant scenarios could be countered by the U.S. in one or more of at least three ways, depending on whether the other state is a friendly democracy or a superpower peer competitor:

- Use diplomatic efforts, and inter-military discussions, to discourage any nuclear weapons states at all from "going first" in adopting such a very broad, draconian counterterrorist nuclear deterrence policy, either before *or even after* they or another state suffers the world's first terrorist nuking. It could be helpful to offer, or withhold, additional military and/or trade assistance, as disincentives to "going draconian," at least if the other state or states are democracies that are basically friendly with America.
- Adopt, or at least *threaten to adopt*, the same sort of draconian policy, as part of U.S. national nuclear deterrence posture—at least, if adversarial peer-competitor nuclear powers officially or de facto do ever adopt such a draconian posture themselves. This could serve as *a deterrent* against any *non-democracy's* draconian deterrence "first adoption," since us doing so too would right away *cancel out* much of the "draconian advantage" the non-democracies would be seeking over the forces of democracy.
- Since Great Power Competition (Cold War II) adversaries tend to compete on the global stage (disingenuously) for perceptions, by those they would suborn, of their *benign friendliness and high morality*, America might seek to dominate the worldwide dialogue, and deter dictatorships from going draconian, by *"naming and shaming"* them into avoiding draconian policies.

Should America exploit strategic ambiguity? As to America's own position on ever "going draconian," this is at least one context in which the U.S. might prefer, at least until other states might force the issue, to maintain what we are here calling "weak form" *strategic ambiguity*: The United States might choose to *not comment, outside classified venues,* about precisely *how* it would or wouldn't react to a successful terrorist nuclear strike against any of our or our Nuclear Umbrella Allies' vital interests. By saying little about specific policy in advance, and withholding final judgment until *after* all the specific circumstances of any actual such attack are conclusively established, America will best keep all its options open. At the same time, it will best give prospective nuclear terrorists—when subjected to the proper deterrence-oriented influencing/education campaign—some very heavy concerns that will surely weigh on their minds.

As already discussed, nuclear counterterrorism via *preventive interdiction* (of terrorists *getting* nukes, and then *delivering* them to targets and detonating them) remains absolutely essential, aided by global nuclear *counter-proliferation* in general. Terrorist *deterrence* via public information and educational warnings, about possible nuclear blowback leading to total human extinction—surely reprehensible to *any deity*, and rather pointless for *sane atheists* too—provides an added, useful methodology. Public information and educational warnings, depicting a global thermonuclear holocaust being triggered by *just one terrorist nuking*, while disturbingly graphic and explicit, would be proactive, productive, peace-protecting, and best of all—through effective deterrence via powerful but nonlethal *messaging*—would *sidestep completely* all the problems of adopting draconian retaliation. One could go even further and, with the support of some progressive imams, point out forcefully that Muslim nuclear terrorists, by the very heinous and indiscriminate nature of their murderous actions, are bound surely for Islamic Hell (*Jahannam*), *not* Islamic Heaven (*Jannah*) with its 72 virgins (*houris*). They will have committed grave and enormous sins (*ithm, al-Kaba'ir*), including the worst sin of all, playing God (*shirk*).

Could Sunni and Shi'a States, or New Caliphates, Ever Want to Nuke Each Other?

For logical completeness, another slice through the multi-dimensional issues-space of nuclear war-and-peace also needs to be considered: Laymen in America might forget that Islam is *by no means monolithic*. Two major sects co-exist worldwide in *rancorous conflict*, Sunni and Shi'a. Bitter state-level power politics blends with these additional enmities, of an historical and theological nature, creating a very volatile mix—not unlike the at-times bloody violence of centuries past between different Christian denominations.

It is not inconceivable that two separate sovereign states in contention, and dominated or ruled outright by Muslim clerics of opposing sects (Saudi Arabia and Iran?), might in future *both* obtain nuclear weapons. The art and science of effective mutual nuclear deterrence, each against the other, would then become just as important as, say, it once was between the U.S. and the USSR.

Similarly, and presumably a lot more unstably, two terrorist groups from these opposing sects might *both* declare modern caliphates, and then might *both* seek to obtain nuclear arms, for self-protection (mutual deterrence) and for possible use against enemies (including unprovoked first-use). If these *fanatical rivals* were to ever get into a competition to be the first to make a nuclear strike (against a non-Muslim target such as "the Great Satan,"—the U.S.—or "the Little Satan"—Israel—or even against *each other*), the consequences could be catastrophic for the whole world. Two observations can thus be firmly stated:

- The broad matter of 21st century nuclear-deterrence rigorous theory, and sound Best Practices, is (and should be) of keen interest—and of more than mere academic interest—to *every* sovereign state, regardless of type of government, geographic region, size, and religious/philosophical mix of the population. The same is true for every *multilateral* treaty group, collaborative-security body, policymaking organization, and "talking shop."
- Nuclear counter-proliferation, and nuclear counterterrorism, are and will remain pressing responsibilities *everywhere*. They need to include vigorous efforts to educate bad actors of every persuasion about the dangers to all humanity of one single act of nuclear terrorism *anywhere*.

We Need to Wargame, Now, the Geopolitical Aftermath of a Possible Terrorist Nuclear Strike

Suppose that a terrorist group does make a nuclear attack, somewhere, against some nuclear power's homeland or its vital interests abroad. Another nuclear power, perhaps a strategic rival of the victim state, might have "serious beef" of its own against the terrorist movement in question. They might even see that movement as an ongoing—and now very emboldened—general threat against them too, one requiring decisive nuclear preemption. That rival nuclear power might then act, either out of felt compulsion or else opportunistically, *and commit nuclear retaliation against the terrorists on its own initiative*. (This would be not quite the same thing as that power declaring draconian deterrence—which as used here, strictly speaking, applies to deterring the *next* terrorist attack against it, *not* retaliating for the *previous* one against a non-allied state.)

It could claim it was acting out of "friendship" and "solidarity" with America, or on behalf of all humanity. It could even cite Hiroshima and Nagasaki as enabling precedents from 1945 for *multilateral* nuclear retribution at a much later date, beyond 2020. It could then claim to have acted out of "enduring alliance reciprocity." After all, Russia (as the USSR) and China (under Nationalist rule) *were* American allies against Japan as the end of World War II, and FDR himself referred repeatedly to the World War II allies as "the united nations."

It could, this way, be argued that the U.S., constructively, nuked Japan on behalf of *all the allies plus the UN*. This line of argument is a thin reed indeed, but an opportunistic dictatorship wouldn't need much justification here. (The direct victim of the terrorist strike, America in this made-up example, does *not* request this hypothesized "retaliation assistance," yet gets it anyway.) The very possibility of such broadly *extended* draconian nuclear *busybody retaliation* ought to weigh very heavily indeed on terrorist nuclear wannabe minds, as well as on the minds and hearts of all their enabling dependents and co-dependents. Again, first realizing these possibilities ourselves, and then educating the terrorists accordingly, is a positive opportunity for *stronger prevention* of nuclear terrorism attacks.

It also needs to be said that just one successful terrorist nuclear strike, let alone two or three at once, anywhere, would be badly destabilizing *everywhere*. This could be especially true if the terrorist group were able to anticipate big-power nuclear forensic techniques, and then managed to somehow obscure the direct origin of the nuke or nukes they set off. By their very nature, successful terrorist nuclear attacks are likely to occur *very suddenly*, with little if any specific warning. (This differs from attacks between sovereign states, which some defense analysts believe would usually be preceded by an obvious *international nuclear crisis*.) Amid the resulting chaos, terrorist-group claims or responsibility might be *non-existent*, or might be *multiple and contradictory*, and would in any case be *difficult to authenticate*.

The world would first know an attack was in progress at all when the nuke(s) was/were set off and mushroom clouds rose over scenes of horrendous death and devastation. The victim state(s) would know only that they had been nuked. It would take time to figure out the source of the nuke or nukes, and to establish the identity of the attacker group or groups.

The victim—and the rest of a horrified world—would not know right way if the nuke was an isolated strike, or *just the first of a few more* terrorist nukings to occur soon, or even the prelude to a *more massive big-state attack* that was disguised (temporarily) as an isolated terrorist strike—or a state's attack that rode opportunistically on the aftermath of a terrorist strike. Lack of friendly defensive sensors detecting any incoming ICBMs or SLBMs or ALCMs could mean nothing: A big nuclear state could easily choose to smuggle in a nuke, for instance via Vladimir Putin's drone mini-sub, or on a disguised North Korean or Iranian merchant ship, or via a commandeered or chartered Third World drug-smuggling submarine. The victim state would have to *assume the worst*, at least as far as moving its own nuclear forces to a higher level of alert, which would be detected by adversaries, who would reciprocate, leading to *global destabilization*. These panicky government reactions could feed on each other a lot faster than state nuclear forensics *could give any hard answers*.

Other nuclear powers that are strategic rivals of the victim state would also have good reason for grave concern. They would know they might somehow come to be blamed for ultimate responsibility for the attack, in the *chaos and hysteria* that could reign post-attack. Their protestations to the victim state over a 21st century Hot Line, no matter how sincere and truthful, might not be believed. Fearing they might suffer a retaliatory nuclear attack from the victim state, and/or might soon themselves suffer a terrorist nuking, these strategic rivals would have to bring their own nuclear forces to a higher level of alert. Hawks among them might argue strongly for making *massive preemptive strikes*. Complicating everything would be the *information warfare tactics* of rabid conspiracy theorists galore, and even enemy state intelligence/*disinformatsia* agencies (military troll farms), with all sorts of morbid motivations and perverse agendas. Making the strategic superpower rivals even more jittery would be them knowing that any of them could easily be the *next* victim of *another* terrorist nuclear attack, *at any moment*.

With people near ground zero dead or dying by the millions, and with radioactive fallout spreading to kill many more, with panic rampant and fear of further attacks pervasive, all heads of state would be under terrible stress and time pressure, *even if* individually each state followed very cautions nuke-release rules including "gold standard" proof of culpability before launching any retaliatory strike. A global thermonuclear war could easily break out. (This might, in the most extreme of extreme scenarios, actually be the ultimately nihilistic goal behind the non-state group's nuclear strike(s) to begin with; since such a massively suicidal *and* murderous hypothetical group *could not be deterred directly*, they could only be stopped by eliciting a circuit-breaker individual from within to act against their *absolutely insane* goal of nuking every human being on Earth).

This chain of logic explains very clearly how a single terrorist nuclear strike could all too easily bring about Armageddon for everyone, including the terrorist group's whole civilization, culture, and theology. *Communicating* this clearly and dramatically to potential nuclear terrorists, *in advance*, is what effective (and moral and legal) nuclear deterrence is all about.

Dealing with the Special Problem of Domestic Terrorists and Hometown Madmen

There is one collection of overlapping bad-actor demographic groups for which the above discussion applies only partly. This deserves special emphasis as to communicating messages of nuclear deterrence: There could be people *within the U.S. homeland*, for instance, who might wish to detonate nuclear weapons on U.S. soil, or hijack them for launching at some foreign target without authorization, who do *not* identify with some non-native extremist ideology such as Muslim terrorism. Rather, they might be violently anti-U.S. government—as in the Oklahoma City bombing. Or, they might be very violently opposed to some *foreign* state or group, such as being virulently *anti*-Muslim, or anti-Israel, or pro-Neo-Nazi, or anti-Communist. They even, as noted above, might be some kind of ultimately nihilistic *"obliteration cult"* that somehow springs up within the U.S. and tries to get its hands on a nuke.

This class of bad actors also includes any persons working within the U.S. nuclear weapons establishment who *lose their minds* enough to seek, via their special access and due to their madness, to commit mass murder and/or suicide using unauthorized American nuclear weapon detonations. A related domestic nuke-attacker category includes the seemingly burgeoning group of individuals who are motivated to take many human lives (up to now, via gunfire) out of *psychotic blind rage*. They might either have employment-based access to nukes, or they might seek to gain such access from outside via subterfuge or force, including by cyber-hacking—or, as seen on TV, by elaborate "Mission Impossible"-style *play acting fake-outs*. (Sometimes, real life does imitate fiction, and even is inspired by it.)

Stringent prevention is the best strategy, wherever nuclear retaliation is entirely *precluded*—as is obviously the case *against our own soil*. U.S. military personnel involved in handling nuclear weapons frequently practice quickly neutralizing any teammate who suddenly loses their mind. Carefully enforced *multi-person* work group requirements assure that any lone nut-job will not get very far. *Air-gapping* key computer systems, that is, isolating them from any outside connections, gives protection in the cyber domain.

American military installations that store, handle, and/or transport nuclear weapons are thoroughly protected and guarded, and any procedural errors or security goof-ups are "autopsied" by authorities to identify causes and best prevent any repeats. America's *open and free press* assures widespread attention and accountability for any such unsafe incidents that do occur. In today's world of *Wikileaks, whistleblowers, and widespread cyber-spying,* it is practically impossible to cover up any nuclear problem (weapon *or* power generation) for long at all. Fame- and profit-motivated journalists and book authors continually seek nuclear scandals and coverups to commercialize for public consumption; this is a double-edged sword for deterrence and Triad funding, but it does make for greatest accountability against *complacent/sloppy nuke custodianship.*

But while it is certainly true that the U.S. would not make a nuclear retaliation against *itself,* it is also true that a *domestic* terrorist's, or *domestic* madman's, nuclear detonation is *just as exposed* to the risk of triggering global Armageddon as is a foreign terrorist (or foreign adversary state's) strike on American soil. This is simply because, in those vital first moments after the blast (perhaps *in situ* on a U.S. base), no one might know the strike's perpetrator motivation *or* nationality—and again, any claims of credit to the media *might be disbelieved,* though if made in advance they would prove the blast was *no accident.* Broadened nuclear deterrence messaging is thus important *within* the U.S. homeland, not just overseas, as *unpalatable and even alarming* as such messaging might be.

There remains the problem of what to do if a *lone madman* or small cult group becomes too crazed to care about *wiping out all humanity* one way or another—or might even have the ultimate lunacy of wiping out humanity as its goal. For these baddest of all bad actors, *interdiction* seems the only adequate preventive. And because all these various posited sub-classes of *domestic* nuclear terrorists are theoretically possible, adequate prevention must remain a *paramount responsibility.*

U.S. law enforcement and security specialists at all levels, as well as civilian and military nuclear establishment guards—and in fact *all* personnel—must maintain *eternal vigilance.* Relevant topics discussed in the unclassified literature, such as stringent background checks; psychological pre-screening, and ongoing behavioral/emotional monitoring; periodic updates of security checks, including lie detectors; multi-person nuclear handling procedures, and mechanical-electronic permissive (really, *restrictive*) action links (locks); surprise drug tests, and financial, forensic-accounting, and other lifestyle-risk surveillance must *all* be sustained at the highest possible levels of excellence and effectiveness. *Complacency kills.*

Research should be carried out continually on how new scientific and behavioral insights, and new technologies and organizational approaches, can keep American nuclear weapons out of the hands of *anyone* with ill intent. This applies equally to all nuclear warheads within the U.S. homeland, plus those deployed overseas that are owned by the U.S. The same should apply for all those nukes owned by our allies, and by all other nuclear powers. America has an excellent track record of aiding other states in securing their nuclear weapons, and this international cooperation simply must continue.

It might be very wise for more countries to share expertise in these matters via diplomatic or intelligence-agency back channels, as was reportedly sometimes done during the First Cold War. Alternatively, the matter could be addressed rather publicly at special conferences and workshops put on by the United Nations. A powerful incentive to stringently avoid loss of control of *any* of a state's nukes or nuclear materials is provided by the very dangerous mess that would occur if control were ever lost long enough for a weapon to be set off by some bad actor. The political stink even if the purloining were foiled in-progress would set *new standards of career-ending media scandal.*

An actual detonation of a purloined or commandeered nuke, regardless of where it took place—even right there, *in situ,* in the owner state's nuke storage bunker—would create a terrible international security crisis. Clearly, the stakes applying to any inattention or ineptitude in securing all nuclear weapons worldwide are truly *almost infinitely grave.*

National Attention to Many Fundamentals Is Needed to Sustain Effective Nuclear Deterrence

It has come up repeatedly in the above discussion that the ability to *accurately attribute* a nuclear weapon (either recaptured intact beforehand, or after its detonation) to a *manufacturer-of-origin* is a critical part of being able to credibly and creditably enforce, post-attack, any deterrence posture using a threat of nuclear retaliation declared pre-attack—at least barring resort to rather loose, draconian standards of "proof" of culpability. It is also clearly essential to have in place, in advance of suffering any nuclear attack(s), a sophisticated framework, skillfully staffed, for intelligence gathering, surveillance and reconnaissance (ISR); reliable indications and warnings processes; integrated multi-domain multi-spectral sensor networks for detecting any hostile nuclear moves; and good diplomatic, military, and non-government back-channel communications paths ("hot lines," trusted neutral intermediaries) for reaching any and all potential foes. Just as important is having the veritable army of law enforcement, customs, intelligence, and special operations personnel needed to help protect state nukes and interdict nuclear terrorism.

These capabilities should be actively maintained, supplemented by working with friends and allies, and even by meaningful cooperation with peer-competitor states, in order to detect, halt, and prevent an occurrence of any terrorist nuclear activity, in its earliest stages. This is out of *enlightened self-preservation* and *pragmatic neo-realism* (power geopolitics) as much as out of any other theories re world order. The full medley of aforementioned capabilities is essential to be able to clearly and credibly *cut through the denials* by state-level bad actors who might otherwise be tempted, someday soon, to enable nuclear terrorists; those same capabilities are needed to quickly and accurately *validate or invalidate any claims* for or against responsibility made by non-state groups themselves.

Two known/suspected conventional-terrorism-supporting rogue states, North Korea and Iran, need especially thorough surveillance, and back-channel forceful warnings, regarding any schemes they might be tempted to hatch to instigate/support a "plausibly deniable" terrorist-delivered nuclear weapon strike. Nor should it be forgotten that, during the First Cold War, the Soviet Union sponsored various (conventional) terrorist groups around the world. China has consistently—and still does—support North Korea as its proxy, and supports Pakistan as a military ally, after reportedly aiding both in their nuclear weapon development programs in earlier years—and both these smaller states *do* reportedly sponsor conventional terrorism now.

All this shows that research and development in assuring security against nuclear attack, for America and any other states, must involve *more than* simply sustaining the adequately-sized nuclear deterrence arsenal—the *all-important Triad hardware itself*—plus its hardened, redundant, nuclear command, control, and communications infrastructure (NC3) and the rest of the laboratory and manufacturing nuclear establishment. The effectiveness of national nuclear posture, whatever the words within it happen to say (or intentionally *not* say), is *also* dependent on the unassailable, unquestioned ability to *implement* the *entire* chain of decisions and actions (including *within enemy minds*) needed to effectively *deter all possible nuclear-armed adversaries.*

This entire chain of effective deterrence is also holistically dependent on continuous research and development into such *broad and multidisciplinary areas* as nuclear power safety and security and non-weaponizable fusion power alternatives, nuclear deterrence theory, human psychology and sociology, diplomacy and arms control negotiations, conflict resolution and peacekeeping, natural- and man-made-disaster relief, humanitarian aid, and post-war reconstruction and recovery techniques.

People are as important to deterrence effectiveness as are hardware. Unlike all the hardware a government or a defense contractor owns, their employees who feel *neglected or mistreated* can try to go elsewhere for better job opportunities; those just starting out who see finer futures outside government service and the defense industrial base can go elsewhere from the outset. A continuing supply of eager, healthy and fit, well prepared, disciplined and resilient *personnel for the military* is indispensable to national security. So is a steady stream of well educated, critically and creatively thinking *civilian researchers* and skilled, proud *industrial craftsmen.*

These staffing needs represent an *ongoing, multigenerational national responsibility and patriotic duty* that requires a pervasive, organic system to teach, and then recruit from, a cadre of student-leaders with sophisticated knowledge of (1) world history, including military history; foreign languages, literature and philosophy; and a respectful overview of varied cultures and faiths, to avoid inadvertent *cultural mirror-imaging* (see the next chapter), (2) "blue collar" specialized fabrication skills such as nuclear welding and molecular-level-tolerance precision machining, and (3) "white collar" expertise in science, technology, engineering, and mathematics (STEM)—not to mention nuclear medicine, physiology, psychology, sociology, and anthropology.

Science-denial, taken too far, is anathema to good national security. Whether in the name of frugal bean-counting for its own sake on the one hand, or in the name of pacifist/isolationist ideologies *or* self-blaming dogmas on the other hand, nuclear-deterrence/Triad *budgetary stinginess* works in both the short-term and the long-term *against* America's national interest—including against our ability to most effectively deter and interdict nuclear terrorism. This is for one simple and stark reason: In the Nuclear Age, with its Great Power Competition, emerging nuclear-armed rogue states, and endless counterterror challenges, there can be no priority higher than assuring the *survival of humanity with permanence of political freedom.* This takes *stable and adequate funding for robust, diversified Triad forces.* Difficult compromises and sacrifices will be needed, especially as our tyrannical state adversaries and various terrorist groups alike aggressively exploit the disruptions and suffering of the COVID-19 pandemic to expand their repressive spheres of influence, all at democracy's cost.

Nuke Modernization Is Essential for Safety and Security

There is another key imperative at work that should drive, and be driven by, all the above concerns. This is the imperative to *modernize* existing nuclear weapons. This is a task that comes around for every generation—and will, presumably, *continue to come around* for foreseeable future generations too.

A nuclear weapon is a complicated device that contains much more than just nuclear fuels and high-explosive detonation stages. The device also has various electric, electronic, and mechanical components that perform a myriad of essential functions. They: provide guidance to the warhead for precise arrival on target; contain and implement advance instructions on just where and when to detonate if ever needed; process multiple sensor inputs to assure the warhead undergoes the correct mix of g-forces, atmospheric pressures and temperature changes, and other environmental factors that assure no unauthorized or premature detonation can ever occur; accept and authenticate the codes and keys needed to confirm any handling and use is fully authorized; and provide a built-in high-performance power supply to make sure everything works exactly (and *only*) as designed.

Just as all other modern technology is constantly advancing in leaps and bounds, so too are the safety and security procedures, interlocking machinery, and computer software and hardware available (and needed) to *assure to the absolute maximum* that an individual nuclear warhead cannot go off erroneously, even by the wildest sort of accident or breakdown or by the savviest sort of misappropriation or sabotage. To deny a national government the ability to continue research, development, and implementation (i.e., *acquiring and installing*) of such safety and security measures makes no sense at all. Such forced obsolescence doesn't make *any* state's nuclear weapons "less useable," it just makes each one *riskier*, and *less dependable* if ever needed to be used—which means that *more nukes* must be kept on hand as individual warhead reliability deteriorates. Forced obsolescence does make nukes *more* useable by all the *wrong* people—including terrorists.

Conclusion: We Must Not Hand Nuclear Terrorists any "Easy Wins"

Nuclear terrorism remains a serious threat to human life all over the globe. There is much that can be done to cut it off at its roots, and America needs to take a leadership role in these efforts. But unilateral nuclear disarmament, to inspire adversary states to follow suit and to deny all terrorists any American nukes to try to access, is most assuredly *not* the way to go. Nor is multilateral nuclear disarmament a realistically achievable goal in today's world. Russia persists in violating international security agreements including nuclear treaties, and China refuses to even talk about nuclear arms control.

The claim that nuclear terrorists cannot be deterred has been deconstructed in detail in this chapter. The use of that bogus blanket claim, as justification for America to dismantle its whole nuclear arsenal as the only recourse, does nothing but play directly into the hands of our well-armed and modernizing nuclear superpower adversaries. Allowing that same claim to lure us into inertia on the counter-terror messaging front will just play into the hands of the terrorists.

CHAPTER 4

With Nuclear Deterrence, Cultural Mirror-Imaging Kills

America's Self-Referential Biases Might Weaken Nuclear Peace

Executive Summary: We All Tend to Do Some Mirror-Imaging Now and Then

Within national defense circles, *"mirror-imaging"* means believing that you know exactly how your adversaries think, when in reality you *don't*. One specific form of mirror-imaging (or "mirroring," for short) is to believe, consciously or unconsciously, that all others perceive and think about vital things the exact same way that you do—without realizing until too late (if ever) how very wrong you are. Mirror-imaging by a state's decision-makers can result from the implicit cultural and psychological biases, explicit prejudices, misconceptions, preconceived notions, and misunderstandings about others, which are latent (sometimes even virulent) within any society's populace and its governing officialdom. These errors can lead to *dangerously misinformed decisions*, and *very counterproductive actions*, within that state's defense policy and strategy sphere. Worse, it might become evident to adversaries that a state is blundering into cultural mirror-imaging *during some international crisis, geopolitical conflict, or outright shooting war*—and then that adversary can exploit the situation to their own advantage.

As shown throughout modern military history, adversaries of America, whether Nazi Germany, Imperial Japan, North Korea, or North Vietnam; or the USSR (and Russia) or China; or Iraq and Iran; or al Qaeda and ISIS; or whoever, can have *heterogeneous systems of values, preferences, goals, and aspirations* that are quite alien—and antagonistic—to

America's free and democratic way of life. These gaps and gulfs in emotions and objectives can prove *particularly treacherous* when it comes to achieving U.S./NATO goals for nuclear deterrence, nuclear counterproliferation, and nuclear counterterrorism.

Values and goals affect a people's *entire approach* to government, diplomacy and trade, international competition, peacekeeping, and especially their approach to war. How We the People and our leaders successfully resolve conflict with other states, and with non-state entities, and how we best defend ourselves and deter others, *or fail to,* are critically dependent on accurate understandings about how our geopolitical opponents think and make decisions.

This chapter explores in detail, using practical examples from current public debate, how mirror-imaging in American and Allied society can insidiously impair the soundness of modern Western nuclear deterrence theory and practice, and *weaken or shortchange the effectiveness of our deterrent messaging to adversaries.* This mirroring can undermine our country's political willingness to maintain a robust Triad nuclear deterrent. It can call into question our united commitment to retaliating in kind, proportionately, in the unlikely event that we ever really do need to respond to a nuclear attack. Worse, mirror-imaging can make us flaunt such divisions to our adversaries—encouraging their Cold War II territorial expansionism, regional conventional aggression, and nuclear blackmail. Chapter 4 will recommend some *practical solutions* to these pressing strategic challenges and fulminating domestic controversies.

This chapter also suggests some *corrections* to several major foreign-policy *misconceptions and misperceptions,* which result from American cultural and psychological mirror-imaging about the *numerous, differing adversaries* at whom our nuclear deterrence posture needs to be directed, individually focused, and then effectively communicated. Chapter 4 overviews: (1) how to better grasp *the differences between nations and peoples and their psyches,* around the world, when developing U.S. "National Nuclear Posture After Next," and, just as importantly, (2) how to more fully adjust, domestically, *for anti-democracy malign influence campaigns* (disinformation by state-sponsored and non-state "troll farms") that are directed at us and our government, and our Allies, continually from abroad.

What Is Mirror-Imaging?

The *core phenomenon of mirror-imaging* is taking for granted (i.e., implicitly assuming) that all other people think and feel the same way you do about something, even (or *especially*) when some of them *don't*—without you realizing you're making this mistake, a sad fact that hobbles you from correcting your error. *Broader aspects of mirror-imaging* include situations when you're sure you know how other people think (which you do realize might be differently from you), but you're wrong about important details, *or* where you're sure *they* know exactly *how* you think, but (again) you're wrong. The *other party* could *also* themselves be guilty of mirror-imaging, in which case *they* believe they know exactly how *you* think—but *they're* wrong.

Committing mirror-imaging is about *much more than* just two parties having differences of opinion; in a specific situation, the opinions held might—objectively speaking—be right or wrong on the part of either, both, or neither party. If both parties clearly and accurately *understand* the other's view, even though they might *disagree* with each other vehemently (violently?), they are *not* mirror-imaging. Mirror-imaging is about one side *not grasping the degree of the other side's fundamentally different mindset over both the details and the whole frame of reference,* regarding the subject-matter (usually, a serious dispute, even a war) over which the specific instance of mirror-imaging occurs.

Mirroring is about this *unrecognized thoughts-chasm* itself, *not* about which side's stance might be more in the right or in the wrong. (*Correctness or lack thereof,* of anyone's opinion on the topic in question, is *not* at issue in the definition of mirror-imaging.) Such *not-grasping* as a behavioral phenomenon, in the midst of some significant geopolitical conflict, can lead to misconceptions, misperceptions, miscommunications, and miscalculations—the "Four *Fatal Mis-es*"—with awful end results for one or both sides *and* for global bystanders.

Mirror-imaging as a deadly problem in world security can be illustrated very concretely with a painful, tragic (though very heroic) example, one which most historians now agree about with 20:20 hindsight: America's long, frustrating involvement in the Vietnam War. The United States and North Vietnam were more than simply engaged in armed combat with each other. They held *violently opposed views* of what the war was even all about—which is a main reason U.S. involvement dragged on for so many years: We viewed North Vietnam's invasion of the South, aided by Viet Cong guerillas, as an *attempted Communist takeover* of one of our democratic Allies, a takeover that was being directed from Moscow and Beijing. North Vietnam saw the *same* conflict as something fundamentally different: a *war of national liberation*, directed from Hanoi, against a corrupt and ineffective, foreign-dominated puppet regime in Saigon.

Mirror-imaging amounts to consciously believing, *or* unconsciously assuming, that cultural and psychological differences between different societies–in their fundamental values, positions, aims, and points of view re governmental, diplomatic, and/or military topics—*don't exist* at all, or at least *don't matter* enough to be reckoned with. While many folks in American society, regarding our own multitudinous domestic affairs, fall for minor mirroring misunderstandings with each other on a continual basis, the consequences can be so small that they might never even be noticed. But major instances of *international* mirror-imaging that creep into national-defense policymaking, like with Vietnam, can be *very costly indeed.* Those costs in blood and treasure are suffered by our *whole country,* even when the *explanations* for those high costs—our own national mirror-imaging errors—are *not properly perceived* at the time by our nation's media opinion-setters and in-power political decision-makers.

Such terrible costs arise because the existence of *important schisms,* in aims and motivations between the two sides, are not understood clearly enough at the outset or even late in the struggle. As a direct consequence of this lack of understanding, *looming differences* fail to be identified, appreciated, investigated thoroughly, and compensated for fully, in the ensuing diplomatic and military peacekeeping decisions, warfighting actions, and—eventually—in the exit-strategy development and implementation. (Solving the mirroring problem is not about us sympathizing with the opposing side, let alone blindly agreeing or making knee-jerk concessions; after all, adversaries *are* adversaries. It *is* fathoming better where they are coming from, so that we can better get to where *we* want to go.)

Mirroring can be especially dangerous in the arena of *effective nuclear deterrence,* because the process of nuclear deterrence depends on *clear communication to, and clear comprehension by,* some *external* (foreign) audience which is the group that needs to be deterred—*in extremis,* via the threat of utter annihilation, if that enemy dares to execute any existentially-threatening attack against our vital interests. Our full and proper understanding of that foreign audience's own viewpoints of itself and of us, and of life and of death, are thus *mandatory foundational prerequisites* for successful ongoing deterrence.

With nuclear deterrence, miscalculations can lead to millions or billions of innocent people dying—which would be the ultimate human tragedy, and the ultimate American policymaking failure. The threat of retaliating with nuclear weapons if some foreign entity makes a first strike using nukes (or other strategic-level WMDs, or overwhelming conventional forces) would seem so straightforward, so simple, as to be a "no brainer." What could ever go wrong?

The answer is: *"Plenty, if we don't think through all the issues very carefully indeed."*

Any important war-or-peace competition and/or containment process (such as a Cold War) can go awry in (as least) two related but distinct ways: (1) An official who commits mirror-imaging can miss the point that there are many parties with whom that official is *in direct conflict* (including via domestic electoral or Congressional voting contests, or during violent international disputes) *who might see important, relevant and fundamental things very differently from him/her.* (Those parties-in-conflict could include individual fellow White House Administration appointees or Members of Congress, or semi-monolithic entities such as entire home-front political organizations, foreign sovereign governments, or sub-state/trans-state armed groups.) And (2) the official who mirrors might also take for granted, *wrongly*, that *third-party individuals and entities on the sidelines of the conflict*—who are also really *not* in agreement with the mirror-er—are simply *uninterested*, or else their opinions *don't and won't matter* to a key outcome—when in fact these third parties *will* play a *big role* in determining lasting success or failure. (This amounts to us dismissing them because "it's not their fight," when some of it *is* their fight.)

Thus, mirror-imaging errors can pile up, with compounding negative effect (or also, sometimes, by sheer accident, even with coincidentally *positive* effect), not just between us and a competing government, but *also* between us and *supposedly independent or neutral "other" organizations or states*—allies, adversary third parties, unaligned countries, even international bodies such as the UN or the EU, or non-governmental organizations (NGOs) such as the Red Cross and Red Crescent.

A key manifestation of this *double-whammy effect* (via direct opponents and via "neutrals"), of important mirror-imaging errors on the political/financial viability of America's nuclear deterrence, is how very heated are the controversies raging, across all the decades of the Atomic Age, (1) within factionalized America society itself and also (2) between the U.S. and even our own NATO (and other) Allies, let alone (3) between us and UN rank-and-file member states, (4) between us and our various adversaries—*plus* (5) the disputes that these different foreign entities all have with each other—regarding many topics relevant to nuclear-war prevention. For instance, precisely this critical nuclear peacekeeping goal is the supposed primary purpose of *both of* two *diametrically opposed* policy propositions, each adhered to by many vehement, passionate advocates at home and abroad: modernizing America's aging Triad, *or* getting rid of it.

Talk about bitter, high-stakes conflicts, prone to lots of mirror-imaging by all the many concerned/interested parties! The challenge here is that the political fate of America's nuclear Triad hardware, and the success of our messaging about deterrence to both Allies and adversaries, are *intimately coupled.* When it comes to nukes, political and cultural mirror-imaging can kill.

Mirror-Imaging re Nuclear Defense Policy Happens Too Often in America

For instance, the proper size, role, and technical makeup of our country's nuclear arsenal are debated endlessly and bitterly by factions in our domestic political system. Our Triad is also at times addressed, sometimes helpfully and sometimes unhelpfully, but in any case with real influence on our own political outcomes, for instance by other NATO states, by Russia and China, by the UN, and by Global Zero. Emotions about *"nukes vs. no nukes"* run high here in America, as do the stakes for big appropriated DC budget dollars and for nationwide governmental and media influence, status, and power. Imagine, then, *how much broader* such chasms of beliefs, perceptions, values, and cognitive processes can be about nuclear weapons, nuclear war, nuclear disarmament—and overt nuclear *aggression*—across the vast entirety of humanity's very diverse and highly factionalized planet. Again, it's not the difference of opinion, it's the *not grasping* the reasons and motivations behind those opinions.

American Mirror-Imaging Creates Weakness and Vulnerability in Our Deterrence

Americans' tendency to mirror in dealing with other countries and cultures is *well known* to our adversaries. They observe us carefully, benefiting from our free press and our frank and pithy political interplay. They see our mirroring behavior, rightfully, as a *strategic weakness* that can *offset* the great strengths of our democratic government, our open society, our free way of life, and the inventiveness and commitment of our troops. This mirroring is reflected in our tending to assume that (1) adversaries mean what they say, and (2) they understand what we are trying to say, in diplomatic negotiations, business/trade dealings, and especially in military operational "signaling."

Specifically, critical blunders can ensue because we think that our subtexts and subtle hints are being received, loud and clear, by a competitor or adversarial entity—when in fact our signal is *missed altogether*, or by being read (and misread) according to *their* own differing precepts, becomes *hopelessly cloudy and muddled.*

Mirror imaging also leaves us vulnerable to being *manipulated* by messaging that "tells us what we want to hear." We then *trust* such messages as being truthful or sincere, when they are in fact a manipulative part of *modern hybrid/asymmetric warfare strategy* in general, and *disingenuous malign-influencing campaign tactics* in particular. This happens because we sometimes don't appreciate how much a foreign-trade or geopolitical rival, or outright military enemy, can *feel strong motivations and then choose to act, surreptitiously and nefariously but forcefully*, in order for them to achieve things that we in the U.S. and NATO consider to be "bad"—and which we would seldom if ever do ourselves. These very bad *objectives* (and, too often, *actual accomplishments*) by our foreign rivals and enemies include: degrade human rights, disregard international treaty terms, disrupt economic stability, overturn good world order and peace, resist rapid resolution of conflicts, selfishly exaggerate and exploit crises, and even (or especially) devalue human life itself.

Nowhere can this be more consequential that when nuclear weapons are on the table.

Mirror-Imaging Errors Fall into Several Broad Types

In the *nuclear deterrence policy sphere*, some mirroring mistakes can fall into one or more of several categories, each with its own unfortunate practical effects and undesirable consequences:

- You wrongly think a fellow countryman is friendly/trustworthy/benign.
- You wrongly think a fellow countryman is incorrigibly bad/evil.
- You wrongly think a foreign person is friendly/trustworthy/benign.
- You wrongly think a foreign person is incorrigibly bad/evil.
- You wrongly think a foreign government grasps your open/direct *messaging* and/or your implicit/tacit *signaling* to them.
- You wrongly think a foreign government wants the same things you do.

Such errors, lurking on the American policymaking scene, can give rise in some quarters to *ill-advised* nuclear posture perspectives and *flawed* political positions. *But forewarned is forearmed.* Seeing that such mirroring is in fact going on, then taking steps to reduce or eliminate it (unilaterally or multilaterally), can help everyone involved in a dispute gain a wiser perspective, as a sound baseline for mutual conflict resolution. This in turn can be very productive for *avoiding* unnecessary controversies, constructively *overcoming* stubborn differences of opinion—and in particular for *strengthening* nuclear deterrence and nuclear peacekeeping, nuclear counterproliferation, and nuclear counterterrorism.

For clarity, here is a concise yet formal definition of mirror-imaging:

Definition of Mirror-Imaging Used in this Book

DEFINITION: *Mirror imaging* is the phenomenon in which one party believes (or at least, behaves outwardly as if they believe) that they accurately and fully comprehend the perspectives and objectives of another party, when in fact they don't.

Belief in Nuclear Un-Usability Is Not Shared Equally by All in the World

The effects of nuclear weapon detonations are genuinely horrific. Photographs, books, oral histories, and films/videos about the *Hiroshima and Nagasaki bombings* make this abundantly clear. So too does declassified information about the many *A-bomb and H-bomb tests* done around the world, on land, at sea, and even (at least once) in space, during the First Cold War. No sane individual questions the utterly devastating effects, on and near the target, of even limited nuclear combat—and globally as well, in the case of less-limited nuclear war. One topic on which intense controversy rages is how best to *prevent* all such combat. The urgency of prevention is emphasized by the existence of various bad actors—such as nuclear-wannabe Islamic terrorists, or the current (Putin) regime in Russia—who believe that nuclear weapons *can* be used to start or escalate a conflict which their side *can* survive and "win," based on their own peculiarly selfish, self-referential, and self-delusive *theories of victory*.

Ironically, deterrence and peacekeeping can be undermined by persons with the *opposite* perspective, too. These well-meaning people react appropriately to their perception of the repugnance of nuclear war, but then they fall victim to mirroring and expect that the world will quickly disarm due to a universal sharing in their repugnance. By favoring utopian pacifism over hard logic about today's plethora of up-arming, expansionist dictatorships, such idealistic folks focus inappropriately on the devastating impacts of nuke-use *in isolation*, overlooking the need, given current real-world conditions, for *effective peacekeeping measures* that reliably protect democracy from those impacts—via mutual deterrence, *not* unilateral disarmament.

Twenty-first-century geopolitics is riven by three-way nuclear *superpower* competition (the U.S., Russia, China), in tension with poorly-coordinated or even mutually-hostile *regional* nuclear powers (the UK, France, Israel, Pakistan, India), further complicated by nuclear *rogues*—North Korea has a few dozen nukes, Iran is an incorrigible wannabe—

all in a world facing significant threats from *nuclear proliferation* and *nuclear terrorism*. Yet some opinion-makers try to argue that international law makes all nukes *illegal*. Some extremist nuclear-disarmament advocates wish to foment a policy that America will *never* retaliate with nuclear weapons—even when a state-level enemy uses them first.

But in the "realist" (i.e., power-driven) system of *pragmatic world geopolitics*, which many historians also label as *anarchic* (ruled by anarchy, *not* by coherent governance), one thing is painfully clear: Such moralistic niceties have clearly *not* dissuaded a number of countries—Russia and China leading among them—from acquiring and retaining large, increasingly modernized and even next-generation (e.g., hypersonic) nuclear arsenals. Worse, Western-style moral niceties *don't apply very much* to rogue states, and *don't apply at all* to the terrorist organizations that have been trying since the mid-1990s to obtain working nukes.

For protection of self and allies, America needs to sustain its own *adequately-sized* nuclear deterrent, as it has done since the First Cold War began. Yet, in part because of mirror-imaging and in part because of malign influence campaigning, Americans cannot agree on what that "adequate size" might be. Meanwhile, in a stark reminder of how much at cross-purposes international-level policies can be between the U.S. and other countries—driven by the differing motivations and emotions that shape state policies—we come back to some recent public declarations by Vladimir Putin: He considers nuclear weapons to be *usable battlefield tools*. Russia might launch them first in any big conventional armed conflict with NATO—triggering a *nuclear* conflict which Moscow believes it could then fight "to conditions of victory." Faced with this adversarial position, any American ought to think that an effective nuclear-deterrence arsenal, in the hands of leading democracies, is *essential as a survival tool*. Even if Mr. Putin is only bluffing when he states this reckless belligerent position, it is *only* our robust nuclear Triad that makes his statement be a bluff.

But as the *"No Nukes"* movement—active to this day through "Global Zero," "Nuclear Threat Initiative," "Ploughshares," and similar non-government organizations—has argued again and again over decades, America should completely disarm on the nuclear front, and should start this process right now, even unilaterally, as the only true route to security. Some United Nations member states—notably, those who do *not* themselves own any nukes—also keep trying to accomplish total world nuclear disarmament.

Arguing for the contrary, for the ongoing sustenance of nuclear-deterrence Triads, is the following *unassailable fact*: No nuclear weapons have ever been set off as a warshot *since the start of mutual superpower nuclear deterrence*, which latter event (upon the USSR attaining the A-bomb in 1949) is now past its *seventieth anniversary*—so far. But even this basic, inarguable historical fact, of total nuke war-shot abstinence for a whole human lifetime, is given conflicting, contradictory, controversial explanations, depending on whom in America (or elsewhere) you ask—in no small part due to mirror-imaging.

Some pundits and politicos, including persistent and vocal Western advocates of immediate and total American (and/or world) nuclear disarmament, have argued that there is, indeed, much more than just sheer chance or random luck to the cause-and-effect mechanism underlying this unbroken human lifetime of nuclear attack abstinence. But, they claim, this mechanism is *certainly not* that nuclear deterrence "works"—something that is, admittedly, hard to rigorously prove *or* disprove other than by surmise from empirical observation of actual history. Disarmament advocates foment instead what amounts to a different *untestable hypothesis*—untestable since the only way to test it properly would be for the U.S. to disarm unilaterally and thus *risk nuclear enslavement or even human extinction*. This latter wrong-headed, untestable theory is that nuclear weapons in war have gone completely unused for 70+ years simply because *they are completely unusable* and *everybody in the world thinks so*—because they are *so* devastating, *so* utterly immoral, and any use at all would trigger inevitable global Armageddon *and everyone on the planet knows it*.

If this un-usability belief were indeed held by all actual and potential owners and users/abusers of nuclear weapons, then complete worldwide nuclear disarmament could and should proceed *with dispatch*. This is because their (supposed) utter un-usability would render nukes quite irrelevant to human affairs—including irrelevant for their two (opposite) *non*-violent "uses," namely (aggressive) blackmail and (defensive) deterrence. And besides them being allegedly irrelevant, nuclear weapons, even if merely resting in inventory, are never entirely harmless. They might be subject to accidental or unauthorized detonation, perhaps after being tampered with or stolen by bad actors such as terrorists.

Worse, two nuclear powers might both, due to misunderstandings (or some other of the "Four Fatal Mis-es" mentioned above), or just through sheer ineptitude, blunder into a nuclear exchange that *neither of them wants*. First Cold War scholars invented a term for this phenomenon: *inadvertent nuclear war*. An entire professional literature on avoiding such things soon emerged, along with great impetus for foreign-relations studies devoted to the science of *negotiating theory* and the art of *conflict resolution*. Inadvertent nuclear war is a clear and present danger that requires eternal care and vigilance to avoid.

So, why hasn't America *already* gotten rid of all of our nukes? It is because our national leaders have understood that the danger of envelopment by and forced surrender to bloodthirsty foreign tyrants, were America to one-sidedly give up our nuclear deterrence arsenal, is a much more clear and much more present danger than inadvertent war, accidents, and/or terrorism. The preponderance of the relative probabilities—the *slim odds* of an accidental, inadvertent, or terrorist nuclear blast, compared to the *sure thing* of Russian and Chinese domination—tells us that we need to retain our effective Triad deterrent.

But what about *universal* nuclear disarmament? After all, nukes, even if never set off, are sources of very long-lasting, toxic nuclear pollution, from the start of uranium ore mining, through warhead manufacture, to any post-arms-reduction phases of scrapping and/or recycling as fission-reactor power plant fuel. Nuclear weapons' safety, security, proper maintenance, crew salaries and benefits, and manpower training, all need funding that might otherwise be spent on social programs, or on much "safer" (though also *much less effective*, hence in fact *much less safe*) conventional deterrence.

A good hint that the No Nukes crowd might be *falling for cultural mirroring* is that America's peer-competitor adversaries show *no sign whatsoever* of being interested in even discussing nuclear disarmament. The massive sums their national budgets keep devoting over decades to modernizing and expanding their nuclear arsenals disprove any suggestions by some Western analysts that these investments are *only bargaining chips to be sacrificed when disarming*. The tremendous sacrifices forced on their civilian populations' lifestyles and standards of living, along with the vast (and very expensive) apparatus of repression needed to suppress the resulting popular dissent, demonstrate those hostile regimes' commitments to permanently owning, and basing regime vitality and permanence on, their nuclear armaments.

A *compelling rejoinder* to nuclear-disarmament advocates' attempted justifications for anti-nuclear *U. S. Government defense-budget parsimony* is this: Without a dependable nuclear Triad deterrent-in-being, all of a democracy's laudable social programs—schools, hospitals, cultural appreciation, solving hunger and poverty, and the like—would soon be quashed completely by overbearing foreign dictatorships.

Why? Because nuclear-armed dictators would most assuredly *run amok* if America ever did get rid of our nuclear deterrent unilaterally, and they would certainly *covertly cheat* on any conceivable future multilateral (universal) nuclear disarmament treaty—assuming one could ever get ratified, to begin with.

Infamous recent history with Iraq, South Africa, Pakistan, Libya, North Korea, the USSR/Russia, and elsewhere has shown that a state can sometimes-to-often *hide* an entire nuclear armaments program *for years,* avoiding detection by U.S. intelligence agencies and UN weapons inspectors alike. *Willfully disobeying* arms-control treaties in secret is not impossible, either—Moscow is a long-habituated master at this. The most stringent, intrusive outside IAEA verifications ("Additional Protocols") might easily miss a few working nukes that were shrewdly hidden from disarmament tallies, especially if those weapons were dismantled into subcomponents and dispersed until the search for them died down; many states' nukes are in fact *designed* to be stored until needed as separate subassemblies, for safety and security.

It seems forgotten by over-enthusiastic anti-nuke advocates that, during the Nuclear Age's and First Cold War's overlapping early histories, many defense experts were concerned about cheating on nuclear-disarmament pacts: During international deliberations on the Baruch Plan (1946) and its subsequent offshoots, then POTUS Eisenhower's Atoms for Peace program (mid 1950s), and then the UN's nuclear Non-Proliferation Treaty's ratification (early 1970s), objections were raised that few (if any) countries would abide fully and honestly with any nuke elimination agreements. (Is such no-nuke thinking—that "history doesn't matter" to *anyone* just because it doesn't matter to *you*—one specific form of mirror-imaging?)

In short, today and tomorrow, cheaters easily could and certainly would conceal some of their nukes until America had altruistically disposed of all of ours. Then they would hold their weapons over our heads, and *freedom would face a losing fight for its life.*

Another Inconvenient Truth: A "Nuclear Monopoly" Enables, Even Encourages Nuclear Use

America's very own military history demonstrates a very inconvenient truth: *When only one state owns any nuclear weapons, they are in fact eminently useable despite (or even because of) their devastating effects on their intended targets.*

Nuclear weapons present such a *difference in degree* of destructive power compared to conventional weapons that they represent a *fundamental difference in kind*: Compared to the *"thousand-plane raids"* by Allied strategic bombers in World War II, a comparable, *near-total obliteration of a large area target*—such as an enemy city—could instead be achieved with *one* fission ("atomic") bomb, delivered by *just one plane.* Worse, once fusion ("hydrogen") bombs were invented, just one bomb on just one plane (or missile) could achieve the equivalent obliterating power of something that World War II strategic-bombing commanders could only dream about (in their wildest nightmares?): *a million-plane raid.*

If a monopoly on nuclear weapons exists, with all of them in the hands of just one country, alliance, bloc, or axis, they are such efficient instruments of death and destruction that to start a war, escalate a war, or end a war, they can be *very attractive* even to the leaders of a democracy. This is proven for all time by how the U.S., late in World War II, when it alone in the whole world possessed any working nuclear weapons, decided to exhaust its entire then-current inventory (of two fission weapons) against its incorrigible enemy, Imperial Japan, in order to force Tokyo's suicidal militaristic regime to surrender unconditionally. We did this, perhaps without even realizing it at the time, because *no one could retaliate against us in kind,* with their own nuclear weapons.

In today's and tomorrow's world, it is only America's unquestioned capacity, for *survivable (assured) nuclear retaliation* against an enemy that attacks us first with nukes, that protects us and our Allies against some enemy dictatorship, with a postulated monopoly on nuclear weapons, doing to us the same thing we did to Imperial Japan. This is proven by listing the horrible things that would not (could not) happen, in this thank-God-hypothetical scenario of a Russia or a China owning *all* the world's extant, working nuclear arms:

- The *immorality* of massive death and destruction would *not* deter that dictatorship, any more than it stopped the wartime U.S. Government from nuking Imperial Japan in 1945. In fact, although there were some lasting negative reputational repercussions to the Hiroshima and Nagasaki bombings, in the immediate sense America *did* achieve all its goals for those nuclear first-uses. Furthermore, earlier Allied conventional (incendiary bomb) firestorm attacks on Axis cities such as Dresden and Tokyo went ahead *despite* (because of?) the tremendous loss of life and property—which those maximum efforts by Allied bomber forces were *specifically intended* to inflict on the enemy. It is also worth mentioning here that the *moral qualms* famously expressed by some of the Manhattan Project scientists, such as Dr. Robert Oppenheimer, did *not* prevent Los Alamos from creating fission weapons in 1945 and then fusion weapons just a few years later.
- *Global blowback worries* such as massive nuclear fallout, nuclear winter, and nuclear summer (as per the *"Three Sources of Nuclear Danger"* from Chapter 3) would be *avoided,* because a

nuclear monopoly would allow the enemy's attack to remain assuredly limited in scope, with *no danger of uncontrolled "two-sided one-upmanship" nuclear escalation*. Such an adversary's whole nuclear-attack campaign could thus, assuredly, staying *well below* the threshold (of many hundreds of megatons) needed to cause a true nuclear-winter and then nuclear-summer catastrophe—while their controlled nuclear attacks would assuredly obliterate America and our Allies.

- The fact that our side could not retaliate with nuclear weapons, if we did not then own any, assures that the enemy's nuclear arsenal and its hardened nuclear command-and-control infrastructure would *remain immune* from retaliatory-nuking damage, thus *avoiding any uncontrolled spasm escalation caused by a triggering of the Intra-War Nuclear Unsafe-User Principle*.
- As discussed further below, the fact that *"life went on"* after the nuclear-fallout catastrophes of *Chernobyl and Fukushima* shows that, to a belligerent-enough dictatorial regime, the risk of their state receiving fallout from their own nuclear attack on us would *certainly not* be enough to deter them.

In summary, there is *nothing* "inherently unusable" about nuclear weapons. It is only *mutual nuclear deterrence* that renders them so. Therefore, it follows as a logical corollary that *seeking unilateral nuclear disarmament by America is not a good idea*. In addition, since in any global nuclear-disarmament effort there would surely be *cheating* by adversaries, who secretly hold onto some of their nukes to achieve a monopoly, *seeking global nuclear disarmament is not a good idea, either*.

Waiting for the whole world to somehow permanently "mellow out," in contradiction to Humankind's longtime track-record of intensifying cycles of industrialized state-on-state violence, might be a nice way for perennial optimists to occupy their time, while the realists among us busy ourselves sustaining effective nuclear deterrence.

Barring Effective Deterrence, Enemy Nuclear First-Use Options Are, Unfortunately, Legion

Worth summarizing for clarity here, the above arguments back and forth are familiar to folks who follow nuclear weapons policy-and-politics current events. These arguments are fine examples of the tensions and conflicts that can arise on the *domestic front*, out of cultural mirror-imaging about conditions and attitudes on the *international front*. An *inconvenient truth* arises, unfortunately, because *not everyone in the world agrees* that nuclear weapons can never and must never be *used in anger*, for either giga-death or blackmail. To fail to grasp the extent of this disagreement is a *perfect example of a mirror-imaging error* in the nuclear peacekeeping realm. It is an example of *failing to understand adversary psychology*, potentially as egregious as the failure of 1930s appeasers to see that the Nazis were, indeed, perfectly capable of perpetrating a multi-continent war and the Holocaust.

See Appendix 2 for a rather long list of different ways in which a belligerent-enough or desperate-enough dictatorial power could be tempted to *initiate a nuclear strike*, to accomplish some specific military and/or geopolitical objectives. This lengthy list shows that the price of too much mirror-imaging can be very dear: If America were to weaken, let alone entirely dismantle, our nuclear deterrent in the face of these multitudinous threats, we would no longer be able to deter such adversary first uses. We would not even have the option to retaliate in kind, after the fact, to try to restore a semblance of mutual deterrence, and to try to salvage some livable strategic stability from the radioactive ashes of our bases, our cities—and our freedom.

Don't Put Lipstick on this Pig, but We Do Need Nukes for Deterrence—and Peace-Restoration

The various complaints about the budget/financial/economic expense of owning nukes for deterrence disregard the vitally important, *truly priceless* role these weapons play in responsible hands as enforcers of nuclear peace—as potent *dissuaders* of nuclear war. Some anti-nuclear rhetoricians have tried to label America's nuclear deterrence posture as "nuclear blackmail" or even "nuclear terrorism," and they condemn nuclear deterrence as "relying on inevitable nuclear war-fighting." These commentators lose sight of three rather important, basic things:

> *First*, they lose sight that the fundamental principle of nuclear deterrence, for a democratic state, is to be fully prepared to dish out punitive retaliation in kind *only after* the offending adversary, *duly warned not to*, has in spite of our warnings, themselves first performed an overt act of *existential-level attack*. Such an attack, a severe threat to the very existence of the United States or our Allies (and, with it, world freedom) could come from nuclear weapons, or from an equally heinous assault via chemical, biological, or ultra-destructive electromagnetic-pulse or cyber weapons, or an overwhelming onslaught using massive conventional forces.

Second, anti-nuclear activists lose sight of a fundamental truth: *"If nukes were outlawed, only outlaws would have nukes."* But nuclear weapons are also an essential tool for "law enforcement" *against* such global outlaws. Nuclear deterrence works because it makes the punishment fit the crime. (This mechanism is *doubly* effective when *both* sides in a geopolitical rivalry each own *mutual* nuclear deterrents.) It is the solid potentiality of swift retribution, of truly Biblical proportions, *clearly communicated and committed to,* that powerfully discourages an adversary's nuking us and our Allies to begin with. Just as essential is the *parallel assurance* that if an adversary *refrains* from making any such attack against us, we will gladly reciprocate by *never* attacking them first, either.

Third: In the event that deterrence does fail, proportionate and discriminating retaliation by a defender (which is allowed under the United Nations Charter) helps limit further attacks being made on the defender by the attacker. In the case of nuclear weapons, especially if America follows the Tit-for-Tat retaliation paradigm of Chapter 3, it puts the monkey on the attacking enemy's back to promptly cease firing and negotiate peace. Nuclear retaliation, as an *exceedingly visible* measure when put in practice, also conclusively discourages any *nuclear copycats* from opportunistically adding to the carnage—either right away, and/or further into the future. A democracy's *always-evolving toolkit,* of responsible techniques for achieving a rapid nuclear cease-fire on politically acceptable terms, forms an *essential pillar* of effective deterrence posture. This is *peace restoration,* not the "war fighting" dreaded by deterrence-naysayers.

Since this three-point pro-deterrence logic is clear-cut and seems unassailable, at least to those officials and commentators who *do* support America's nuclear deterrence, one likely, at-least-partial explanation for the *persistent opposition* by nuclear-disarmament/Triad-budget-parsimony advocates is that *they are mirror-imaging* about (1) the domestic pro-deterrence advocates (perhaps *believing wrongly* that they are all "power-mad suicidal warmongers") and/or (2) the foreign nuclear-armed adversaries (perhaps *believing wrongly* that they really just want to be our friends).

Another Case in Point of Mirror-Imaging: Tactical Nukes on Our SSBNs

The excerpt-quote below was first published in my *INTERESTING (NUCLEAR) TIMES* e-newsletter, Issue 4 (20 June 2019). It is included here to give a *real-time working example* of how the research behind this book tried to make inroads in alleviating some of the deterrence policy controversies arising (in part) from American cultural mirror-imaging.

> Part of America's evolving nuclear-deterrence toolkit in 2019 and beyond should be a hard, pragmatic look at the need for a few low-yield (5 kiloton) tactical nuclear weapons deployed on our highly survivable SSBNs (strategic deterrent submarines). Their submarine-launched ballistic missiles (SLBMs) can deliver any warheads to distant intercontinental targets in barely 30 minutes—much faster than using bomber aircraft, and in certain deterrence scenarios this greater speed could be vital. This change, to one missile per sub, would *not* significantly reduce our *strategic* deterrent, now fielded on the aging fourteen subs of the Ohio class. Our strategic deterrent relies exclusively on thermonuclear warheads yielding roughly 100 or 500 kilotons each—up to *100 times as deadly and destructive* as the proposed tactical warheads.
>
> Later into the 2030s and beyond, our survivable undersea leg of the strategic deterrent Triad will still reside on the remaining fifteen MIRVed (Multiple Independently-targeted Reentry Vehicles) Trident II D-5 missiles aboard each of at least 12 Columbia-class submarines.
>
> This change *would* give the *additional option*, on one missile per sub, of retaliating with tactical nukes. This would more fully (and proportionately, discriminately) deter all conceivable nuclear-armed adversaries—by being able to hit back, in exact like kind, with *any* mix of high- and low-yield weapons that an enemy might decide to use against our vital interests first.
>
> *Russia owns many more tactical nukes than we do.* Our deterrence is incomplete unless we specifically dissuade them from ever putting into practice something that would be exceedingly dangerous to both them and us. This strategy, stated in their own public national defense posture, would be for them to use low-yield nukes to prosecute a "sub-H-bomb" conflict that they believe they can win. (We are badly handcuffed from retaliating with nukes at all, if we can only respond to a tactical nuclear attack with a strategic thermonuclear counter-blow; it would seem to signal on our part a desire to *drastically escalate the conflict.*)
>
> This need to plug a conspicuous gap in America's defensive arsenal is one more point where *avoidance of mirroring* becomes a crucial cog in the gears of our effective nuclear deterrence infrastructure. Our adversaries are not entirely averse to using nuclear weapons,

> to possibly taking huge casualties themselves in consequence, and they don't make the mistake of thinking all nuclear warheads are created equally horrific.
>
> How do we institute a culture that avoids our country acting as if all possible enemies think about nukes the same way some of us at home do? It is a matter of having the right open-ended, pro-diversity mindset, the right all-encompassing, opposition-force- (Red-Team-) and Devil's-Advocate-embracing "intellectual macro-culture." Then, using that mindset and culture, we must grasp that a very belligerent enemy might decide to tangle with us while holding two views we would never hold ourselves: a lack of aversion to massive own-side losses, and a hope to defeat us by willingly fighting in the nether "atomic bomb" region that lies between conventional conflict and the ultimate, inhuman horrors of all-out thermonuclear war.

The operant phrase at the end of this Newsletter quote, which *directly illustrates* the broader problem of mirror-imaging within the nuclear deterrence sphere, is where it says *we need to grasp* that adversaries might act badly "while holding two views we would never hold ourselves."

There is *also* mirroring involved in a related issue: Opponents of America's basing low-yield nukes on our SSBNs say that doing so would make our nuclear arsenal *too usable*, that this action would tempt us to *go first* in ever violating the "nuclear taboo." Here, opponents claim that an American president *would* think as our adversaries do—i.e., that low-yield nukes are "the same" as conventional bombs and bullets, that low-yield nukes can safely be used with no risk of escalation to thermonuclear holocaust. This claim *fails to perceive* how very aware every POTUS is made by his/her senior military advisors (such as STRATCOM) regarding (1) *the awful destructive effects* of even a "small" nuclear attack (and bear in mind that so-called low-yield/tactical nuclear weapons *do rival in power* the murderous, city-busting Hiroshima and Nagasaki bombs); (2) the *terrible risks of escalation* to thermonuclear Armageddon; (3) the deadly effects of globe-circling nuclear fallout; and (4) the human extinction event resulting from nuclear winter and then nuclear summer. (In a very real sense, POTUSes personally receive briefings with some of the *same "Three Sources of Danger" messaging* that Chapter 3 recommends be used to support nuclear counterterrorism.)

In early 2020, the U.S. Government confirmed that it *had* in fact recently begun to put low-yield nukes on one Trident missile aboard each U.S. Navy Ohio-class SSBN going out on deterrent patrol.

Another Case in Point of Mirroring: At Least *Some* Nuclear Terrorists *Can* Be Deterred

As was discussed in Chapter 3, it has been something of an article of faith to some, during the modern era of Islamic terrorism, that (proposition "A") nuclear terrorists are not subject to effective nuclear deterrence *because they are all totally suicidal*. This "fact" has even been used by some hardline anti-Triad advocates to admonish that (proposition "B") the U.S. should eliminate its entire nuclear arsenal unilaterally, immediately, to prevent terrorists from ever stealing and using an American nuke. But these conclusions are not entirely true—and such ill-advised admonishments arise to begin with, in part, due to mirror imaging. In the terms of symbolic logic, proposition A is *not* true, and proposition A does *not* imply proposition B; therefor proposition B is *definitely not proven*.

Where, then, did this false (and potentially dangerous) A-B one-two punch against Triad funding come from? I posit that it derives from one form of psychological mirror-imaging that some Western defense pundits fell into—and as always with mirror imaging, this falling-into mistake was *inadvertent and unrecognized* at the time. The mirroring error here was rather subtle: It was to think that by defense pundits simply modeling *the suicidal psyche of individual nuclear terrorists in isolation*, such pundits could derive reliable *aggregate* conclusions, ones that would apply just as well at the level of *entire belligerent social groups* as they do to *individual suicide-bombers*. What the pundits *forgot to take account of* in going from the small to the large were *decisive wider* societal motivational issues: family relationships (the "Lysistrata Effect" below), whole-of-group cultural identity pragmatism, survivable vice un-survivable community goals, and collective cognizance of the consequent aftermaths of over-drastic actions.

In effect, these pundits came to think about nuclear terrorists in overly simplistic terms, *in isolation at the very moment of attack*, as if they were just *suicide-bomb-vest wearers with very, very big bombs*. The pundits didn't consider the *wider implications*, to all Islamic society everywhere, of any use at all of nuclear weapons, anywhere, by Islamic terrorists.

The point here, which is not impossible to communicate to terrorist communities who don't already "get it," is that nuclear first uses *do* present, to *all* humanity *including all Islam*, a truly existential risk–of the extinction of our entire species, planetwide. The death of every Muslim and the wiping out of all Islamic culture cannot be in the interests of that religion, its adherents, their sought-after caliphates, and their Deity. In fact, this risk of extinction when conveyed clearly and dramatically (visually?) gives counterterrorism professionals important leverage to achieve good nuclear deterrence. The requisite risk messaging is based upon extremely relevant terms that terrorist-supporting social groups can be persuasively influenced by. This positive outcome can occur because those stark terms speak to the groups' most fundamental *fears* (utter defeat and total death)—while complying with deterrence(i.e., *being* deterred) much better supports their most cherished aspirations (a thriving, secure, respected modern Islamic multi-national community).

The failures of some defense analysts, to (1) have not recognized the *crucial difference/disconnect in perspectives and objectives* when passing in scale and scope from the *spear-carrier individual* to the *decision-making collective*, and then to (2) have not factored that disconnect usefully into their counterterror strategy-study findings, is an example of *mirror-imaging* according to the broad definition (above) that I am using in this book.

Do Not Forget, Ignore, or Downplay the Value of the "Lysistrata Effect"

This oversimplified "leap of faith" directly from *individual suicidal terrorist behaviors* on the one hand, to supposed *aggregate community motivations and goals* on the other hand, without adjusting for the *discontinuity* in scale and scope, misses the complete picture of *exploitable nuclear-deterrence social-psychological dynamics*. The mirror-imaging mistake in this syllogism (train of logic) is to forget that, even among a foreign, medievalist, religious-fundamentalist group devoted to the fall of Western civilization, *the whole is not just the simple sum of some of the parts.*

In summary, no individual terrorist mullah's or rogue-state despot's power is truly infinite. Restraint among an overly belligerent leader's top lieutenants and their enablers, *against committing the ultimate crime against humanity of extincting the entire species*, really does matter as a shaper of operational results/effects. And as Aristophenes dramatized in his anti-war play *Lysistrata* in 411 BCE, lieutenants' and generals' *families* matter too. (Generals' wives withheld their affections, to successfully persuade their husbands to cancel plans for ill-advised aggression.)

As detailed in Chapter 3, many people—in the chain of command or behind the scenes—are involved to get from ordering any nuclear strike to actually carrying it out. Like an electrical circuit, or a railroad track, *one break in the line* can be enough to stop nuclear weapon delivery. This is especially true on the part of terrorist organizations, which lack the checks-and-balances, deeply inculcated discipline and loyalty, and multiple redundancies of Peer-Competitor-level state nuclear establishments. (American military professionals, in dramatic contrast to terrorists and rogues, are thoroughly indoctrinated on the distinction between a legal order and *an illegal order*; they are trained to refuse *illegal* ones. A justified *retaliatory* nuclear strike, duly ordered by POTUS after some enemy strategic-level attack on our vital interests, would be recognized throughout STRATCOM as *legal*, and duly implemented.)

This *"Lysistrata Effect"*—a successful intervention against excessive belligerence, by concerned family members—though imperfect and not guaranteed, should not be dismissed outright. It can provide another valuable layer to the *overall layered defenses*, already recognized (and diligently implemented) by experts as essential to preventing nuclear terrorism. A keen, piercing appreciation of *discontinuities between small- and large-scale adversary psychology*, shared within our defense establishment, and a targeted process of *communication and education* about deterrence, directed at all relevant levels of *adversary societies* by all of our foreign-relations capabilities, are essential parts of sustaining nuclear peace.

How to help deter nuclear terrorists, and whether to deploy low-yield nukes on SSBNs, can be seen as case studies in *problem solving for more-effective nuclear deterrence*, via the technique of *"applied mirror-imaging avoidance."*

More Applied Mirror-Imaging Avoidance: Putin's Nuclear Blackmail Threats Are Bluffs

The exposition above, of how POTUS's advisors would graphically articulate to him/her how low-yield nukes are definitely *not* "easily usable" in an unprovoked first strike, is quite likely "mirrored" in the cautions likely expressed privately, by their own experts, to adversary peer-competitor heads-of-state such as Vladimir Putin and Xi Jinping, and possibly also to adversary rogue-state leaders such as Kim Jong Un and Ayatollah Khamenei. If this is the case, then in particular Russia's various recent *nuclear intimidation attempts*, along with their supposed *"escalate to deescalate"* strategy, are really just *"dual-use bluffs"* designed to (1) frighten Western audiences, while at the same time (2) justifying Moscow's sizable nuclear-weapons budget to its own long-economically-suffering, now-restive citizenry, in both cases by posing these ultra-expensive armaments-in-being as "genuinely useable."

This same *bluff strategy* is also very likely the basis of Russia's claim, in summer 2020, that they would view any and all ballistic missiles launched against them as being nuclear armed. To launch a nuclear counterstrike, before verifying (by the incoming missile's detonation) that it was actually nuclear tipped, would be to commit national suicide—and Russia surely knows this.

A wise and effective U.S./NATO counter-strategy, for dealing with such belligerent *nuclear bluffs,* is to politely ignore them, sidestepping direct confrontation *without* being intimidated. America should then carry on with the nation's normal business of *sustaining solid and robust nuclear deterrence*—such as installing some low-yield warheads on US Navy SSBNs.

Even More Mirroring-Avoidance: Nuclear Deterrence Workers Should Be Well Supported

One insidious form of mirror imaging is to imagine that your own *ill-founded fears and hatreds* of another group are actually justified by the motivations and intentions of that group, when in reality that group's desires and goals are *completely benign, even beneficial to you.* A way this sort of *misguided psychological projection* takes place *in American society is by the paranoid reviling, within anti-nuke pop culture, of both* uniformed and civilian nuclear-deterrence practitioners. The people who study and carry out our nuclear deterrence have been repeatedly (mis-) characterized in pejorative terms as "Dr. Strangelove types," as "wizards of Armageddon," as "trigger-happy nuclear warfighters," or worse.

In reality, sustaining an effective national nuclear-deterrent infrastructure is a serious and weighty duty, requiring great commitment and personal sacrifice. It is about proactively preserving human life, *not* reactively dealing mega- or giga-death. As such, studying the subject should be seen by our nationwide society and our higher-educational system as *laudable and essential.* As just one good example of a multidisciplinary arena for researching and developing cogent new theories and modern best practices, it forms a key aspect of beneficially applying America's national prowess in Science, Technology, Engineering, and Math (STEM)—as well as our leadership in the "softer" sciences (such as psychology and marketing) and in the humanities (such as history and theology). This broad effort *deserves support, not denigration* within our national defense budget, proportionate to the indispensable "deliverables" that such effort can contribute to our society and to the world–lasting and reliable nuclear peace.

Dissipating any paranoia about the good intent and noble aims of U.S. Nuclear Triad leaders and crews, to help dispel fears some folks share concerning our Military's vital deterrence mission, deserves a bit of discussion, in the vein of applied mirror-imaging avoidance:

> We can demonstrate the genuine value of our Triad logically, via a simple "thought experiment"—one that involves recognizing how an adversary's *perspectives* on preserving human life (or *not* preserving it) might *differ drastically* from our own good intentions. (Domestic and international mirroring-avoidance do overlap here!) Posit some future aggressor against which our nuclear deterrence would fail. If our nuclear deterrence were ever to fail, resulting in the aggressor's nuclear attack, consider how *very intensely belligerent* that hypothetical nuclear aggressor against American vital interests would have to be. And if our nuclear deterrence against them failed, then *conventional deterrence* against their nukes would certainly fail. Knowing this, and allowing for the adversary's craving to unilaterally own nukes as a source of *ultimate God-like power on Earth*, Americans should come to clearly see that this adversary would *surely disobey or cheat* on any worldwide nuclear disarmament plan.
>
> With many governments either (1) facing the *mere latent potential* for such a hypothesized *nightmare aggressor*, or (2) themselves *embodying* the bad actors who *crave* such aggression, any total world nuclear disarmament plan, no matter how well meant and idealistic, would fall apart from the outset. *Denying that such nightmare aggressors do or might exist is a form of psychological mirroring that amounts to wishful thinking bordering on the delusional.*
>
> Imagine a world in which some intensely belligerent entity, possessing nukes, could run rampant, unopposed except by conventional arms—the biggest of which would be only a *thousandth or a millionth as potent* as said belligerent's *individual* A-bombs or H-bombs. You say you'd *rather not* envision such an appalling world, for you or your kids or your grandkids? Frankly, neither would I.
>
> A good way to start a practical *"to do list,"* to correct for such mirroring errors, is this: Make very sure that America's voters, and our elected/appointed officials, *robustly support* continuing national investment in STEM education and STEM-related job training for our students and our workers. Only in this way can We the People be sure that our government is able to sustain the prowess and leadership in nuclear deterrence and nuclear peacekeeping that our precious freedom needs and certainly deserves. (Volume 2 of this book will have an entire chapter devoted to sustaining STEM primacy as an essential backbone of nuclear peacekeeping.)

Mirroring Can Impact Treaty Negotiations, and Treaty Compliance too

Arms-control treaty compliance is challenging to verify and will always be subject to covert cheating (especially by suicidal or nihilistic terrorists, callous criminals, and sociopath dictators—all of whom definitely do *not* share our own ways of thinking). Necessarily invasive nuclear arms-control treaty compliance verification processes are *very expensive*, and as seen with Iran and North Korea these processes really do *require host cooperation*; at best verification effectiveness will always be *vulnerable* to the good guys' bureaucratic inertia and infighting, to their budget cuts during times of austerity, and to their tendency—like all humans—to complacency. At worst, emerging ways to deceive IAEA sensors and surveillance cameras, new deep-underground covert bunker construction methods, emerging "deep fake" video techniques, and other artificial-intelligence-based *dissembling methods* yet to even be contemplated, *will enable ever-more-serious* cheating, rendering arms-control and disarmament treaty-compliance enforcement moot altogether.

(As mentioned elsewhere, perfection of *commercial/civilian "hot" fusion power* would help solve world energy shortages safely and cleanly, while *"diverting"* countries away from the fission-power expertise and infrastructure that studies show are *leading enablers* of proliferation to nuclear weapons.)

As of this writing in early 2021, New START is still in effect and requires both Russia and the U.S. to allow nuclear arms inspectors to enter each other's relevant facilities to check treaty compliance "on the ground." New START is due to expire in February 2021; it is vital, in avoiding a wasteful, dangerous new warhead-count arms race, that its limits at least be tacitly obeyed by both sides, until a new treaty can be negotiated and possibly include other countries such as China. Yet *Russia, like the USSR before it,* has not always obeyed arms-control treaties once it ratified them: *They cheat, a lot.* Examples include their ignoring the Nixon/Brezhnev ban on biological weapons, then blatantly violating the ban on MIRVing land-based ICBMs, and more recently cheating on the Intermediate-Range Nuclear Forces Treaty (INF) and the Open Skies Treaty. America *withdrawing* from an arms-control treaty due to Russia cheating, as has happened several times, is at best a pyrrhic victory: It does "impose negative consequences" on the cheater, but only after the fact, and only nominally/mildly at best. At worst, our adversary gets exactly what they want from the lapse of the treaty.

China has declined to participate in any serious nuclear arms-control discussions at all.

The beliefs that either of our Near-Peer Competitor adversaries (1) *share* America's seeming (notorious?) craving to consummate disarmament treaties no matter what—even at the cost of merely symbolic provisions, and/or with disadvantageous terms for U.S. interests—and that they then (2) *mimic* our tendency to obey such "bad" treaties quite honestly, form another cluster of mirror-imaging errors in American foreign policy and national defense.

One More Time: It's Only *Our* Deterrent Arsenal that Makes *Their* Nukes "Unusable" to Them

Ironically, it is only the possession of a strong, survivable nuclear deterrent by the forces of freedom—creating the ultimate, unavoidable risk that any calculatedly "limited" enemy attack could inadvertently escalate to radioactive Armageddon followed by global nuclear winter and summer—which creates the *belief* by some in America that adversary nukes are "unusable." *Take away* democracy's nuclear deterrent, or *reduce it* to an ineffective minimum, and adversary nukes could (would?) in fact be *used with abandon*, with only acceptably negative consequences (if any) to that attacker—and/or to the evil copycats sure to follow their ugly example.

(*Proportionate* nuclear retaliation, in and of itself, might *not* be effectively deterring enough to an adversary that is *very much not* casualty averse—ala the next Mao, Castro, or Hitler. It is the *truly existential threat* to the attacker him/herself, of likely-unavoidable Geophysical Wipeout triggered by their own unprovoked nuclear first use, which provides an *essential added layer of compelling protection* to the whole "nuclear-war-danger package.")

The credible threat of effective nuclear retaliation is thus foundational, nay *indispensable* to preserving world nuclear peace. Without that threat, an adversary's nukes can in fact be eminently usable—up to a point that would be *utterly catastrophic* for democracy: There is a rather large intensity to a one-sided nuclear attack required for it to produce *true global nuclear winter and summer*. Below that terrible threshold—*several hundred megatons or more* detonated in the open air on land—local ecological catastrophes would abound, but (1) global hard freezes and months-long, famine inducing sunless/moonless/starless 24-hour darkness, along with (2) destruction of Earth's protective ozone layer leading to subsequent killing daytime hard-UV overdoses, would *not* occur.

Hundreds of megatons ever actually *used* against America and our Allies would reduce us and our various civilized national cultures to *irrecoverable oblivion*.

To repeat here for emphasis, doing away with our nuclear deterrent unilaterally, due to exaggerated fears of our own Triad, would leave America wide open to the 100.0% risk of domination by a nuclear-armed enemy dictatorship. Sustaining our Triad deterrent is a very smart tradeoff, a grim necessity due to mankind's *incorrigibly aggressive, occasionally sociopathic nature*—and an unavoidable consequence of inevitable human technological progress, coupled to our universe's physical laws which say that nuclear weapons are possible at all.

Logical Discipline and An Open Mind Can Help Prevent Mirror-Imaging

To mirror-image, or perhaps more tellingly "to commit mirror-imaging," is very much a part of human nature—especially, it seems, for Americans. This is perhaps because our world leadership in creating a modern democracy (1776), followed by more leadership as the twice-successful Arsenal of Democracy (two world wars) and (even despite COVID-19 recession effects) the world's biggest economic powerhouse, leaves us thinking that our preconceived notions are inherently right and proper. I think they are too, but mirror-imaging is something else.

It takes tremendous self-discipline and mental effort to remain always cognizant of how vast the gulf can be between values, precepts, goals, and creeds of different groups of human beings all around our very populous and complicated planet.

Dehumanizing other groups because they are feared minorities, or are the despised enemy, just serves to make cultural mirroring even worse. It makes those "out group" members seem to be *objects*, not people, i.e., to be inanimate *things*. As such, they are fantasized to not have any thoughts and feelings at all, let alone thoughts and feelings that need to be thoroughly understood (though not agreed with) to effectively influence their behavior and avoid mutual tragedy.

Perhaps this requisite discipline and effort are best sustained in any large American or Allied organization by having culturally and ethnically diverse co-workers backing up one another, on polyglot planning and melting-pot strategy *teams*, under particularly insightful, inclusive leadership—of the sort the U.S. military has learned it needs to strive for.

Sidestepping that disciplined work, by simply *demonizing an adversary*, provides few useful insights and effective action plans, if any, for how best to productively, positively influence adversary behavior for *good own-team outcomes*—short of declaring war and *killing all the adversaries*. Sometimes, of course, as in World War I and World War II, precisely this is the necessary and appropriate strategy. But in the *nuclear-armed modern world,* talking is very much preferred to fighting against any adversary with a sizeable, deliverable nuclear arsenal.

Strong deterrence readiness and savvy engagement dialogue, practiced *together,* comprise the wisest course today and tomorrow. Effective deterrence and productive engagement are the very anathemas of blind mirror-imaging and dehumanizing objectification.

Diving Deeper: Unrecognized, Overlooked, or Neglected Differences Can Cause Mirror-Imaging

There are a large number of *sources or causes* of the many potential differences between different peoples' viewpoints, aspirations, or habits, and their perception-forming, conclusion-reaching, and decision-making processes. These traits, these "ways of doing business"—which some defense analysts call the *operating code* of those peoples—help shape whatever specific package of *warnings, inducements, threats, promises, and compromises* might best influence them diplomatically, militarily, and economically, i.e., overall-geopolitically. This is true in all aspects of life, not just on the topic of nuclear weapons and deterrence.

These variations within and between different social groups derive from the many permutations and combinations possible among the *numerous parameters* that characterize any complex human community. Those parametric differences include varying economic systems of the group (for example, communism or market socialism or capitalism?) and socio-economic status of its individuals (rich or middle class or poor?); different demographic characteristics (male or female? young or old? fit or disabled?); different political systems (democracy or dictatorship or a hybrid?) and relative political power and influence (privileged, engaged, or disenfranchised?); different natural resource-, education-, and technology-access (abundance or scarcity?); and different ecological/meteorological environments (mild or harsh? hot or cold? arid or damp? thriving or threatened?). Different concepts of "my nation" and of that nation's culture and history–including *its military history, its proud achievements (as self-perceived), and its lasting beefs with others*—are also formative of geopolitical conduct.

Effective Nuclear Deterrence Cannot Sidestep Issues of Human Psychology and Sociology

Two very important sources of differences, together, make implicit mirroring treacherous indeed, for all governments and citizens involved on *both* sides of any interaction distorted by that mirroring. The interaction/outcome might, for instance, be the especially critical fork in the road between successful deterrence leading to peace, or a failure of deterrence leading to war. These two sources are differences in: (1) *interpersonal* (social) behaviors pertaining to *culture*, and in (2) *internal* (personal) emotions and choices pertaining to *psychology*. Both of these topics, sociology (social anthropology) and psychology (clinical psychiatry), represent vast areas of study in the theoretical and the clinical realms. But in managing international relations for peace and prosperity, they are neglected at any diplomat's, military advisor's, or politician's peril.

While many cultural differences are reasonably open to study by sociologists and anthropologists, *psychological differences are not so easy to fathom* decisively and accurately. This is because outward cultural differences such as language(s), manner of dress, available transportation modes and infrastructure (such as, donkey cart or maglev train), preferred architectural styles and available building materials (glass skyscrapers or mud-brick houses), local cuisine (ingredients, cooking methods, even table manners), and religious observances—as alien as these sometimes appear to be to visitors/outsiders—are evident to any reasonably attentive observer.

But psychological differences are *largely invisible*, and often—for nefarious purposes—they lurk within a devious adversarial subject's thoughts, *stubbornly disguised*, at least until a highly trained, objective psychologist's prolonged face-to-face observation and probing of the subject can eke them out. Even with such skills and tools brought to bear on a clinical or criminal case (including *a war criminal or terrorist*), a subject's true motivations and intentions can remain rather murky and speculative. (This is one reason why *complete and current eavesdropping intelligence* on adversary leadership's—and followership's—unfettered communications, with one another, is so important to what the Pentagon calls *Indications and Warnings* of enemy attack. Such revealing intel amounts to direct and candid *quasi-internal observation* of the persons of interest—at least, once adjusted for enemy spoofing or counter-intel disinformation "plants.")

Many wars might have been prevented altogether, or at least ended on a more lasting, positive basis, had one or both sides involved not committed mirror-imaging (and demonizing) while conceptualizing about each other. Examples range from the American Revolution to the Vietnam War and beyond. It is very difficult to know what an adversary who must be deterred is really thinking, and *how* they will actually behave. It is also very difficult for an adversary needing to be deterred—and needing to deter *you*—to know what you are really thinking, and how *you* will actually behave.

One seeming advantage enjoyed by practitioners of specifically *nuclear* deterrence is that the weapons are *so starkly destructive*, and the consequences of their use *so immensely threatening* to sheer human survival, that unambiguous interlocution between deterrer and deterree *ought to be inherently straightforward*. Why, then, is the history of relations between nuclear powers so *fraught with misunderstandings and crises*?

In the real world, no one can read minds, and no one has a crystal ball. Chronic liars tend to also be very distrustful people; your own honest statements, that you make to them, will not be heard as credible by them. Wishful thinking, distortions by domestic political agendas, even occasional intellectual laziness, contribute to this dangerous *"fog of peace."*

To mirror unduly about adversary opinions concerning nuclear-weapon usability and nuclear-retaliation effectiveness in the 21st century could have terrible consequences. To weaken national nuclear-deterrence readiness and potency, as a result of such mirroring, could very well put us all on the *slippery slope* to the nuclear Armageddon that Americans and our friends and partners worldwide all want to avoid. (The importance of human psychology to effective nuclear deterrence is the subject of an entire chapter in this work's upcoming Volume 2.)

Zeroing in on "the Problem of Mirror-Imaging" vis a vis Effective Nuclear Deterrence

Effective nuclear deterrence is something that, fundamentally, needs to occur in the minds of the adversaries to be deterred. *Only they* can form the decision that they shall refrain from attacking because of their fear of the net negative consequences to them and to their goals of making a nuclear attack. As a consequence, *deterrence is an inherently psychological process*. The most brilliant planning and policies, and strongest concrete measures, taken by a state to protect *itself*, by establishing a "good" system of deterrence against adversaries, will all come to naught if those adversaries, *in their own minds*, decide to attack despite what the *defender* perceives as the "obvious" unacceptable net negative consequences to the attacker of doing so.

The *adversary's* own overall evaluation of attack-related odds, near-term and longer-term goals and objectives, cost/benefit tradeoffs and effects, gain/loss tallies, and other absolute and relative estimates, forecasts, and projected outcomes, might lead them to believe—even if falsely—that they will (or at least *might*) achieve more than they sacrifice by some atrocious act of nuclear belligerence. The state trying to protect itself can attempt to influence these important adversary cognitive perceptions via conducting proactive diplomacy, promulgating educational information, issuing pro-peace propaganda, and/or conducting visible military-preparedness exercises, even holding public displays of *deterrence-readiness strength* and, by implication, *national will*. The latter could include televised public military parades, conspicuous personnel drills, and *in extremis* even (as North Korea has done in recent years) conducting detectable underground nuclear tests. But ultimately the decision whether to attack a defender (such as the U.S. or our Allies) is up to the prospective enemy, *not* the defending state.

As a result of this, a state's fundamental duty to *engineer and maintain* a good system of nuclear deterrence, as part of its overall national defense apparatus, is inherently subject to the *pitfalls* of cultural and psychological mirror imaging. This mirroring is always at work, insidiously, in *both* directions (since our adversaries mirror-image too). This is so even within the *implicit cooperation* behind any stable, mutual nuclear deterrence situation between two or more near-peer-competitor nuclear-armed states.

When push comes to shove, just because your own best judgment tells you that your deterrence is sound and your adversaries ought to feel the same, the adversaries might in fact *feel differently*. They might, conceivably, find your deterrence *even more effective* than you thought, and handle you at all times with figurative kid gloves, even showing you appeasement. But they might on the other hand see your deterrence as *less effective* than you thought, or even as *ineffective altogether* against them. They might, in error, *underestimate your will to retaliate in kind*, leading them to confidently make a nuclear attack against you. Your nuclear retaliation, which you yourself *never for a moment doubted* would occur if ever needed, would then come as a terrible shock to them—but only *after* it was *too late* for them to reconsider. The results of such an outcome would be tragic indeed for *everybody: Armageddon.*

Nuclear deterrence should never be taken for granted, and should never be bad-mouthed and neglected as "recidivist" or "old fashioned" or "a First Cold War relic." It should *never* be shortchanged in favor of illusory short-term budget savings, which only open up avenues for some adversary's belligerent aggression (nuclear or, more likely, heightened proxy/regional conventional and/or cold-war-style pervasive "hybrid" aggression).

One even has to wonder, in this era of fake news and malign-influence attacks galore, how much of nuclear disarmament talk in the West is directly or indirectly reflective of adversary disinformation warfare against the security interests of democracies. And given modern money-laundering "technologies," one has to wonder how much of the funding for sincere Western unilateral nuclear disarmament movements actually originates unknown to them in Moscow or Beijing—or even in Pyongyang or Tehran.

In a previous chapter, I referenced President Teddy Roosevelt speaking about deterrence in terms of what in his day were the world's most powerful, mobile weapons systems. He said, *"Battleships are cheaper than battles."* We might paraphrase him today by saying *"Nuclear deterrence is cheaper than nuclear war, and a heck of a lot cheaper than post-nuclear-war reconstruction—with mass burials beyond counting."*

Mirror-Imaging Can Be Mitigated, Because (Again) Forewarned Is Forearmed

To avoid the deadly pitfalls of *deterrence denigration* (i.e., deterrence parsimony and neglect), *proper cognition* is essential by *both* (1) those to be protected against attack, *and* (2) those to be convinced to never attack. Such vital cognitive awareness, if ever weakened or lost, must be swiftly *regained, retained, and refined,* regarding all the ins and outs of the cause-and-effect mechanics underlying safe, sound, truly effective nuclear deterrence.

If two states in a position of mutual rivalry and competitive distrust *both* seek to deter each other, then all these processes go on *in both directions at once.* This does not alter the fundamentals, although it produces more factors and variables to keep track of. Such *mutuality* probably *improves* the effectiveness of deterrence in each direction, since each party has the opportunity to observe the other's deterrence establishment, both overtly and covertly, *noting and learning* from comparisons and contrasts between the two approaches. Further, each party's military experts are forced to most keenly understand *both* operant points of view, that of the deterrer *and* that of the deterree. Mutual effective deterrence is inherently stabilizing, because the security of well-conceived and well-implemented deterrence postures *dispels undue paranoia* in both directions simultaneously.

Proper safeguards for survivability of both side's own deterrence forces allow a sense of security on *both* sides. Some inevitable minor disagreements allow for a bit of *saber rattling* while respecting *nuclear taboo-and-norm "guard rails,"* letting the competitors test each other, "let off steam," and court unaligned states who might choose sides—but without unbalancing the coherent whole.

Theoretical research and plain common sense, in an ideal situation, ought to guide both parties to avoid deterrence tactics that can be too destabilizing. These *"worst practices"* include (1) having only non-survivable nuke weapons systems, forcing exceedingly reckless launch-on-warning rules of engagement (ROEs), or (2) creating overly tempting targets for *preemptive attack,* by heavily MIRVing one's land-based ICBMs, or (3) deploying mobile ICBM launchers near or in cities, inviting a "counter-force" barrage that amounts to a tremendously murderous "counter-value" barrage, too.

When one party goes for destabilizing the world nuclear-arms balance via their hardware and/or procedural changes, as Putin's Russia has done with *land-based MIRVs* and *ground-launched IRBMs* and *mobile ICBMs*—and more recently with his boasting of long-range *drone submarines* and *nuclear-powered cruise missiles*—the other party (the U.S. and NATO) should see this as what it is: callous attempts at *nuclear blackmail,* and calculated attempts to sow friction and dissent for its own sake—by a *disruptive enemy of good world order and democracy.* The best, wisest, safest response to such fear-factor coercive tactics is to *refuse* to join in any *destabilizing, wasteful arms race,* while ensuring that America's and NATO's adequate, effective, and Best Practices-based nuclear forces remain *fully ready and well sustained.*

Diplomatic containment, flexible and modernized deterrent forces (within New START limits even if the treaty is not renewed), plus more-stringent *economic sanctions*—and *in extremis,* withdrawing from a treaty that the other side insists on violating—are also proper responses. What is definitely *not* the best counter-move to Russia by the US/NATO alliance is any *inflation* in the size of our strategic nuclear warhead counts (H-bomb inventory)—unless the future global threat environment is *significantly different from today's.* The persistent Russian treaties-cheating and norm-busting behaviors should also make it abundantly clear to U.S. policymakers and budgeteers that America "going first" *with any further cuts* to our deterrent arsenal size and readiness is *a very unwise course indeed.*

It never hurts to remind the world that the *surety of swift retaliation,* with its ever-present danger of escalating to Armageddon, working *both* ways, puts *helpful dampers* on crises and *discourages* major acts of conventional aggression or of successful nuclear blackmail. And because with *mutual* nucler deterrence *each* side gets to be *both* the deterrer and the deterree, it can be a lot easier to appreciate the all-important *other guy's perspectives* as *both* the deterree and the deterrer.

The most important thing is to *not* assume that the other guy's perspective is, underneath his saber-rattling and attempted blackmail threats, *the same* as your own. As discussed below, American democracy's and Russian dictatorship's experiences (or lack thereof) of *existential conventional invasion*, and of resulting *scorched-earth strategic defenses*, in both World Wars I and II, are *so fundamentally different* that we certainly *cannot* safely conclude that Mr. Putin "doesn't meant it" about using his nukes to "win" a war against NATO. Nor can we safely assume that if we dismantled our nuclear arsenal in a sign of friendship, he would follow suit.

What We Mean Here by Nuclear Weapon "Use"

One key variable in the dynamic, pushing-and-shoving contest of ideas that shapes deterrence effectiveness (or the lack thereof) is a comparison between the defending and potentially-attacking parties' different belief systems as to *nuclear weapon usability or un-usability*.

First, we need to make a *semantic distinction*: nuclear weapons can be said to have three fundamentally different "uses":

- for *deterrence*, as weapons-in-being backing up retaliation threats,
- for *blackmail*, accompanied by intimidating messaging about possible use,
- for *attack*, by actually detonating them on a defender's target(s).

There is also a *potential fourth use*, as was (1) discussed with POTUS Truman before the Hiroshima and Nagasaki bombings, and as was (2) used by both sides during the Cold War. This fourth use is for *signaling*, via a *demonstration* or a *test*. A military "demonstration" amounts to a *very serious warning*, setting off a weapon *relatively harmlessly yet near to and directly visible from enemy territory* (such as was considered for Imperial Japan's Tokyo Bay, but was rejected in favor of an actual attack on Hiroshima). A messaging (as opposed to purely scientific/engineering) *test* is less aggressive than a demonstration, detonating the weapon on one's *own* territory, but also sends a *pointed message* to adversaries (as the USSR did in a "strategic comeback gesture" after its setback in the 1960ish Berlin Crises, using its tremendous open-air *57-megaton* King Bomb test in 1961).

This fourth use was put in abeyance by all the major nuclear powers with the end of the Cold War, as per the *norm against any full-up nuclear weapon tests* established by the *Comprehensive Test Ban Treaty* (CTBT)—which the U.S. has not ratified and which has not taken effect worldwide. Rogue state North Korea has, as of early 2021, violated the CTBT norm on six occasions. The U.S. alleges that Russia and China have also violated the CTBT norm recently, via extremely-low-yield underground test blasts which are very difficult to detect.

For clarity, in the further discussion below, by "use" and "usability" of nuclear weapons we mean, specifically, in the narrowest sense of *actually setting them off in attacks.*

Nuclear Usability/Un-usability Belief Systems Are Not All Simply Nothing or Everything

Returning to a general discussion of mirror-imaging, different beliefs about whether nuclear weapons are "usable" or not, in different situations of combat offense or defense, derive from the sum total of all the myriad differences, *ranging from the identified to the unidentifiable,* between individuals and groups in the world population. It seems fair to say that usability and un-usability viewpoints thus lie along a *spectrum*—just as does the range of potential effects of different types of nuclear weapons potentially used to attack an enemy in different ways, in different places, in different numbers, for different specific military purposes, in different imaginable future geopolitical scenarios.

In other words, nuclear weapon usability belief and its opposite, un-usability belief, are not either-or absolutes. *Everything is relative.* It will be beneficial to 21st century effective nuclear deterrence theory, and Best Practice development, to pick apart these *various "relativities,"* and sweat the details of what makes each such phenomenon tick.

There is a Crucial Binary Distinction in Nuclear Deterrence

There is a very important binary distinction about nuclear usability, and usage, regarding *who sets one off first,* or (equivalently) *who commits first some other existentially-threatening act of strategic aggression.* A person or a state might rightly believe that, whereas it is (1) *utterly unacceptable* for them (*and anyone else*) to make an unprovoked detonation of a nuke in anger or even just in a test (barring some overwhelming existential threat), rather it is (2) not merely acceptable but in fact *necessary* for them to, in advance, declare the righteousness and the full intention of going *second,* to sustain nuclear deterrence via the promise of nuclear retaliation—*and then exercise that right to retaliate, if ever need be.*

(*Counter-proliferation efforts* can sometimes lead to *seeming doctrinal contradictions* here—or even to a much resented *"haves vs have-nots"* global system re nuclear-weapons ownership—when states that *do* own nuclear-deterrence arsenals *seek to deny* nukes to currently non-nuclear-weapons-owning states. See Chapter 7 for a discussion of how this contradiction might be constructively resolved: View nuke-ownership as *the weighty deterrence/peacekeeping responsibility of a dutiful few*, each of which must pass extremely high qualification hurdles, rather than as a privilege or right that should be open to anyone, without any standards of training, attitude, and teamwork. An analogy will be drawn to persons who serve as their community's First Responders: "Not every kid can grow up to be a cop or a firefighter.")

As embodied in our current National Nuclear Posture Report—and despite naysayers' sensationalized allegations to the contrary concerning POTUS Trump versus Kim Jong Un alluding to "fire and fury" *vis a vis* "seas of fire"—the U.S. clearly *does* make this essential binary distinction as to who goes first vice who goes second using nuclear arms. We would *never* nuke first without being sorely provoked by *severe* enemy aggression; we *would* nuke second in retaliation for a strategic attack. And as embodied in its own public statements of nuclear posture, Russia is clearly implying that it might indeed nuke *first* during armed conflict with NATO which it might in fact have started *itself*. (There is ample room in both country's posture positions for some *"weak form" strategic ambiguity* here, although some of it is perhaps being caused, not intentionally, but via *ill-considered* and/or *poorly-drafted* official statements—or by more-than-borderline *attempted-coercive "nuclear diplomacy."*)

It does behoove the U.S. and other free, peace-loving nations to understand deeply the implications of this *"who nukes first"* binary distinction. The *asymmetry* between democracy and tyranny arises from the ways in which a dictatorship can intentionally or unintentionally distort basic realities (as democracies see them) to serve its expansionist, repressive political and geopolitical purposes. Certainly, those totalitarian purposes include *propaganda* and *psychological warfare*, both *domestic* (inward focused, at the dictator's own citizens) and *foreign* (outward focused, at American and Allied audiences).

The conundrum underlying this is fundamental: Nuclear postures are statements using words, *not* attacks using nukes, and—again—*"weak form" strategic ambiguity* prevails as to (1) what is being said, (2) what is at present really *intended*, and (3) what in practice (during a nuclear crisis, or conventional or even nuclear war) would/will actually be *done*. This last and very crucial matter, item (3), is something that even the state's government itself *cannot be entirely sure about*. Robust deterrence is clearly of the essence, to live well given this conundrum.

Prior Disasters and Recoveries, in War and Peace, Play Important Roles in Nuke Usability Views

Across the international arena, views are by no means completely uniform about how "usable" nuclear weapons might be, in the future, as tools for fighting *wars of aggression*.

There are at least *two dimensions* to the ways in which nuclear-weapon usability beliefs, and resulting warshot decisions and actions, can vary along *broad spectrums*, among America's various 21st century nuclear-armed (or nuke-aspiring) adversaries. A lot depends on their past experiences of participating in, or remaining neutral from, aggressive and/or defensive wars, civil wars, and international peacekeeping/peacemaking efforts; these experiences all can differ drastically in many ways between different groups of people (such as the winners versus the losers in each particular conflict).

One difference is social-emotional driven. This parameter concerns the adversary's own experiences and collective memories, if any, of *prior events* of massive damage they suffered from various causes, natural and/or man-made. These memories will be intertwined with those of *subsequent recovery/rebuilding experiences*, which could be successful, unsuccessful, or mixed.

This damage-and-then-recovery pairing influences psychological profiles about future martial aggression, risk taking, and especially about "societal pain-tolerance." *These profile factors can have an impact on how best to deter that nation from starting a nuclear war. A single, blanket messaging paradigm—what* is said and *how* it is delivered—might not work equally well everywhere. Similarly, the same U.S. Department of Defense's *power-projection mix*, of conventional and unconventional *weapons hardware and operational doctrines*, might not be best employed in exactly the same way to deter all possible aggressor states or non-state entities around the globe. STRATCOM planners are taking a hard look currently at how to optimally custom-fit deterrence capability and capacity, out of America's supremely flexible and adaptable toolkit, to very individualized, focused "deterrence challenge areas" worldwide.

Here, by *pain tolerance* we mean a group's *ability and willingness* to carry on with an armed conflict, rather than giving up, in spite of suffering the terrible costs of ongoing war: military and civilian casualties (killed, missing, sick or wounded), destruction of housing and personal property, destruction of workplaces and transport, physical deprivation (fuel rationing, starvation, medical shortages, etc.), and mental anguish (gnawing anxiety, bitter grief, depression and loneliness, raw rage, stark fear, etc.).

Defense strategists have often said that societal pain tolerance—whether high or low and how it changes with unfolding events—*is a critical parameter for shaping deterrence effectiveness*, both conventional and especially nuclear, at every stage of any war-and-then-peace cycle. Pain tolerance also heavily influences other warfighting postures (such as willingness to *take more combat losses*), military truce (cease-fire) bargaining tactics, and international armistice (peace treaty) negotiations.

Varied experiences of prior military victories and defeats can even, in complex ways, influence perhaps the most telling benchmark of all for cultural differences around the world. This is the *value attached to human life* (both one's own and that of others, domestic and foreign). Also important is the relative value attached, in different situations, to *individual* welfare within a group or state, versus collective own-group and own-state dogma and primacy *overall*. (Think "My life belongs to our Emperor," or "I would gladly die for the *Fuhrer*.")

The other dimension of nuclear-weapon use/non-use belief pertains to a government's or society's expectations for the *netting out of the various broad outcomes* of their nuclear aggression, both (1) those expected to be *beneficial* to them, and (2) those expected to be *detrimental* to them. The *first set, of beneficial outcomes,* is summarized by the relative amount of death and destruction and suffering, and the relative diminishment on the world stage, expected to be *inflicted upon the enemy*. The *second set, of detrimental outcomes,* amounts to the perceived potential for costly retaliation, death and destruction and suffering, geopolitical diminishment, and especially for *severe escalation*, expected to be *inflicted upon the government and the society* by its enemy and its enemy's allies, due to that government's own nuclear first-use and subsequent events.

The whole set of possible outcomes will be very broad-ranging, reflecting the many uncertainties: The actual outcome of a *nuclear military "adventure"* is extremely unpredictable. The outcome can vary tremendously, to say the least, based in part on the random dictates of *chaos theory* (the butterfly effect). Chaos will be great because the weapons are so immensely destructive and the combat so fast paced. This is true *even if* the nuclear war does in fact, somehow, remain "limited" in scope and duration–something an overconfident attacker may be counting on.

How the outcomes vary will depend in part on *how* exactly the aggressor nation plans to attack their enemy, using some or all of their available nuclear weapons inventory. Details of that attack plan would include selections, and sequencing, of particular strikes chosen out of the sizable number of different military-purpose/specific-target/weapon-yield options available to them. (A lengthy detailing of various such attack options–short of making one gigantic "spasm" nuclear strike–is discussed in Appendix 2 below.) Also, just as with conventional war, *"the plan goes out the window upon contact with the enemy."* How the defender responds, blow by blow, to being attacked with nuclear weapons is a *great imponderable*, but one that will *profoundly* affect the course and ultimate outcome of the conflict.

This discussion, and that which follows below, *has a point*: If a nation suffered a prior very destructive enemy attack/invasion, and was able nevertheless to defeat that attacking enemy and then rebuild its population and property, it is more likely to 1) think that a nuclear war it wants to stay limited *will actually stay limited*, and to 2) believe it will harvest ample *net geopolitical benefits* from starting said war.

It should therefore be of interest and concern to all Americans that both Russia and China have each suffered *precisely* such war experiences, not once but twice in the 20th century. Russia was invaded by Germany in World War I and again in World War II, each time in what was as close to *"total war"* as each era's technology and national resources would allow. China experienced massive military upheavals and great loss of life, *first* in the prolonged invasion and occupation by Imperial Japan, and *soon thereafter* during China's immensely bloody Communist-versus-Nationalist Civil War.

It thus behooves America to make very sure that Russia and China: (1) do *not* believe that any nuclear war they start will necessarily stay limited, and (2) *do* believe that even if it does somehow stay limited—which is a *fatal gamble* to take—they will *not* by any rational criteria turn out to benefit enough to say that they "won." We in America need to draw from this little analysis some *vital cautionary self-admonishments*, about applied mirror-imaging avoidance. Such avoidance is critical to our *deterrence messaging and Triad effectiveness*, which are heavily dependent on us having accurate understandings of adversary *perspectives*, and accurate expectations of adversary *behaviors*.

The abovementioned, straightforward case studies about Russia and China—founded in recent world history which is *not* subject to very much controversy—admonish America and our Allies against (1) inadvertently relying, in our nuclear deterrence posture, on cultural/psychological *mirror-imaging*, (2) inadvertently overlooking how *profoundly different* from ours (and from each other's) the basic perspectives can be among different of America's adversaries, and (3) inadvertently neglecting how working to elucidate and prioritize *adversary-focused* informational/influencing initiatives, in our diplomacy and our international public outreach, can substantially strengthen the effectiveness of American and Allied National Nuclear Posture.

The Demographic Processes of Aging and Forgetting Can Dilute Deterrence Effectiveness

Before saying more on the possible impact of differing *disaster rebound experiences* vis a vis mirror-imaging and nuclear deterrence, we note for emphasis another pairing of simple, universal, but—in this context—*unfortunate* demographic facts about human life and human nature as clocks tick, calendars change, and years and decades pass.

- People being mortal, the persons who experienced first-hand, and survived, terrible devastation from a major military catastrophe will gradually *die out* with the passage of time. They will be replaced by offspring who learn of things only *second or third hand.* Important and expensive lessons on war and peace will be *lost,* and will need to be *learned anew* by the next generation. Those who survived the original devastation but suffered permanent injury or serious disease may be *socially isolated or ostracized* and/or will often be among the first to die out, taking their *cautionary oral history legacies* with them—especially if steps are not taken swiftly to record, preserve, and publicize them.
- If subsequent, post-disaster reconstruction was generally successful, many people will focus primarily on that positive success, as a *mental offset* to the negatives of the catastrophe(s) that happened *earlier* on the timeline of shared memories. This *further erodes lasting cognition* of the original disaster's lessons on the high costs and foolhardiness of making aggressive war and/or unpreparedness for defensive war.

These twin factors themselves can make effective nuclear deterrence of some countries (and sub-state/trans-state entities) significantly more challenging for the U.S. and our Allies. This is especially so as *post-post-First Cold War* world history gradually moves forward along the timeline of mankind's existence, carrying all living people with it until they age and pass away. Their direct knowledge of the horrors of war (*whether conventional, nuclear, or counter-insurgency/counter-terror*) thus *will get diluted* with next generations of newborns, leading to a new era of forgetfulness and unawareness, and perhaps also of dangerous naiveté. Also, the collective consciousness might retain better recollection of the rebound from the catastrophe than of the *military recklessness* that preceded it and the *pain* that accompanied it. This can further dilute the potential *deterrence effect* of the old timers' experiences upon that society's newer national security policy. It is by this temporal and demographic *memory-delete mechanism* that excessive nationalism, jingoism, "yellow journalism" (a class of fake news), and authoritarian military adventurism—whether fascist or socialist—can *rise anew* in a subsequent generation, one that acts as fresh *death-dealers* in the perpetual war-and-peace human "game"—a generation whom outside, objective observers would think ought to really know better.

There is another effect of population aging and replacement via human reproduction. This effect can also weaken deterrence, but it operates on the collective consciousness not of the attacker society, but on that of the *defender*, that is, the one that is seeking to *achieve* deterrence of others. To be truly effective and successful at deterrence and defense, a state's elected-or-appointed leaders, voters, and general population all need to remain aware of exactly how *duplicitous and bloodthirsty* aggressor states can sometimes be.

People who love peace, who are basically honest and benevolent in their day-to-day dealings, can have trouble conceiving of how *not* like them an expansionist warmonger regime can be. Lovers of peace thus tend to inadvertently "round off" the sharp edges of others' aggressive intent, even when that intent is to profligately draw their blood. For instance, a foreign adversary's declarations of belligerent intent are often dismissed via such pabulum as *"he doesn't really mean it"* or *"she's just pandering to her domestic politics."* This is one reason why it takes *constant effort* and some *real sacrifices* (peace of mind and social-program funding) for open, democratic states to maintain effective deterrence against *genuinely evil but sweet-talking, two-faced forces* in the harsh outside world. One eternally relevant example is that of Neville Chamberlain, prime minister of the UK in the late 1930s, who jubilantly declared *"Peace in our time!"* shortly before Adolf Hitler attacked Poland and started the mass death that was World War II and the Holocaust.

History Revisionism Is Not Good for Anybody

History revisionism is the intentional or unintentional distortion or denial of operant motivations and relevant facts from a prior era, sometimes for commercial profit and/or political gain. Revisionism can leave a society vulnerable to further, *very ill-advised military adventurism* as it willfully (but *not* mindfully) *leaves old adventurist blunders behind.* Is the 21st-century world *endangered* in a bad new way, now that eyewitness accounts of the mid-20th century's deadly upheavals are becoming forgotten or distorted? Does the *dying-out* of Holocaust survivors, Hiroshima Maidens, and America's own Greatest Generation of World War II combat survivors alike—along with a *perverted reemerging and romanticizing* of neo-Nazism and similar race-hatred cults—heighten the future's nuclear dangers? Perhaps it does.

The foisting of revisionist *geopolitical and socio-economic falsehoods*—by belligerent national heads-of-state, by nihilist sub-state/trans-state (terrorist) leaders, and by vicious demagogues of all ilks—has long been a favorite way for warmongers to manipulate base/ugly mass emotions through the popular media, in order to engender widespread popular support for prolonged aggression and bloodshed. Just one example is Propaganda Minister Josef Goebbels's skillful, heavy use of commercial radio broadcasts in the 1930s to spread *appealing but toxic—and viciously anti-Semitic—lies* about why Germany lost World War I. Such threats to world peace are worsened by modern psyops techniques and information-warfare technologies, such as "deep fake" false-but-convincing, full-color HD videos being engineered via artificial intelligence to then spread, Internet-wide and beyond, various *aggression-feeding myths and misrepresentations.*

These kinds of *disinformatzia* and *dehumanization* grudge/hate politics and identity-nationalism tactics can lead directly to extremely deadly armed conflict. In the example of Goebbels and Hitler turning Germany from Weimar democracy to Nazi totalitarianism, *tens of millions of soldiers and civilians* were killed by World War II in Europe, the Soviet Union, and North Africa—a purely conventional armed conflict whose end on VE Day arrived *before nuclear weapons were even invented.*

How a People Have Endured Prior Catastrophes Affects Their Nuke-Usability Views

Major disasters causing truly awful collective experiences for millions of people can take one of two different forms: non-nuclear, or nuclear. *Non-nuclear mass destruction* can be either *naturally-caused,* such as an earthquake-induced tsunami or a volcano eruption or an especially devastating hurricane/typhoon season, or *man-made,* such as a war or a terrorist attack. Deadly disease pandemics, such as AIDS or COVID-19, can be seen as *hybrid events,* since pathogens *can occur and adapt naturally, or can accidentally escape a laboratory, or can be intentionally released in a bioweapon attack,* but pandemics spread—and are contained and treated successfully, or not—via *human* agencies and behaviors. Another type of catastrophe, part natural and part (man-made) nuclear, took place at Fukushima, Japan, in 2011: An earthquake triggered a tsunami which in turn caused a massive reactor meltdown with breach of multiple radioactive cores—a genuine *hybrid "perfect storm."*

It will help our further exposition of effective, up to date nuclear-deterrence ideas and suggestions if we now carefully categorize some representative, genuine disasters, that humanity has recently lived through, or died in, within living memory. Especially in today's age of malign influence campaigns and "fake news," *these totally real headline events,* of massive death and destruction, can (and sometimes *do*) unfortunately serve as the raw ammo for dangerous disinformation propaganda spewed by truth-vandalizing trolls, nefarious conspiracy theorists, and conniving dictators. At a minimum, these genuine "megadeath" events can cause people in any society to become inured (*deadened?*) to the short-term and unnecessary loss of millions of strangers' lives—thus weakening the vital taboo/norm against unprovoked nuclear-attack first use.

Previous Non-Nuclear Death and Destruction Have Lasting Emotional Effects

As detailed above, mass destruction could occur to a society, a region, or even the entire world from one of several causes: a natural catastrophe, or a man-made attack or accident, and hybrid events are possible. Within the same society, different people will react in different ways to such drastic loss of life, destruction of property, and creation of many injured requiring ongoing care. These differences evolve in part from the varying "mental constitutions" with which different people are born, and from the varying, lasting formative experiences of their developmental years and beyond. These processes remain murky, and predictions for any given individual are notoriously unreliable.

Speaking overall, although adversity can inspire *personal growth and optimism* in some survivors, others will wish to *escape* the need to actively contemplate the catastrophe in any constructive way. The latter group might instead exhibit *passivity and withdrawal,* reflected in existential despair and fatalism (regarding further natural disasters) or quick and abject surrender (to avoid further enemy attack). The former group, however, will feel *mobilized* to take corrective and preventive action, in the form of (1) building better structures and systems to *mitigate* future natural disasters, and (2) supporting stronger military deterrence and defense (including *civil defense and resiliency* measures) against further, future enemy attack plus *more reliable checks and balances* against own-country military adventurism.

Whichever individual choices are made, many people who experience around them devastating loss and destruction, or who are forced to make impossible choices about the death or survival of others (e.g., as First Responders), will become somewhat inured/resigned, at least unconsciously—but also *emotionally damaged.* (The process compares to post-traumatic stress disorder—PTSD—suffered by those who wear the Uniform in combat.) The civilian victims of a catastrophe will know for the rest of their lives, with dreadful new certainty and haunting vividness, that such horrors can and do indeed occur—*and could (will?) occur again,* to them and their friends and loved ones. This can impact their worldview, wreck their normal complacency and contentment, and possibly result in *low expectations* regarding any future personal/family peace of mind and local-neighborhood quality of life—and can also lead to low expectations and even bitter cynicism about the fate of their nation and the state of humanity.

Bad mental health, substance abuse, failed marriages, even suicide can ensue, if help and treatment by trained professionals are not made quickly available. In a worst case, the sufferers can feel compelled, in part because of *unconscious survivor guilt,* to turn such poor expectations into *self-fulfilling prophecy* (acting out), to punish themselves and those around them. This pathological guilt-shame complex can even lead to an unconscious *death wish,* made manifest by *indiscriminate acts of interpersonal violence.* In particular, we need to ask, since American popular culture has become all-too-cognizant of so-called *suicide-by-cop* and *mass-shooting* incidents, is there also sometimes—in some people—an impulse to *murder-suicide* by *warfighting*?

Sometimes, disaster victims will carry inside themselves such grief, resentment, rage, feelings of helplessness, anxiety and depression, or emotional regression to a dependent, childlike (but violent) state, that they nurture an insidious desire for "getting even," for *revenge.* This is especially true if the agent of their suffering is seen as human nature rather than Mother Nature. Their trust and confidence in government leaders—domestic *and* foreign—can become reduced. Even in the case of an obviously unavoidable natural disaster, any perceived failure of government authorities to have been better prepared in advance, or to provide timely rescue and recovery aid, will lead to pent up resentment—directed at certain *scapegoat sub-groups* at home and/or abroad. This creates social unrest that opens opportunities for feloniously manipulative *sociopathic demagogues* to rise to power. They can make political capital from their followers' ugliest street-brawler instincts, by *dehumanizing and demonizing out-groups* that they say are somehow to blame. This puts a high premium (gaining rewards, avoiding punishments) on joining, and staying loyal and obedient to, the demagogue's belligerent in-group.

Whether individual citizens who were once victims of a catastrophe feel lasting passivity or lasting aggression, or some of both or maybe (ideally) neither, many will become *enablers*, perhaps inadvertently, of future *intra- and inter-national violence*, such as war and terrorism. Their preexisting mental scar-tissue, from the earlier experienced catastrophe(s), can significantly raise their pain threshold, and collectively make them *much more difficult to dissuade and deter.*

This problem can be further compounded by their learned/acquired awareness that *recovery and reconstruction* have been *possible and successful*, at least up to now, *in their own community*.

Next, we need to look carefully at some examples of *non-nuclear-war* mass destruction, and then at *specifically nuclear* destruction. There are important lessons to be drawn from both.

Past Reactions to Man-Made Non-Nuclear Attack Can Yield Some Valuable Insights

It is a fact of military history that the most immediately deadly and destructive attacks of World War II were not the fission bombings of Hiroshima and Nagasaki, but the *conventional* strategic firestorm bombings of Hamburg and Tokyo. Although the latter events did not involve nuclear radiation effects, the number of deaths and square miles of destruction in each of these two firebombed cities rivaled what a single 15- or 25-kiloton atomic bomb could inflict. The descriptions of blast and burn injuries to individual victims who survived, or didn't, are quite as harrowing to read; looking at old photos is just as bad or worse. In fact, lacking Geiger counter readings, it is difficult to distinguish between the destruction wrought by one A-bomb against Hiroshima from that wrought by repeated conventional bombing raids against Tokyo or Berlin.

Conventional world war does take much longer to inflict comparable death and destruction compared to nuclear war. But on a cumulative basis over several years of immense national efforts, both World War I and World War II killed *many tens of millions*, maimed huge numbers of survivors, and destroyed vast tracts of terrain and property. The massive bloodshed did not stop there. Since 1945, *regional wars* have been fought intermittently across a vast *"arc of instability"* ranging from *the Balkans* (Serbia versus neighbors x3), through *the Aegean* (Turkey vs Greece re Cyprus), *the Middle East's Fertile Crescent* (Israel vs Arabs x6; civil wars in Lebanon, Syria, Libya), *the Caucasus* (Chechnya, Georgia, Nagorno-Karabakh), through *Mesopotamia* (Iraq vs Iran, then vs Kuwait, then x2 vs U.S.-led coalitions), through *Afghanistan* (vs the USSR, then vs the U.S./NATO), and *all across Asia* (Nationalist vs Communist China; India vs Pakistan x3; the UK in Malaya; North vs South Korea; North vs South Vietnam). *Many parts of Africa* have also been wracked repeatedly by costly wars, civil wars, intertribal or inter-ethnic massacres and genocides.

Deadly terrorist attacks aside, the United States is *uniquely fortunate* among major nations to have not in living memory—or in its immediately-preceding (the Greatest) generation—suffered wholesale slaughter from *civil wars and international (state-on-state) wars* that were *fought on America's own mainland territory*. Standing in stark contrast, with profound implications, is that Germany, the USSR/Russia, China, Japan, France, Italy, Israel, Poland, the Netherlands, Belgium, Spain, and to some extent the UK all *did* suffer such prolonged, collective military catastrophes. India and Pakistan, Iran and Iraq, and North and South Korea also fall into this most-unfortunate group.

This distinction alone renders Americans *particularly prone* to the pitfalls of *cultural and psychological mirror-imaging* in the realm of foreign relations and national-security affairs. In the U.S., it can sometimes be hard for our leaders and elders, our media pundits and politicos, and our residents and voters to see things the way their wise and wizened counterparts in these other countries do; we might sometimes even seem childishly naive, while they might in contrast be bitterly cynical. There are thus dire implications for the U.S. regarding *both our deterring strategies and our defending tactics* in today's widespread *hybrid-war*—which includes, far beyond the purely military sphere, a very hard-fought information-vs.-disinformation global contest.

Concerningly, the above-mentioned class of nation-state *war-fought-across-own-turf* sufferers includes *all four of the other Permanent Members of the UN Security Council—all of whom own nuclear arsenals.* That war-torn class also includes one or both sides in some of the world's *most intractable, and now nuclear-armed, regional conflict zones* in the Middle East and in Asia.

All of which says something essential, which ought to be glaringly obvious, and yet which can be dangerously obscured by the "noise" of 21st-century pro-unilateral-nuclear-disarmament news-media argumentation: So long as nuclear weapons do exist in the hands of many such countries—inured as they are to massive war-losses by their own experiences of (sometimes multiple) devastation/reconstruction cycles—America needs to (1) modernize and sustain a diverse, well-dispersed, assuredly-survivable Triad nuclear arsenal as an *effective deterrent force-in-being*, and also, in support of it (2) pursue a diligent and all-inclusive, multi-cultural-focused program of *nuclear-deterrence cautionary education and messaging*. This two-fold *foundational dialectic-aphorism of nuclear peacekeeping* will be further supported by the logic exposed in the rest of this chapter.

Some Natural Disasters Mimic Nuclear-War Death Counts—and Life Does Go On

The AIDS epidemic is an example of a recent, prolonged global pandemic that has caused the death of *tens of millions* of people, before effective treatments became possible; it remains a very serious threat to public health. The recent, still-ongoing COVID-19 pandemic is another example; as of year-end, 2020, almost 2,000,000 people worldwide had died of COVID-19 in *one year*. The 2004 tsunami that devastated the entire region around Aceh, Indonesia by some estimates killed 250,000 people *in one day*. These death tolls are comparable to those that could be inflicted by a single nuclear weapon, or a nuclear war.

This gradual worldwide experience of prolonged illness, followed by fatality, over the past thirty or forty years, for tens of millions of AIDS victims, can be viewed as a (perhaps comparatively mild?) analogue to the long-term deadly effects of a nuclear war's radioactive fallout and/or a nuclear-winter/nuclear-summer climate disaster. The lesson that can be drawn from what we might label as an *"AIDS + COVID/Aceh Analogy"*—both good *and bad*—is that civilization *survives and recovers*. This is good because it shows that humanity is indeed very resilient. It is *bad* because it permits a cynical warmonger to anticipate (or at least proclaim far and wide) that triggering a nuclear war will—as least for him/her and their loyal retinue—have *a survivable outcome filled with Earthly rewards*.

Effective nuclear deterrence can in this way be *fatally undermined*, if the U.S. ever grows complacent regarding its hardware-and-messaging deterrence responsibilities—which are *de facto obligations* of the world we Americans live in today, a nuclear-armed world that we ourselves helped create in 1945. And we in a real sense made things worse by fomenting the World-Wide Web and the Internet, decades later: They are abused now as *weaponized delivery platforms* in the ongoing, internecine, international *Disinformatzia War* that is raging between science-based truths and insidious fake news, between defending democracy and advancing tyranny. This undermining info-war poses a constant danger to the mass comprehension and uptake of honest nuclear-deterrence messaging.

Today's Cold War II information war is *a genuine war*. America's adversaries invest very heavily in their constant assaults on our perceptions of objective reality, to make us "lose the bubble" of where our pro-freedom, national-defense duties lie. Such offensive pressure must be resisted ably and strenuously. The U.S. needs to keep seeking *a moral and benign form of information-warfare dominance*—what could also be called *"believability superiority"*—in the face of so much seductive but nefarious anti-Triad propaganda by so many persistent adversaries.

The financial cost of supporting this pro-deterrence duty, which America shirks at our own deadly peril, is not nearly as "unbearable" as domestic and foreign naysayers would have the American public believe: To modernize the U.S.'s nuclear systems over the next generation would really cost our society *less than an additional* 5% of the annual National Defense Budget. Yet China and Russia, North Korea and Iran, and others all maintain troll farms busy trying to shoot yet more poisoned arrows at the supposed Achilles hell of our country's security: the willingness of voters to pay for this cost.

In particular, the *enticing falsehood* that "were America to abandon our nuclear arsenal, then untold riches could be poured into social programs instead," is, sadly, just *wishful thinking*: Total U.S. Nuclear-Weapon Infrastructure recapitalization costs are budgeted at about $1.3 trillion in constant 2020 dollars, but this seemingly monumental fortune is to be funded and spent gradually at a steady rate over *three decades*. Those costs would actually amount to *under 1% per year* out of the U.S. Government's *entire Annual Federal Expenditures*, which total $4.7 trillion for 2020. Freeing up such an amount would not change the world. *An extra $45 billion per year* for social programs would certainly be a handsome sum, but we need to be realistic about how far it could ever go. Diverting this money from a vital defense capability would *not* be anywhere near enough to pay for poverty-ending aid programs, would *not* solve world hunger, and would *not* cure all cancers. For perspective, $45 billion is only 7% of *one year's* state and federal Medicaid Program costs. (All dollar amounts are from Wikipedia.com.)

But to shortchange nuclear peacekeeping *would* have *astronomically bad consequences,* in terms of encroaching adversary authoritarianism, enemy repression of human freedoms—and *terrible loss of life* via undeterred wars big and small, both conventional and even, yes, nuclear.

It would be far better for democracy, and far more effective for funding greater social progress, were Americans to focus on squeezing *waste and inefficiency* out of U.S. Government expenditures, *without* disarming our nuclear-deterrent infrastructure—a fact *conspicuously absent* in the anti-nuke propaganda that adversaries direct at U.S. Homeland audiences.

The Lack of Much Hard Data Enables Bad-Actor Distortions, and Even Delusions

Actual experience of nuclear-reactor and -weapon radiation leaks (in accidents) and nuclear-weapon detonations and fallout (in attacks, or tests) among human populations is fortunately limited. The medical effects, both immediate/acute and long-term/chronic, were studied after the attacks on Hiroshima and Nagasaki (one fission-bomb air burst each), and after the various tests and accidents of the Cold War and since then. These different incidents, spread around the world, include: several fissile U or Pu spills from missile, aircraft, or submarine mishaps such as Damascus, Arkansas; Palomares, Spain; and *K-129* off Hawaii; several severe reactor meltdowns ala Chernobyl and Fukushima; and over one thousand A-bomb and H-bomb test detonations, ranging in yield from sub-kiloton to multi-megaton, set off underground or underwater or in the open air or in outer space. Long-term results for 2011's major Fukushima reactor disaster are in still progress, and the health effects of North Korea's 21st-century underground tests, at least some of which vented to the surface, are open to investigation.

The numerous, highly unpleasant and often lethal symptoms from these human exposures are well documented elsewhere. (See for instance a Wikipedia.com search on "List of military nuclear accidents.") Suffice it to say that for those not *killed promptly by the initial blast or meltdown* (or non-nuclear effects of the accident such as submarine sinkings), a *slow but certain, agonizing death* from incurable cancers years later is a definite possibility—and wondering whether one will sooner or later also take sick and die can itself be *very debilitating.*

Statistically credible experience data was garnered in studies of those individuals who were caught by the fallout from U.S. nuclear weapons tests conducted in the South Pacific or in the continental United States—the group of so-called Down-Winders. (One has to wonder what went on in the other countries that developed and repeatedly tested nukes, especially the Soviet Union and China.) In some cases, national governments (including the U.S.'s) sent large formations of soldiers across fresh nuclear test-site terrain, on foot or in jeeps, to measure the impact of radiation exposure on *short-term combat capability*. Many soldiers did remain fighting-fit for at least a few days, which was taken as *good news* in military circles. Further empirical data was obtained by studying the grim aftereffects of uncontained nuclear reactor disasters, notably Chernobyl and Fukushima. (The Three Mile Island partial meltdown, in contrast, was well contained.)

Experience data on the lasting *group-emotional* and *sociological/political* effects of nuclear weapon detonation exposure is harder to analyze rigorously, since these factors are by nature *more nebulous*, and also because they are contributed to by *other influences* that cannot be separated out (see next paragraph). Nuclear reactor disasters (and by extension, future nuclear attacks) can also lead to *forced temporary evacuation and/or permanent relocation, loss of economic productivity, and family separation and other social disruption*; some analogies could be drawn with the various effects of non-nuclear disasters such as AIDS + COVID-19/Aceh discussed above.

But the exact impact of any past nuclear-catastrophe events, regardless of specific cause, can be hard to assess precisely (and even harder to project forward at all accurately), in isolation from other human factors that were (or might in future be) at work simultaneously. Such factors could include (as in the case of World War II-era Japan) exposure to prolonged conventional strategic bombing, suffering of heavy losses in overseas combat theaters, and home-front rationing and deprivation, or (as in the case of the late Cold War-era USSR) suffering of serious combat losses in Afghanistan, separatist agitation among many Soviet republics and Warsaw Pact states, and general economic-system failure.

Nevertheless, two examples, *Hiroshima/Nagasaki*, and *Chernobyl*, are very telling. They carry important *applied mirror-imaging avoidance lessons* for all Americans. At the same time, as we caution readers below, they might provide adversaries of democracy with *nuclear-blackmailing and war-mongering ammunition* to fuel expansionism-enabling malign-influence campaigns, which could all-too-easily lead to very deadly consequences for aggressors and defenders alike.

Hiroshima and Nagasaki Deserve a Closer Look, for Effective Future Nuclear Deterrence

Both cities were able to rebuild after World War II, with significant help from the occupying United States plus some resources brought in from elsewhere inside war-ravaged Japan. Hiroshima and Nagasaki are both thriving major metropolises today. However, the twin nuclear attacks were formative events in a massive *regime change* in Japan, away from militant imperialism. Post-war Japan was rapidly transitioned into a *largely pacifist national culture* with a demilitarizing constitution, which then prevailed for two or three generations. Only recently has Japan moved away from these values—in large part due to aggression by nuclear-armed China and North Korea—and Japan's defensive remilitarization remains controversial, at home and abroad.

Caveats re Hiroshima and Nagasaki:

Perhaps obscured by Japan's own (like West Germany's) post-war Economic Miracle—propelled in part by America's *massive foreign-aid largesse* (e.g., the Marshall Plan in Europe)—was the fact that relatively quick recovery by the two nuked cities Hiroshima and Nagasaki was enabled by *special local/immediate circumstances.* For one thing, both weapons were intentionally set off by the U.S. at medium altitude, to *minimize their dirty fallout effects* (and yet maximize overall Mach Y-stem blast-force damage). And while Japan had been subjected to very damaging conventional strategic bombing for months by the U.S. Army Air Corps (as the U.S. Air Force was then organized), the Imperial homeland (unlike Germany) had *not been invaded, fought over, and occupied,* except for some outlying islands. (The U.S. Navy Submarine Force's highly successful anti-*maru* campaign against Japanese shipping led to widespread deprivation, but did *not* directly cause great death and destruction in the Home Islands.)

After the surrender, enough of Japan's civilian population and infrastructure *remained intact,* and all of it was *safe* from more American nuclear (or conventional) weapons, which helped greatly in local reconstruction. Furthermore, the United States, whose foreign aid to Japan, as mentioned above, was crucial to the defeated country's recovery, had *not* suffered any serious attacks at all on its continental landmass, leaving the rich U.S. able to also, simultaneously, focus on the Marshall Plan for rebuilding Western Europe.

But in the *severely contrasting case of any future widespread nuclear war,* it is possible (likely?) that *none* of these favorable factors would apply, making post-war reconstruction and recovery much more difficult and prolonged for everyone involved, *if not impossible.*

Thermonuclear weapons—which didn't exist in 1945—set off directly against hardened targets, such as ICBM silos and command bunkers, would create miles-wide radioactive craters and throw *huge amounts* of dirty debris and fallout into the stratosphere, to spread far and wide, globally. Nuclear weapons set off against commercial nuclear power-reactor cores, because of the complicated nuclear physics involved, would produce *particularly toxic* fallout effects. In any major nuclear armed conflict, dozens or *hundreds* of cities at once—if only due to being near military bases, industrial complexes, and other "valid" strategic targets—would suffer severe blast, heat/fire, and/or radiation/fallout damage and injuries—thus *completely overwhelming* local surviving first responders and national assistance resources alike. And foreign countries, that could otherwise provide recovery support, would have their own *terrible nuclear aftermaths* to contend with.

In short, the recoveries of Hiroshima and Nagasaki are *not representative* of the prolonged-to-permanent *worldwide devastation and population crash* likely to result from any future nuclear war—especially once the Intra-War Nuclear Unsafe-User Principle, and the ensuing Three-Fold Geophysical Wipeout, take hold around our planet.

Chernobyl also Deserves a Closer Look re Future Effective Deterrence

The Chernobyl nuclear reactor disaster of 1986, and subsequent sub-optimal response by the Soviet government, are seen by some analysts as having been pivotal to speeding up the collapse of the Soviet-style communist economic and political system. While different in nature from the twin U.S. nuclear attacks on Japan, the net effect was comparable: massive *regime change*. Sadly, tyrants can draw this lesson just as well as can proponents of democracy. A nuclear attack or nuclear war could be seen by any number of evildoers as an effective way to bring down any government (*including America's*) to which they are belligerently opposed.

Caveats re Chernobyl:

While recovery and decontamination proceeded apace at Chernobyl, with some assistance from other countries, the immediate area of the reactor explosion and fire still remains too contaminated for practicable re-habitation—except for a small number of elderly, widowed Chernobyl babushkas, and other hardy (foolhardy?) returnees. Perversely, now that the area is less "hot" a generation later, it has become a *lurid tourist attraction*—most recently, for Instagram selfie-seekers inspired by a TV show. While this might be seen as good collective post-catastrophe adaptive entrepreneurial behavior, it further obscures one key aspect of Chernobyl's recovery that made reconstruction look deceptively easy—and a *bad consequence* of this obscuration is to erode effective nuclear deterrence going forward.

That key aspect is that Chernobyl was *a single nuclear-reactor disaster*, not part of a widespread nuclear war. Recovery aid (including medical aid) was available from far and wide outside the local area of the disaster (including from the U.S., and from within the USSR itself), in ways it would probably *not* be during any nuclear war, or after one.

Any Nation's "Selective Misperception" Is a Serious Problem for *All* Nations

Expansionist autocrats are human beings first. As such, beneath their overbearing manipulativeness and imperious brutality, they can be subject to some of the *same* conscious and unconscious motivations and behaviors as other people. One adverse human behavior is called by psychologists *selective misperception*. This is the tendency to see only what one wants to see. (Democratic leaders are infamous for sometimes committing this same mistake.)

While not wishing to here plumb further the profound depths of Freud-based (or other) psychiatry, it is safe to say that unconscious conduct in others is familiar to most of us, namely, the visible tendency for someone to act in a certain *suboptimal (even self-defeating)* way for a certain emotional reason without them even realizing it at the time. Of course, the unconscious mind need not be pathological. In a well-adjusted, self-aware person the conscious and unconscious can work together for peace, health, and happiness of self, family, and community.

Selective misperception can have particularly negative effects when a bad actor possessing nuclear weapons seeks ways to *rationalize* those nukes' unprovoked first-use for his or her own selfish political gain. As discussed above, they can believe that nuclear attacks could be efficient means of triggering major *regime change* among their foreign opponents. They can tell themselves that their own in-group's *swift reconstruction* after any retaliation will be *readily achievable*—and that they will even enjoy a *bounty of newly-acquired* riches and power galore.

A more cogent (i.e., less purely unconscious) dictator on the warpath can still use these *same* (objectively highly questionable) arguments, intentionally and misleadingly, as *jingoist rhetoric*. This provides the dictator with information-warfare ammunition to use to seductively deceive, recruit, exploit, and control followers, both senior and rank-and-file. Some loyal followers will have their own cogently opportunistic, and/or unconsciously morbid, motivations and appetites for mayhem, and will eagerly sign on along the dictator's journey to unprovoked nuclear war—even if these sycophants, very cynically, might not much buy into their leader's particular brand of phony rhetoric.

As an extreme for-instance of *purported regime-change strategy*, some (hypothetical, thought-experiment scenario's) delusional neo-fascist egomaniac might believe that, if he/she launched a surprise nuclear strike against the United States, then in the ensuing socio-political disorder—rather than our SSBNs (and numerous other surviving nuclear-Triad forces) launching a devastating nuclear counterstrike–sympathetic fascists in America could come to seize control of a much-diminished America's new government, turning our country into one of his/her *loyal vassal/puppet states.* Whatever the dictator's particular ideology, he/she might count on exploiting this *fifth column* consisting of local malcontents, infiltrated operatives (sleeper agents as on the TV show *The Americans*), and ideological "fellow travelers" to bring down a badly weakened U.S. from within. This "magical thinking" does *not* need to bear any relationship to objective reality for the idea to be tempting to some power-mad narcissist, making the deluded scenario *quite dangerous to the world.*

For instance, recall that Adolf Hitler somehow managed to convince himself that after his armed forces overran and occupied the continent of Europe, he could make peace with the UK, with whose people he felt an *ethnic kinship* that he thought was nicely reciprocated. What a purblind hypocrite!

And Hitler wasn't alone in such fantasies. While his preparations for invading the Soviet Union (Operation Barbarossa) reached a fevered pitch, and the Jewish Holocaust was already in gear, Hitler's arch-disciple Rudolph Hess, acting on his own, in 1941 hijacked a Luftwaffe fighter and bailed out over Scotland to act as an "emissary of peace." The *denoument* of Hess's craziness, unfortunately, is *military* history, not diplomatic history.

Former UK Prime Minister Neville Chamberlain, perhaps himself *clinically delusional*, had already tried to appease Hitler, and (as referenced above) he failed miserably. Fortunately, Winston Churchill (and America's FDR) understood the true nature of the enemy. Hitler died in the *Fuhrerbunker*, and Hess of old age in Spandau Prison decades later. One can ask if either of these Nazi villains got the earthly punishment they deserved. Their grandiose scheming, even in an era restricted to *conventional* weapons, led to the horrible deaths of tens of millions—*many of whom followed Hitler's sick leadership willingly, even eagerly, into their own vast slaughter.*

When nuclear weapons are on the table, delusions and deceptions can be even more deadly. The belief that everyone else in the world is as *sane and rational*, and *as "nice" and honest*, as you yourself are—and values the *very same values*, and strives for the *very same goals*—comprises one *particularly lethal* form of cultural and psychological *mirror-imaging* that American society and government seem to be prone to.

Especially now (early 2021) that the serious economic ravages of COVID-19 are giving added fuel to domestic nuclear deemphasis-and-disarmament advocates—and to their adversarial foreign enablers and reinforcers—America's voters and leaders need to remain *very clear-eyed* about the necessity for effective conventional and nuclear deterrence. Numerous *egregiously false narratives*, grossly and shamelessly exaggerating both the expenses and the dangers of *essential, every-generational* U.S. nuclear-Triad infrastructure renewal, need to be "exploded." They must be assertively, persistently debunked in persuasive, *truthful* layman terms—all across those popular media venues in which the same old anti-nuclear myths keep rearing their ugly, disingenuous heads.

Conclusion: Unrecognized Mirror-Imaging Can Weaken Deterrence's Effectiveness

This chapter has sought to expose some of the *risks to nuclear peace* that can result from cultural and psychological mirror-imaging, and it has overviewed some suggested ways to *avoid the perceptual errors* that can heighten such risks. *Applied mirror-imaging avoidance*, always a crucial prerequisite of successful foreign policy and effective national defense, demands a *cogent awareness of how very differently from us* various foreign adversaries might emote and act.

This awareness, by Americans and our Allies, must include a pragmatic recognition of *how very depraved* some belligerent overseas leaders have sometimes truly been during recent world history. The willful, even ecstatic genocides engineered by the likes of Heinrich Himmler, Pol Pot, and Slobodan Milosevic help elucidate the truly terrible depths of the envelope of human-on-human, mass-violence potentials. It is essential that during the 21st century, we never lose sight of the regrettable fact that such atrocities might occur yet again, *if dedicated countermeasures are not adequately sustained.*

A top priority among such countermeasures, now that nuclear weapons are available to a number of democracies and tyrannies alike, is to deploy sufficiently powerful, survivable nuclear deterrence capabilities.

We discussed how some of the *emotion-based naysaying controversies* within U.S. domestic politics regarding nuclear peacekeeping—e.g., about the supposed unaffordability of sustaining the future viability of America's nuclear Triad, really costing *just 7%* as much as Medicaid—can be explained in part by widespread domestic mirroring *errors* about the threat of nuclear blackmail and attack from abroad. We exposed how these controversies are *magnified by* adversaries' canny use of our own *sometimes-utopian wishful thinking* against us, within their prolonged, concerted, and insidiously manipulative malign-influence campaigns. We also discussed various delusional psychological processes which foreign dictators can be prone to *themselves*, and/or can use to mislead their own citizenry, duping one and all into acts of deadly aggression—including potentially, in the future, *nuclear aggression*. Accounting for and taking *active countermeasures* against those foreign-bred delusions and manipulative deceptions, *wherever* they try to take root, is indispensable to combating the *widespread propaganda and disinformation* that adversaries use more and more, in the Internet and social media age, to foment their own brand of belligerent nationalism, and also to undermine democracy's resolve.

This chapter also looked at several specific examples of ultra-high-mortality events and their *successful reconstruction/rebound aftermaths*, ranging from the AIDS pandemic and the Aceh tsunami, to Hiroshima/Nagasaki and Chernobyl/Fukushima. We used these case studies from recent history—and thought-experiments looking at autocrats' misguided temptations to try to *force U.S. regime change and reap rewards for aggression*—to derive some relevant practical lessons. These lessons concern American awareness of, and thus avoidance of, some archetypical mirror-imaging mistakes that we might otherwise fall into concerning how overseas persons could react to the prospect of successfully rebuilding and eventually thriving after martial catastrophe. The main point, which it is definitely *our* job to make sure both we *and* all our potential adversaries never forget, is that any past events—whether a Hiroshima or a Chernobyl, or a pandemic or tsunami—are not truly relevant to 21st century nuclear war. The latter would be the ultimate global human catastrophe, one which is *almost certainly irrecoverable*, since it would probably escalate uncontrollably into a human-species extinction event.

These various *actionable cautions* can help further evolve, in the right and necessary direction, America's ongoing development of *two crucial national-defense capabilities,* namely (1) maximally effective, adaptive 21st-century *nuclear-deterrence weapon systems and national posture,* and (2) peacekeeping-focused *positive-influence Internet (and other) messaging counter-disinformation/anti-psywar campaigns.* Both of these foundational pillars for preventing nuclear war will be considerably strengthened by *avoiding cultural mirror-imaging,* thereby facilitating *more-accurate assessments* of different nuclear armed adversaries' varying perceptions, aspirations, and expectations. The latter always play a *huge role* in shaping enemy military strategies, capabilities, and intentions. They should thus also shape *America's (and France's and the UK's) firm commitments to investing in their nuclear-deterrent infrastructure renewal, and also to furthering effective global outreach and education programs using genuinely truth-based nuclear-peacekeeping messages.*

When it comes to nuclear war, it is the safest course by far to *assume nothing* about peer competitors', rogue states', and terrorists' sometimes-disordered cognitive processes, their conscious objectives and unconscious impulses, their potentially-malignant plans, their degree of trustworthiness (or decided lack thereof)—and their willingness, even *psychotic eagerness* to use nuclear weapons aggressively, *if not constantly and very effectively deterred.*

CHAPTER 5

Simple Math Shows the Need for Nuclear Arms Controls

Some Equations Quantify Nuclear Testing and Proliferation Dangers

Executive Summary: Counterproliferation and the Test Ban Norm Deserve Maximum Support

As we leave the 21st Century's second decade behind, we see two ominous trends along that crucial, always-active *world peacekeeping front* of preventing any sort of nuclear attack or nuclear war. *One ominous trend* is the rising belief in some quarters that low-yield (tactical) nuclear weapons could actually ever be used to initiate, or intentionally escalate, a "winnable" war—i.e., one that doesn't expand uncontrollably into global thermonuclear Armageddon. *The other ominous trend* is the rising count in the number of countries that have or want their own arsenals of nukes—a process called *"nuclear proliferation."* That number, which was stable at *five* (alphabetically: China, France, Russia, the UK, the U.S.) for a whole generation from the mid-1960s, has since the end of the Cold War *increased by four* so far (Israel—unofficially/ambiguously—plus India, Pakistan, North Korea), and Iran is a threatening wannabe.

South Africa also once possessed six or seven working nukes—deliverable by transport aircraft to potential targets in the Communist-led, aggressive "Front-Line States" on Johannesburg's northern border. But South Africa—partly because of the end of both the Cold War and of apartheid, and partly because of mounting pressure from economic sanctions—gave up their small nuclear arsenal in the early 1990s. This nice historic fact has, ever since, *inspired nuclear-disarmament advocates around the world,* who wish that all other nuke-owning states would soon do the same. I think that, sadly, this is a forlorn hope, as now, despite the UN's recent ratification of a treaty calling for a total worldwide nuclear-weapons ban, *not one of the nine current nuclear powers has the slightest interest or intention to comply.* In fact, the U.S. recently called for the fifty-plus smaller countries that signed the UN treaty to change their votes and annul it.

However, as mentioned earlier, I do think that the Global Zero movement and its *confreres* deserve meaningful support, and much thanks, for all their efforts promoting *nuclear counter-proliferation*—a critical process, and an essential, everlasting goal. This goal will be discussed further, and justified by basic math, in this Chapter 5.

It is important to recall that ongoing counterproliferation efforts, going back to the 1950s, *have actually had some considerable successes.* Witness, President Kennedy in the early 1960s stated seriously that he estimated the number of nuclear-armed states in the year 2000, denoted symbolically/algebraically as "N," would grow to *thirty-five.* The fact that twenty years into the 21st Century, N = *only nine,* with upward pressure toward *ten* (Iran), should be a source of encouragement and optimism for nonproliferation and arms control workers everywhere.

(An optimally pragmatic, practical, practicable *alternative model* for effective long-term global nuclear peacekeeping—elaborated on and justified in Chapter 7—develops a Best Perspectives package based on *"competitive strategic stability."* This notion aims to *redirect* current resentful views re a "nuclear glass ceiling" or "nuclear haves-vs.-have-nots" or even a "nuclear apartheid," based instead on the *professional sports norm* of having both *athletes* and *spectators* in the arena. The hoped-for effect would be to hold N at the current nine—itself a world Goldilocks Zone—and have these states' teams of experts vie in World Cup or Olympics style *deterrence Best Practices "test matches."* The UN's objective IAEA inspectors could act as referees and judges. Similarly, we will try to support U.S. and world counterproliferation goals by looking at a *"call 911 (or 999)" model,* in which all countries—like all the people living in a city—*delegate* First Responder protective duties to a well-trained, properly-equipped—and *small*—elite corps of professionals.)

However, the rising belief in some quarters in nuclear weapons' *"limited usability,"* for (supposedly) productive battlefield purposes—even when said belief is just discussed in *professional defense journals,* or is (more tellingly) also expressed in *diplomatic signaling/messaging* (including nuclear blackmail/coercion attempts)—helps explain why more nations might want to have nukes. Naturally enough, they would wish to own their own to assure their security, via establishing some viable nuclear deterrence. But, at the same time, and very dangerously, any further rise in the count—JFK's "N"—in the number of states (countries) that do own them would increase the chance that deterrence somewhere, somehow will fail, and nukes will actually be used for war.

Furthermore—comprising serious threats to maintaining good world order and nuclear peace—the double dangers of (1) nuclear *testing* (by those who do own nukes), and (2) nuclear *proliferation* (by those who don't own them, yet), *cannot be addressed and mitigated separately* by concerned world players. Nor can they be coped with adequately via inwardly focused "benign neglect," isolationism, or science denial.

Robust and determined, pragmatic *arms control negotiations* are clearly needed to halt both of these dangerous trends, as are renewed and expanded *global education campaigns* about the dangers to all humanity of even limited, local nuclear aggression. Both these negotiations and this education can by aided by *properly explaining the value of and need for* the existing small number of states—a "just right" Goldilocks Zone—who do now *sustain global strategic stability* via effective mutual nuclear deterrence.

The negotiations and the education can also be reinforced by use of some theoretical but nonetheless powerful "thought experiments"—illustrative exercises worked out on paper, and in our minds, about the perverse motivations behind, and unchecked consequences flowing from, nuclear testing, nuclear proliferation, and (God forbid) nuclear combat.

This chapter uses some simple math to illustrate how *drastically destabilizing* to world survival it could be to have even (1) the slightest further spread of *nuclear weapon ownership* among *more* nations, and/or (2) the slightest further violation of *nuclear weapon test bans* (let alone violation of *nuclear attack-abstinence norms*) by any nations. Chapter 5 then summarizes a series of logically rigorous, aspirational policy suggestions (i.e., some "Best Practices for a Nuclear-Posture-After-Next"). These are being offered here for *consideration, modification, and possible adoption in some form, if appropriate* by the U.S. and other world nuclear powers and non-nuclear powers alike—some of these suggestions were exposed in the previous chapters and/or will be built on more in subsequent chapters and appendices.

These policy aspirations include eventual ratification by the U.S. of the Comprehensive Nuclear Test Ban Treaty, *realpolitik* amendment/renewal of the Non-Proliferation Treaty, and introduction at the UN of a sheaf of other Best Practice treaties, protocols, and norms, all embodying a pragmatic world system for *"competitive but stable, sustainable but affordable, contained but right-sized mutual nuclear deterrence."* In an ideal (and *attainable*) world, this system would both (1) replace the various current, unwise and unworkable (though well meant) treaties, and social/political movements, whose top-level objective is the forlorn (hence counterproductive) hope of *total world nuclear disarmament*, and (2) reduce the rising pressures causing the *lapse* of many existing nuclear arms-control treaties as Russia and/or China *cheat* on them and America is forced to *reply* to this cheating. (The dangers inherent in *existing nuclear powers significantly increasing the number of warheads in their arsenals* is a problem of a different sort, as was covered in Chapter 2 and will be discussed further in Chapter 6.)

The Norm of Nuke-Attack Abstinence Is Threatened in This Century

A consensus among commentators supports two conclusions about nuclear weapons usability in combat in the 21st century. One is that the worldwide abstinence from use in acts of war over the past 75 years has established a significant *norm* of international behavior—what classical-geopolitical theorists would label a *status quo*—which helps constrain states to continue obeying that norm, namely *nuclear attack abstinence*. As with other norms of the post-WWII "Modern World Order," this particular one is supported by most (if not *all*) states, and it benefits from significant *de facto* hurdles to ever being violated—hurdles that were not so evident back during the worrisome height of the Cold War.

(Worry is good; it foments *care, caution, and safety*. Nuclear weapon ownership by *some* nations—necessary to restrain the world's inevitable *existential-threat aggressors*, and to prevent another *"big" conventional world war*—is a weighty stewardship/guardian responsibility that, like other burdens of "state adulthood/maturity," comes with an unavoidable element of worry.)

The world's history to date—from the invention of nukes in 1945 through this writing in late-2020—has been that, once *at least two rival states* both owned nukes, a nuclear war never did break out, either on purpose, or inadvertently. Certainly, there were operational false-alarm close calls, some quite hair-raising, but cooler heads always prevailed. A nuclear bomb never did detonate by accident, either, though there were mishaps, including bomber crashes or sunken missile subs, where sometimes the high-explosive initiator and/or the missile's chemical fuel did explode. The fact that in the same long span of years there were several major nuclear *reactor* disasters involving core fires and meltdowns, both in the East and in the West, suggests that the added *military discipline* and high-level, direct *civilian political control* in place for nuclear weapons really does add a significant level of ultimate-failure prevention.

Stringent mutual deterrent-threat (i.e., survivable second strike) mechanisms are now in place more and more, to support maintaining the norm of nuclear-attack abstinence, going into the future. Any nuclear attacker, especially any *first* such 21st-century violator (hopefully none ever!), can anticipate a wide range of painful retaliations and harsh punishments—up to and including, in the most extreme case, their own *existential obliteration.* Though an aggressor's remaining, post-strike nuclear arsenal (if any) might discourage actual counter-invasion on the ground—involving traditional occupation, with regime change, by vengeful defenders—many techniques are available to "reach into" the violator's turf and government, to "cut off" the violator within a (radioactive) *cordon sanitaire.* These various techniques include, above all, proportionate nuclear-weapons retaliation ("retaliation in kind," i.e., second-strike nuking), plus reinforcing this—across a much less destructive spectrum—by all sorts of diplomatic steps and conventional weapons-strike options. These include harsh international opprobrium and ostracism, cyber-punishments, high-explosive cruise missile barrages, economic sanctions, naval and aerial blockades (quarantines and no fly zones), trade boycotts, special operations (commando) pinpoint direct actions, and International Criminal Court prosecutions. In fact, even those states that might, in future, neither own their own second-strike nuclear arsenals, nor are unwilling to join an international coalition that resorts to *conventional* military force to punish the aggressor, can *still* participate actively in the *diplomatic and economic retaliation/retribution measures.*

Why Is Total World Nuclear Disarmament a Forlorn Hope—and the *Wrong Goal* for Arms Control?

Many people—especially some of the folks (voters) living in (what at least seem to them to currently be) secure, peaceful, prosperous "status-quo" states like America—devoutly wish that all the world's nuclear weapons could be eliminated. They see them, rightly, as threats to human survival. But this sincere wish overlooks the existence, in the real world, of nuclear-armed or nuclear-wannabe *terrorists, psychopaths in power, warmongering tyrants,* and various other bad-actor leaders and their conniving enablers, all of which/whom will simply *never* give up their nukes or their nuke ambitions. All these bad actors simply must be nuclear-deterred by the good actors. Overly naïve or utopian disarmament treaty goals also ignore the sad but oft-proven fact that ratified international disarmament treaties *always have cheaters.* Were nuclear weapons to ever be outlawed, then—truly—only these terrible outlaws would have *all* the nuclear weapons, and they would *not* be constrained in any effective way from using them for heinous acts of mass murder and untold destruction. Nuclear deterrence is the *only* reliable way to deter nuclear bad actors.

The relative preponderance of, *not* simply probabilities (*odds* or *chances*), but of resultant mathematical *expectations* (factoring in also *severity* of losses) is an important tool for making *truly relevant comparisons.* In other words, when ranking different policy options and/or scenario outcomes, advisors and decisionmakers must compare the relative magnitude of (1) the *small chance* and *relatively localized, "limited" devastation* of inadvertent, unauthorized, or accidental nuclear detonations by major states who do pay attention to safety and surety, and (2) the *virtual certainty* and *widespread,* "un*limited*" *devastation* of nukes being used for intentional aggression and mass murder if any unconstrained bad actors are allowed to run rampant, undeterred, on the world stage. Such *mathematically meaningful comparisons* argue *decisively* in favor of the following as the only effective solution: Have a few large, rich, populous states, each protecting *huge vested interests in nuclear peace,* each of which own right-sized (for them) nuclear arsenals, to competitively maintain effective mutual nuclear deterrence arsenals—including all necessary supporting infrastructure, such as hardened, redundant NC3; nuclear early warning, and intelligence-gathering capabilities; and well-maintained nuke stewardship/sustenance facilities. (This theme of "the few standing in for the many" will be expanded on in the concluding Chapter 7, below. The importance of considering the *resultant expectation of loss* from nuclear "events" during sensible policymaking, not simply their *probability of occurrence,* is discussed in detail in Appendix 1, which advocates for using *sound actuarial-science practices* as underpinnings for development of nuclear postures.)

"Revolutionary" Powers Want to Take On, and Displace, the "Status-Quo" Powers

As the classical foreign-relations academics argued, not all state (or sub-state) powers are status quo powers. Some are labeled "revolutionary"; they seek to disrupt the status quo, perhaps using great violence, for their own benefit at home and abroad. Modern clinical and organizational psychology teach us that (1) all too often—as with Adolf Hitler, Josef Stalin, Saddam Hussein, or Slobodan Milosevic—states fall under the control of a *sociopath dictator*, and that (2) such a person is driven by a *lack of any empathy* for other human beings, coupled with a deep-seated urge to *obliterate human social institutions* and *extinguish human life*. In consequence, the norm of nuclear weapons abstinence requires constant, fervent work to maintain. *Deterrence, not disarmament,* is the only way to preserve, protect, and defend the American Way of Life, along with worldwide nuclear peace, on a permanently sustainable basis.

Any Future First Nuke First-Use Will Not Be the *Last Such* Nuke First-Use

Another general consensus of nuclear strategy commentators is that any unprovoked, initiating, aggressive/offensive use of nuclear weapons in the future could very well open the floodgates to *further nuclear weapons proliferation*, and also to a wave of *nuclear weapons combat-usage aggression*. Any such trends could easily lead to a nuclear Armageddon, which whether it unfolds quickly (spasmodically, in "half an hour") or slowly (intermittently, over months or even years) would sound the ultimate failure of the human species to perpetuate itself. What is best done to prevent this?

No state lives, works, exists in splendid isolation, and no state can depend solely on its own nuclear-deterrence resources (let alone plaintive protests of "neutrality") for total protection against conflicts between other parties—*nuclear fallout and nuclear winter and summer* are planet-wide afflictions that obey *no* national boundaries or security walls. A broader, comprehensive system of treaties and norms *between states* is clearly needed. They must collaborate despite some native mistrust, out of simple necessity. This *international nuclear peacekeeping system* must come equipped with *benefits* for complying non-proliferators, and with *deterring punishments* for non-complying proliferators and aggressors. I.e., an effective world system of nuclear peacekeeping needs both carrots and sticks.

A basic mathematical exposition can lend further emphasis to help justify the investments and sacrifices of time, cost, effort, and aggravation necessary to strengthen and sustain the existing, so-far-successful but currently-strained world nuclear peacekeeping system.

Simple Math Can Illustrate Effective Nuclear Deterrence's Urgency

The set of simple equations derived below, taken together, dramatizes rather explicitly that the ultimate sought-after norm, nuclear abstinence, is *very brittle*. It is subject to sudden shattering, *opening the floodgates of profligate nuclear-weapons usage*, if prevention via deterrence and counterproliferation is ever neglected. It is now and will remain, in practical terms of money, property, and lives, *infinitely better* to work to preserve the abstinence norm unbroken, than it would be to neglect it—and then have to pick up the radioactive, smoldering, festering pieces left from a nuclear war.

Fundamental Cautionary Equations of 21st Century Nuclear Peacekeeping

The *open floodgates problem*, of future nuclear attack abstinence-norm violation, is so significant that it deserves statement/display in mathematical form. Except for some elementary probability theory—and one formula that uses a bit of differential calculus notation for shorthand—the equations below use only basic algebra knowledge. We'll review the meaning of special symbols as we go. Readers who prefer to skip the formulas can just read the accompanying verbal elaborations, which do of necessity interweave *policy implications* with the equations.

These equations are based on simple common sense and mathematical deductive logic. They use symbols to express their conclusions for clarity, for those readers who might be conversant in math. They are *not* meant to be accurate predictions, nor do they in any way account for the actual, real-world ways in which individual nations (and alliances/coalitions), and their advisors and decision-makers, might ever behave. The equations *do* represent a concise, approximate summary of relative, qualitative cause-and-effect chains; by using the "calculus of inequalities" these equations lead to some general conclusions about the *urgency of controlling international nuclear-conflict risks.*

The equations all refer to nuclear-test and warshot counts occurring *in the future only*. They do *not* count the two nuclear weapon warshots used in 1945 by the U.S. against Imperial Japan. *Nor* do they count the numerous nuclear-weapon tests, by states ranging from the

U.S. and the USSR/Russia before 1950 through to North Korea in the 21st century. That is to say, their entire perspective is *prospective only*.

Now for some simple algebra:

> In general, let PW represent the probability that nuclear-weapon warshots are used in the future, between some user-specified future starting date of interest, and some user-specified further off ending-date. Setting these two user-chosen date parameters ("independent variables") establishes the future time horizon to which all the subsequent formulas are meant to apply.
>
> As always, the lowest possible probability is 0, and the maximum possible probability is 1, represented by 100%.

Probability Equations for Nuclear-Weapon "Use" in Combat/Warshot Strikes and Counterstrikes

Now, let N represent the number of nuke warshots possibly/potentially set off, during that user-specified, relevant-to-them interval of future time for which PW is to be calculated.

[For you math mavens, we could have used the fancier notation $PW_{(t1,\ t2)}$ (note the subscript $_{(t1,\ t2)}$, denoting the start and end dates of the relevant time interval, within a timeline dating system where today—actually right now—is represented by 0). This would have highlighted—for purists—the user-specified time-dependency of the various probability quantities in the equations below. But we omitted said subscript to simplify the notation, since the focused-upon time interval in question, whatever it is chosen to be, is then *fixed* as background to all further discussion here about the probability inequalities.]

N could be any non-negative integer (whole number) such as 0, 1, 2, 3, etc. (The maximum possible *N* would relate to the total number of nukes in all the world's nuclear arsenals.) A and B below are user-chosen specific values for N.

[Note this N is not the same variable as the number of states that own nukes, which is also sometimes also denoted by N, per JFK, as mentioned earlier.]

Next, let PW(A or more | B) represent the *conditional probability* that some future (user specified) *total* number of warshot nukes, in the (rather) wide range of numbers "A or more," (where A is chosen by the user) *does* subsequently get used during the specified future time interval, "given that" (the meaning of the "|" symbol) the (user-specified) total number of warshot nukes "B" have *already, so far* been used *when the chosen time-interval first begins*, that is, between $t = 0$ and $t = t_1$. (Or, as in the conditional probability of equation 3 below, let "B tested," when B is so labeled, represent the future total number of attempted-full-detonation nuclear weapon tests conducted before the given time interval (t_1, t_2), *without any* actual warshots *yet* being used after "actual now, today," i.e., time $t = 0$.)

The symbol ">" means "is greater than."

The symbol ">>" means "is much greater than."

Again, the symbol "|" means "given that."

Then:

$$PW(N = 2 \text{ or more used} \mid 1 \text{ used}) >> PW(N = 1 \text{ or more used} \mid 0 \text{ used})$$
[Equation 1]

What this inequality signifies is that the probability of 2 or more nukes (in total) being used in anger, given that the first future "warshot" *does* get used (as opposed to any nukes "just" used in tests) *is much greater than* the probability that one or more do get used when *none* have been used yet in anger.

Equation 1 embodies, in stark math terms, what most people would see as common sense.

We can go a step further. If indeed at least one nuclear warshot does get used in the future, various national nuclear-deterrence postures (specifying retaliation in kind), and mutual defense alliances (such as NATO) with their "nuclear umbrella" *extended deterrence* treaties, make it *extremely likely* that *at least one more* warshot will be used, in retaliation, by or on behalf of the party against which the future first-ever warshot was used. Thus we can say that:

To a first approximation,

$$PW(N = 2 \text{ or more} \mid 1 \text{ used}) = 100\%$$
[Equation 2]

Now, as discussed elsewhere both in this book and in other nuclear-deterrence literature, if at least one nuke is used in an attack, and then retaliated against, there is some probability that *uncontrollable escalation*—contributed to by the Intra-War Nuclear Unsafe-User Principle—will be triggered, leading in the worst case to *total global thermonuclear Armageddon*—the combat use of *huge* numbers of nukes. Thus, we can write as follows:

$$PW(N = \text{all the world's nukes} \mid 1 \text{ used}) > 0 \text{ and maybe is } >> 0$$
[Equation 2.1]

Probability Equations Relating to Nuclear-Weapon Test Dangers

The same sort of logic can be applied to *nuclear weapons tests* as to actual nuclear combat warshots.

Let PT represent the probability that nuclear weapons tests are conducted in the future. Then by PT(A or more | *B*) we mean the conditional probability of *A* or more nuclear weapon *tests* occurring in the future (underground or otherwise), given that *B* such tests have occurred already in future *before* the user-specified time interval (t_1, t_2) under study. (This notation is the direct analog of *PW* re nuclear weapon warshot use.) Again, one test raises pent-up geopolitical, defense-related, and emotional/psychological pressures for additional tests by various parties. (Shame on North Korea!) We can thus anticipate that:

$$PT(N = 2 \text{ or more} \mid 1 \text{ tested}) >> PT(N = 1 \text{ or more} \mid 0 \text{ tested})$$

[Equation 3]

What Equation 3 says is that any further nuclear testing at all is *very likely* to trigger a large amount of further testing. This clearly demonstrates the vital importance of nuclear test ban treaties and norms. This probability inequality will be "especially unequal" (and *especially stark*) when the start of the time interval under study is "today" ($t_1 = 0$).

Also worth pointing out, we can anticipate that any future nuclear weapons *testing* (especially by a state *in addition* to North Korea, which has recently done 4 tests—so folks are sort of used to Kim Jong Un doing that) will have *an undesirable effect* on the likelihood that one or more future nuclear weapons will *actually be used in anger as warshots.*

[Algebraically—again for you fellow math mavens—this means the following: The calculus derivative of the probability of *weapon use* in an attack or counterattack (a warshot), with respect to the probability of *weapon testing,* is greater (much greater?) than zero. Thus we obtain Equation 4, where "df/dx" means the instantaneous rate-of-change influence (graph's tangent slope) of the independent variable "x" on the dependent variable "f," as in differential calculus:

$$d\,PW(N = 1 \text{ or more} \mid 0 \text{ used}) / d\,PT(N = 1 \text{ or more} \mid 0 \text{ tested}) > 0 \text{ or} >> 0$$

[Equation 4]

This Equation 4 calculus derivative being positive, or very positive, makes a strong statement supporting the same broad conclusions as the other equations.]

Some *Rather Critical* Policy Implications, in Plain English

The slightest further violations of the nuclear-weapons Test Ban norm (whether by North Korea or by any other entity) and/or slightest violation of the nuclear-weapons attack abstinence norm, could indeed very well open the floodgates to *additional copycat and me-too violations, retaliations, escalations—and induced population collapses.*

It is therefore vital that the U.S. (and our Allies) retain a very strong conventional *and nuclear* deterrence force. (Our adversaries, for their own best sense of security—which enables the best *worldwide strategic security*—really should observe these same Best Practices, too.)

This is not only to best help prevent any norm violations. It is also, if necessary, to be able to use a flexible and proportionate spectrum of military interventions to punish actual violations—in highly visible and truly painful ways, with lasting negative consequences for the violator's regime. This *capability and intent to punish* (whether by a nuclear *or* a conventional counter-strike, as appropriate given the adversary and their degree of violation) is necessary to restore and enforce the worldwide nuclear abstinence norms as quickly and as stringently as is practicable, against the dastardly conduct of the norm-violating ("revolutionary") power.

In particular, it is absolutely vital that the U.S. and other major states and international authorities continue their laser-sharp focus on convincing North Korea to dismantle its small but menacing nuclear arsenal, or at least to permanently refrain from any more nuclear testing and to focus exclusively on *deterrence.* Keen attention must also be paid to defeating Iran's ability to ever obtain nuclear weapons.

These Equations Argue for the Very Strongest Nuclear Counter-Proliferation Efforts

Counter-proliferation experts argue that it is vitally important to keep *the number of countries with nuclear weapons* to the bare minimum. Why is this so? One simple answer is: The more states that do own nuclear weapons, the more are the various unpredictable, confusing permutations and combinations by which two entities could get into a nuclear war which could then spread to more and more other entities. In an absolutely worst case, every state or sub-state armed group on the planet with nuclear weapons could end up shooting them all off at each other.

Reasons for this wild escalation (hinted at above) could include—and this is a very long list—sheer panic, mad rage; invocation of various interlocking alliances, and nuclear-umbrella commitments (ala World War I's uncontrolled defense-treaty free-for-all); wider incursions of nuclear delivery platform trajectories, of radioactive fallout, and even of sun-obscuring (nuclear winter) pollutants onto previously-uninvolved sovereign territory; accidents and errors when systems are badly degraded by the raging nuclear combat; terrible side effects of nuclear combat, such as EMPs, stray shots (with errant nuclear detonations) when combat-damaged in-flight guidance and fusing systems go badly awry; attempts to halt the fighting which fail; attempts to restore intra-war nuclear deterrence which fail; and other factors that normal people (let alone nuclear strategist professionals) can't even conceive of during happy, peaceful times.

Some Permutations-and-Combinations Equations Warn about Nuclear Proliferation

Perhaps one way to express the nuclear proliferation "problem" is to come up with a simple formula that roughly expresses:

> C = the number of *distinctly different* ways in which a long chain of nuclear conflicts and escalations can draw in more and more entities, one by one, among all the various different possible subsets of owners of nukes (out of the superset of all world nuke owners) who do sooner or later get dragged into the nukings,
>
> as a mathematical function of:
>
> N = the total number of countries and sub-state entities that do own nukes.

Let us denote this function as $C = F(N)$. What is the mathematical "function" F?

Only the vaguest estimate of the relationship F between C and N can be given here. Let's think this through in stages. First, we ask, is C equal to the number of entities N, any one of which might start a nuclear war? That would mean $C = N$. But surely this is way *too low* an estimate, as it ignores all the ways in which more entities can jump in or get dragged into the nuclear war, whenever $N > 2$.

Does C = N * 2? (The "* 2" notation means "to the second power," i.e., squared.) This would make more sense, since any entity might be the one that starts the war, and they might (objectively speaking) start it with any other one entity. (Also, when N is 1, they might get into a civil war with themselves, in which nuclear weapons come into play by both sides.) But N * 2 is *also too small*, again because it ignores the potential *chain* of spreading of the war further, to even more nuclear entities—at least if N is bigger than two. (Recall that as of this writing, in 2021, N equals nine, and Iran presents a clear and present danger of N becoming 10.)

To first keep things comparatively simple, while still making our basic point here, let us first, in Equation 5 below, count up *only the scenarios* in which, eventually, *every one of the world's nuke owners* does end up participating actively in the war. (We are not yet, in Equation 5, counting all "smaller" nuclear wars, i.e., those in which at least one nuclear power stays uninvolved throughout.) We do in Equation 5—and in the more inclusive Equation 7 which follows it below—count *as distinct* each scenario in which the various nuclear combatants come in *in a different order.*

To elaborate on the counting rules we are going to use in the following calculations, we are *not* even counting here the situations of nuclear powers attacking, with nukes, countries that do *not* own nukes. We are only counting any involvement at all for *actual nuclear weapon-owning states.*

Nor are we even counting the ways in which the outbreak of nuclear war could motivate *further* states to first gain their own nukes (i.e., proliferation)—which would *increase N itself.*

Thus, what we come up with in Equation 5 will be *only a lower bound* on the total different number of ways a nuclear war could play out. The actual number of different ways would be *much larger,* if both "smaller" nuclear wars (fewer entities involved) and further proliferation (increase in "N") were counted as well.

But we *will* count smaller wars, too, in Equation 7.

Now then, the number of different ways in which a nuclear war can start and then spread until it involves *all of N* different nuke-owning entities equals:

$$N \times (N-1) \times (N-2) \times \ldots\ldots \times 3 \times 2 \times 1 \qquad \text{[Equation 5]}$$

This particular function of N is called in mathematical language "N factorial." It is denoted in standard mathematical symbolism as N! The exclamation point, as algebraic notation, denotes "factorial," but it also puts very useful emphasis on the *true (immense) speed of growth* of the problem of preventing nuclear war as the number of nuclear weapons-owning states expands.

As simple algebra will show, it is a fact that:

$$(N+1)! = (N+1) \times N! \qquad \text{[Equation 6]}$$

This is to say, whenever a *new member joins the "Nuclear Club"*—thus increasing the member count from N to N + 1—the number of total-war scenarios jumps by a *multiplicative factor* N + 1. I.e., the more nuke-owning entities there already are, the *faster* the number of total war scenarios inflates *each* time a new nuke entity arises. For instance, if *one more entity* such as Iran joined the current nuclear club, raising N from 9 to 10, the number of ways total nuclear war could spread would rise by a *factor of 10.* Add another nuclear weapons-owning state, and it would go up by a *further* factor of 11. And so on. If we ever went from 9 to 11, an increase of *"just" 2 countries,* the number of horror scenarios would go up by 110 times! (And this is an understatement.)

So far we have assumed, to estimate "F," that (in what we are thinking of as a *single* nuclear war), eventually *every* nuke-owning entity does join in. But what if, within a hypothetical future "single" nuclear war, *fewer than* every possible entity in "N" ever joins in? This would give us a less-approximate, not-as-overly-low sense of what the mathematical relationship "F" looks like. That will give us a less inaccurate (not as badly underestimated) indication of how "F" behaves, as "N" might—in some rather ugly future counterproliferation scenarios—grow bigger and bigger over time.

In other words, we will now *also* count (as separate individual scenarios for how a possible future nuclear war might play out) *every* distinct situation (as to *which* entities join in, in *what* order) in which *fewer than all of the world's nuke owners* do join in the nuke combat over the course of the war.

Equation 7 below shows that the total "counted" number, of different nuclear-war scenarios, would then go up *significantly more rapidly* than when F uses the above, much simpler counting rule of Equation 5.

Let us designate the number of such scenarios, defined by this more pessimistic (but more complete, more realistic) counting rule, given the number of nuclear entities N, as the function FF(N). Using simple algebra—and also, as previously, including nuclear civil wars (between two domestic factions, in one state, who both grab some national nukes)—we see that:

$$FF(N) = N + N \times (N - 1) + N \times (N - 1) \times (N - 2) + \ldots.. + N!$$

[Equation 7]

And thus:

$$FF(N) = N \times (FF(N - 1) + 1)$$ [Equation 8]

Equation 8 shows that for this more all-inclusive way of counting all the different possible lineups of nuclear wars, if the nuclear club increases from 9 members to 10, then the scenario count inflates by multiplying by 10, and then by adding 10 more on top of that. If an 11th member joins the club, the total number of nuclear war scenarios would go up by a *further* factor of 11, plus adding 11 more on top of that. And so on.

By this fuller definition of "counting" all the different horror scenarios, if the world went from N = 9 to N = 11, the total would increase by a factor of 110 times (as before), and *then* would jump further, by an *additional 231 different scenarios*!

More Counter-Proliferation Policy Imperatives

Clearly, the more states (or sub-state/trans-state entities) own nukes, the *tremendously harder* it becomes to engineer threats and inducements, custom-fit to each party, that would deter or resolve *all* conceivable international crises and conflicts *without nuclear war ever breaking out.*

It also becomes *vastly harder*, as the number of entities in the world owning their own nukes does go up much at all, to *restore a semblance of nuclear peace* in the unfortunate case that deterrence ever does fail, by nuclear war breaking out.

To repeat for emphasis, these equations don't even begin to take account of how the outbreak of any nuclear combat is *very likely to cause even more states to proliferate,* sooner or later getting their own nukes if they are even still alive, thus increasing N itself.

To summarize, the above simplified Equations 6 and 8 demonstrate conclusively that, for its own survival, the civilized world must (1) make maximum effective efforts to *prevent any further nuclear proliferation,* and (2) make maximum efforts to assure that *today's mutual nuclear deterrence line-ups remain fully effective,* to insure forever preserving nuclear peace.

Nuclear Treaties Are Living Documents Always Needing More Work

The first purpose of the above simple math is to help illustrate the grave relevance of effective nuclear deterrence and ally assurance to enforcing the global norms of both nuclear-test and nuclear-attack abstinences. *The other purpose* of the equations is to show the importance of worldwide compliance with those provisions of the UN's Non-Proliferation Treaty (NPT) that forbid the further spreading of nuclear weapons to any more countries. As the 21st century unfolds, the latter treaty is best seen as a work in perpetual progress, *a living document*—one whose life extension will clearly be a very long-term process and a pressing international responsibility. (Arms races between existing nuclear powers, which can also seriously endanger nuclear peace, are the direct and indirect subjects of other, currently endangered—or outright violated—treaties and norms, such as the ABM Treaty, New START, the INF Treaty, Open Skies, and the CTBT.)

The best foundation for inclusive discussion of modernizing the NPT in a real-world, pragmatic way, i.e., one that is likely to both (1) *be agreed to and ratified* by relevant states, and (2) *then actually achieve its nuclear peacekeeping goals*, is to draw on a rigorous logical development of what nuclear deterrence, ally assurance, and nonproliferation seek to achieve, how they can work given current and emerging technologies and geopolitical concerns, and what pitfalls exist to threaten good implementation and long-term success. This "NPT Treaty life-extension negotiations process" itself, and the updated treaty-draft amendment enhancements it could deliver, have to be robust and resilient, with "impact attenuators" and "guardrails" that allow for a limited amount of the inevitable diplomatic pushing and shoving, and military saber rattling and jousting, that do inevitably occur between competitive and even adversarial states. One specific topic demanding very careful, thorough discussion is how to prevent occasional attempts at nuclear blackmail—an extreme form of psychological warfare—from going too far and exploding into outright nuclear combat.

Several ways of updating the NPT treaty, to better control nuclear proliferation among states (and possibly among some terrorists as well) in the 21st century, include:

- Perfecting civilian, commercialized *hot-fusion power reactors*, as a highly attractive alternative to always-problematic (unsafe, polluting, bomb-fuel using/making) nuclear fission power. Fusion-power technology assistance could be given (to replace fission power) to states that do swear off nukes. Ample, safe hot-fusion electric power availability for everyone could be a significant stimulus to *lowered world strife, a "greener" and healthier planet, and universal prosperity*. Treaty language precedent for this exists, in that the NPT now provides for making fission-power technological assistance available to nations that swear off nuclear weapons via ratifying the NPT.
- Promulgating, and realizing, a world system of *Best Practices* for mutual effective deterrence and ally assurance among existing nuclear weapons-owning states. As discussed in earlier chapters, this would include two "aspirational" require-

ments, perhaps to be enforced by time-limits for compliance: (1) that all nuclear states field *stealthy, survivable deterrence submarines*—nuclear powered SSBNs if affordable by their national economy, or alternatively, air-independent propulsion SSBPs, which are available for export to those states that can't build their own—for assured, survivable second-strike capabilities, and (2) that all nuclear states set a cap *and* floor to national nuclear arsenal warhead counts at the *individually-optimized numbers of nukes* which each such state truly needs, to be able to meet/assure its own and its nuclear-umbrella ally(ies) deterrence needs, by being able, if necessary in a last extreme, to inflict decisively deterring (i.e., existential-level) "massive" damage on any and all likely adversary nuclear powers *no matter how many casualties and own-property destruction the bad-actor might be willing to accept.* This two-part deterrence mechanism, combined with explicitly allowing R&D *and deployment* of now-burgeoning and even unanticipated future technologies—to (1) make deterrent second-strike Triad legs (SSBNs and SSBPs, ICBMs, DCAs and strategic bombers) *even more survivable,* and to (2) make retaliatory weapon-delivery vehicles (ballistic missiles and their RVs or MARVs, cruise missiles, hypersonics) *even more mission-reliable (i.e., able to assuredly reach their targets)*—would recognize the realities of how to assure nuclear peace while avoiding any more wasteful and dangerous nuclear warhead-count arms races. (The ultimate survivability of SSBNs or SSBPs, along with a robust national system of Nuclear C3 and leadership succession, would then be a reliable mechanism to deter any state-level adversary from making any surprise, unprovoked first-strike or "decapitating" nuclear attacks.)

- Rationalizing a *UN-recognized network of nuclear-umbrella alliances, with clear provisions for participants to join and change or end their membership,* for those non-nuke-owning states that truly believe they do need nuclear protection for their own national security. This would involve officially accepting what is right now on the face of it true, that a few large countries ("superpowers") owning right-sized, effective nuclear arsenals are absolutely needed in the current (competitive, factionalized, divisive, anarchic) world to deter both *nuclear aggression* by any belligerent party aiming at them or their allies, and to deter *another big, bloody conventional world war.* Such a protocol, a *"realist" update/revision* replacing the (neglected/ignored)

NPT clause re *universal* nuclear disarmament, would also require either "grandfathering in" all *existing smaller/regional nuclear states*, or more optimistically, eventually alleviating *root causes of past proliferation* by working to resolve certain regional existential conflicts in the Middle East and Asia that now cause certain smaller nuclear states to believe they continue to need their own nukes. To repeat for emphasis, a state unable to field a survivable deterrent fleet of SSBNs or SSBPs on a timely basis would not be permitted to retain a nuclear arsenal long term—it would be required to make nuclear-umbrella arrangements instead.

In this way the Cold War accusation, that the NPT instituted "nuclear apartheid" in favor of the five founding nuclear weapons powers (the main victors of World War II), might be dispelled once and for all. The recently ratified UN Nuclear Weapon Ban Treaty, attempting yet again to eliminate all nuclear arms worldwide—which is supported by *only some* of the non-nuclear-weapon states, and is being ignored by all nine current nuclear states—would have a *sound and manageable alternative*: a global system of "competitive nuclear peace-keeping" founded on effective mutual deterrence, implemented by (1) the three rival nuclear superpowers or alliances (China, Russia, and the U.S./NATO), and (2) at least until regional and religious existential threats are greatly reduced, by the variously-situated current/de-facto regional nuclear powers (India, Pakistan, Israel, DPRK, all of which deploy or are working to get SSBNs or SSBPs). Of course, there also must be provision to deal satisfactorily with nuclear-wannabe Iran, and with any other potential proliferating rogue states. Also note importantly that such nuclear-arsenal rightsizing and readiness, plus ally-assurance diplomacy/messaging, are vital to prevent further nuclear proliferation, even (or especially) by any of America's (or another superpower's) current umbrella protectees.

Here Are Key U.S. "Best Policy" Implications of the Nuclear Testing and Usage Equations

The above equations, especially Equations 3 and 4, also help reinforce and reemphasize the tremendous importance of worldwide ratification of, and compliance with, the Comprehensive Nuclear Test Ban Treaty (CTBT), which is currently hanging fire. Several countries that own nuclear weapons still need to ratify the treaty before it can take effect. The United States is one of them. America's then-President did sign the treaty, but since then the U.S. Senate has not ratified it, over concern that our and our nuclear-umbrella Allies' national security *might in the future require additional nuclear weapons testing.* This is a very good point. But perhaps also, at this point, the U.S. has now certainly withdrawn from *enough* nuclear arms-control treaties as a necessary way to *censure adversary cheating.* We should retain at least *some* worldwide nuclear-weapon proliferation (NPT treaty) and testing (CTBT norm) bans/strictures, to sustain the essential underpinnings of global nuclear peacekeeping.

It would perhaps be better were the U.S. to ratify the CTBT (which like all international treaties does have a *unilateral-escape clause*), and then focus on (1) strong support for our rapidly-aging Triad's necessary hardware and NC3 replacement and modernization, plus (2) continuation of the American Government's existing, ongoing National Nuclear Stockpile Stewardship Program, and (3) renewal and modernization of the Department of Energy's and the National Nuclear Security Administration's nuclear-weapons laboratories, and manufacturing and maintenance infrastructure.

The Stockpile Stewardship program uses sophisticated supercomputer modeling, combined with non-nuclear or sub-critical bomb-components testing, in lieu of actual nuclear weapon full-detonation testing. Continuing innovative research into the computer capabilities and modeling needed to be able to *perfect any required new weapon designs, or to validate modification and/or maintenance of existing designs,* but (per the CTBT norm) *without* actual full-up weapon testing, seems very wise. This should include taking things to the next level of computing and modeling in the years to come, including use of truly astonishingly fast and powerful, *emerging quantum computer capabilities.*

Overall, the stark nuclear-usage equations above also help clarify the vital importance of powerful, perseverant, well-funded, globally coordinated measures to dissuade, deter, and/or (in the last extreme, if ever required) interdict (shoot down) any belligerent adversary's future limited, unprovoked nuclear strike. The United States must continue providing essential leadership on this front, in both *missile shield deployment and hypersonic interceptor* nuclear-defense R&D.

To summarize from previous chapters about logically-rigorous, modern nuclear deterrence theory and Best Practices, two crucial points relevant to the present discussion are:

- Because of *varying* actual and potential viewpoints on nuclear-weapon *"first-use usability"* around the world, plus the ineradicable vastness of publicly-available information on *how to manufacture nuclear weapons*—combined with the proven tendency of some human beings to *cheat* on treaties, laws, and norms, along with the difficulty of *rapidly finding and stopping* all such nuclear cheaters—the only really viable way to prevent any, ever, future adversary unprovoked warshot usage is via perpetually vigilant, robust, survivable, safe and secure nuclear deterrence-in-being–with a *fully adequate, but not excessive,* number of nuclear warheads in the right-sized national defensive arsenal. Some simple modeling calculations, presented in the next chapter, suggest that, in the *current threat environment,* the current U.S. arsenal size, of 1,550 deployed warheads per New START, with a comparable number stockpoled, is the right number—*whether or not* New START is extended somehow, or is instead allowed to expire.

- America's deterrence-in-being absolutely *must be supported* via vigorous, cutting-edge stockpile stewardship programs, rather than through full-up warhead testing—and (very importantly indeed) *must not be weakened via unilateral (one-sided) U.S. nuclear disarmament.* The latter would only have the direct effect of undermining universal respect for the global norm of nuclear-weapon-use abstinence—by leaving treaty cheaters *completely undeterred,* and America's non-nuke-owning Allies (and other states, too) *frightened into profligate proliferation.* Significant *bilateral* arsenal downsizing would also be badly destabilizing, since with relatively few nuclear warheads on each side, aggressors might conclude that such a war was *practicably winnable*—the massive damage ensuing, though very dire, could be regarded as *acceptably limited by a truly desperate or sociopathic enemy regime.*

Several significant *defense policy corollaries* (logical consequences) of these main points are:

- It is vital that Congress and the American people sustain robust annual and multi-year funding for all twelve (at a minimum) of the new Columbia-class fleet ballistic missile submarines (SSBNs). Similarly vital is the funding for all forty-eight (or more, if necessary) Virginia-class nuclear powered fast-attack subs (SSNs)—as many as possible of the latter with the Virginia Payload Module (VPM) SSGN-capable hull extension—so that these SSNs can, among all their many other essential 21st-century missions, help protect our SSBNs and defend against adversary SSBNs. America also needs to continuing analyzing, very carefully, to exactly what extent there are or aren't genuine risk/benefit tradeoff gains to returning to the First Cold War's posture of basing tactical nuclear weapons on U.S. Navy surface warships and fast-attack submarines: Precisely how much would America's (and NATO's) nuclear deterrence *truly be strengthened* over and above its present effectiveness? Would a nuclear arms race, and nuclear proliferation, be *unnecessarily yet detrimentally encouraged?*

- It is likewise vital to sustain stable, robust multi-year funding for the *other legs* of the strategic U.S. Nuclear Triad, namely next-generation land-based ICBMs (the Ground Based Strategic Deterrent—GBSD), and nuclear-capable heavy strategic/stealth bombers (the B-21 Raider) plus the latter's payloads of stand-off (crew-survivable), stealthy (strike-reliable) Long-Range Stand Off cruise missiles (LRSOs). LRSOs, which might have either a conventional or a nuclear warhead, are *really no more nor less "destabilizing"* (as some anti-nuke pundits allege) than *long-existing* U.S./NATO (and adversary) airborne deterrence platforms (delivery vehicles) and their ordnance: The Dual-Capable Aircraft (DCA) that launch them, and the cruise missiles and/or gravity bombs they can launch—ever since the First Cold War started, and throughout various major brushfire wars since then—*always* might have incorporated *either* a conventional *or* a nuclear warhead. (The Reagan Administration's deployment of the superbly capable, *dual-capable* B-1B Lancer supersonic strategic nuclear bomber—an adjunct to the venerable, dual-capable B-52—is credited by some ex-USSR officials with helping end the Soviet Union in a *peaceful, internally-fomented* regime change.) Also very important is sustaining adequate capacity of a joint and combined U.S./NATO fleet of *dual capable* fighter-bombers, for making any necessary retaliatory *tactical-nuclear second strikes* within Europe or other geographic theaters.
- It is vital that America support strong ongoing funding for all of the various government departments and agencies, and those genuinely effective international cooperative bodies too, that work to keep nuclear weapons out of the hands of rogue states and sub-state/trans-state armed groups (terrorists), who all should *never* be allowed to obtain or possess them. It is just

as critical to sustain the current, vigilant, layered defenses against nuclear proliferation and nuclear terrorism. The world of law enforcement and the defense world must make *very sure* that any bad actors who do obtain nuclear weapons or their fuels and other components are *never permitted* to retain (or sell on) those materials, assemble working weapons, deliver them to a target, and detonate them–or commit nuclear blackmail, intimidation, and coercion.

- All official studies of possible future so-called "nuclear warfighting" (more properly, *nuclear peace restoration*) should continue to make it very clear that those studies are intended solely and specifically to *reinforce and maintain effective nuclear deterrence*, and (just in case) to end any nuclear conflicts with other countries, that the enemies start, *as rapidly as possible on acceptable political and humanitarian terms*. To neglect or omit such studies within U.S. National Nuclear Posture would leave a *serious loophole or gap* in our deterrence and defense: It might telegraph to adversaries that, although we did own nukes, we had *no good plan* re what to do with them if an enemy ever did hit us with a nuclear strike. It is precisely the perpetual need for effective nuclear deterrence that necessitates preparedness for the not-entirely-inconceivable situation where such deterrence might fail. The ability, in the last extreme of any nuclear war, to *reliably and quickly reestablish intra-war (and then post-war) nuclear deterrence, strategic stability, and nuclear peace* is a critical part of overall Pentagon and State Department capabilities. Chapter 4's suggested retaliation paradigm based on Tit-for-Tat, to be elaborated upon in Volume 2, might provide a useful adjunct (or at least, a helpful elaboration/explication) to existing U.S. Strategic Command plans and targeting paradigms.

Conclusion: Simple Equations Highlight the Importance of Sustaining Arms-Control Norms

The simple equations developed above help to dramatically, starkly emphasize the utterly vital importance to worldwide nuclear peace-keeping of the *nuclear test-ban norm* and of *nuclear non-proliferation*. These imperatives translate into a few interrelated Best Practices for America's and NATO's nuclear deterrence strategy, policy, and posture—Best Practices which will help maximize the beneficial utility, to all world citizens (people *and* countries), of all the considerable effort and expense needed to implement effective, modern nuclear deterrence-in-being.

In particular, the *better demonstrably prepared* America's nuclear deterrence Triad is in *every conceivable necessary respect,* then the *less likely* it is that an enemy will ever dare violate the ultimate geopolitical taboo, namely the nuclear-aggression abstinence norm. The *more modern our equipment, the more thorough and flexible our contingency planning, the more focused and cogent our messaging and signaling, and the more ready our personnel,* the less likely it is that our prospective strategic military capabilities might ever need to be used in combat in the real world. And the *smarter our nuclear policies, strategies, and postures, and the more comprehensive our preparations to mitigate the very worst,* the more likely it is that, even in the very worst case, peace can be restored rapidly—with a minimum of death and destruction, and the minimal advancement of tyranny—after any such nuclear violation is ever committed by some badly-misguided foreign entity.

Having a strong, robust, modern and safe, secure nuclear deterrence Triad, *always at hand and immediately ready,* is what lets free people sleep soundly at night. It lets all Americans and our Allies (and everyone else on planet Earth) enjoy the full fruits of peace and prosperity while we're awake.

CHAPTER 6

Too Few Nukes Are Worse Than Too Many

America Should Stick to the New START Warhead Counts

Executive Summary: U.S.'s Defense of World Nuclear Peace Is Both Selfish *and* Altruistic

Having *too few* deployed and stockpiled nuclear weapons to, without fail, achieve one's essential strategic-deterrence purposes can be just as risky to peace, or even *more* risky, than having an unnecessary, excessive number of nukes. *Rightsizing* America's nuclear arsenal is the key to preserving global nuclear peace without triggering wasteful, dangerous *warhead-count upward arms races*. What's more, the nuclear peacekeeping benefit of rightsizing is *not* a zero-sum game: If we succeed at continuing to be truly "great" at it in this Cold War Two era of nuclear tensions galore—thereby successfully protecting our sacred Way of Life, as America always has since 1776—then *the rest of the world* gets to enjoy the *same* nuclear peacetime that America's modernized, effective deterrence Triad sustains for ourselves, and the world benefits *at no extra cost to the U.S.*! (This is distinct from the vexed issue of *"free-riding"* by America's Allies, in which they do *not* meet their side of NATO—or other—defense-spending obligations.)

Recall that the U.S. and USSR did get into an *extremely expensive* arms race in the 1970s and 1980s. At its peak, a few years before the USSR collapsed in bankruptcy, the two countries together owned something like 70,000 nuclear weapons; Greenpeace estimated that this was enough to wipe out all of Humanity *seven (7) times over*!

In retrospect, those inventories were wildly excessive. Near the end of the First Cold War and then afterward, the U.S. and USSR/Russia both, in stages, reduced their arsenals by very considerable amounts, sometimes by *ratifying bilateral, legally-binding arms-reduction treaties* and sometimes through *coordinated but independent and voluntary initiatives* by both heads of state.

Then, amid the West's triumphalist celebration of "the end of history," it seemed as if the two nuclear superpowers were even getting into a "race to the bottom," to *completely denuclearize*—or so some over-optimistic commentators believed. Then belligerent dictator Vladimir Putin came to power in 2000 in Moscow. International relations, *always unpredictable, inherently cyclical, and deeply competitive,* have progressively worsened since then. A belligerently expansionist, anti-democratic Russia is now well into growing and modernizing its nuclear arsenal—and is using the *inherent self-protection* of that arsenal to repeatedly violate peace and freedom *below the nuclear threshold*: in Chechnya, Georgia, Ukraine, Syria, Libya, and elsewhere.

Despite these facts, and despairing of ever achieving total *global* denuclearization, some American pundits and politicos now seem to want the U.S. to continue its nuclear disarmament *unilaterally*, on sheer, blind momentum. They fail to understand the absolutely crucial difference between (1) *eliminating excessive nukes that aren't needed for effective deterrence* and (2) *retaining a sufficient number of nukes that* are *needed for effective deterrence.* Some of those misguided influencers argue for what is called a "minimal" (or "minimum") nuclear deterrent. This would be sized *well below* the current New START Treaty's allowed level of a bit more than 1,550 "deployed" strategic warheads in our Triad, with a roughly equal number "stockpiled" as backup—for a total right now of something like 3,000 or 4,000 American H-bombs. We also own around 500 tactical ("battlefield") A-bombs. Such *tactical* nukes are *not* regulated by New START—or any other treaty—and Russia actually owns about 5,000 of these "low-yield" A-bombs, some *ten times* as many as we do!

Those unilateral disarmament advocates urge that America go down to as low as 200 or 400 *total* strategic nuclear warheads, *period*—with *no* quid pro quo from Russia. They say this is to save money, and because it would (supposedly) be "less dangerous" for the world. But the former would be true *only in the short term*; the latter is not and never would be true *at all.*

No "End of History": Too Small a U.S. Triad Is *More* Dangerous Than One That's Too Big

The U.S. having *"just a little* nuclear deterrence" would, in some not-inconceivable geopolitical scenarios, be just as bad as us having none at all in today's (and tomorrow's) heavily-armed "multi-nuclear" world; *big wars, both nuclear and conventional, would become enabled* for the first time since the dawn of the *"Mutual Nuclear Deterrence Age"* in the 1950s.

Why? As we will explain more below, a nuclear deterrent *only* effectively deters *at all* if it is able, even *after* the attrition of a massive enemy surprise attack, to *get through* the enemy's strongest defenses to inflict upon that enemy damage *so severe* that the attacking regime's political and military assets cannot possibly hope to survive—and the potential attacker *knows this in advance* in no uncertain terms.

The sad fact is that a "smallish" U.S. arsenal could only inflict lesser damage, even when using nukes—*especially* in the face of enemy missile-shield and other defenses, which could become increasingly effective in the foreseeable future. Such lesser damage *might not be enough to deter* a very belligerent enemy who opportunistically, ruthlessly (or just plain desperately) sees "lesser" as being *too mild* to dissuade them from making an overwhelming nuclear first strike—at our fatal expense. *This scenario isn't so farfetched: Both Mao and Castro advocated it to the USSR during the First Cold War.*

What Do I Mean By "Rightsizing" the U.S. Nuclear Deterrence Triad?

I first learned the term *rightsizing* back in the early 1990s, while I was a partner in a global management consulting firm, when it was in vogue to describe (and justify to the media) what usually amounted to a corporation's personnel layoffs. The idea is this: For a company's given goals and objectives, needs and resources, profitability and access to capital, etc., there is an *exactly right total* count of employees that it should have on its payroll. If a business has too many employees—so the management consultants would say—then that firm should "rightsize"—by laying off the excess number of employees.

While the term *rightsize,* in this corporate context, is really just a euphemism for job cuts (with resulting unemployment), the "rightsizing" concept could serve well in the rather different context of national-defense strategy and nuclear-deterrence Best Practices. Thus:

DEFINITION: To *rightsize* a state's nuclear arsenal means to, *first,* determine the number of nuclear warheads that is *"just right"* for that state's strategic deterrence and defense needs, and then, if the actual current warhead count is *different* from what is needed, to carry out a program of either (1) "laying off" *(safely dismantling)* any excess, or (2) "hiring up" *(expanding)* the warhead count if there is a shortfall.

This Chapter 6 will in particular illustrate, using some simple mathematical modeling, the importance—to nuclear peacekeeping, nonproliferation, *and* counterterrorism goals—of America continuing to rightsize our nuclear arsenal according to our own *genuine strategic security requirements*, given the current and foreseeable threat environment that we face. (The same or similar little models could be formulated for *any* state, whether an American ally, adversary, or neutral.)

Note that this idealized, simplified rightsizing formula for nuclear-arsenal warhead count determines a Best Practice number *only in the abstract*. As developed below, the formula is isolated from various *pressing real-world U.S. (and Allied) government concerns* regarding assurance of our Nuclear Umbrella Allies, denuclearization of North Korea, counterproliferation in Iran (and elsewhere), and *securing warheads from thefts and accidents* in less-stable and/or less-experienced nuke-owning countries (such as the former USSR, or modern-era Pakistan). The rightsizing paradigm derived here is also independent from various other, wider U.S.-domestic political and overseas geopolitical issues. These issues might in future include targeted government spending, and investing, to *stimulate* a recessionary national economy—due to COVID-19, or for some other reason—and to *regenerate* infrastructure and skilled workers for the defense industry.

Some Policy Implications of Rightsizing America's Strategic Nuclear Warhead Count

The all-important *arsenal rightsizing question* has recently taken on great urgency: The 2010 New Strategic Arms Reduction Treaty (New START) ratified between Russia and America will expire at about the same time that this Volume 1 is being published—unless the two nuclear-superpower adversaries can agree to renew it. Chapter 6 makes a case—using simple calculations based on *modeling assumptions* which follow First Cold War *deterrence strategy norms* given in the literature—that the number of *deployed* strategic nuclear warheads, with comparable amounts further *stockpiled* as backup, that are specified by New START as maximums allowed for the U.S. (and for Russia)—whether by planning, or Providence, or both—are in fact the *exactly right amounts* to sustain effective mutual nuclear deterrence.

Either state's reserve-inventory "nuclear stockpile"—similar in quantity under New START to the warheads actually "deployed" (available immediately)—provides a *necessary margin* for various uncertain future contingencies. For America—indeed, for *any* nuclear-weapon-owning state—just one of these contingent scenarios is that we *lose* our nuclear-weapons manufacturing infrastructure in a future nuclear war but somehow we survive as a country, and then need *further* nukes for deterrence and defense against—or during—a *second* nuclear war *later on.*

The New START numbers will be mathematically demonstrated below to be *both necessary and sufficient* for *survivable strategic stability,* between the U.S. and one or two superpower adversaries (Russia and/or China). A key logical consequence is that *the same numbers* are *at the same time* also necessary and sufficient for *assurance of our Allies* that America's *"extended deterrent"* (Nuclear Umbrella) will be able to protect them *as well*: Even if Russia and/or China were to nuke some of our Allies but *not* America, our (intact) arsenal would surely then be able to inflict existential destruction on the attacker(s) in return.

This *numerical-adequacy finding* supports the following four-fold policy/strategy and budget/acquisition recommendations:

1. The U.S. should seek to renew New START at the *same* 1,550 deployed strategic warheads level as is specified now by the treaty. The U.S. should *not* reduce its strategic warhead stocks below the levels of the treaty, either unilaterally or bilaterally, *whether or not* the treaty is renewed or expanded. (Reduction would mean *we would no longer have the survivable option* to assuredly inflict retaliatory damage of decisively daunting *(i.e., effectively deterring)* catastrophic, existential magnitude on a very determined, very populous, richly endowed, geographically extensive—and massive-casualties accepting—belligerent/aggressor adversary superpower bloc.)
2. If Russia and America cannot agree to renew/extend the New START treaty—as seems quite possible as of this writing at the end of 2020—the U.S. should *not* get into an upward arms race over warhead counts with Russia (and/or with anyone else, such as China). America instead must *continue recapitalizing/renewing and modernizing* our entire existing technically and domain-wise diversified, geographically dispersed, numerically robust and thus resilient, mutually protecting and holistically survivable three-legged strategic Triad: SSBNs carrying SLBMs, silo-based ICBMs, and strategic bombers carrying ALCMs. If Russia were to commit a *small* upward violation of the New START caps, *Moscow would gain little*: whichever of our possible land assets they might attack with "a few extra nukes," our SSBNs could *still* assuredly obliterate their regime in our retaliatory second strike. If Moscow were to push upward

into the *tens of thousands* of warheads, as they did in the First Cold War, we should *not* again seek to keep up warhead-for-warhead. We should instead give priority to *building additional Columbia-class SSBNs, to further disperse our existing submarine-launched ballistic missile (SLBM) warhead inventory* against any possible enemy *strategic anti-submarine barrages*—which seems to be the only "useful" thing Russia might possibly hope to do with such a ridiculous thousands-strong warhead *buying binge*. (Even that *massive expenditure* of hard cash, and then of expensive weaponry, would only make sense if Russia could ever, somehow, localize our super-stealthy SSBNs, submerged on quiet deterrence patrol, to within a few hundred nautical miles within the vast world oceans.) To see the logic behind this "more subs, not more nukes" recommendation, let us look at representative cost figures: Additional *Columbia*-class SSBNs, bought in quantity—and *without* acquiring extra SLBM missile bodies *or* warheads—for an added "marginal" cost of about $6 billion each (once serial production is already well underway), come at a *small fraction* of the all-in "sunk" cost of a 1,000-plus H-bomb anti-submarine ICBM barrage, needed to try for a mission kill once *one sub* is vaguely localized. At the Russian *rouble* equivalent of roughly $200 million and up for *one* heavily-MIRVed ICBM plus its hardened silo or mobile launcher—even when bought in quantity—Moscow would *go bankrupt* long before it could threaten America's at-sea survivable deterrent fleet (of *at least four subs* at any given time) via any purported, massive H-bomb warhead-count "advantage." Russia's most powerful ICBM, the Sarmat, can be MIRVed with ten heavy warheads; 100 such ICBMs would cost them *more than four times* what one SSBN would cost us; Russia's gas-and-oil-exports-dependent, COVID-19-damaged national economy would not long survive this *four-plus times* cost disadvantage. *Balanced U.S. Triad force structure* would continue to be essential during any such future spending/building arms race; the *whole U.S. nuclear-defense industrial base* can support this balance by building additional next-gen ICBMs (the GBSDs), next-gen B-21 Raider strategic bombers carrying next-gen ALCMs (the LRSOs), plus late-block *Virginia* SSNs to protect our *Ohio*-replacement next-gen *Columbia* SSBNs. The key is for America to do so, if ever really needed, with *appropriate restraint*, updating and achieving that total warhead count which is *genuinely rightsized* given *actual U.S. requirements* in that particular, rather unpleasant *future threat environment.* We should, most assiduously, *avoid* getting into another H-bomb-building "overkill orgy," like the one the USSR instigated back during Cold War I. As in (3) below, we must during Cold War II resist acquiring any new nuclear weapon system simply because "the Russians (or the Chinese) are getting them," if those systems are not actually necessary to adequately meet all America's strategic deterrence-and-defense objectives.

3. The U.S. should keep to the arms-control-treaty practice of *not overly specifying internal limits* on *different types* of nuclear delivery vehicles, to allow *national deterrence-Triad flexibility*—with certain *notable exceptions*: Destabilizing, sneak-attack weapons such as Russia's Poseidon long-range "drone sub" (nuclear torpedo), its heavily MIRVed, heavy-lift Sarmat ICBMs, or its new "nuclear-powered cruise missile" design should all be *banned*, because they are *completely unnecessary, inappropriate weapons useful only for intimidation and terror.* Intermediate-range, ground-launched missiles should be limited or eliminated by an agreement replacing the lapsed Intermediate Nuclear Forces Treaty, since this would restore a further *nuclear-peacekeeping buffer* in certain regional theaters such as Europe. On the other hand, maneuverable hypersonic vehicles, when meant for *assured delivery* of retaliatory second-strike nuclear warheads, should *not* be banned; as these maintain the mutuality of effective deterrence, and with it *strategic stability*, amid Russian and Chinese avowed concerns about advancing American missile-shield capabilities and capacities. *Hypersonic flight* is certainly one area where the U.S. *should* use its STEM supremacy (Science, Technology, Engineering, Math) to achieve, at a minimum, *complete parity* with any other states; the field of hypersonics R&D is *not* an "unnecessary, overkill/terror weapon" but rather it represents a valid, useful, fundamental advancement of mankind's transportation capabilities and humanity's future horizons.
4. The U.S. should *not* significantly increase its count of low-yield, tactical (battlefield), "non-strategic" nuclear weapons, even though Russia owns about *ten times as many* as us (5,000 versus 500), and these are *not* regulated by New

START or any other agreement. (The "ST" in START stands for "Strategic"—*only*.) If Russia were ever to be reckless enough to start a tactical nuclear war, or escalate a conventional one to the tactical nuclear level, the U.S. can respond *Tit-for-Tat* with our own low-yield weapons. If our inventory of these were ever nearing depletion during some major, ongoing tactical-nuclear conflict, we would always have the options to respond to further Russian A-bomb strikes by either (1) using our 100-kiloton H-bombs, on a "Tit-for-Tat equivalency" basis of *comparable total warhead yield used*, or (2) as is being done *now* for the new low-yield (8-kiloton) nukes installed in our SSBNs, removing the fusion fuel from an H-bomb to retain only the "trigger" A-bomb. We should, when relations become amenable enough, negotiate with Russia to reduce their tactical nuclear stocks—and also get them to officially, formally *renounce* any first-nuke-use "escalate to deescalate" posture.

Some Domestic Political Pressures Could Also Push U.S. H-bomb Counts Upward *Unnecessarily*

To repeat for emphasis and clarity, America's and NATO's overall baseline deterrence strategy *in the current global threat environment* should be to hold pat—unilaterally if necessary—relying on the U.S.-, UK-, and France-owned nuclear arsenal sizes we currently have. We must *modernize*—as is now absolutely necessary—both the obsolescing First Cold War-vintage warheads themselves *and* their delivery platforms, their command and control (NC3), and their various delivery vehicles, but *not* increase the total numbers of strategic warheads we and the rest of NATO own. If Moscow were to significantly increase its deployed strategic nukes beyond New START's "counted" 1,550 plus about the same number in additional reserve stockpiles, America's *most actionable concern* should be over the safety and security of this expensive and wasteful Russian nuke-warheads surge—*not* over "keeping up" with the profligate, provocative, foolhardy adversary. We should, instead, rely on our skill in building, and manning and commanding, superior (in fact, world beating) SSBNs, and fund and build more than twelve of them if necessary, to disperse our existing SLBM warheads among a larger fleet.

The same thing goes for America's responses to any large upward push in China's nuclear arsenal, which right now seems a *likely occurrence* given Beijing's steady growth in their nuclear arsenal—from about 280 in 2020 to their stated target of about 700 (*or maybe even 1,000*) by 2030.

However, there may in practice be *political pressures* to raise America's arsenal size by joining in such a nuke-warhead arms race, including but not limited to pressures from (1) private sector *weapons manufacturers*, (2) *hawkish pundits* inside and outside the then-current Administration, (3) *Allies* who wish to feel even more strongly assured, and (4) elements in the *American public* who may be misled to think that "parity" at such an excessive level enhances security. (It does not do so, as *unnecessary warheads unnecessarily raise the risks* of national overspending on military acquisition, and of accidents, terrorist thefts, unauthorized uses, and organized-crime diversions.) Any action taken by U.S. Congress and POTUS to knuckle under to such arms-race pressures should be understood as a purely political, destructive, instant-gratification vote-getting response, *not* one with underlying justification derived from any *logic-based effective-nuclear-deterrence Best Practices*.

Furthermore, some of Russia's current crop of nuclear blackmail threats, and their blame games about the U.S. withdrawing from the Intermediate Nuclear Forces (INF) Treaty because Russia cheated on it for years, are designed to sow further (and exploit existing) *divisiveness* on the American political landscape. These disinformation and psyops tactics by Moscow—just like back in the First Cold War—are also meant to engender in our citizens *a paralyzing fear of America's own strategic deterrence arsenal*, in order to *trick us* into partial or total unilateral (U.S.-only) denuclearization—while Moscow continues aggressively expanding and completely modernizing their own nuclear forces.

The *same disingenuousness* is rampant these days in Beijing's numerous, egregious lies about their real intentions—as they too rapidly modernize and aggressively expand their nuclear forces, seeking every advantage to gain militaristic hegemony in what Chairman Xi and his minions call "China's Century."

Key Question: How Many U.S Nukes Are Enough but Not Too Many?

How many total deployed (i.e., quickly deliverable) strategic nuclear warheads (if *any*) does any state really need, in today's *very nuclear-weapons-savvy world*? This depends on a number of factors: the state's *national endowments* (geographic, military, economic, STEM), its *geopolitical role* (superpower, smaller ally of one, unaligned/neutral) and its *security situation* (global or regional "policeman," secure or unsecure borders, friendly or hostile neighbors). In some cases, as is borne out by actual world history, a nation will indeed conclude that these factors both require it *and* enable it to have nuclear weapons—and *also* (importantly) to conclude that possible changing conditions in the foreseeable future will *not* get that nation to change its mind, as South Africa did when it gave up its small nuke arsenal in 1994. The decision to build any nukes is *only the beginning* of a long and complex process to actually obtain at least one working weapon, confirm this fact to its citizenry and announce it to the world in a successful underground test, and then ponder the deep issues of "proper" arsenal size and national nuclear purposes, strategies, and posture.

To try to estimate in this chapter an answer to the big question of *"How Many?"* for the United States, first remember a crucial fact: The U.S. would *not ever* be making an *unprovoked* nuclear first strike.

America making a necessarily-nuclear retaliation to an *enemy's actual nuclear first use,* and/or to a strategic-level or even an existential attack that an enemy makes using *overwhelming conventional forces* or *other WMDs (weapons of mass destruction)* is *not* really an "unprovoked American first nuclear strike." It will have been *highly* provoked indeed! Our retaliation would most safely be done, for strategic crisis stability and to guard against false alarms, *only* on a *launch-after-attack basis*—i.e., *only* when it has been *positively verified* that enemy nukes (or other strategic-level or existentially-threatening weapons) have *already actually gone off* against American/Allied vital-interest targets. The U.S. nuclear Triad hardware and personnel will by then have taken losses due to enemy strategic fire, possibly *very significant losses.* America needs to plan for the very worst, for a situation where our ICBMs and our nuclear-capable aircraft have suffered many hits with enemy H-bombs—and even where one or more of our SSBNs at sea have somehow had their stealth compromised and then suffered a mission kill from enemy SSN nuclear torpedoes and/or ASW nuclear-missile saturation barrages. Then, to reach their own assigned deterrence targets, our surviving retaliatory fire will have to first run the gauntlet of *fully alerted enemy multi-layered defensive systems* (i.e., enemy ballistic missile defenses against our ICBMs and SLBMs, and their anti-aircraft/anti-cruise missile systems against our strategic bombers, fighter-bombers, and air-launched cruise missiles.)

As the old saying goes, *"There's many a slip between cup and lip."* It ought to be clear, from this rather hellish characterization of the "elimination rounds" our nuclear-retaliation weapons would have to endure, in the awful transition from nuclear peacetime to wartime, that *by no means all* of them can be counted on to ever "live" long enough to detonate successfully on their intended enemy targets, in our absolutely-vital proportionate counter-strike. Only by us owning a large-enough, modernized-enough, diversified-enough, and dispersed-enough (in both longitude and latitude) always-ready deterrence Triad can America be sure that enough of our nuclear forces will survive a worst-case enemy first strike for us to be guaranteed to be able to dish out a proportionately massive retaliation. And only by owning such a robust, survivable Triad can we, in advance, demonstrate the absolute readiness to retaliate in kind that we need to be able to deter any nuclear (or other WMD) first use to begin with.

Nuclear Arsenal Rightsizing Involves both Ceilings *and* Floors

A very approximate *needed-warheads-deployed* calculation for the U.S. is elaborated in this chapter as one means to set an overall *ceiling* (cap or maximum), to help prevent any further, pointless worldwide nuclear arms races in the single parameter that matters most: *strategic nuclear warhead count*. (Any negotiated bi/multi-lateral or voluntary unilateral restrictions on technical aspects of delivery vehicles for those warheads, as from time to time in the past have been agreed to by DC and Moscow, are beyond the scope of this model.)

The simple model below, explained step-by-step, establishes caps at levels which turn out to *closely resemble the New START deployed-strategic-warhead limits* already in force (for now) between the U.S. and Russia. We will explore the policy and budgetary implications of this key finding, below.

It is important for readers to be aware that *these same calculations*, along with good understanding of cause-and-effect linkages behind (1) inadequate deterrence and (2) a deterrence-violating actual enemy attack, also establish a *floor*.

This is to say, the modeling here establishes a *minimum* number of warheads, below which America starts to take *very serious risks* if it makes any further cuts, *even if* other nuclear powers *do* follow along with similar cuts. (Such so-called "minimal" nuclear deterrence would allow any very belligerent and non-casualty-averse adversaries to believe they could prevail in an all-out surprise nuclear attack against the U.S., by them "riding out" our perforce-very-limited retaliatory counter-strike.) America would be taking *very grave risks indeed*, in case other nuclear powers *don't follow along with our one-sided arsenal size cuts—or say that they will but then cheat.*

Here Is a U.S. Arsenal Rightsizing Estimate Based on Open Sources and Simple Math

To estimate a proper nuclear arsenal size for America, we (as would anyone else attempting such estimates) need to make some reasonable starting assumptions.

We can take our deployed SSBNs to be highly survivable—*provided* we also have a big-enough (hundreds strong) ICBM fleet to absorb many enemy ICBMs—which (among other things) might otherwise be used to saturate large sea areas in an ASW "barrage strategy." We can think of our ICBMs, in hardened silos, as in part acting like invaluable fly paper, "attracting" the bulk of the enemy's counterforce nuclear warheads. This is simply because our silo locations would be precisely known, and all our very accurate, powerful ICBMs together are a huge retaliatory second-strike threat, to any enemy who dares nuke us but for whatever reason leaves our Ground-Based Strategic Deterrent force alone.

America's long-range strategic bombers, and shorter range fighter-bombers, would need to rush to become airborne (good *escape time*) when the inbound enemy nuclear strike is first detected (this amounts to *safely recallable* aircraft scramble-on-warning takeoff rules). Then they would have to run a vicious gauntlet of enemy integrated air defense systems, to ever be able to fire their stand-off cruise missiles, and drop their bombs, against U.S. STRATCOM's assigned retaliatory targets—if and when their crews do get the final, POTUS-authorized go-ahead codes to attack.

Let us assume, lacking finer data, that the enemy's national integrated air defense system (NIAD) is about as effective against our in-atmosphere, "air breather" (flying) warhead-delivery platforms, as the enemy's overall ABM, BMD, and other missile shield systems (ground-, sea-, even space-based) are against our ICBM and SLBM space-transiting, ballistically-plunging warhead-delivery platforms. In other words, we posit the hypothesized enemy's different (current or future) strategic defenses can each achieve roughly the same U.S.-weapon-system-class attrition rate, against our different retaliatory Triad platform classes. The attrition rate will in practice never be 100%—which would mean *none* of our warheads get through—for a variety of practical reasons. But we dare not assume that this attrition rate is zero, either, which would mean that *all* our warheads get through.

Next, some additional technical preliminaries need to be laid out.

As already hinted at by our discussions of New START, properly reckoning the *adequate grand national overall-arsenal strategic-warhead-count total* requires us to look at *two* numbers. The first is the total number *deployed*. This is the number ready for quick use in a dire enough scenario. The second is the total number *stockpiled*. These warheads are deeply secured in long-term storage against unpredictable, contingent eventualities further down the future timeline. Those contingencies include (1) additional nuclear wars in future years, *after* our nuclear-weapons manufacturing infrastructure is destroyed in the initial war, *or* (2) individual Triad-class systemic technical failures, that require additional warheads be uploaded on still-functioning platforms in the hopefully-still-working, other Triad classes.

We'll look at estimating the needed number *deployed*—as in the 1,550 of New START. *Stockpile* levels would be of roughly the same magnitude, so we won't specifically model them or mention them more.

One input variable we need to specify for our model is the *number of shots* an enemy nuclear superpower's overall ballistic missile defense system is allowed by treaty, or is capable of by design and by logistical capacity. I pulled the figure of *200 available shots per country* from the 1970 U.S./USSR arms-control anti-ballistic-missile (ABM) Treaty.

Something else to reflect in the model is the need for any state's surviving deterrent's retaliatory second strike to always get through against *any attacker's own defensive systems*; enough of America's second strike must be able to get through, no matter what, to for sure inflict proportionately severe damage on any attacker. This must be true even *after* the attacker succeeds in launching a *devastating surprise nuclear counterforce (disarming) first strike* against the U.S.'s entire nuclear arsenal, at which point in the conflict the attacker's own defenses against our retaliatory strike would surely be at their own *highest-possible alert/readiness status.*

The simple arithmetic, and working formulas below, also take implicit account of the very mobile sea-based portion of America's current Aegis Ashore Ballistic Missile Defense (BMD) anti-boost-phase system, with its supporting fixed, land-based radars. This *mobility* of the launchers allows BMD to effectively *protect large regions simultaneously.* We assume that, in the imaginable future, other peer competitor states will develop comparable systems, or perhaps will somehow share ours in a credible way (as President Reagan suggested to Mikhail Gorbachev).

(*Boost-phase interceptors* are those which target the *entire enemy missile* soon after its launch, while it is *rising* under engine power through the atmosphere. They might utilize a *kinetic interceptor* such as a homing anti-missile missile, or *a directed-energy weapon* such as a high-power laser. In contrast, *terminal-phase interceptors* target the nuclear warheads within their *individual reentry vehicles*, after those RVs have been released by the missile's payload bus and they are *plunging back down* through the atmosphere. *Space-based interceptors* are those which target the *warhead bus before RV release*, as it zooms through the vacuum of space.)

We also know that the *stealthy mobility* of SSBNs permits them to maneuver around between ocean areas and thus *evade* the reach of adversary boost-phase anti-missile launchers, whether the latter are based on land or at sea. (This is another important aspect of SSBN retaliation *survivability*.) However, SLBMs would *not* be immune to space-based and terminal-phase interception, due to the similarity in final trajectories to those of our ICBMs, as the sub-launched weapons converge on enemy territory. Thus, the model does not explicitly distinguish between enemy attrition rates against our ICBMs vice our SLBMs.

Arsenal Rightsizing Needs Some Worst-Case Pessimism, and Some Disciplined Futurism

In all this modeling, a level of *"pessimism"* about our second strike's ability to penetrate to assigned targets is *de rigeur*, to establish *genuinely adequate* arsenal size as a *stable figure* for the *foreseeable future*. (The derived figure is meant to be largely immune to fluctuations over time in *national perceptions*—always potentially inaccurate—and in *national political moods*—prone in the U.S. to roller-coaster gyrations.)

The modeling also needs a level of "futurism," meaning a disciplined look ahead at what plausible/emerging near-future technologies (owned by the U.S. and/or our Allies, and/or by our adversaries) might imply about U.S. Triad rightsizing right now.

We continue in this appropriately cautious vein, to further set up our model:

> What about possible future enemy types of *additional* anti-ICBM/SLBM weapons? At present, these types of systems are mostly still under development, or are at best only theoretical possibilities. For instance, the U.S. Army's Terminal High Altitude Area Defense (THAAD) is not (yet) designed to be able to intercept ICBM and SLBM incoming warheads; it works against shorter-range, lower-speed theater ballistic missiles.
>
> Nor do magnetic rail guns, laser cannon, or particle beam guns, powered perhaps by a ground-based electric grid or by a nuclear-powered shipboard-turbogenerator electric supply—for boost-phase or terminal-phase defense—*or* powered instead by space-based nuclear blasts—for knocking out warhead buses or released RVs, maybe via X-ray lasers—currently exist at all in deployed strategic-nuclear-defense form, though some do exist in laboratories and in some military systems serving other purposes. If and when such emerging technologies do begin to take the place of, or supplement, the older boost-phase and terminal-phase kinetic-interceptor missiles for strategic defense, negotiations might be needed to somehow limit their (potentially infinite) "ammo supply" and (potentially extreme) rate of fire. Estimates of adequate nuclear-deterrent arsenal size would then

need to be reassessed. To the extent such next-generation systems could achieve *additional attrition* against defender retaliatory nuke warheads in flight, the rough estimates below of U.S. deterrence Triad arsenal size would be *too low.*

Because no system can be trusted to achieve 100% effectiveness during actual wartime, it is alas a utopian pipedream that any defensive system will be so reliable and all-encompassing that it would ever render nuclear weapons "obsolete and irrelevant," as in President Reagan's Star Wars idea. More on this in the next section.

The Above Points Demand a Quick Aside

Before we go on with our calculation, we need to think a bit more about what the above *emerging future anti-nuke defensive technologies* could mean. Suppose that directed energy and particle beam anti-missile and anti-RV systems eventually become advanced enough that their mechanisms and their power supplies do allow *a very high and very sustained rate of fire.* What we are talking about then is the BMD equivalent to a *"Rambo-style machine gun that never needs to reload."* If and when this ever occurs, the world might actually achieve the dream that President Reagan had, that science fictional missile shields would become science fact and would render ICBMs and SLBMs obsolete.

Not so fast!

That sounds like an outcome devoutly to be wished—except for the serious loss of nuclear deterrents against big *conventional* world wars. This alluring future does, however, still have the *same flaw* that the original Star Wars system had: There would almost certainly be *leaker warheads* getting through, even amid the nuclear projectiles that the system is designed to stop, and each leaker will have *terrible lethality.* In fact, achieving a very-high, successful attrition rate against even *large scale* (whole arsenal at once?) missile strikes, by any sorts of deployed, proven future missile-shield systems, would motivate nuclear-armed states—especially the aggressive dictatorships and rogue states—to deploy nukes with truly *immense* warhead yields, maybe 100 megatons each or even a *gigaton (1,000 megatons)* each. This would be flirting must too close for comfort with nuclear winter, but aggressive-enough states might do it anyway, at a minimum as a means of nuclear blackmail and brinkmanship.

Also, these hyper-modern missile shield systems ala President Reagan *still* would not be of *any* use against enemy nukes delivered in slower, lower-altitude, more clandestine ways, such as by submarines (including Russia's putative unmanned Poseidon "drone nuclear sub"), or by contraband-smuggler submersibles, merchant ships, small boats, civilian airliners, or small planes or helicopters (manned or unmanned), parachutists, or cars or trucks.

Many of these, being delivery modes that even today would appeal to any terrorist group that succeeds in getting their hands on a nuke, need to be guarded against very carefully right now. What we might see in the future is that various nuclear states might seek to perpetuate their nuclear-aggression and nuclear-deterrence capabilities alike, by resorting to these simpler, older, cheaper covert platforms—or to hyper-modern (autonomous drone) derivatives. What we would then have is more akin to "Forward into the past" than "Back to the future." Nuclear deterrence and defense against large-state and rogue-state or terrorist dangers would then all *converge and homogenize* into ever more elaborate, expensive, and inconvenient *hurdles to travel and transport* anywhere by any means, as necessary to enable interdicting nuclear contraband across such a very broad spectrum of delivery methods. Alas, nuclear weapons would *not* have been obsoleted *at all*, after all. So much for real-world Star Wars ever "rendering nukes irrelevant."

Thus, the calculation estimates below will probably remain very relevant for the foreseeable future, and probably also for the un-foreseeable future, too.

Another Aside, Which Is Actually *Less* Relevant Than It Might Seem

Knowledgeable commentators, some of whom can say this because they were there, have related the history that America's Triad system has arisen not just from any theoretical ideal about mutually supporting diversification but also from pragmatic *turf rivalries* between different branches of the U.S. Armed Forces. The Triad that the U.S. now owns has grown out of decades of *inter-service political battles and budget fights*, some very acrimonious, in which "everybody wanted a piece of the nuclear-deterrence pie." Another contributing factor to building out our Triad has been the ongoing efforts of multiple defense contractors, lobbyists, and consultants, all of whom had (and have) various useful deterrence *hardware for sale*.

This is a fact, but it is also in a real way an *irrelevancy*. How we got to be where we are today in Triad implementation is interesting as an historical footnote, but from the current point of view of effective nuclear deterrence *Best Practices and Best Perspectives*, the essential thing is that America *should* (must) and in fact *does* own a diversified, dispersed, overall-exceedingly-survivable Triad of nuclear deterrent systems. That we got here "politically" as much as "theoretically" is a *boon*, a sign perhaps of Providential guidance. Now and going forward, the currently diverse and robust American nuclear-deterrence Triad needs to be preserved and modernized, period.

More Reasons We Need All Three Triad Legs, Each Itself Purpose-Rightsized

The full Triad is so important because the three separate legs each exploit *different* hardware, based around our Homeland and abroad, including at sea, in *different* manners; some are highly mobile, while some are fixed. They use *different* software systems. They travel through *different* global-commons mediums (land, sea, air, space). They follow *different* sorts of trajectories through those mediums to reach their targets. They use *different* types of propulsion systems and guidance systems.

All this *differentness* helps assure that the probabilities of failure of the three legs are truly independent of each other, i.e., are *exceedingly unlikely* to be subject to *simultaneous, collective failure "risk contagion."* The same essential differentness *vastly complicates* the chance that any adversary or adversaries, not matter how technically advanced and superbly equipped, could *ever* succeed in making any small, medium, or large scale nuclear or other-WMD attack on American and Allied global vital interests without us being able to *retaliate proportionately* via our nuclear-deterrence Triad.

How Much Assured Retaliatory Damage Is "Enough" to Deter Utterly Relentless Adversaries?

To assure that *each separate leg* of the Triad on its own (in case *only one* is functioning properly and can successfully penetrate enemy defenses) will *always* get through to its targets in *"adequate numbers"*—to sustain successful strategic deterrence—we need to set up a model parameter to specify (quantify) *what this adequacy means in numerical terms.* Cold War commentators seemed to agree that any state that had already launched a massive first strike (so that its hundreds of ICBM silos would then be *empty*) would be horrifically crippled, by our retaliatory second strike, if it ever suffered the destruction of *about 200* carefully selected strategic targets (political-control assets, military and naval bases, armaments factories and other industrial/manufacturing centers, and natural-resource concentrations such as mines). Such "horrifically crippled" level of damage is in fact *vital* to, in advance, effectively deter the most dangerous types of adversaries, including those:

1. who are (like clinical sociopaths) *not own-casualty averse,*
2. who are (through ignorance or miscalculation) *not sufficiently risk averse* (about the downsides to starting nuclear war),

3. who may perceive themselves as being politically or militarily *cornered and desperate,*
4. who (perhaps through narcissistic psychosis) pride themselves as *consummate, can't-lose gamblers.*

One *extreme scenario,* alluded to earlier, needs to be guarded against carefully via effective nuclear deterrence. This actually almost happened *twice* during the First Cold War. Both Mao Zedong and Fidel Castro, at one time or another, advocated that the Soviet Union start an all-out nuclear war with the U.S. and the rest of NATO, because—so they calculated or assumed—after all the terrible death and destruction that would ensue worldwide, the Communist side would have *more survivors* than the Capitalist, and the power of the Communist dialectic would let their side *rebuild faster* and *take over* the entire post-nuclear-war world. This *documented fact* of Cold War I history is a truly horrifying thing to think about even today, decades later. But *it could occur again* in the future, and anything like this needs to be very effective deterred against indeed. (The USSR declined Mao's and Castro's invitations—because U.S. nuclear deterrence *worked.)*

Back to An Estimate of America's Needed Warhead Counts

So, we will assume for now that, in a worst-case scenario, *a full 200* is the number of our retaliatory nuclear warheads which the U.S. must, prospectively, (1) *itself* be totally sure about, (2) definitively warn *adversaries* about, and (3) convincingly assure *Allies* about being able to get through to their intended targets *no matter what.* (It is only a coincidence that this is the same number as the 200 treaty-allowed ABM shots. Below, we will soon consider a more general formulation, in which these two numbers can differ and can be any user-specified independent variables.)

Cold War conventional wisdom also held that it would take *two* nuclear warhead hits against each of an adversary's *very hardened* (missile silos, command bunkers) and/or *very spread out* (air bases, resource complexes) targets, to be sure of destroying almost every one of the various targets on US STRATCOM's lengthy, solidly-deterring ("countervailing') second-strike target list. (It is not adequate to merely *deploy* enough such missiles; this fact must be clearly *communicated* to any and all potential nuclear-armed adversaries in advance, during peacetime.) Some recent commentators have tried to argue that the improved accuracy of current nuclear weapons means that only one warhead, set off against each target, is sufficient. But weapons experts have responded that this claim must be disbelieved for purposes of planning effective Triad deterrence capabilities and postures.

All of the above tells us that if you need to get past a gauntlet of 200 enemy missile-shield shots, to survive to be able to hit 200 enemy strategic targets twice each, you would need on average, for *each* of the three separate triad legs, fully *600 warheads* to send into the teeth of enemy airspace defenses. Why?

In a rapid-fire exchange, neither side has a chance to reload from stockpiles (including missile-shield reloading stockpiles) before cease-fire negotiations hopefully kick in—or civilization is *de facto* destroyed. But we need to be cautious, by presuming that *every allowed adversary anti-missile interceptor shot* is successful against one of our counter-strike missiles, warhead buses, or RVs. We also need to assume that, on average, *only one of our triad legs* survives the enemy's initial attack (or a major technical flaw, or a pandemic much worse even that COVID-19, or whatever) to be able to launch retaliatory missiles.

Therefore, additive to each of our missiles that does get shot down must be a *pair* of additional missiles, that both get through and so have the chance to hit that particular strategic target that they both are aimed at. The total per leg thus needs to equal 200 (shot down) + 200 × 2 (double hits per each of 200 targets). This is 600, *per each Triad leg.*

The exact calculations used by the U.S. Government for this type of estimate should be determined by the National Nuclear Security Administration (NNSA) and the other, coordinating parts of the Department of Defense (the Pentagon)—including but not limited to STRATCOM—and the Department of Energy, which together address America's nuclear weapon issues. They need to use all the information available to them about own-nukes performance, and about adversary missile-shield intercept capabilities and silo/bunker hardening performance. U.S. planners and strategists also need to take account of the effects of *warhead fratricide.* (This is when the first-to-arrive of several friendly warheads, launched at the same enemy target at close to the same time, could destroy the others when it detonates, via radiation and/or lofted rubble.) Presumably, the most accurate, well-informed of all this nuclear-capabilities data is top secret, to protect America's security interests and to protect our various intelligence sources giving us insights into adversary capabilities.

Now, what about the *losses* our peacetime deployed Triad would take from an *enemy's incoming first nuclear strike?* We are implicitly building-in the *gross attrition* to America's peacetime deployed warhead/platform counts, caused by the worst-case incoming enemy attack, by considering that *only one leg, or roughly one-third of the total number deployed, are available for attempted retaliation, after suffering a surprise "bolt from the blue" massive attack that the U.S. only retaliates against using very cautious launch-after-attack ROEs, at the same time that our Triad is already suffering from serious multi-leg unavailability due to internal technical problems and/or serious environmental downside outcomes.*

Note that if, in future, our Triad does in fact ever suffer such serious unavailability, and this unfortunate fact is somehow perceived at the time by America's adversaries, then one or more of them might be very tempted to launch *exactly such an unprovoked bolt-from-the-blue against us.* This "risk contagion," or "dangerous coupling" of fluctuating relative strengths and weaknesses between the U.S. and our potential nuclear-armed enemies, is an *ongoing challenge* to achieving good strategic stability—a challenge than can only be effectively met by exactly the diverse and dispersed, survivable Nuclear Deterrence Triad that America has long sustained through thick and thin.

Now, accepting for purely illustrative purposes this 600-count estimate of needed warheads launched (rather, attempted to be launched assuming not yet destroyed) on average *per leg*, an "ideal" number of total deployed strategic nuclear warheads for America—or for any major world power whose geopolitical situation is very comparable to America's and which demands its own Triad—would be 3 × 600 = *1,800.* I say "attempted to be launched" here because, strictly speaking, we are allowing for some technical failures and enemy attrition at any point *between* the crews getting their validated launch orders, *and* when the ballistic or cruise missile's engines ignite and it takes off from the silo or the submarine, or from the strategic bomber, and flies on to where it is supposed to set the warhead off.

Based on the assumptions that went into it, this 1,800 deployed warhead-count assures—with the necessary high confidence—that 200 separate retaliatory second-strike targets, as selected by the U.S. for retaliatory nukings, *will* be destroyed among the attacking enemy's various strategic assets.

Since this very simple formula does not look into the *complicated counting rules* used by New START for different delivery platforms' warheads, this estimate is not out of line with the 1,550 "counted" deployed warheads allowed under New START language current as of late 2020. This says at least one of two things: Either America's leaders and their negotiating counterparts in Russia know what they are doing and the negotiated New START limits are based on *sound underlying deterrence principles,* or else, again, *Providential guidance* has been at work. Or maybe *some of both.*

The next part of this chapter will look at some "traditional" nuclear-deterrence concepts, which were developed of necessity during the First Cold War—in order to talk about, make sense of, and strategize for that monumental and dangerous struggle. These pages will update those foundational concepts (as is *certainly necessary*) to the modern, 21st-century era—i.e., to a period of human history that is both *"multi-polar"* (two or more current, competing superpowers) and *"multi-nuclear"* (nine diverse states currently own nukes, and Iran is a wannabe).

A Quick Review: Basic Targeting Strategies and Different Measures of An Adversary's "Size"

Recall that back during the First Cold War, as American deterrence strategy matured from its earliest days and its earliest ideas, the Pentagon shifted from countervalue (against cities) or counterforce (against silos and sub and bomber bases) to *countervailing* strikes, as its foundational retaliatory (hence, deterring) threat/promise directed at nuclear-armed adversaries.

Presumably, the most modern NC3 capabilities and nuclear weapon systems fielded by the U.S., now or in the future, allow for meaningful real-time flexibility as to nuclear-combat target setting, especially regarding *intra-war targeting tactics* that are responsive to H-bomb damage-assessment information (on both ours *and* the enemy's strikes) *after* any previous nuclear strikes that have occurred. Furthermore, details of strategic deterrence targeting plans are top secret, for obvious reasons. But the U.S. does continue to follow the basics of countervailing policy. Why? Because indiscriminate countervalue policy is by nature *immoral*, while counterforce policy for retaliation is likely to be *ineffective* as explained below.

So, what are "countervailing" targets? They encompass the general category of targets that an adversary, presumably authoritarian regime needs to remain intact and functioning, in order for said regime to be able to continue to run its government effectively; mount viable, organized and sustained armed/military resistance against external threats; and communicate with, control, and repress its populace. Such a target set could, in practice, include (but not necessarily be limited to) various national and local government meeting places, ministries, and offices; military headquarters, C4I and other sensor-and-communication assets,computer centers and command bunkers; plus secret-police facilities, radio and TV stations, and the like; physical assets that are especially valued by the regime-supporting-oligarch owners thereof could also be included here.

(Of course, in practice, a nuclear weapon's indiscriminate destructiveness might make it impossible for any detached observer to know if such retaliatory detonations were aimed at countervalue, counterforce, countervailing, or other types of targets. But the moral quandary here would largely land in the lap of the aggressor regime, who made the original WMD strike for which the U.S. needed to retaliate.)

Next, note that each different targeting-set paradigm above inherently relies on a *different* notion of what exactly measures *a particular adversary's "size."* Is national "bigness" (size), for instance, measured (maybe?) by the number of separate civilian conurbations ("greater metropolitan areas"), and their population totals, within the enemy country; *or* by the number of ICBM silos, and nuclear-submarine and strategic-bomber bases, it owns worldwide; *or* by the number of separate (dispersed) concentrations of national-governing-and-control assets within its territory, each of which would need a separate strategic (or tactical) nuclear warhead to be destroyed?

Triad Rightsizing Depends on Size of Adversary's "National-Control Assets", *Not* Its Arsenal

Now, if more than 1,550 deployed strategic nuclear warheads are ever deemed by the U.S. Government to be necessary, to successfully deter an "extremely big" adversary or axis of adversaries—i.e., one with a *very large number of widely dispersed high-value national-control assets*—then a larger total deployed and stockpiled U.S. nuclear arsenal *would* be called for. What is important to recognize though, as explained in this section, is that the adversary's total number of nuclear warheads owned in its arsenal *actually "drops out of the equation,"* i.e., it is really not a significant factor in America's own Triad-rightsizing calculations:

> The U.S. does not need to build a whole bunch more nuclear warheads that we have "now" just because an adversary builds a whole bunch more nukes than they have "now." (We instead ought to *better disperse our existing* survivable submarine-launched deterrent by building more SSBNs—and maybe also more SLBMs, with which to de-MIRV the missiles we do deploy now, spreading their multiple warheads out to more Trident II missile bodies. In fact, the U.S. Navy emphasizes publicly and to Congress that the upcoming Columbia-class fleet will consist of *at least* one dozen boats; *more than twelve* might prove necessary for effective deterrence, depending on *unpredictable* future world conditions and *unforeseeable* adversary behaviors—such as the ones mentioned here.)

Some *restraint* in ever building many more warheads is also called for, because it might (in practice) prove to be completely effective as a strategic-deterrence retaliation threat for America to be able to destroy "only" 200 *carefully selected* strategic-deterrence adversary targets, even out of a *much larger* potential set of adversary targets—even within the *biggest and best-defended* future adversary state(s) or alliances *ever imaginable*. This is because *modern micro- and macro-economic* models, run on today's supercomputers (or tomorrow's quantum computers), can select individual targets that, as a group, if obliterated, would *thoroughly cripple* the entire enemy military-industrial-political system—while *protecting* innocent enemy civilian populations, and leaving top leadership *functional to negotiate peace*. Such *optimization modeling*, which might be classified, would indicate if, say, 200 nuke hits is enough, not enough, or even conceivably unnecessary overkill.

Saying that *how many nukes a potential adversary owns is not an input variable to this simple warhead-count rightsizing model* is tantamount to claiming that the First Cold War's concept of an *American "counterforce" nuclear strike* has become merely an *historical curiosity*. (This was the idea of the U.S. using our nukes to destroy the enemy's nukes "on the ground," to limit the damage the enemy's nukes might otherwise do to America. It dates back to a time before the USSR had much of an SSBN fleet and Moscow lacked effective early-warning radar coverage.)

This bold claim now requires clarification:

> Even if a hypothetical enemy could make a surprise attack with enough nuclear warheads to preemptively destroy *all* of our ICBMs and strategic-bombers and tactical DCA aircraft, our secure, survivable (rightsized) SSBN Triad leg hiding stealthily at sea would remain viable to make a devastating counterattack. This fact is what enables America to follow a necessarily cautious *launch-after-attack strategy*. This shows how important having a robust SSBN fleet is for (1) *sustaining strategic stability* through effective nuclear deterrence, while (2) *reducing perverse motivations* for nuclear arms races and (3) *assuaging* unstable use-it-or-lose-it pressures and *avoiding* overly paranoid surprise-attack phobias. In particular, having enough very fine, survivable SSBNs *decouples* (1) America's own nuke-arsenal rightsizing calculations from (2) the size of the potential enemy's nuclear arsenal.

(But SSBNs are *not* like a Reagan Star Wars shield: their missiles *deter* an enemy from attacking us first, but they do *not* interdict the incoming strike if he/she does attack us, *nor* do they prevent or mitigate the massive damage the enemy would do to us via such an attack. They *do* make absolutely sure that we will be able to *get even*. And, providing that our deployed SSBNs can maintain stealth against any enemy ASW barrages and SSN trailing, all that an excessive number of nukes would let the enemy do in an attack, whatever *their* targeting strategy, is make our Homeland's already-radioactive rubble bounce even higher.)

In the worst case, of an enemy actually starting a nuclear war with the U.S., were that enemy to first build an excessively large nuclear arsenal, those unnecessary nukes would be *the only assets remaining* to the (former) hostile regime, after our survivable retaliatory strike against its 200 top strategic targets; the enemy population we spared direct nuking, out of our own guiding morality, would alas tragically succumb to the ensuing global nuclear winter and nuclear summer—brought on by the enemy regime itself. Once we have the capacity to inflict this level of damage whatever the enemy did to us first, additional large numbers of U.S. nukes would *not* serve any truly useful added purpose—in technical terms, they would *not add significant additional utility at the margin*.

Think it through: Since our Ballistic Missile Defense by design stands a decent chance to interdict a "small" enemy ICBM strike, any actual enemy "bolt from the blue" surprise attack is likely to be a very large strike using *all* its ICBMs—so as to try to immediately cripple our own ICBMs and other retaliatory nuclear forces as much as possible. No matter how many of them there then were in the enemy's homeland, the *now-empty enemy missile silos and mobile launchers* would *not* rank highly on America's list of strategic assets we would at that point need to target for prompt destruction. Rather, instead, the attacking enemy's so-called *"countervailing"* or *"regime control"* assets—centralized warhead-backup stockpiles (*many fewer* in number than operational launch sites), missile factories, aircraft factories, submarine shipyards, other nuclear weapons support facilities, airbases, naval/marine bases, army bases, C4ISR bunkers, secret-police infrastructure, and other political-control assets—would and should be the primary strategic targets for the U.S./NATO counterstrike.

Now granted, an aggressor might choose to make a surprise attack using *fewer* than all of their ICBMs *initially*. In that case, the defender (America) might wish to target the un-launched ones, still sitting in their enemy silos, for retaliation. However, since the aggressor *knows for sure* that a nuclear war has already been started (by them!), he/she is *practically guaranteed* to launch the *entire remainder* of their ICBMs the *very moment they first detect* that the attack victim (the U.S.) is launching retaliation against those yet-unused ICBMs. That is, in this *intra-war context,* the attacker would feel *completely free to use "launch on warning" ROEs* to make *another* strike, based upon *then-completely-valid "use-them-or-lose-them" thinking.* If the defender *did* target those silos, they would *all be empty* by the time those retaliatory warheads reached them.

America's National Nuclear Posture declares that we would retaliate against *any other type* of "strategic" (massively destructive, existentially threatening) WMD attack (chemical, biological, EMP, cyber) with a *nuclear* counterattack. This virtually guarantees that any nuclear-armed peer-competitor adversary that wishes to make a strategic-level assault on the U.S. would do so from the outset with their nuclear weapons. (During the First Cold War, the USSR planned to use its biological weapons as a *second* wave, *after* a nuclear first strike.) This in turn virtually guarantees that if a peer-competitor (Russia and/ or China) ever wanted to "take out" the U.S., they would do so using their *nuclear* weapons from the getgo—so we come back to the fact that their ICBM silos, mobile launchers, and bomber airfields would all be *empty* by the time our retaliatory nukes could hit them.

Put differently by using an historical analogy, nuclear warhead counts, in the deadly-serious game of mutual nuclear deterrence, are *not* much like counting both sides' (immediately reloaded) cannons in some big conventional artillery duel. In the latter, the two sides' *same* artillery pieces kept shooting away at each other as fast as they could, suffering some gradual attrition in the process. One side's numbers and calibers compared to the other side's numbers and calibers definitely did matter; artillery superiority could win battles and wars. But nuclear deterrence is not like that. Both sides' ICBM silos (grouped in missile fields) and mobile launchers (some with multiple tubes) do *not* as individual units keep blazing away at each other—reloading a silo or mobile launch vehicle tube is a *painstakingly slow* and *very vulnerable* process, requiring extraction of the delicate reload-missile from its secure stockpile location and transporting it *under nuclear fire.* This process generally takes much longer than the thirty minutes it would take for a few American ICBMs to destroy the attacker's centralized missile-reload stockpiles—which would certainly be top priorities for retaliatory destruction.

If the enemy were to try to overcome this issue by removing many missiles from stockpile in advance of need, to *preposition* them near their launch points before starting the war, it would be *totally conspicuous* to our Indications and Warning assets, and *profoundly provocative,* triggering an American high alert and even risking us making a *preemptive strike*—but even then, the enemy forewarned would *already* themselves be on high alert, and would *shoot off* their silos and mobile launchers the moment we launched our preemption.

So, unless the U.S. ever wanted to ourself make a surprise, unprovoked "bolt from the blue" nuclear strike on an adversary, which is a totally preposterous notion, then no matter how one slices this Armageddon pie, deployed adversary nuclear weapons will already be in the air, on the way toward us, before our retaliatory nukes could hit their launch points.

CONCLUSION: America's deterrence-retaliatory nukes *should*, as reasoned above, be aimed at crucial adversary strategic targets *other than* the attacker's (almost certainly by then empty) nuke silos or mobile ICBM launchers. Arms races over warhead counts and nuclear supremacy, *beyond* the New START number adequate for deterring a large adversary, are *very counterproductive*. In fact, the above discussion helps show that First Cold War-style *"nuclear supremacy,"* purported to give some sort of overwhelming strategic military/political and psychological advantage, is a *dangerous fiction*. And, as we will discuss further below, both sides realizing that this is nothing but a dangerous fiction *eliminates* whatever purely psychological advantage some misguided nuclear blackmailer might seek—and thus should eliminate that belligerent aggressor's motivation for bloating its nuclear arsenal to begin with.

Here Is a More General Rightsizing Formula that Takes Account of Adversary "Size"

The general formula here for destroying an enemy target list of size T, using 2 nuke shots per target for surety, is that the number of friendly warheads *that succeed in being launched*, X, must satisfy $(X - 200)/2 = T$. This holds as long as the old ABM norm of 200 shots is used to size a national BMD system. If the actual size of an enemy BMD system's shots is S, then use

$$(X - S)/2 = T$$

If the number of hits per target to be sure of target destruction is N, use

$$(X - S)/N = T$$

Then, for sure-shot performance of the overall Triad, given the various risks of failures to one or two legs, A = total nuclear arsenal warhead count should = 3 × X.

Solving for X gives

$$A = 3 \times (S + (T \times N))$$

Track Enemy Assets to Be Held at Risk, *Not* Perceptions of Détente or of "Peace Dividends"

For a sufficiently bloodthirsty, warmongering, and defiant, perseverant tyrant, regardless of his/her country's size, suffering a lot of terrible destruction overall—but where many of his/her own prized personal assets survive (especially those he/she is able to hide in other countries for future access)—might *not* be deterring enough. A stronger deterrent goal is to assure that he/she suffers a genuinely crippling blow to *all* wealth, power, and control assets belonging to his/her belligerent state, to him/her personally, to other regime leaders and oligarchs/plutocrats, *and* to any "cutouts" they might use to try to hide wealth. This is exactly what *countervailing deterrence posture* aims to achieve, but a question is *how far and wide* to take the search for such assets to be held under threat (by nukes or by other means) in the globalized 21st century. Forcing some personal sacrifices on a dictator, as can be done currently via U.S. and UN economic sanctions, is certainly proving to *not* be much of a sufficient deterrent against even "mere" conventional aggression. When it comes to nuclear and strategic-WMD aggression, then the ability to retaliate with utterly massive damage, putting any regime that dares to nuke us literally "*stratospherically* out of business," and their dictator permanently in the poor house or very much worse, are clearly essential.

Nuclear-deterrent arsenal rightsizing—which basically means strategic retaliation *target-list right-choosing and rightsizing*—is a tricky, esoteric, and dynamic field of endeavor. What ought to keep New START's allowed strategic-warhead inventory sizes adequate for some years ahead is the built-in, cross-protective survivability from having *three separate Triad legs*, backed up by adequately numerous SSNs and BMD systems.

It is a *bad idea* to dismantle nukes and then build more nukes later, over and over, while trying to *chase perceptions* of the "exactly ideal" arsenal size *of the moment*. Perceptions and moments alike are *ephemeral and transitory*. They are too vulnerable to adversary propaganda *manipulation* and to homegrown, domestic political *opportunism and over-optimism*. (The twinned needs for *stability of geopolitical perspectives*, and for *immu-*

nity from emotional roller-coasting and from *funding-and-readiness whip-sawing*, are discussed in rigorous detail in Appendix 1.)

Resist Fake News and Triumphalism/Over-Optimism; Harness Punitive Economic Sanctions

In today's unsettled, unsettling world of *fake news* and covert information-warfare *malign influence attacks*, perceptions in the moment are very vulnerable indeed to nefarious outside influence. Given the *evident and unending* need to hold at risk numerous enemy-regime assets, some of which can be sheltered in neutral states immune from *any* directly military retaliation (without bad horizontal escalation), today's methods of *global financial sanctions enforcement* become an essential part of the overall toolkit of effective nuclear deterrence.

A *Three*-Player Strategic-Rivalry Game Changes Everything for the *Worse*

The potential for having to face off against multiple nuclear-attacker entities *simultaneously* (at the *same* time) or *sequentially* (one *after* another) gives an additional strong reason to maintain an *additional warhead stockpile* sized at least equal to the *deployed* portion of the total arsenal's warhead count. This is certainly a nuclear-deterrence Best Practice, and is permitted by New START.

For instance, let us examine a nasty scenario on the timeframe of 2030 to 2035.

Let's Consider an Unpleasant Future Scenario

We posit in this "thought-experiment" scenario that Russia has continued modernizing its nuclear weapons, and continues to boycott efforts such as America's recent Nuclear Security Summit and other U.S. and UN arms control initiatives. We also posit that China continues to modernize its nuclear arsenal without transparency, and also grows it significantly in size, to rival those of *each* of the U.S. and Russia considered *separately*.

Let us also posit in this scenario that such factors as U.S. Congress *gridlock*—including rigid and inadequate *continuing spending resolutions* forced by budget impasses, renewed budget *sequestration* (or something even worse?), and the ongoing threat of federal government *shutdowns*—leave America's Columbia-class SSBN building program badly behind schedule.

In real life (as opposed to in this thought experiment), it has long been projected by the U.S. Navy that there will be, between 2025 and

2036, a *deep shortfall* in deployed U.S. Navy SSNs (our fast-attack, hunter-killer subs). What if, on this later-2020s to mid-2030s time-frame, in order to effectively deter simultaneous nuclear attacks against U.S. vital interests by Russia and China *working together*, our National Command Authorities determine that 200 is an insufficient number of retaliatory targets that need to be held under threat? (Keep in mind that 200 is a First Cold War guesstimate that is now *stale*, to say the least.)

To provide for such contingencies, the deployed stockpile might need to be *a lot larger* than the above simple model's suggested deployed warhead count of some 1,800-ish actual warheads. Suppose that China develops a full-blown BMD system, and Russia fields one as well, each with its own (nominal, speculative) 200 defensive shots available. There is a serious risk that the 1,800 deployed American warheads, possibly needing to be launched in a retaliatory second strike against *both countries at once*, might be badly diluted in several different ways.

First, no matter how good America's BMD might then be, many of our GBSDs and B-21s that we would need to have and use to help us retaliate, would suffer about *twice* as severe a mauling in a combined Russian and Chinese surprise nuclear first strike. *Second*, our surviving strategic missiles would have to get their warheads past not 200 but *400 total* (Russia + China) enemy BMD shots. Third, they would have to do this in order to be sure of destroying the allowed-for 200 attackers' total assigned countervailing targets—except this 200-target quota would have to be *spread out* now against the vast assets and land areas of *both* Russia *and* China—and China is and will be *hugely more developed* than it was during Cold War I. If Russia and China did attack us together in this scenario, they might even have enough deployed warheads *between them* to attempt a crippling ASW barrage against one or more of our *Columbia* SSBNs!

In other words, our Triad warheads that survived a combined, *gigantic* bolt-from-the-blue nuclear pummeling would then face a daunting task. They would need to somehow survive *twice* the intensity of a surprise attack, get past *twice* the intensity of ABM shots per each of our in-flight retaliatory warheads, while achieving only *half* the target-list bombardment intensity per enemy country, compared to what we could manage if we ever had to defend ourselves against only one of Russia or China at a time.

This multiple-big-attackers downside scenario implies that there might be serious upward pressure on America's nuclear warhead numbers, both deployed and stockpiled, in some future crystal-balling downside scenarios. This says that America simply *must revamp* and sustain the full infrastructure (command-and-control, administrative, scientific, and industrial) needed to quickly manufacture additional nuclear warheads and delivery platforms, *just in case.*

But wait. There's more.

Who Says the First Nuclear War Will Be the *Only* Nuclear War?

There is another significant source of *upward pressure* on American nuke arsenal rightsizing, in *any and all* future scenarios. A nuclear crisis or conflict facing America, at some point on the future timeline, might not be the *only such* crisis or conflict (or outright nuclear war) to ever occur on the whole future timeline. (Again, see Appendix 1 for a technical discussion of this issue, from the *actuarial perspective of forward-looking deconstruction of protracted future timelines, across multiple future not-inconceivable downside scenarios.*)

The U.S.'s facilities for manufacturing any new nuclear warheads, even based upon existing, old designs, have been *mothballed.* They would need at least ten years to be fully reconditioned and reactivated. The longer that the present global nuclear peace prevails, the more this crucial ten-year horizon will likely keep being *extended* by a budget-strapped Washington, *indefinitely ahead* of us on the timeline. Ten years would be an awfully long time to wait for more nukes if we ever did need them, as we very well might in today's and tomorrow's volatile, multi-polar, multi-nuclear and proliferation-prone world.

Our nuclear weapons factories would almost certainly be *obliterated* in any future First Nuclear World War. This would leave us unable to make more nukes with which to try to prevent or get through any future *Second* Nuclear World War—assuming Democracy survived the first one, assuming even that Humanity survived the first one. All of this provides good reason to be *very cautious* about further unilateral nuclear-arms reduction initiatives by America. Such caution is *critical,* whether said unilateralism is driven by funding parsimony, or utopian pacifism, or selfish isolationism, or all three, and whether or not America figures out how to resist and deflect foreign anti-nuclear malign influence manipulation.

Nuclear Parity is an Elusive Thing When There Are Three or More Major Competing Players

The real possibility during the 21st century, of China becoming more like Russia on the thermonuclear-arsenal front, that is, acting as a very serious nuclear-arms numerical rival of the U.S., gives *great urgency* to maintaining and updating diplomatic, economic, cultural, and other tools, procedures, and expert staffing regarding *global nuclear arms-control negotiations.* In late-2020, President Trump attempted (unsuccessfully) to fold China into the needed discussions with Russia about renewing New START. As the discussion above helped establish, some sort of alliance or partnership, or even just informal, opportunistic cooperation, between Russia *and* China in competition with the U.S. would be a *major game changer* from the original Cold War situation, of *only two* key big players bargaining while in simple opposition to one another—while China was *very much less* developed as an economy and a military power than it is today.

The People's Republic of China is something of a global nuclear *wild card.* One reason to not discount this concern is that China, under President Xi Jinping, is showing a persistent, even worsening pattern of picking and choosing, and even distorting, what international laws and norms it chooses to rely on, obey, ignore, exploit selfishly, or violate outright. The constellation of nuclear arms-control and arms-reduction treaties ratified, or signed but not ratified, or withdrawn from, or cheated against, by other world powers exclusive of China could give Beijing a wide strategic armaments "playing field" on which to *run rampant* by all sorts of shenanigans *short of* actual nuclear war. Recall that, unlike Russia, China has no practical experience of negotiating nuclear arms-control or arms-reduction treaties with the U.S.—let alone of having to then *obey* them.

The whole notion of what *nuclear parity* means is *importantly different* when there are *three (or even more)* major negotiating factions. So long as there were only two significant players, the USSR and the U.S., it was not impossible to agree that *maintaining parity* was a good thing. It was comparatively easy to negotiate toward what "parity" actually meant, and what the actual numbers should be (such as 1,550 each): Parity, in that era, meant *equality* in nuclear-armaments numbers between the two big competitors. (Complicated counting rules had to be negotiated, because the two blocks, NATO and the Warsaw Pact, fielded different, not exactly equivalent weapons systems. Also, as noted above, New START does *not* apply to tactical, battlefield atomic weapons; in this important category of *allegedly more-useable,* low-yield nukes, Russia outnumbers the U.S. by some *ten-to-one*; this remains a serious challenge to achieving genuine nuclear parity.)

Consider a possible future world in which China might continue growing its nuclear arsenal, to rival in size those of both the U.S. and

Russia (each taken separately, or even both taken together). What does *three-way parity* mean, especially given that at different times for different reasons two of the three states might *gang up* against the third, in *different* combinations? This "triangulation" of shifting two-against-one rapprochements and alliances *did* happen more than once during the First Cold War.

If parity is taken in arms control discussions to mean "actual numerical equality," simple arithmetic shows that *instability* and *hyper-inflation,* in both *shifting alliances* and *rising warhead* counts, would quickly occur if China, Russia, and the U.S.—in an unstable, nobody-wins three-player game—did *all* seek to achieve "mutual parity" against all comers. The international situation would easily become *dangerously chaotic and wasteful*—unless, that is, the UK and France join with the U.S. in standing against China and Russia, as is the intent behind NATO's joint defense clause, Article Five. Then a notion of parity-as-equality, at the *current* armaments inventory levels, becomes *safely and soundly* achievable.

Put in simple equations, the *problem* of having *three-way equality* in the future is that it would result in:

Russia + China = 2 × USA, *and*

China + USA = 2 × Russia, *and*

Russia + USA = 2 × China, *all at the same time*

The *solution* to this particular nuclear conundrum is preserving something like the *current equilibrium* between East and West "blocs," in which (since according to Wikipedia, the UK, France, and China each own about 300 nuclear warheads, while the U.S. has 6,200 and Russia has 6,500):

USA + UK + France = Russia + China, *so things remain stable*

This equation shows another important aspect of why, right now, the world is in a *"Nuclear Goldilocks Zone"* where strategic parity and strategic stability hold, with exactly the right level of nuclear arsenal sizes needed for effective mutual deterrence.

Various scenarios and calculations, which this writer omits here, demonstrate that it is in fact *essential* to a stable, manageable outcome when seeking "parity" to take account of the UK and France, both of which deploy their own small fleets of SSBNs. That analysis *also suggests that the U.S. should do everything it can to dissuade China from asserting a right to build up to equality of warhead counts with Russia and America*. It is important to note that, like China, neither France nor the UK are parties to the 2010 New START.

Strategic Nuclear "Superiority" is a No-Go for Everybody

There is a serious paradox about three or more nuclear weapons-owning states all seeking *nuclear superiority* over each other at the same time. Arithmetically, the only way to do this would be via an insane nuclear arms race where they all tried to build *an infinite number of nukes*. It was bad enough during the First Cold War, where despite concerted efforts at arms control in some quarters since the 1950s, in fact by the mid-1980s the U.S. owned about 30,000 nukes and the USSR about 40,000. This was said (by Greenpeace) to be enough to kill every human being on Planet Earth seven (7) times over. What a waste!

Conclusion: America's Triad Is in a Goldilocks Zone that We Need to Renew and Sustain

Simple mathematical modeling shows that the U.S. should maintain our strategic nuclear warhead count at the *current New START level*, diversified and dispersed over a renewed and sustained *three-legged deterrence Triad*, for the foreseeable long-term future. We should *not* go any lower on *either* our hydrogen-bomb inventory or our number of (individually and collectively rightsized) Triad legs, as doing either would impair the effectiveness of our Triad to decisively deter even the most threatening current and future adversaries. Nor should we go *above* New START in our warhead inventories, *even if* an adversary seeks to provoke us into a wasteful warhead-count arms race. If that ever happens, we should focus on building more Columbia-class SSBNs in order to *further disperse* our existing SLBM stocks—if necessary even de-MIRVing all those warheads onto *more* individual SLBMs uploaded into *more* separate SSBNs, to achieve even better survivability of each warhead and of our whole Triad.

However, if China actually does ever move to increasing the size of its nuclear arsenal to equal those of the U.S. and of Russia, then

Congress, POTUS, STRATCOM, and the American electorate *must reevaluate* America's strategic requirements and our options, and we *might need* to do more than just further disperse our existing H-bombs onto more SSBNs. We might in such a case *also need* to manufacture and deploy *more H-bombs,* plus more GBSD, more B-21, and more LRSO *delivery platforms.* By far a *better* way to deal with any such dire future arms-race scenarios is to *dissuade* our near-peer adversaries from starting such nuke arms-races *to begin with.*

To succeed at this dissuasion, the U.S. needs to very conspicuously and committedly *sustain the vitality* of its entire strategic-deterrence infrastructure, including not just our weapons inventories and their NC3 but also our weapons laboratories, our defense industrial base, and our deterrence intellectual capital. We also need to *diplomatically but pointedly message* to our adversaries that if they ever do try to beat America in a nuclear arms race, then their own *déjà vu* of national bankruptcy and fragmentation awaits them just up the road.

CHAPTER 7

CONCLUSION

A Pragmatic Vision of Nuclear Peacekeeping: Competing for Strategic Stability

Executive Summary: What is the Most Viable Path to Durable, Worldwide Nuclear Restraints?

The ongoing behaviors of sovereign states, and terrorists, that do now or would like to own nukes suggests that President Obama's call, in his 2009 Prague Speech, for global nuclear disarmament will not be answered any time soon. In that case, it would be *very unwise* to in any way degrade America's nuclear-deterrent Triad infrastructure unilaterally. If—just as during the half-century First Cold War's *bipolar* matchup—mutual nuclear deterrence *and* counterproliferation can prevail in today's *tripolar, multi-nuclear* 21st Century—then *nuclear restraint* will also continue to self-dissuade large states from ever fighting an *ultra-lethal Conventional World War III*. Considering that many tens of millions of people were killed in World War I and World War II, this is an *extremely valuable* added benefit to Humanity.

The most viable foreseeable future—call it *"lasting nuclear peace with honor"*—would then be one in which the current *non-rogue* nuclear weapon-owning states all sustain effective nuclear deterrence-in-being, each against their particular set of potential nuclear-armed adversaries. Each of these deterrent arsenals needs to be adequately rightsized unto itself, while also being thoroughly safe, secure, and survivable. Only then could the nuke-owning states *also* extend *genuinely-assured* protection to their various Nuclear Umbrella Allies, thus *significantly damping* pressures for proliferation—at least by *non-rogue states* that have concerns re their national security.

More to the point, all responsible nuclear powers can—and *need to*—channel their geopolitical animosities into vying competitively for *cultural, intellectual, and political prestige* in the arena of *open-book (not top secret) global nuclear peace maintenance.* "Thought leadership" here can be—and should become—as important a venue for *venting safely international tensions, rivalries, and aggressions* as it ever was during the First Cold War. Clearly, in the realms of theory and practicality, strategy and doctrine, in *ideas* and not just in *hardware,* there is a lot of fresh terrain on which to hold *contests* for Best Practices acuity and for world-class scholastic/analytical "thought experiment" excellence. One might even think of holding a global competition every year or four years, *like a World Cup or Olympics,* except in this realm of *unclassified intellectual product/content* (like a quiz show?): effective nuclear-deterrence and nuclear-peacekeeping postures and messaging techniques, crisis-resolution and peace-restoration methodologies, nuclear-weapon designing for safety and security, efficient cleanup/disposal of excessive nuclear-warhead stocks and other nuclear wastes, and reliable nuclear counter-proliferation and counter-terrorism cooperation paradigms. The UN's International Atomic Energy Agency (IAEA) staff of disciplined and objective experts could provide the referees and the judges for these A-league "test matches," these world grand-master "chess championships."

Arms-control treaties—viewed as living things, *not* set forever in bureaucratic concrete—are also needed, to dictate reasonable *parity in total warheads,* with reasonable *inventory sizes,* between near-peer competitor groupings, thereby *helping prevent senseless, insecurity-driven arms races.* Fortunately or unfortunately, the world currently seems to fall into several *"tectonic plates"*—geopolitical blocs instead of geological blocks—where peer-competitor(s)-against-peer-competitor(s) nuclear *"earthquake zones,"* and peace-or-war *"subduction or separation seams,"* need to be more rationally depressurized, their forces-in-conflict resolved away from disastrously colliding together *or* destructively pulling apart.

The U.S., France, and the UK (i.e., NATO) vis-à-vis Russia is one such *nuclear-weapons tectonic plate seam-in-tension-or-compression.* The U.S. and its Asian allies vis-à-vis China is another. Russia vis-à-vis China is a third. India vis-à-vis Pakistan is a fourth. Israel vis-à-vis Bad Future Iran is a fifth. And the world vis-à-vis rogue state North Korea is a rather problematic sixth. This *interlocking-tectonic-plates* analogy helps emphasize how very important it is to sustain worldwide nuclear non-proliferation efforts. To *add a new plate* (another nuclearized state or even a caliphate) to the crowded roster of current ones could *wreck the geological stability* of the whole. It could, just like with planet Earth's real tectonic seams, lead to *dangerous H-bomb hot spots and deadly radioactive rings of fire.*

How Can We Keep the Big Picture During the Stresses of Current Events?

This book has tried to lay out nuclear deterrence Best Practices and Best Perspectives that mostly change slowly over the years, if they ever change much at all. But sudden headline events can tear our focus away from broader horizons, tempting us too much into the moment. We might fixate on the short-term, and lose sight of the forest for the trees—even lose sight of the trees for the leaves. Sometimes, terrorists or dictators pull off something shocking, precisely for the purpose of distracting democracy from its own best, wisest course. Other times, events seem to take on a life of their own, amplified and distorted perhaps by the rhetorical legerdemain of *self-seeking demagogues* and the manipulative machinations of *"Daddy Warbucks" conflict profiteers.*

It is important to proceed always with patience and dignity. It is important to build tenacious capacity to *balance* between pressing issues that *crosscut* through different scales of reference in time and space, and that *intersect* between different segments of world society. Examples of potentially disruptive events in recent years are the Hague arbitration tribunal's decision completely in favor of the Philippines and against China in the South China Sea; the deadly terrorist vehicle rampages in France and elsewhere; the attempted military coup in Turkey; and the blame games and science denial during the COVID-19 pandemic. We live in turbulent times. But this is no excuse to manage ourselves and events ineffectively. Turbulence is part of the modern world. We need to deal with it.

This 2 × 2 Matrix of {Attainable(?) × Desirable(?)} Futures Is Full of Bad Nuclear No-Nos

This book has offered suggestions for a near-future world that seems most achievable, workable, and livable, one that could be implemented and stabilized based on conventional deterrence and nuclear deterrence executed for the world at large by, in effect, a "Global 9-1-1 Corps" of competing nuke-owning states and blocs that have SSBNs. But we also have touched on four possible future worlds, advocated by some in the literature and the popular media, that seem dangerously unworkable in our lifetimes:

- *Unilateral Zero:* (Also sometimes called Solo Zero): An *attainable yet undesirable* world, in which the U.S. eliminates all its nukes and hopes that other countries follow its fine example. Many of them *won't*, any more than aggressive countries followed President Wilson's peace initiatives after World War I. Deterrence against nuclear wars and also against big conventional wars would be *dangerously weakened* from the current relatively stable world situation.
- *Global Zero:* A *not-safely-attainable*, and also *undesirable* world. Too much cheating is likely. It is mathematically impossible to properly coordinate an accident-free and public-health-preserving process of nuclear disarmament, among multiple states with very differently sized arsenals, in such a manner that multi-way parity is constantly sustained over all the years needed to get from here to global zero. It is not even clear what parity would *mean*, when warhead counts vary among different nuclear weapons-owning states from 1,550 *deployed*—with many more stockpiled—down to the low *hundreds*, down to the mere *dozens*. Should all inventories be reduced *simultaneously* in *geometric proportion*, or in *arithmetic proportion*, or by some other disciplined scheme—and if so, *what* scheme? None obviate the *extremely destabilizing nuclear-security dilemma* resulting when, say, one superpower has only 10 nukes left while another has 20—giving a deadly 2-to-1 advantage, yet *without* the deterring risk of possible uncontrolled escalation to Armageddon. *And*, it can't be overemphasized enough, Global Zero would also leave the world with *no* reliable deterrent against a big, *mega-lethal* Conventional World War III.
- *Minimum Deterrence:* (This means arsenals so small that states can only do each other relatively "minor" nuclear damage.) This is *attainable*, at least unilaterally, but is *highly undesirable*. Effective mutual nuclear deterrence depends essentially on arsenals adequately sized to hold at *existential risk* the very *big-sized* strategic-assets inventories of states that are *large* in the financial and geographic senses, such as the U.S., China, and Russia. If nuke states could *only* inflict on

each other, either in a first-use or in retaliation, *minimal* nuclear damage, then there would be no mechanism to effectively prevent a nuclear war from appealing to a very aggressive or cornered/desperate gambler or gamesman (let alone madman) despotic regime. In a world with minimum deterrence, nuclear weapons would become *all too useable* by *all the wrong people.*

- *Multiple-Overkill: Attainable,* but *very undesirable.* It is ironic, even tragic, that during the First Cold War, despite successful negotiations by the U.S. and USSR to control nuclear weapons in the 1950s, '60s, and early '70s via a series of treaties (Limited Test Ban, ABM, NPT, SALT), nevertheless a combination of *mutual distrust, fear, and sheer acquisition mania* led the two superpowers to acquire by the 1980s, between them, some 70,000 nuclear warheads. Pundits pointed out that this was enough to kill everyone on the planet *seven (7) times over,* or more! This sort of nuclear warhead acquisition "MAD-ness" should *not* be allowed to ever occur again. It is *wasteful* of money, *polluting* to the environment, and *pointlessly dangerous.* While it is essential to have a *genuinely adequate* number of warheads for effective deterrence, continuing to manufacture tens of thousands more really needs to be *avoided.* It does *not* increase security for anyone, beyond that (by definition) magic number of the *adequately sized* effective arsenal—such as *today's "just right" Goldilocks Zone* between the U.S. and Russia under New START.

The point of this tabulation—which can be thought of by more mathematically-inclined readers as falling into a 2 × 2 matrix—is *starkly straightforward:* Each of these scenarios, advocated in the mainstream media by different interest groups, is *either genuinely unattainable, or seriously undesirable, or both.*

"Either/Or" Thinking Should Be Avoided; Many Key Things Fall Along a Broad Spectrum

This book's chapters and appendices have tried to show that a number of aspects of successful nuclear deterrence, and of nuclear peacekeeping and peace-restoration more generally, require thinking along *continuous spectrums* rather than simply in terms of pairs of polar-opposite extremes. Future-scenario or thought-experiment potentialities, and therefore national policies and postures, need to take account that *few* conflicts or controversies involve solely a 0% or 100% answer or outcome. More than just true/false or multiple-choice issues, we are dealing here with *difficult "essay questions."*

It is vital that humanity *pass the test* of deterring all nuclear strikes *with flying colors*. For instance, by delving into the treacherous waters of "draconian" counter-terror deterrence, of proxy-sponsored or chain-ganged nuclear conflict, and of autocratic (even democratic) nuke-usage options, we saw that some common propositions, encountered in media screeds here and there, are *not true*: The odds of nuclear war in the future between big states and/or their proxies is *not inherently/inevitably either* 0% *or* 100%; it depends tremendously on the success—*sans* cultural mirror-imaging—of nuclear-deterrence posture and messaging. The odds of someone finding an acceptable way (to them) of deterring nuclear terrorists is *not* 0%. Membership in a Nuclear Free Zone (NFZ) does *not* mean that safety from any future nuclear war is 100% guaranteed. The potential usability of a ground-penetrating tactical nuke in some future armed conflict is *neither* 0% nor 100%, especially as adversaries large and small dig deeper and deeper underground.

Above all, the probability that the U.S. Congress will enact *full, stable, multi-year funding* for the *prompt and rightsized* renewal of America's vital nuclear-deterrence Triad—with all legs adequate in numbers, and *all* infrastructure revitalized—is *somewhere in between* 0% and 100%, due to political divisiveness, gridlock, and a lack of focus. The necessary budget appropriations therefore need the *urgent attention and support* of *all* voters, in the U.S. electorate at large, and especially on Capitol Hill.

If Nuclear Conflict Is Come as You Are, the Forces of Freedom Had Better Come Strong

Throughout the First Cold War, various commentators said that if a nuclear war ever did break out between NATO and the Warsaw Pact, it would be over in half an hour—the flight time of incoming and outgoing ICBMs. Of course, in some scenarios a nuclear shooting war could drag on for weeks or months, of devastating salvoes and counter-salvoes punctuated by lulls while the combatant states licked their wounds, along with sporadic negotiations toward a lasting cease-fire. Since weapons depots and arms manufacturing plants would be high on all combatants' target lists, it would not be possible to manufacture more major weapons systems for a very long time once such a war broke out, even if it were ended quickly while it somehow stayed limited. Given these timing and damage issues, nuclear war was said to be truly "come as you are."

Thus, the U.S. and other nuclear weapon-owning defenders of democracy require nuclear deterrence-by-retaliation systems that are *fully up to date* and *sufficiently numerous*—including secure *backup stockpiles* that make adequate provision for a *long and uncertain future.* To be effective deterrents-in-being, America's deployed Triad assets and their elite crews need to be *immediately available and ready at all times.* Weakening America's deterrent forces, by letting them become *too slow* to bring online from a *de-alerted* status, or *inadequate* in numbers, or *obsolete* in capabilities, or all three, is a very bad idea. Intentional obsolescence in nuclear-weapons safety features, delivery platforms, and guidance and fusing systems makes no more sense than asking modern armies to defend their countries using *biplanes and flintlocks.* Such *negligent leadership* would allow, and even encourage, *belligerent adversaries* to launch a *surprise nuclear attack* that they could *expect to get away with.* Short of that, it would leave America and our Allies *seriously exposed to nuclear blackmail* (extortion, coercion), which would be bad enough. It could even expose us to *"big" non-nuclear warfare* of the sort that could eventually *kill a few hundred million people,* reverse the West's brilliant First Cold War victory, and *bring down democracy in favor of world tyranny.*

Fact of Life: Not All Kids Get to Be Police Officers, EMTs, or Firefighters—Only *Some* Do

We can make an analogy that the various countries of our world are like different people within a city. A city has definite needs for various community services. Among these are certain First Responder services: police, fire-and-rescue, and ambulance/EMT. Not everyone in the city can or should or needs to be a First Responder, but enough of the right sort of people, with the right kinds of personalities and training and the right kind of equipment, definitely do need to answer this call to service—as Chiefs, Lieutenants, Sergeants, or as rank-and-file—or else there will be crime and disorder, conflagrations and avoidable deaths, much pain and tragedy in the city.

A democracy owning a right-sized nuclear weapons Triad, with the proper sort of highly trained professionals to command and crew them, *can and should* play a very necessary global peacekeeping-via-deterrence role within the Community of Nations—to arrest and punish "law breakers," to extinguish potential "brushfires and conflagrations," and in a very real way to save the imperiled from unnecessary injury and death.

It makes no more sense for America to discard its Triad, in some *hollow move* toward "world peace" or "equality with the have-nots," than it does for a city to discard (or "defund") all its First Responders, in some hollow move toward "public safety" or "equality with the have-nots."

In the other direction, it also makes no more sense for America to join in an international *nuke-count "race to infinity,"* than it makes sense for any civic jurisdiction to buy so many fire engines, police cars, and ambulances that it has to park one in *every residence's driveway*, let alone in *every single space available in every parking lot and parking garage in town.*

Having a few large and rich nations maintaining mutual nuclear deterrence arsenals, competing against one another over only those parameters and characteristics which are wise and good—strategic stability, weapons safety and security, nuclear-policy sophistication and nuclear-posture maturity, foreign-relations comity via viable crisis-mitigation processes—is the best way to *permanently enjoy* the special benefits which only nuclear weapons in *the hands of the responsible, more-mature few with the most to potentially lose* can provide for all: no nuclear or strategic WMD wars, no conventional big wars, no nuclear blackmail or nuclear terrorism, and no unnecessary nuclear proliferation.

How Can We Best Balance Nuclear Non-Proliferation with Nuclear Deterrence-in-Being?

It will be an ongoing, probably impossible and certainly misguided challenge to ever reconcile (1) non-nuke states' repeated calls for all the nuke states to eliminate all their nukes, in order to satisfy the *long-ignored* Non-Proliferation Treaty's Article VI and thus end *so-called "nuclear weapons apartheid,"* and (2) the *evident continuing need* perceived by nuke states to *sustain* their nuclear arsenals. This quandary exists because any concerted worldwide nuclear disarmament campaign faces various hurdles that at present, at least speaking from realist pragmatism rather than idealist utopianism, seem *insurmountable*:

> The nuclear disarmament campaign would be too difficult to enforce against *inevitable cheating*. The campaign would *drag out over time*, and lead to serious *numbers-based disparities* and *dangerous instabilities*, as arsenals shrank from *adequate deterrence size* down to minimal, *ineffectively small yet non-zero size*. As the numbers all shrank, rather small disparities between intractable adversaries (such as 250 versus 260) would take on *monumentally destabilizing* significance (such as 10 versus 20), leading to *inevitable catastrophe*. And such global disarmament, even if it could somehow be made to work, would deny humanity

> the ultimate and indispensable firewall against a *murderously big* Conventional World War III. Putting the few last allowed world nukes into the hands of the United Nations, an idea which *failed* in the late 1940s (the Baruch Plan), would be *paralyzed* by intra-UN politics and bureaucracy.
>
> Non-nuke states have a valid point about the *"nuclear glass ceiling"* between *the nuke haves and the nuke have-nots.* However, it should be recognized by all that, in the world of hardball international relations and give-and-take diplomacy, there can be a *workable calculus* of negotiations to *redress such complaints.* It helps here to be aware that some states seek nukes of their own not simply for *security*, but for *global prestige*, or as *bargaining chips*, and/or in order for their in-power regime to *aggrandize itself* in domestic politics, and/or for internal scientific, industrial, and bureaucratic factions to *gain more influence* and *command larger budgets.*

A workable calculus of positive inducements, not just negative sanctions, for negotiating new universal principles for a happier world with both nuke states and non-nuke states in it, can include accelerated R&D and foreign aid in the area of *commercial fusion power generation.* Such technology, utilizing high-power laser ignition and intense magnetic-confinement chambers (tokomaks), is of late advancing in leaps and bounds in many national and private laboratories around the world, This could be a very beneficial add-on (or even better, *revision*) to the NPT's existing inducement, which now offers peaceful fission-power generation help to those countries that do not proliferate nukes. The *huge differences* would be that (1) fusion power, unlike fission power, *cannot* be weaponized, even nefariously/covertly, into deliverable nukes, while (2) fusion power, unlike fission power, is *not* subject to active-core meltdown catastrophes and spent-core environmental toxins.

Another inducement can include a more systematized approach to gaining *protective nuclear umbrella ("extended deterrence") memberships*, as well as to re-confirming and strengthening *("assuring")* all the commitments behind existing umbrella treaties.

A third persuasive element, possibly leading to UN ratification of a waiver of or amendment to implementation/enforcement of NPT Article VI as written, could come out of *wider exposition and discourse* re the *unsolvable problem* of how to prevent a third, *guaranteed-to-be-horribly-lethal* conventional world war, in a world without nuclear weapons-in-being serving to *effectively deter* superpower and regional-power big conventional attacks and invasions.

A further talking point as a soft negative inducement, against more states acquiring their own nukes, can be the *horribly expensive* yet in-for-a-penny-in-for-a-pound *indispensable SSBN (or SSBP) fleet* needed to deploy nukes with the requisite *overall survivability*—which, in comparison, *no* mobile land-based ICBMs can offer. SSBNs (and SSBPs) can be better characterized in the world's view as *hyper-essential, hyper-expensive tools of global peace enforcement,* paid for, owned, and deployed by the handful of states that can most capably support and sustain them. That is, SSBN or SSBP fleets are a national *obligation* from the states that do own them, to the *whole world*; they are *not* just acquired to flaunt national prestige and military-industrial muscle; rather than "competing" with domestic social programs, they *complement those programs* by defending *all that Human society enjoys.*

Perhaps the clincher argument demonstrating clearly the need to continue long-term with the world's current, effective mutual nuclear deterrence-in-being—an argument *reinforcing and amplifying* all those others offered above—is the persistent presence in our world of both (1) violent, raw, visceral *human impulses of rage and hate,* and (2) sociopathic national leaders who resort to *over-nationalist or over-populist demagoguery* to harness those mass impulses and instigate *genocidal massacres and bloodthirsty world wars.*

The aforementioned inducements and arguments do deserve wider attention, especially to help "lubricate and inform" more productive dialogue between folks who see the need to renew America's Triad and folks who seek to eliminate it. Then, maybe, more widely as well, the nuclear-deterrent have-nots of the world will come to understand that the haves are *not* a specially privileged class to be resented or emulated, like "trust fund kids" or "one-percenters." Rather, they are *self-sacrificing servants of safety and prosperity for all, planetwide,* like 9-1-1 First Responder crews and their vehicle fleets are for the *entire* city they serve.

We Need to Draw "Profiles in Outrage" to Stop Potential Nuclear Aggressors Early

It is not rocket science to perceive that aggressors on the international scene—such as the *sociopathic demagogue warmongers* mentioned above—tend to evince a distinct set of behaviors as they gear up to seize wider power and do more harm. Spotting this cluster of attributes *early in the game* can help motivate democracies to take necessary steps to limit the problem behaviors *early on.* Some systematic discipline to this monitoring of bad behaviors might help democracies avoid the natural tendency to give a budding bad actor *the benefit of the doubt* about their intentions, until it is too late to prevent great bloodshed. This is especially important in the modern era, when troublemakers the world over can cloak their *anschluss* and *lebensraum* tactics in a whole *multi-dimensional cloak of fake news.*

Here is a list of traits that a review of recent history suggests correlate with an entity on the international stage having *genuinely, seriously ill intent.* These traits are *openly observable*; that is, they are *not* hidden with that entity's internal organization and operating culture, *nor* are they dependent on our detection via covert intelligence sources. One can think of these as a *Dirty Dozen*:

1. Identity nationalism by ethnic majorities, with persecution of minorities.
2. Military buildup beyond legitimate defensive needs.
3. Forceful territorial expansionism.
4. Trumped up, paranoia-feeding accusations about external threats.
5. Propaganda provocations, negative info war, and recurring cyber-attacks on "enemies."
6. Increasing autocracy at home.
7. Denigration of human rights.
8. Simmering border conflicts made to flare up.
9. Strict control and surveillance of domestic media and of foreign Internet access.
10. Proxy-conflict instigation and exploitation of other states, sponsorship of terrorism.
11. Supporting troll farms, clandestine malign-influence (divisive fake news) campaigns.
12. Interference in other countries' electoral processes, domestic voter suppression.

These traits and behaviors do *not* specifically look at whether a "revolutionary" state seeks to alter the "status quo" international order. This Dirty Dozen list of behaviors *does* look directly at a state's belligerent, deceitful, and destabilizing conduct *per se.* There are nations, the United States among them, that demonstrate subsets of these behaviors at times, yet do so for *valid, positive, even noble reasons*: seeking constructive change via peaceful, diplomatic means. And while wars are usually started for political or economic reasons, not all wars are fought over changes to the international order, so much as over the size of shares in the goodies of an *existing order.*

The U.S. Does Have Good Ways to "Seize the Initiative" for Effective Nuclear Deterrence

It is an old and time-honored adage of military strategy that to succeed at one's national security and geopolitical goals, whatever they might be, it is essential to *hold the initiative,* rather than allow an adversary to keep the initiative for themselves. The "initiative" means the ability to dictate the *terms* of the contest and the *time and place* of competitive encounters, and to maintain overall *freedom of action.* The idea is to not be passive or reactive, but rather force the adversary to react to *you.*

The problem with anyone trying to successfully fight a nuclear war is that once it gets going, *nobody* holds the initiative. Massive death and destruction take on a momentum, an *"entropy"* all their own. *Everyone* must react to events, until the events halt themselves because *everyone is dead.*

But effective nuclear deterrence is all about *preventing any* nuclear war. As Martha Stewart would say, "It's a good thing." In the context of good nuclear peacekeeping, and urgent nuclear peace-restoration capabilities if worse ever does come to worst, this book has tried to show that there are in fact a number of *productive, positive steps* that America can take to hold and apply the initiative in effective nuclear deterrence.

Such *benign, life-preserving* actions and measures include:

- Updating and amending existing global nuclear arms-control treaties and norms, negotiating and ratifying new ones, and fomenting perfection of commercialized non-fission-reactor, renewable energy sources—especially "hot fusion" power, which ought to be talked up more now in a nuclear nonproliferation context, to lay the groundwork for when it becomes commercially practical.
- Continuing to periodically develop and publicize the Congressionally-mandated updates of U.S. National Nuclear Posture Review Reports, which can serve as a world role model for Best Practices and Best Perspectives in effective nuclear deterrence-in-being.
- Sponsoring and/or directing truth-based public education and scientific information, via the Internet and in other ways, about the benefits of sound nuclear deterrence—and the very real dangers of devastating nuclear-attack blowback/escalation effects—to everything that even Islamist nuclear terrorists cherish.

- Modernizing America's nuclear Triad forces while avoiding, and proselytizing globally against, both senseless international arms races, and various foreign nuclear deterrence approaches and strategies that are definitely "Worst Practices" for world peace, prosperity, and survival—such as MIRVing land-based ICBMs, or using launch-on-warning rules of engagement.
- Providing, perhaps through the new U.S. Space Force, leadership for international cooperation to study and mitigate the risk of large asteroid and/or comet impacts with Earth. By using a series of stand-off nuclear blasts all to *one side* of a threatening space object, the combination of gentler blast force, plus intense photon pressure and surface-vaporization ablative recoil, can provide a useful but nondestructive shoving aside onto a safe trajectory. MIRVed warhead buses mounted on heavy-lift space vehicles are ideally suited for such efforts. This work will probably in the near term need to look at the responsible/necessary use of nuclear weapons in deep space, until other space-rock diversion technologies can be operationally perfected. These efforts perforce unite the vital interests of all states, in the name of their very survival. The problems of *non-nuclear* space-rock deflection are two-fold: (1) they will probably not be ready for reliable operational deployment without many years of effort and billions of dollars of investment, and (2) the conventional impactor and hard-shove methods might not work against the preponderance of asteroids, now understood via robotic spacecraft probes to be structurally weak "orbiting rubble piles."
- Helping foment a new global culture of *competitive nuclear peacekeeping*, especially in the realm of open-book sound nuclear deterrence, peacekeeping, and peace restoration (conflict cessation and resolution) theory and practice. This intellectual product is just as important to effective deterrence as are the retaliatory systems themselves, i.e., the Triad assets and their dedicated crews. One can even envision periodic international contests in which different state teams, of academics, think tankers, military folks, and government officials, together vie for top global standing just like at a World Cup, or Olympics, or chess-master championship—or Nobel Peace Prize.
- Both the *competitive nuclear stability* model and the *First Responders* model, offered above, can help explain the pressing

need for the world to sustain today's counterproliferation and existing-arsenal-rightsizing Goldilocks Zones—with all world citizens accepting and enjoying their individual current positions as either a nuke owning or non-owning state. Via the analogies to (1) *a sports arena* that has *both* athletes *and* spectators, and to (2) *a city* that has *both* police/fire/ambulance crews *and* civilians, we can hope to banish permanently the *pro-proliferation bugaboos* of a "nuclear glass ceiling" and of "nuclear apartheid."

Conclusion: Ideally, "Winning" at Nuclear Deterrence Really Means *All Humanity* Wins

For solidly effective mutual nuclear deterrence, some of the lines of reasoning that need to be thought through can seem Byzantine. Perhaps the contemplation of motivations and counter-motivations, of moves and counter-moves, plans and counterplans, should be compared to an ongoing battle between world chess champions. But this exacting, grueling (and very competitive) work is worth it—so long as banning all world nukes *and* all conventional world wars remains hopelessly out of reach—simply because of the absolute importance of preventing an adversary's unprovoked first use of nuclear weapons. The essential need for prevention—the need for some larger peace-loving, technologically-capable democracies to maintain robust, flexible, survivable nuclear retaliatory second-strike arsenals—is regrettable. But it ought to be viewed for the foreseeable future as an unavoidable cost of living, and of staying alive, in today's highly volatile world. Perhaps the *"nuclear peacekeeping Olympics" model* and the *"Elite First Responders" model*, both offered above, can help communicate these opportunities and imperatives to those good folks who do not yet "get it."

The 9/11 Commission's final report criticized U.S. authorities for "unprepared mindsets" and "failures of imagination." Only careful evaluation of a wide range of what-if *thought experiment* scenarios—including ones that by design push the envelope of possibilities—can combat such weakness. Only in this way can we prevent some future nuclear Pearl Harbor.

U.S. Government war-gaming is definitely *not* meant to advocate intentional nuclear war-fighting by choice. But staying fully cognizant and prepared, regarding *all* requirements for nuclear deterrence, does seem the only responsible course to follow. In case America and our allies, partners, and friends ever do suffer an adversary's nuclear first strike, we would have no acceptable alternative but to retaliate in kind, proportionately and discriminately—along with making an urgent push to *contain and terminate* the conflict on politically acceptable terms, and then *restore* effective deterrence, before the whole human race is wiped out.

To sustain, and keep secure, America's necessary leadership of an *open, rule-based global system* that remains readily accessible to all law-abiding entities and peoples, the U.S. needs to continue to promulgate up to date, in-tune-with-the-times National Nuclear Postures. Those postures need to be *holistically integrated with,* not stovepiped away from, America's various other *multi-domain strategic defense needs*—such as deterring war in outer space, and protecting our cybersecurity. We also must have declaratory defense policies (and *de facto* action plans) that are clear, complete, concise—and that don't rely on bluffs which might get exposed by overconfident adversaries, "freelancing" trolls, or even by concerned domestic whistleblowers.

Strategy experts such as Dr. Henry Kissinger argued during the First Cold War that intentional nuclear policy *ambiguity* can help to reinforce and amplify effective nuclear deterrence. That ambiguity—leaving some things *unsaid* and/or *unspecified*—can further complicate an adversary's risk/reward calculations, thus enhancing that adversary's keen perception of the fatal dangers to him/her of making any unprovoked nuclear first strike. But in the 21st Century, *some* ambiguities might lead to a nuclear armed adversary making strategic miscalculations that we *do not* want them to make. *More comprehensive messaging*—backed up by *fuller logical rigor*—in updated U.S. nuclear postures might be appropriate, even essential, to successfully, all across the foreseeable future, most thoroughly *preserve, protect, and defend* world peace, American-style freedoms, human rights, and human life itself.

APPENDIX 1

NUCLEAR POSTURE'S BASICS SHOULD BE BASED IN ACTUARIAL SCIENCE

Executive Summary: Actuaries Plan for *Long* Timeframes across *Multiple* Downside Scenarios

What do Best Perspectives and Best Practices for *preventing nuclear war* have to do with actuarial science? *Here's what:* The actuarial profession, traditionally, specializes in setting *sound financial standards* and developing *risk mitigation practices* for the insurance industry and for pension funding. Beyond just the tricky challenges of balancing powerful opposing imperatives—setting adequately-*high*-yet-marketably-*low* pricing for policy premiums and pension-plan contributions, and calculating sufficiently-*strong*-but-*not-excessively-cautious* corporate loss reserves—actuaries need to think clearly and carefully about some *very bad things*. These so-called *"life contingencies"* (deaths, illnesses, fires, hurricanes; investment market drops, interest rate crunches, insurer bankruptcies) might (or might not) happen over an *extremely long future timeframe*. Some insurance policies and pension plans—including Social Security—make promises that will take *a few decades* to fulfill, and the insurers or pension planners themselves want to avoid insolvency for *much longer even than that.*

The resulting ever-evolving body of actuarial Best Practices stand in stark contrast to the *short-term thinking* and *constricted time horizons* inherent in America's competitive political processes. It is precisely within this highly pragmatic, (re)electability-oriented "culture" or "operating code" of our country's sacred Democratic Way of Life that some behaviors and viewpoints which actuaries take for granted, in their own work, can intersect beneficially with drafting the "U.S. National Nuclear Posture After Next."

It is my considered professional opinion, as a fully qualified Fellow of the Society of Actuaries since 1980, that U.S. National Nuclear Posture Review Reports, going forward, could benefit from certain fairly straightforward logical and/or semantic fine-tuning. This effort, which is more than mere wordsmithing, could be applied to *what the postures are,* and, within U.S. Government documents and messaging, to how they are expressed to the world. The global audiences for such indispensable *nuclear-peacekeeping information* include near-peer competitor states, rogue states, and adversary non-state groups such as terrorists, as well as various electorates and private citizenries in America, our Friends and Allies and Partners abroad, and also neutral or "nonaligned" states. I.e., basically *everybody.*

To explicate and exploit more fully this relevant nexus of The Actuarial and The Political could be a very valuable exercise indeed. America's nuclear-deterrence effectiveness is the *last bastion* against suffering a nuclear or other strategic-level WMD attack—which if we ever let it happen, would then place on our POTUS the *terrible burden* of needing to order a retaliatory nuclear strike. Effective nuclear deterrence is also a strong—and essential—*dissuader* against major conventional wars and nuclear blackmail; furthermore, a robust Triad *assures* our Allies that they *can* rely on America's (and NATO's) Nuclear Umbrella, thus *discouraging* those allies from any further nuclear proliferation.

Any rational person would want to do these many crucial jobs *as well as humanly possible.* Note that America making the investments necessary to sustain over time U.S. STRATCOM's Nuclear Deterrence Triad provides an *all-in-one solution,* one that for a whole human lifetime has indeed *worked rather nicely* and promises to continue to do so *if not now taken for granted, denigrated, or shortchanged.*

The "bumper sticker" or "elevator-pitch take away" here is simple:

> ***Either America can continue to invest over time the giga-dollars needed to sustain our Triad, or we and the whole world could all too easily suffer the giga-deaths of a nuclear war.***

Organization of Appendix 1; A Basic Definition; Overall Goal of this Appendix

This Appendix details *five recommendations,* each expressed in **bold type** below, that are derived from *actuarial first principles of risk analysis and risk mitigation*—ones that have proven important for identifying and managing some of the fundamental dangers inherent to the human condition and the good functioning of modern society. Such suggested nuclear-posture R&D *methodological enhancements* derive from what I label as *"actuarial-style contingent timeline deconstruction,"* a common-sense variant of which might be more familiar to some readers under the guise of the more computer-intensive *"long range Monte Carlo simulations."*

DEFINITION: *Actuarial-style contingent timeline deconstruction* is an "enterprise navigational paradigm" in which *multiple* unpredictable happenings, and their various possible cause-and-effect (action and reaction) *linkages*, are *all* taken account of along a *very protracted* future timeline, in many different happenstance scenarios. Then *different* possible coping strategies are assessed against each other by testing their various outcomes all across the same *large set* of different future downside scenarios. Only then are *superior risk-mitigation tactics for today and tomorrow* selected and acted upon, after knowing what *might* come to pass across a widely-encompassing range of *possible dangerous futures.*

The five key recommendations will be offered below, after a brief retrospective on some aspects of prior and current U.S. Nuclear Postures, based on my close reading of their texts in the unclassified literature. The overall goal of this Appendix 1 is to demonstrate the value, nay the necessity going forward in a dangerous world, of the nuclear-deterrence community learning to see and think more as actuaries do.

Prior Nuclear Postures

Since the end of the First Cold War, updated National Nuclear Postures have been issued a total of four times: by the Bill Clinton, George W. Bush, and Barack Obama Administrations, and then the Donald Trump Administration in 2018 promulgated its own National Nuclear Posture Review Report—which is the most recent one extant as of this writing. Some time after Inauguration Day 2021, the Biden Administration will issue the next NNPRR.

The Clinton and Obama postures had unclassified versions. The Bush posture was classified but portions were allegedly "leaked" and discussed in the media. Each in its own manner and style included an appreciation of the strategic threat environment in the world at the time. The first three, strictly speaking, might have relied on less than fully rigorous thinking in making the causal link that, because the Soviet Union was no more and Russia was now deemed rather unlikely to nuke American interests, the U.S. did not need as large a nuclear arsenal as when NATO and the Warsaw Pact stood in direct, bi-polar opposition. The Trump Administration's Nuclear Posture Review's unclassified version somewhat made up for this potential shortcoming, but still could be seen as subject to some *whipsawing* due to its own lack of a long-term actuarial view.

There were really, and still are, *two distinct things* in play here. *One* was the question of whether Russia (and/or another entity) *was at that time, or would soon again become,* nuclear-ly belligerent—or not. *The other,* the main focus of this Appendix, is whether said short-term belligerence being *perceived* of by America as higher or lower ought to, *"in the moment,"* lead to significant actual or anticipated changes in the U.S.'s deployed and stockpiled strategic nuclear warhead-count level—a basic Triad parameter that, for several good reasons discussed below, really needs to be *kept stable over long periods.* (Perhaps, gentle reader, you're starting to see what I mean about "whipsawing.")

The fact is that arsenal rightsizing, being a very *"sticky"* statistic—one that takes years to either increase (by building more nukes safely under real-world funding and industrial-base *constraints*) or decrease (by *safely and securely* dismantling excessive existing warheads)—should ideally *not* be changed simply according to the latest, *possibly incorrect or overoptimistic* perception of possible adversary threatening-vice-benign behaviors. For instance, despite the Reagan/Gorbachev disarmament moves and then the collapse of the USSR, some U.S./NATO (and other) commentators in the 1990s remained concerned that post-communist Russia might become as confrontational and/or belligerent as the Soviet Union often was—if not even more so. In addition, new threats of a nuclear nature *might* emerge, demanding a bigger U.S. nuclear deterrent arsenal—and might emerge faster that America's Triad can modernize to keep up with events. *Exactly such bad things have indeed occurred.*

To amplify this particular point, *a very fundamental prerequisite* to successfully enjoying the short-term and long-term benefits of effective nuclear deterrence-in-being is to *recognize explicitly* that the most dangerous threats of all to successful U.S. Triad effectiveness can arise from unanticipated, unpredictable *discontinuities* to national and international technological, environmental, and/or political conditions.

One especially destabilizing type of discontinuity is a *sudden regime change in an adversary*: Germany's peaceful Weimar Republic because Hitler's warlike Third Reich very suddenly, due to a bad political-economic crisis that came to a head in 1933; The Shah of Iran was deposed quite suddenly by Islamic extremists in 1979. Moscow's regime unexpectedly changed *thrice* in the last generation: from adversarial Communists, through reforming Mikhail Gorbachev, to conciliatory Boris Yeltsin, to adversarial Vladimir Putin.

Another extremely destabilizing type of discontinuity is an *enemy conventional-weaponry surprise attack*: Ranging from Pearl Harbor and the Battle of the Bulge, through China entering the Korean War, then the Vietnam War's Tet Offensive, to 9/11/01, with *perhaps more to come in future*, such shocks can almost instantaneously fracture U.S. and world equilibrium, and alter the whole direction of global history.

It is (in part) because of the *always-present risk*, of precisely such dangerous but unanticipated disruptions to the international system, that America's nuclear deterrence must *always be sustained in a steady state of full readiness.*

Rightsizing versus Overkill

There is a fundamental difference between (1) reducing nuclear arsenals because a prolonged arms race has led to *unnecessarily huge* nuclear weapon inventories, and (2) reducing an arsenal, perhaps on sheer momentum and under anti-nuclear political pressures (fed by covert adversary information warfare), to the point that *too few* nukes are owned to be able to severely-enough damage an enemy state *after* it launches a devastating first strike against American interests. Eliminating overkill is very wise for all sorts of solid reasons—though in hindsight, it would have been much better to not build tens of thousands of excess nuclear warheads in a wild contest for illusive "nuclear supremacy" to being with, and then need to spend even more funding on dismantling most of said warheads.

But to reduce America's arsenal *below* a certain *minimum effective number*, which is in fact at the current New START Treaty level of 1,550 accountable warheads deployed each, for the U.S. and for Russia, is potentially very destabilizing: An aggressor regime in Moscow might think that in this case a nuclear war is survivable and winnable by their side, because the damage from America's first-strike-blunted retaliation would *not* be completely devastating to the Russian Motherland. Remember that sociopath despots are not especially casualty averse; too often, they will tolerate *huge losses among their own populace* in return for large anticipated geopolitical gains, and perceived permanent job security, *for themselves.*

The distinction between eliminating overkill excesses, and weakening an arsenal too much for effective nuclear retaliation, is very important indeed; the first case productively *eliminates harmful waste*, while the second counterproductively *undermines strategic stability*. In drawing this distinction, it is particularly important that American decisionmakers not fall for the fatal trap of *psychological mirror-imaging.* In this behavioral phenomenon, an American unconsciously (and very wrongly) takes for granted that all foreign people and peoples see everything in life and in the world in exactly the same (American) way as he/she does. In fact, emotional "cultures," cognitive "operating codes," and concepts of "ultimate fulfillment in life (or in death)" can vary considerably in a single "nation," let alone within one sovereign state made up of many ethnic/tribal sub-nations, and these characteristics can all vary *very considerably* between *different* sovereign states. When it comes to being nuclear-ly peaceful and keeping the nuclear peace, some foreign entities, whether superpowers or regional powers or rogue states or terrorist groups, could genuinely present dire threats to the American Way of Life.

Some Technical-Mathematical Clarifications Could Help Strengthen Nuclear Deterrence

Examining from first principles the fundamental cause-and-effect linkages between preceding and subsequent events along a timeline, as actuaries do in their work, can be edifying. This is especially true regarding the pushing-and-shoving, of historical and geopolitical forces, that can affect nuclear-deterrence outcomes, good or bad. It is important to *consider separately, and in balance, two basic steps* that, though separate, also *work together.*

The *first step* is to maximally discourage anyone—including one's own self—from making a nuclear first strike (other than in justified response to a *genuinely existential threat* that comes from *overwhelming conventional weaponry* or from *non-nuclear strategic WMDs*—in which case the *first-nuclear-as-such-but-actually-retaliatory* defensive strike is *not* a true "first-use"). This maximal-discouragement step is accomplished via a rigorous, vigorous campaign of communicating about the whys and wherefores of America's nuclear posture, and about sound deterrence theory and Best Practices; it is a matter of issuing declarative statements, practicing diplomacy, and conducting aggressive outreach education about *nuclear peacekeeping requirements and imperatives.*

The second step is to very publicly be seen to possess all the many capabilities and capacities needed to prevail via *nuclear retaliation*—along with well-prepared and rehearsed plans for politically-acceptable *conflict resolution* (war termination) *after* the essential Tit-for-Tat second strike—to be used against any adversary *who ever dares* to start a nuclear or other existential or strategic-intensity WMD war. This very-public-possession step is all about fielding sufficiently numerous, diverse and dispersed, survivable *weaponry hardware and command-and-control infrastructure, wielded by top-notch commanders and crews*: collectively survivable Triad delivery platforms, redundant and jam/spoof-proof NC3, enough SSNs to protect one's SSBNs, thorough coverage by ground-based and space-based early-warning sensors, finite-but-effective ballistic missile defenses, and thriving scientific/industrial establishment.

Both these steps to owning an effective nuclear deterrent are indispensable. They are also somewhat *independent*: Different policies/postures can go with different hardware sets, and vice versa.

Much of American national attention, and national spending, have gone into the vital second step, the nuclear weapons and NC3 and other apparatuses, without which no superpower-like entity can claim to have achieved effective nuclear deterrence. But the first step, achieving full clarity and impact as to all and every means of decisive deterrence *outreach education and messaging*, for discouragement of nuclear *aggression* and subsequent discouragement of unbounded *escalation*, seems in some ways to have been relatively neglected. This neglect of *deterrence intellectual product* has, just maybe, been particularly prevalent at times since the end of the First Cold War.

Thinking along a protracted and volatile future global timeline, as actuaries always do and as American defense decision-makers must, it appears that this vital first factor, revolving around declaratory U.S. Nuclear Posture, could in some regards be strengthened by more *logical/technical rigor of formulation*, and *completeness and clarity of statement*. By taking a more critical yet proactive perspective on risk mitigation—one that doesn't just *identify* problems but also tries to help *solve* them—a close reading, and reading between the lines, of various U.S. National Nuclear Posture Review Reports and related U.S. government documents leads to several suggestions for possible future nuclear posture updating. These can be achieved at *low expense* to taxpayers, and *without disruption* of current acquisition programs, via a straightforward refinement of *key wording (and thinking) alone*. None of these five suggested enhancements, below, would alter the intent of any current (or, for that matter, prior) Nuclear Posture clauses. Nor would these five points call into question (or modify) any of America's current hardware and procedural Triad modernization matters.

These suggested sorts of logic and wording enhancement could have several benefits. Making them could avoid the real danger of "telegraphing," perhaps inadvertently, to actual or potential adversaries, as well as to Allies and partners who demand assurance, some (1) *over-optimistic expectations* about relations between states, some (2) *misunderstandings* of how geopolitical discontinuities can mesh dangerously along the timeline, and some (3) *reluctance* to live up to burdensome but unavoidable nuclear peacekeeping and peace-restoration (threatened retaliation) responsibilities. (The positive *assurance* of allies, that America's Nuclear Umbrella is sufficiently large and survivable, and stands always ready to protect them, is absolutely vital to nuclear peacekeeping and non-proliferation efforts, which also crucially support nuclear counterterrorism.)

1. Nuclear Deterrence Posture Should Not Be Reticent That It Is About Punishing Aggressors Who Deserve and Need to be Punished.

Effective nuclear deterrence requires both (1) the *ability to deny* an attacker precisely all his/her military-political goals, *plus* (2) the *willingness to, in addition, punish* him/her forcefully for committing the attack. In practice, during any actual nuclear war, it could be difficult to separate these two components of a counterstrike, but we will do so anyway here, at a theoretical level, to elucidate the underlying concepts.

Why are both effects, (1) and (2), required to effectively deter in advance an aggressor who is thinking about starting a nuclear war?

If the intensity of America's counterstrike does *not* achieve both effects (1) and (2), an aggressive "gambler" has no disincentive against gambling. The worst case for them then would be that their attack goals fail, and the only immediate military cost to them would be those *weapon-assets* they *expend* in making *their* attack, plus those *other assets* they *lose* absorbing *our* proportionate and discriminating counterattack. Merely promising unspecified, overall "massive damage" or "unacceptable costs" to an enemy, via our nuclear retaliation, is *not* strong enough wording; this is in part because the *fear factor* of the *mere mention* of nuclear retaliation *at all* might *not* work on enemy minds the same way that it does within U.S. pop culture. (This pertains to the issue of cultural mirror-imaging, per Chapter 4.)

Note that the promise, that our retaliation will always be *strictly equal*—in *our* nukes expended to make our counterstrike, plus *their* targeted assets destroyed by our counterstrike—to the damage the enemy first inflicts on *us*, plus *their* nukes expended to make their first strike—might *not* necessarily be *daunting enough* to a calculating or desperate enemy. This is analogous to an *exchange of queens* in a chess match: In some scenarios the aggressor *wants exactly such an exchange*.

One advantage of incorporating the Tit-for-Tat escalation/de-escalation-management paradigm into nuclear deterrence posture development is that it creates a *clear-cut baseline of reference* for the U.S. and our Allies, and against our adversaries, all at the same time. Doing so then allows (and helps clarify) an appropriate *scenario-specific* added *component* (which might be zero, moderate, *or* massive, depending) which is *fine-tuned* by POTUS/STRATCOM specifically to inflict "enough incremental punishment to fit the crime"—while our *total* counter-strike magnitude/intensity does still remain proportionate and discriminating (as required by International Law).

Note that the weapons expenditures *used up* in a nuclear exchange take on significance due to those weapon inventories being *rather finite in numbers* (from 2 digits to 4 digits per state or bloc), compared to a superpower's much more numerous conventional forces.

In symbolic terms:

U.S. Counterstrike Intensity = *Equalizers* for Damage-We-Suffer
& for Enemy-Nukes-Expended
+ *Added* Punitive Component
[Equation A1.1]

Note that in this Equation A1.1, the portion of America's nuclear counterstrike labeled "Equalizers for Our Damage Suffered & for Enemy Nukes Expended" might *not* be *strictly equal* to the *very same* number of warheads and their yields as *used up* in the aggressor's first strike, and to the *very same* types of targets as the enemy *hit* with their nukes (as that portion *would* be in exact Tit-for-Tat). This is because, in scenario-specific circumstances, the intensity of U.S. Triad forces' counterstrike, needed to deny the aggressor *all* their military-political goals, will need to be *carefully calibrated and fine-tuned*, maybe upward or downward somewhat from the Tit-for-Tat baseline's exact equality. Ditto for calibrating and fine-tuning the portion labeled Added Punitive Component. The utility of Equation A1.1 is that it tries to break out clarifyingly and elucidate clearly such *distinct* mathematical functions within our counterstrike's overall makeup.

Nuclear deterrence, as a razor-sharp tool for global peacekeeping, is far too important to America and to humanity to admit of (i.e., allow to creep in) any effectiveness-undermining loopholes in the messaging semantics or obfuscation in the procedural concepts.

It needs to be clearly spelled out that these stark reckonings of damages, expenditures, and punishments must include *more than* just the immediate military (and civilian) devastation of such attacks and counterattacks themselves. The long lasting, broader political and geopolitical gains and losses to both sides must also be included. In some cases, an attacker might obtain lasting geopolitical benefits even if they clearly "lose" the immediate nuclear exchange that they started.

As a hypothetical example, Iran could achieve great leverage over its perceived enemies via mass fear, along with a great gain in status and legitimacy among rogue-state cronies (e.g., North Korea) and non-state/terrorist proxies (e.g., Hezbollah), for having shown the courage to take on "the Great Satan." At the same time, the U.S. and NATO might "lose face" terribly, by the fact that they suffered a destructive and deadly nuclear attack from upstart Tehran—us nuking them back might just strengthen further extremist-Muslim militancy. Perhaps just as bad, or even worse in the long run, the U.S. could suffer widespread condemnation in some quarters for "allowing" its nuclear deterrence to fail. A great propaganda and morale victory might be handed to advocates of mayhem and destruction all over the world.

2. Nuclear Posture and Triad Sizing Must Not React Impulsively or Opportunistically to Short-Term Geopolitical Swings or See-Saws. Temporary softening of nuclear deterrence messaging just to be "politically correct," and gaps in Triad arsenal readiness accepted to save some budget money, are terrible ideas. They degrade the effectiveness of the deterrent, thus provocatively inviting nuclear attack or nuclear blackmail.

If the probability (inherent likelihood, inclination, or temptation) of any enemy making a nuclear attack—or simply committing an egregious case of nuclear coercion—is *at any point(s) in the foreseeable future* going to be *greater than zero*, meaning there is indeed some chance that such an attack or coercion will *eventually* occur *without* a strong deterrent, then the need for an effective deterrent-in-being *at all times* is *not* a rising/falling function based on own-side political perceptions of enemy attack-or-coercion-likelihood "today, in this moment" rising or falling. The need for a deterrent will *always* be 100%, if the attack or coercion likelihood is *ever* above 0%.

I.e., "a little nuclear deterrent" does not "go a long way." It goes nowhere but to perdition. *Au contraire*, a visibly unwavering commitment to a steady-state (mathematically "constant") full-fledged Triad-stands-ready-in-being status is indispensable as an Armageddon-preventive *at every point on the timeline*, to damp *any and all* adversary nuclear aggressiveness with maximum, permanent deterring effect. Such adversary nuclear belligerence must be decisively squelched *at every point* "from here to eternity," in order to *at all times* suppress its possible birth (within enemy minds), its possible burgeoning (within the enemy leadership regime), and its possible covert nuclear-arsenal expansion (let alone said arsenal's *expenditure* in a surprise attack).

The "foreseeable future" *planning horizon*, over which to sustain *arsenal size constancy*, is in reality very long. Deconstructing the dips and rises over the timeline in our ability to make new nukes after disposing of existing nukes, we can make a theoretical, mathematical statement that has crucial real-world implications: Our arsenal constancy planning horizon needs to *substantially exceed* the time in years realistically required to *resurrect or reconstruct* America's full nuclear-weapons (warheads *and* delivery platforms) manufacturing infrastructure, after its post-Cold War mothballing, dismantling, and neglect, to the point of being able to then, quickly—if ever actually necessary—*undo* any potential, further nuke warhead-count cuts, via *restarting serial production* and then over further time *manufacturing many hundreds* of new, fully safe and reliable modern warheads and delivery platforms.

Allowing for multifaceted and unforeseen challenges to U.S. Defense Budget funding, various new/untested technology risks, the difficulty of redeveloping key civilian and military weaponeer and industrial base and laboratory skills, and Washington, D.C.'s known bureaucratic/political inertia re recognizing and responding to international crises, this *constancy planning horizon* for the U.S. is now *certainly longer than a decade*, quite possibly longer than *two decades*. If the U.S. makes big Triad cuts because we think the bad guys have suddenly become good, and they revert to being bad within twenty years, we run the serious risk of not being able to sustain a nuclear arsenal that is rightsized concomitant with effective deterrence of the renewed adversary threat.

In short, going forward, America should not make any large cuts to its nuclear arsenal in anticipation of a more benign international threat environment—which encompasses adversary nuclear, other WMD, or existential-level conventional attack or blackmail—if there is any chance that the threat environment will deteriorate again within twenty-plus years.

3. Deterrence Arsenal Rightsizing Is Not Much Affected by Near-Term Adversary (Real or Perceived) Attack Likelihood, nor by Adversary Nuclear Arsenal Sizing.

The adequate sizing of an effective nuclear deterrent force is not a function of either the perceived or the inherent/actual probability of an enemy attacking American/NATO/Other Allied vital interests *soon*. Nor is it solely (or even much at all) a function of how many nuclear weapons adversaries possess. It is primarily a function of the overall size of the potential enemy's most prized (and ethically/morally targetable) "countervailing" endowments, such as military-political control assets, command bunkers, and strategic weapon stockpiles; financial, industrial-manufacturing, and technology-R&D centers; and natural-resource concentrations (such as mines, oil fields, and refineries).

Arms reduction to avoid excessively large "overkill" arsenals is highly desirable; hence the mutual ratification of the 2010 New START treaty by the U.S. and Russia. But it is very unwise to continue further reductions on sheer momentum.

Excessive nuclear disarmament, whether unilateral or multilateral, erodes arsenal size to the point that mutual deterrence against both nuclear/ WMD and conventional big war is very dangerously compromised.

Even with parity (rough equality) of nuclear warhead numbers between peer competitors, too-small nuclear arsenal sizes would fail to deter a gamesman/gambler or desparate belligerent who is not very casualty-averse. He/she might see the retaliatory damage possible with any "minimal"—and thus perforce very limited—U.S. nuclear Triad as, again, akin to an acceptable exchange of queens in chess, i.e., as being to their strategic advantage. They might not see our minimal retaliation as at all akin, in contrast, to the *ultimate deterrent* of an effectively sized (larger) arsenal, the possession of which by America confronts the adversary with risking uncertain but plausible *unlimited Armageddon*—human extinction triggered by their attack.

There are three important underlying processes at work here. The *first*, as discussed above, is that, given American nuclear weapon-factory mothballing and dismantlement after the Cold War, the number of workable U.S. nukes is very "sticky" against upward changes in desired warhead counts. The *second* is that American perceptions of the probability of an enemy attack or lack thereof can be *badly wrong*. The *third* is that even American *actions*, based on a momentarily accurate perception of enemy attack probability being low, can trigger enemy *reactions*, raising that attack probability very rapidly in very detrimental ways. In particular, the *action* of us dismantling our Triad could trigger the reaction that an adversary nukes us.

On the other hand, looking in the upward H-bomb count direction, our necessary deployed and stockpiled nuclear warhead counts are not really affected if an adversary significantly increases their own nuke warhead counts.

This is for four compelling practical reasons:

1. Since the U.S. would never make an unprovoked first nuclear strike on another country, we have no real need for a large "counterforce" first-strike arsenal able to *preemptively* destroy (for "damage limitation") all the adversary's land-based Triad assets.
2. If an adversary does make an unprovoked nuclear first strike on America and/or our Allies, then regardless of whether that first strike is "large" or "small," the adversary's Triad forces will be fully alerted and their personnel "hyper-ready." They will be watching with their full spectrum of early-warning capabilities for the first sign of an American reaction to us being nuked. Thus, *all* the adversary's land-based nuclear weapons will already be well on the way toward their U.S. targets before *any* American land-based retaliatory second-strike weapons can reach the adversary's at-that-point-empty ICBM silos and bomber bases. *In short, our ICBMs and strategic bombers would not be able to usefully attack an adversary's nukes, if a nuclear conflagration ever did break out. The same logic applies to our SSBNs.*
3. The total number of nuclear warheads needing to be deployed on American SSBNs is *not* a function of the numbers of adversary SSBNs or of those submarines' SLBM warheads, since our SSBNs and their SSBNs are extremely unlikely to ever be used to shoot at each other—their stealth makes them as a fleet essentially impossible to target while at sea, at least before they "make a datum" by launching their missiles. *Once their nuclear-armed ballistic missiles have been launched, sinking an enemy SSBN during a nuclear war would be a Pyrrhic victory—if not a waste of badly-needed remaining American firepower.*
4. Our BMD capability should continue to focus on "small" rogue, terrorist, accidental, or harrassment level attacks. It is not meant to stop a large-scale attack now, and does not need to be expanded in an arms race.

4. Deterrent Arsenal Rightsizing Must Provide for Multiple Nuclear Wars on a Very Long Timeframe.

The adequate sizing of an effective national nuclear deterrent force must include a secure, sustainable reserve against possibly having to deter or fight more than one *nuclear war over the full timeline of the 21st century and beyond.*

Otherwise, an earlier nuclear war in the future, though survived, could have already seriously eroded America's existing deployed *and stockpiled* nuke arsenals (via use, or combat destruction), and also thoroughly destroyed our (currently largely mothballed or dismantled) nuclear warhead and delivery platform new-manufacturing infrastructure and personnel. Thus, we could be left defenseless against some future nuclear-armed tyrant regime, at an all-too-foreseeable time when the global norm against nuclear-weapon combat strikes has already been utterly shattered.

In addition, beyond needing to deter any and all nuclear/WMD attacks, big conventional wars, and nuclear blackmails against us and our Allies, *for decades to come* in a very unpredictable world, we require something further. We must have an *extra* margin of secure nuclear weapon stocks *today*, to protect us against and/or credibly intercede in nuclear war(s) that might occur *in the future*, between *other* nuclear-weapons possessors at war *with one another*. Modern Game Theory warns us that conflicts involving more than two parties can be extremely unpredictable. But an outside party (America) that steps in to *end* a two-player conflict (Russia vs. China? India vs. Pakistan? Israel vs. Iran?), *not* turn it into an ongoing three-player one, benefits everybody. This compelling fact, exposed to clear view by actuarial-style timeline deconstruction, places a solemn duty on America's shoulders that we can never escape:

There is a powerful onus on us to lead the world in ongoing nuclear peacekeeping and peace-restoration, since we led the world to nuclear weapons in 1945 and we are the only country to ever use them in war.

Similarly, we must have a strong reserve of *additional* deliverable nuclear warheads surviving, after any "first" nuclear war against us in the future, because once U.S. vital interests and defenses have been significantly weakened in *that* war, *another* adversary might opportunistically be tempted into starting a "second" nuclear war against us—wherein their own nuclear arms and defenses, and their society, are all (so far) fresh and intact, and ours *aren't*. The violation of the ultimate nuclear taboo by the *first* aggressor could open the floodgates to *yet more* aggressors.

Any apparent unpreparedness for at least two future nuclear wars could leave America open to multiple adversaries colluding with or manipulating each other into delivering an insurmountable one-two punch against us and world freedom.

5. Compare Nuclear Dangers Using Event Loss Expectations, *Not* Just Event Probabilities

A fifth basic principle of actuarial science deserves explicit articulation here, because following it can help a lot in setting public policy, to rationalize the U.S. Government's *and* the American electorate's approaches to properly evaluating and comparing the relative dangers of different sorts of nuclear-weapon catastrophes that might occur in the future. Such evaluation and comparison, as performed *within rigorous mathematical probability theory*—which is after all an *indispensable pillar* of sound actuarial practices—uses the concept of "Expectation":

DEFINITION: The expectation pertaining to some unfortunate event is equal to the probability of that event occurring multiplied by the magnitude of the loss resulting were that event to occur. (For those initiated in calculus, more precisely, it equals the integral of the probability distribution function multiplied by the loss-intensity distribution function.)

In *both* the insurance industry *and* in nuclear deterrence, "magnitude of loss" is measured in terms of the number of *people killed* and/or injured, and the monetary value of *property damaged* or destroyed.

Using estimated calculations of expectations, *not* just of probabilities, can help to usefully *inform public policy choices* regarding how best to mitigate (control, reduce, even eliminate) two *different sorts* of Nuclear Dangers: (1) the danger of an outright nuclear war, and (2) the danger of a nuclear terrorist attack or an accidental nuclear detonation. How America can best minimize these two dangers is perhaps the *most controversial conundrum of today*, affecting as it does *all* of our nuclear policy, strategy, and posture development; part of this vexing conundrum is that the different strategies for coping with these Nuclear Dangers 1 and 2, advocated by various commentators and pundits, stand in *direct contradiction* to one another. This is perhaps most easily shown by comparing two statements, which summarize the prevalent sentiments in different segments of the general public, the mainstream media, and Congress:

- "The Best Practice for preventing any adversaries from starting a nuclear war is for America to *maintain* a robust, diversified nuclear-deterrence Triad."
- "The Best Practice for preventing any terrorists from obtaining nuclear weapons, and for preventing any nuclear weapons

> from being detonated by accident, is to *eliminate* all nuclear weapons worldwide—or at least in America."

Obviously, these two lines of argument lead to *directly opposite* conclusions about what to do. So, to try to decide which course of action is the wiser one overall, nuclear-disarmament advocates seem to say, "Compare their *probabilities*. The probability of a nuclear war actually breaking out is *low*, since everybody in the world understands that this would lead to a nuclear holocaust followed by a nuclear winter and summer, and human extinction. But the probability of a nuclear terrorist attack is *high*, since we know terrorists are trying hard to obtain nukes, yet an isolated terrorist nuking would cause only localized devastation, *not* a global holocaust or nuclear winter, and besides, terrorists are suicidal anyway; the odds of a single nuke going off by accident somewhere, given the thousands upon thousands of them still in existence, is *also high*, since a bad technical glitch in one, somewhere, eventually, is only a matter of time."

The key to resolving this apparent conundrum is to do what actuaries do in such situations, which is *compare the expectations of loss* of the different negative outcomes, *not* just their probabilities of occurrence. Regarding America's and the world's proper, nay *necessary* approach to nuclear weapons, it is thus essential to recognize some basic Points:

1. Though *relatively unlikely*, at least so long as effective mutual nuclear deterrence were sustained between the potential adversaries, a nuclear war, by resulting in the detonation of hundreds or thousands of warheads, *could cause deaths numbered in the billions.*
2. Though seemingly *more likely* to occur, a nuclear terrorist attack or an accident, by resulting in the detonation of only one or perhaps a handful of warheads, *could cause deaths numbered in the hundreds of thousands, or millions.*
3. In addition, were the world to give up all nuclear arms, then nuclear deterrence of a big conventional World War III would be forfeited, leading to the *almost inevitable* occurrence of such a war, and a future, conventional Third World War *could cause deaths numbered in the many tens of millions.*

Combining these general statements about relative death tolls *if* the events occur, with the general statements about relative likelihoods of their occurrence, and *looking not just at relative probabilities of occurrence but at relative expectations of loss*, we can now see that:

- Points 1 and 2 say that a nuclear war, overall, in cold mathematical terms, is a more deadly event to try to prevent (via effective deterrence) than is a nuclear terrorist attack and/or a nuclear-weapon accident (via Global Zero). (Obviously, it is essential to prevent *both*, via good weapon safety and better deterrence of terrorists)
- Point 3 shows that Global Zero would be *much less beneficial* than might at first appear, since a thorough evaluation of *all* of its likely downside timeline-deconstruction outcomes shows that total world nuclear disarmament—even if ever really achievable without cheating by bad actors—could easily lead to a death toll *expectation* rivaling that of a medium-sized nuclear war.

Thus, we can elucidate a *fifth* basic principle of actuarial science, as adapted to apply to nuclear deterrence Best Perspectives and Best Practices:

> **In Choosing Between Contradictory Public Policies for Mitigating Different Nuclear Dangers, it is Essential to Compare the Different Downside Events' Mathematical Expectations of Loss, *Not* Just Their Relative Probabilities of Occurrence.**

Conclusion: Nuclear Deterrence Benefits from an Actuarial Risk-Mitigation Perspective

The actuarial profession has spent decades developing and testing points-of-view, conceptual approaches, and specific techniques and methodologies for identifying, measuring, and mitigating the *multifaceted, simultaneous dangers and risks* involved in providing insurance and annuities, which help recompense a large population's *potential for losses* due to life, health, and property downside events and outcomes. Whether an insurance company happens to be a for-profit stockholder corporation, or a mutual company owned collectively by its policyholders, the combination of pressures to *properly balance two mutually contradictory forces*, namely (1) to not overcharge (which would impair good sales) but also (2) to not undercharge (which would impair solvency), together mandate a *percipient and continually-evolving approach to setting the key interlocking parameters* of an enterprise that protectively benefits society greatly, via reducing the negative impact on families and on businesses of downside "life contingencies."

Similarly contradictory forces—not overspending and not underspending—need to be properly balanced when rightsizing the socially-beneficial enterprise of sustaining America's protective nuclear deterrent.

This Appendix has sought to demonstrate that some of the fundamental Best Perspectives and Best Practices of continually evolving actuarial science ought to be evaluated more closely, as useful tools to help in the development of America's "National Nuclear Posture After Next."

APPENDIX 2

MANY ENEMY FIRST-USE OPTIONS NEED DETERRING

Executive Summary: First-Uses Might Aim for a Daunting Spectrum of Military Purposes

Adversaries of freedom and peace who possess one, or dozens, or hundreds, or even many thousands of nuclear weapons face a number of tempting ways in which to make a nuclear first-strike against America and/or our Allies, partners, and friends—and against other states or sub-state/trans-state armed groups. Appendix 2 will present an extensive, though not exhaustive, list of such enemy first-strike options. The purpose of this long list is simple: to show the utter indispensability of the U.S. sustaining a *rightsized* and *very diverse, survivable* next-generation nuclear deterrence Triad—including (1) the highest-possible quality Submarine Force (of 12+ Columbia-class SSBNs, guarded by about 72 Virginia-class and/or "SSN(X)" follow-on SSNs/SSGNs), along with (2) 650 (including backup/reserve) well-dispersed Ground-Based Strategic Deterrent (GBSD) ICBMs in hardened silos, plus (3) about 180 modern, B-21 Raider stealthy strategic bombers armed with highly-survivable Long-Range Stand Off (LRSO) stealthy cruise missiles.

In essence, Appendix 2's listing below of *potential geopolitical objectives with specific target descriptions forms just one essential part of the knowledge and information infrastructure—the intellectual product—*supporting America's overall system of effective strategic deterrence. Many of these hypothetical enemy options could be attractive to a despot who *takes big gambles and who is not casualty adverse.* They could also be attractive to an authoritarian strong-man who thinks that America is too "squeamish" to retaliate with nukes if they use nukes first against us *"just a little."* They might even appeal to a desperate, politically cornered tyrant who wants to *"wag the dog"* very dramatically, even apocalyptically, for his/her own domestic job security. This is because the options would, at least initially, use nuclear weapons in combat in very limited ways. But there can never be a guarantee against a *"limited"* nuke first-use escalating to global thermonuclear holocaust, and the extinction of Humanity:

> Since any nuclear-armed state might secretly possess a ***doomsday "suicide switch,"*** as the Former Soviet Union is reported to have done—a system to automatically set into inexorable motion a spasm, all-out nuclear counterstrike triggered by any incoming nuclear attack (or just by an overwhelming existential conventional invasion)—it is an ***incontrovertible theorem of deductive logic*** that the best (***and only***) time to end a nuclear war with 100.0% confidence in Humanity surviving is ***before it ever starts.***

Effective nuclear deterrence is *absolutely crucial.* All potential nuclear belligerents *must* clearly understand, through a process of continual education and dialogue by America and our Allies, that even a small, tactical battlefield nuking is really and truly *not* the same as just using a "really big artillery shell." Rather, *any* unprovoked nuclear weapon first-use in combat, *at all,* should be viewed as the unleashing of an *abomination,* a violation of ultimate norms, taboos, and red-lines—one which will be righteously counterpunched against, with alacrity and great power, by America's nuclear deterrence Triad.

The enemy themselves will have *given us no choice* but to make such a second-strike response, to *valiantly defend* ourselves from enslavement or annihilation, while *trying unflaggingly* to force an armistice on terms favorable to continuing democracy. *Hesitation on our part* over this grim calculus of deterrence-and-retaliation, during peacetime or during war, could amount to our *abject surrender* to relentless, endless, incremental nuclear blackmail. Worse, to *not* retaliate would invite *further* nuke strikes, and copy-cat nukings *galore.*

The Worst Nuke-Use Effects Include the Longer-Term Ones

As amply discussed in the literature, the severity of the effects of any particular, specified, hypothetical nuclear weapon usage (say, a 10 kiloton tactical nuke or a 10 megaton strategic nuke), as to the human deaths and injuries, and property and environmental damage it would cause, can be characterized via various sets of computer-modeling output data. This appendix seeks to emphasize the *bigger-picture, longer-term effects,* which sometimes seem to be less often mentioned in the literature and in pop culture. (Early in the First Cold War, when Global Nuclear Winter was not yet understood, and computer modeling in general was relatively primitive, U.S. Strategic Air Command (SAC) might omit even mentioning those "out-year" effects simply because they were so much harder to calculate than the immediate blast effects.)

Modern ultra-high-energy explosion dynamics, meteorology, public health, macroeconomics, and other supercomputer modeling nowadays using AI and Big Data can give a more complete picture. The various horrific aftermath effects include:

- added mortality and morbidity from permanently impaired human immune systems, plus the longer-term effects of (1) the immediate blast injuries and burns, (2) the exposures to prompt weapon-burst radiation and neutron activation, and (3) the exposures to subsequent, long-lasting radioactive fallout;
- psychological stress and mental depression, which can cause permanent emotional disability;
- global human and animal sterility and terrible birth defects, caused by genetic damage, leading to serious medical and caregiving dependencies, and mass starvation;
- local or planetwide climate alterations with resulting severe windstorms, downpours and floods, droughts, deep freezes, prolonged darkness, broiling heat waves, deadly hard-UV from searing sunlight after the ozone layer is destroyed and the nuclear winter eventually clears (*nuclear summer*), and famine due to worldwide livestock deaths and crop failures from all these causes;
- *major setbacks to human civilization* caused by the loss of essential technologies and facilities, and the death and destruction of important scientific and cultural expert knowledge, skills, designs, equipment, and artifacts;
- *long-term collapse of gross national product* caused by all the above effects, with numerous direct and indirect economic/financial/social costs, with very harmful impact on health-care affordability and on standards of living in general; and
- *long-term collapse of human population,* permanent damage and destruction to the human gene pool, badly impaired species fertility with collapsing reproductive success over generations, *and even eventual extinction of the human race.*

Here is a Long List of Nuke First-Use Options Bad Actors Might Be Tempted to Use

High-Altitude Nuclear Explosion (HANE): One or more nuclear weapons might be set off intentionally in space. A near-Earth orbital nuclear blast would generate a very destructive electromagnetic pulse (EMP). This EMP would destroy much earthbound, unprotected electrical and electronic equipment in a "footprint" on the ground far below, potentially on a continent-wide scale. It would depend on the yield of the warhead and the altitude and location of the blast.

A near-Earth nuclear blast would also produce prolonged and highly destructive particle-storm effects in the near-vacuum of space, around Earth's radioactive Van Allen belts. (We now know of three such belts.) These effects would gradually knock out all orbiting near-Earth satellites, and prevent the functioning of newly launched replacements, for a period of *several years.*

The important thing is that few people if any would be killed by the blast itself, and the fallout would mostly, eventually, dissipate into deep space. This low lethality could significantly weaken the threshold to enemy nuclear first use in this manner. Note that retaliating in kind, by the victim of such an attack, would somewhat "even out" the damage. But the crippling of so many electronic systems on and near Earth would *reduce* reconnaissance, communication, and calculation abilities (including *de-escalation and cease-fire negotiating abilities*) to a situation like that in World War II or even World War I—which were *notorious bloodbaths* even *without* the availability of nuclear arms.

Non-Lethal Military/Political "Demonstration": Another less-lethal first-use option is to detonate one or more nuclear weapons in the atmosphere, in a manner that is conspicuous, but tries to minimize the various bad effects other than the psychological/emotional ones. This way, a nuke can serve as a quasi-diplomatic but powerful gesture (signal) of national will, and as a strident negotiating tactic during a serious international crisis. Perhaps this would be one workable way to end a conventional war that was getting out of hand, to jar the nerves of the other side and pressure them into a peace settlement. (Russia's "escalate to de-escalate" posture is different, contemplating the first-use of low-yield, tactical nuclear weapons against actual NATO battlefield targets.)

Examples of such "demonstration shots" could include setting off a nuke on the defender's own territory, but in an unoccupied desert or mountain range area, or in a designated weapon testing-range reservation, or out at sea away from main shipping lanes. A shot set off just beyond a defender's oceanic Exclusive Economic Zone (EEZ), usually defined as 200 nautical miles from their shoreline, could be a nervy hybrid between "on defender territory" and "sending a message from international waters." For an aggressor to make such a demonstration shot on their *own* territory, not underground but rather *in atmosphere*, could give it a sort of "plausible deniability" camouflage as a "mere nuclear test"—*but an extremely provocative one.* There is nothing like live video of a brand new, always extremely iconic nuclear mushroom cloud thrusting high into the air to get the world's negative attention.

Defensive "scorched earth" tactics: Nuclear weapons, despite their obvious disadvantages, do make excellent mass-demolition and incendiary charges. Conventional weapons, even the highly controversial area weapons of hyperbaric fuel-air explosives ("MOABs") and cluster munitions, will leave surviving pockets of infrastructure throughout the sector that is bombarded. (In fact, conventional bombardment of an area often *improves* its defensive qualities, as happened when the Allies bombed the Monte Cassino monastery in Italy in World War II.)

Nuclear weapons, in contrast, completely "sanitize" any along-the-ground, not overly hardened target area, with a radius measured in miles or even tens of miles. MOABs and cluster bombs would create *Swiss cheese,* while nukes would create a *thorough moonscape.* In the last extreme, facing serious defeat that threatens national survival (or at least regime survival), an adversary losing a big conventional war might be motivated to use nuclear weapons to create an instant, wide and badly contaminated, scorched-earth zone, to *cover its retreat* against enemy ground troops and armor.

The "Swiss cheese vice moonscape" conundrum also applies to thoroughly disabling any sort of *resources*—such as forests, farmland, open-pit and under-mountain mine industries, oil fields and petroleum refinery complexes, the Internet, or a national railway and highway system—which are spread out or highly networked, and thus have many redundant pathways and nodes, and backup infrastructure sites, with which to sidestep only-partial destruction. The threshold to nuclear first-use in this manner might be *particularly low* if the enemy created the scorched earth no-man's land on its *own* (near-border?) territory.

Ethnic cleansing or religious holocaust depopulation tool: This option would be particularly inhuman, but for that very reason needs to be articulated for prevention. Recent world history has seen too many instances of a bigoted dictator using conventional means to try to exterminate "out groups," or at least terrify them into fleeing away across international borders as refugees.

If a modern Hitler, Stalin, Milosevic, Pol Pot, Idi Amin, or Bashar al-Assad were to possess nuclear weapons and plan such a mass depopulation campaign, their very sociopathic inhumanity would remove barriers to such evil action. They might calculate that in certain circumstances the use of one or more nukes of limited yield, set off so as to *kill and uproot thousands or millions,* could produce results worth any negative consequences to them. Unfortunately, this would be a genuine "madman with nukes" nightmare for the Free World, one demanding potentially draconian preventive or preemptive measures. Along similar lines, a nuclear-armed despot faced with a *huge influx of foreign refugees,* due to some other international crisis or disaster elsewhere, might be tempted to *stem the flow* using a *nuclear border wall,* by setting off a tactical nuke in front of or along the refugee swarm's path of migration.

A "Holocaust-buster" munition: The flip side of using a nuke for ethnic cleansing is to use a nuke to *prevent* ethnic cleansing. A nuclear demonstration or actual nuclear strike can be used in some extreme cases by a democracy or coalition, to very forcefully *dissuade* a foreign tyrant from persecuting an ethnic or religious group.

A border "fallout war": A belligerent dictator armed with nuclear weapons might seek to launch a "less lethal" nuclear first-use attack against another state, perhaps one with which it shares a border, by setting off nukes in-atmosphere on its own territory, in such a way that the deadly radioactive fallout mostly drifts across the border to harm the target state, the latter's troops, and its citizens. Such a dictator, whose moral compass might be deranged to begin with, could argue that he or she has not really violated international norms against first-use attack, since the detonation(s) on his/her own soil was/were "mere weapons tests." Further, he/she could argue that the noise of the blast and the sight of the rising mushroom cloud constituted *sufficient warning* to evacuate to people across the border, and beyond.

Highly-capable ground penetrator munitions: Unfortunately, the effective depth of even the latest designs of conventional (high explosive) ground penetrator (GP) weapons—such as America's developmental 30-ton conventional GP bomb—is significantly exceeded by the depth at which hundreds of high value, hardened underground military bunkers have been constructed around the world. (A number are several thousand feet, or even *miles* deep.) A nuclear ground-penetrator round promises to still be able to disable such installations: While the weapon itself might penetrate the earth no further than a conventional round can, the subsequent nuclear blast would be powerful enough to *reach down* hundreds or thousands of feet farther and *cave in or shatter* the intended target.

Because the weapon would penetrate dozens or hundreds of feet before exploding, depending on the local geology and the bomb's final flight path and kinetic energy, its detonation would have some similarity to an underground nuclear test. (Collapse of rubble behind the warhead, especially if the nuke uses a time-delay fuse, would help play the same role as the *tamper "plugs"* installed in test shafts before an underground nuke test-shot is set off, meant to "block the chimney" against toxins leaking to the surface.) While some fallout could be expected to vent upward, and local groundwater and underlying aquifers could be badly contaminated, the escaping heat, blast, and radiation effects might be *significantly less* than with a surface or air detonation.

To some aggressive adversaries, this might excuse the first-use in anger of a nuke in the form of a ground penetrator round. In fact, an adversary might drop such a weapon in a full-blown *tactical exercise test,* in an unpopulated area or a military reserve on its own territory—as a form of non-lethal demonstration *distinct in world eyes* from a normal underground test. Such an act would put *more emphasis on the military than the political* in the tone of the "diplomatic" negotiating message being sent by the "harmless demonstration."

"Catalytic" Nuclear War, and the related "Neo-Classical" nuclear war: The possibility of a nuclear war that breaks out because of the *devious meddling and/or violent influence of a third party* was recognized during the Cold War. Scholars sometimes called this *"catalytic war."* Now we face a phenomenon of the *post-post-Cold War era*: a possible return to one or another Cold War-style nuclear conflict. The two may be hard to tell apart. The whole *Indo-Asia-Pacific* area could be ripe for this in the future, especially with North Korea, China's serious "Uighur problem," the Russian Federation's (separatist) far east territory, or the Russia/Japan "frozen conflict" in the North Kuriles. India versus Pakistan is another possibility. So could the *Middle East* (including a bitter rivalry between Sunni and Shia caliphates who get The Bomb), the *Caucasus,* and *Anatolia.* Some new *Russia/China* border conflict, like the one that came close to going nuclear in the late 1960s, is another distant but troubling possibility.

Then there is the geopolitically-reshuffled *Eastern Europe Theater*, from the Balkans to the Baltics to the Arctic—and beyond. And don't ever forget *Israel and Iran.*

First-Use Effects Partly Mitigated by the Weather: Local weather conditions at the time of detonation of a nuclear weapon can have important effects to either *exacerbate or mitigate* the overall level of death and destruction. If visibility is obscured by fog or smog, smoke, mist or haze, or heavy rain or heavy snowfall, then the radiant heat of the blast will be blocked from starting fires and burning people as far away from ground zero as would otherwise occur. Rain, snow, in fact any recent or current humidity and/or precipitation, can reduce the combustibility of everything in the target area. If the precipitation occurs soon *after* the blast, it can help extinguish fires that might get started, will remove some fallout from the air to the local ground instead, and can to some extent help wash down the area to aid in post-blast decontamination.

First-Use Militarily Demanded by (and/or Facilitated by) the Terrain: There are various natural environments and terrain conditions in which it is conceivable that a conventional conflict will bog down to the point that a frustrated autocrat in possession of nuclear weapons might be sorely tempted to use them first. If said autocrat sees his or her reign in power as threatened by embarrassment or defeat due to such a *21st century quagmire* for their regime, threshold norms against actual nuclear first-use might collapse into ineffectiveness. Furthermore, some natural environments lack major sources of *conflagration fuel*, reducing the risk of nuclear winter. These include the Arctic landmasses, the Arctic Sea, and Antarctica and its surrounding Southern Ocean, plus any large, undeveloped desert or mountain range above the tree line.

An epidemic among a dictator's military personnel: Suppose that an aggressive dictator were handcuffed from using his/her conventional forces effectively because a crippling epidemic was spreading fast among his/her people in uniform, for which vaccines or treatments did not exist or were not available in sufficient quantity quickly enough. In this scenario, he/she might be motivated out of desperation to make a first-use of nuclear weapons instead. Fortunately, the COVID-19 pandemic is raging at a time that major powers, including nuclear-armed ones, are not at hot war.

To Get Around Serious Population-Aging Manpower Problems: Some nations, including but by no means limited to China, face an accelerating trend of the overall *demographic makeup* of their citizens shifting relatively quickly to the *older age ranges.* Some commentators have pointed out that this trend could impair not just their economic productivity, but also their military vitality. Unfortunately, greater reliance on nuclear weapons could be seen by some state leaders as an offset to this manpower problem.

Tactical nuclear war at sea: According to the English-language open literature, France conducted a study in the 1950s regarding whether it might be feasible to fight and survive a nuclear war limited to tactical weapons used only out at sea. The French argument went that if only low-yield weapons were used, by and against aircraft and warships, then only combatant personnel would be directly affected. The *tactical* fallout would mostly be local (lower-altitude tropospheric, not higher-altitude stratospheric), and would dissipate on the local winds and dilute in the seawater over vast trans-oceanic distances. With comparatively little to burn, and little to vaporize except seawater, there would not be a major nuclear winter aftereffect (something which was not known about in the 1950s).

The continental coastlines present a natural, major *dividing line* between war-fighting domains, which might very well serve both physically and psychologically to confine the nuclear warhead detonations, though *not* their radioactive fallout, to the ocean battlespace only. Fallout would occur not just from vaporized weapon parts and targeted military assets, but also from *neutron activation* of elements present in abundance in seawater and in the bodies of copious sea life.

Perhaps most importantly, it was found that, if not too close to a nuke ground zero, well-sealed-up warships could protect their battened-down crews from the worst effects of blast, heat, and radiation. They could avoid being capsized by any nuclear "tsunami," by turning toward it, just like they would ride out severe storms or rogue waves at sea—nuclear-detonation surface ocean waves die out fairly quickly. Most ship contamination would be confined to the *outside* of the vessels.

While the local ocean area would be *very badly contaminated,* if the vessels were able to steam to or get a tow (upwind?) to clean water, then *good decontamination* could be done simply by washing down thoroughly with clean seawater mixed with detergent, and then painting a sealant over exposed surfaces. Warships expecting a nuclear attack can further protect themselves by activating a system of external firefighting nozzles around the ship, to create a drenching mist that cools and cleanses. Old films of U.S. Navy warships practicing this *protective drench-down* are available on-line.

Destruction of a natural (or artificial) island military base: Winston Churchill once called the UK "an unsinkable aircraft carrier." One might also regard a small-sized island's naval or air base as *"an amphib or aircraft carrier that can't move."* But the potential for an adversary to use nuclear weapons means that such an island base *isn't unsinkable*. This option might become irresistibly attractive to a belligerent, who knows that while conventional weapons can knock a runway, say, out of action, the damage is quickly repairable (see U.S. Navy Seabee operations in the Pacific in World War II, and Argentinian operations in the Falklands War). The air base can usually be returned to action in a matter of hours.

A nuclear weapon set off at ground level in the middle of a modest-sized island can obliterate the entire island, by *excavating the underlying geology* (whether it be natural, or artificially dredged and land-filled, or some of both) down to a large and lastingly-radioactive *underwater crater*. Especially if the island is isolated from civilian populated areas, and *prevailing winds* can be counted on to carry fallout "safely" out to sea to be dissipated and diluted and *half-life aged*, the costs/benefits tradeoff of such first-use might seem irresistibly attractive.

As a potent deterrent or defense against an amphibious invasion: An amphibious invasion across any large body of water (as opposed to a combat river crossing) is *very vulnerable* while approaching the target shore and during landing ops, until a large lodgment is established. Inevitably, to be effective the invading force will have to *concentrate* (bunch up) along the water's edge and the beach. This presents an ideal target for a defender to nuke the landing force. The nuke would be set off on the defender's own frontier/seaside territory, and territorial waters. A determined defender could easily invoke *rights of sovereignty to drop The Bomb on its own territory* in a defensive move.

Nuclear blackmail/extortion (part 1): A nuclear weapon does not need to be actually set off for it to have useful effects for a belligerent. The *mere threat of use* can be very intimidating. That hostile threat does not need to be 100.0% credible for it to be *very worrying* to the targeted national leaders, diplomats, military commanders, and highly vulnerable civilian citizenry. So long as the belligerent is *perceived* by his/her target audience(s) as having at least some of the technical ability, the will and determination, and the aggressive intent necessary to perpetrate such an actual attack, the nuclear blackmail can be very effective. It can gain military and political *concessions*, and favorable *dispute settlements* for the blackmailer.

During the Cold War, both the U.S. and the USSR made to each other more-or-less-veiled references to their possession of nuclear arsenals—and their willingness to *use* those nukes—on dozens of occasions when they were at geopolitical loggerheads. Such tough talk came to be seen as a special class of negotiation tactic, which defense analysts called *coercive nuclear diplomacy*. There were (and are) some unwritten rules of how such bullying should or shouldn't be attempted: (1) try to formulate the threat using semantics graded so as convey the genuine *degree of displeasure* with the adversary's stance or behavior, just as has long been the practice for non-nuclear diplomatic spats, (2) be keenly aware of the adversary's actual red-lines for triggering their nuclear preventive or preemptive strike, and make sure to never cross those red-lines, (3) preserve for oneself a face-saving *"off ramp,"* to be able to back away from the brink—rather than become trapped into starting an *inadvertent nuclear war.*

The empirical evidence from decades of confrontations and crises between East and West was that the participants were able—using common sense, appropriate caution, plus back-channel diplomatic messaging—to carry out nuclear tough-talk *"jousting"* while remaining safely within implicit-but-effective *"guard rails"* that maintained *nuclear peace.* Whether *nuclear newbies,* such as India and Pakistan or North Korea, or *nuclear wannabes,* such as Iran, will be able to mimic this during their own possible future nuclear crises with adversaries remains to be seen; superpower caution, and state-to-state *"tutorials"* about responsible, safe nuclear-arsenal custodianship, are clearly called for; this is one subject where bi- and multi-lateral talks might be better than *hard line shunning* of an adversary or rogue.

Nuclear blackmail (properly, *coercion*) tactics themselves fall along a spectrum of seriousness in at least two dimensions, which can blend together in practice: how they are *communicated,* and how their communication is *backed up* by displays of nuclear readiness visible to those being threatened. Communications can run the gamut from veiled references, to outright and explicit threats. These can be conveyed via televised speeches, media interviews, press conferences, back-channel conversations, "leaks," stern diplomatic notes (*demarches*), or complaints to (or about) international bodies.

Demonstrations of readiness to *in extremis, follow through* on the extortionist threat can include observable nuclear weapons *alerts* of various scales (bomber aircraft are very good for this purpose, due to their gradual, flexible deployment processes); *exercises* of nuclear weapon delivery platforms with or without warheads being seen to be uploaded (installed) on them; *military parades*; and conspicuously performed *tests of nuclear weapon subsystems*, such as high-explosive implosion triggers, or unarmed but nuclear capable versions of ballistic missiles or cruise missiles being *test launched* (with or without advance notice)—on established national firing ranges or on menacing trajectories against neighbors (such as North Korea has done against Japan). An *underground or even in-atmosphere full-up test* is an extreme form of readiness demonstration, but such tests *would badly* violate international test-ban norms and treaties.

A certain amount of *bluffing*, and of *"crying wolf,"* are to be expected in such nuclear extortion/coercion attempts by a bellicose entity. But the onus is on the threatened party to interpret them correctly to avoid a major geopolitical loss, or even an actual nuclear strike. Thus even bluffs and crying wolf by a habitual nuclear extortionist will *command defender attention*, and carry an intimidating message—one amplified by paranoid conspiracy theorists and sensationalized popular media outlets alike. This is in part because defending policy makers know that any bellicose extortionist might talk himself/herself into a corner, one where his/her regime's survival might become dependent on actually carrying through on a nuking threat. (The U.S. tried such nuclear bluffing against North Vietnam during the Nixon Administration, but Hanoi appears to have seen through it—always a risk when someone bluffs.)

Nuclear-diplomacy tough talk, and nuclear blackmail/extortion (part 2): Nuclear weapons technology is very expensive, but when it comes to nuclear weapons, talk isn't cheap, either. *Talk has consequences*. Nuclear blackmail (strictly speaking, extortion) has been seen in action during the First Cold War, and also since then, for instance in a threat by Vladimir Putin against Holland. Although no nuclear weapon is (necessarily) actually set off even in a test, a public threat or reminder is issued by an aggressor about how he or she owns many nukes, and he/she might very well detonate some in an angry first-use if feeling provoked or pressured enough.

This exercise in *psychological warfare* propaganda does represent a state's genuine "use" of its nuclear arsenal, to get its way on the geopolitical stage by a *disinformation influence campaign*. This is achieved via coldblooded intimidation of weaker states and of superpower rivals alike. At the same time, by sowing fear of a *belligerent nuclear "backdraft" response* against *opponents' conventional posturing or pushback*, the tyrant tries to create a tight, fully believable *red-line*—against any *other* state's use of economic, diplomatic, or even conventional military counter-tactics that might try to limit the dictator's expansionism.

Superpower competition for more Nuclear Umbrella client states: Any nuclear weapons-owning state can benefit the security and defense of its conventional-weapons-only allies by providing to them *extended nuclear deterrence* via a *nuclear umbrella*. This amounts to a publicly declared agreement that any nuclear aggression against the ally or allies will be deterred, and retaliated against if necessary, by the big power's nuclear arsenal.

During the Cold War, and since then, the U.S. has provided such protection to the other members of NATO, in coordination (complex and controversial at times) with the UK and France (who own their own nukes). Similarly, the USSR provided this protection to Warsaw Pact countries, and now appears to do so on a more limited basis, primarily to "the Stans," via the Collective Security Treaty Organization (CSTO). In contrast, China, a significant nuclear power, does *not* have a nuclear umbrella arrangement with any other states, which is perhaps one reason why North Korea has developed its own nukes. (China supported Pakistan's nuclear weapons program development, and it is generally assumed that China has an interest in protecting Pakistan against any sort of serious threat from India or elsewhere.)

It is not inconceivable that during the 21st century, one way that actual or "wannabe" superpowers will *compete with each other* could be in trying to garner allies for their own extended deterrence nuclear umbrella *"protection services."* Success at such competition by a nuclear weapons-owning state would *increase its status, influence, and security* on the world geopolitical stage, and benefit the regime's *prestige and power* at home. This deterrence comes without the expenses and other disadvantages of the smaller country developing a nuclear arsenal itself—but it might nevertheless come at some very real price to the dependent protectee. For instance, to prevent the junior partner from dragging the senior into a catalytic nuclear war, the senior might exercise *stringent control* over the junior's foreign policy. This interfering domination might occur in general out of the superpower's desire for *hegemony*, especially if and when it uses its nuclear umbrella to try to turn smaller allies into outright *puppets*.

Asteroid hits as nuke false alarms: All states with nuclear weapons must assure that their early warning sensors, and launch-only-after-attack rules-of-engagement (ROEs) for nuclear retaliation, can *distinguish* swiftly and reliably between an actual nuclear attack and a major *space-object impact*. Otherwise, a natural tragedy could lead to the man-made one of an uncalled-for nuclear counter-strike, either by accident or (as a horrible, opportunistic nuke first-use option) even on purpose—to *level the* *playing field* of national damage and pain when one side in an adversarial match-up does suffer an asteroid/comet strike.

The U.S. and some other nuclear powers have used "ground truth" *detection/verification systems* to confirm, before considering launching a nuclear counter-strike, whether a hostile nuclear detonation has *actually occurred* somewhere in the state's homeland, or at one of the state's foreign military bases or upon a treaty ally. These defense systems must *go beyond* simply reporting a huge explosion in the air or on the ground, with great heat and blast, and unearthly isotopes and even radioactivity. If the cause was in fact an *infernal act of nature*, of solar system orbital mechanics—an unexpected asteroid or comet hit—this fact *must be established* very promptly, with extremely high reliability. Private and commercial media must in such a situation avoid the temptation to speculate about nuclear war, alien invasion, or other sensationalized conspiracy theories. That is because, especially in a country lacking advanced nuclear-attribution forensic capabilities, a *civilian nuclear facility* (nuclear power plant and/or nuclear-waste storage site) that *gets hit and obliterated* by the space rock could be *mistaken* for an enemy nuclear attack—because of the massive deadly radioactivity spread far and wide when said nuclear facility is breached and its toxic contents spread far and wide—which would have truly dreadful consequences way beyond the space-rock impact itself.

The ever-present possibility of Planet Earth being lethally pummeled by a space object should be used among diplomats and arms control advocates as an *important talking point*. It ought to move any owner of nuclear weapons far away from a retaliatory defense posture based on *hair-trigger* launch-on-warning ROEs. It ought to go even further and shift states with launch-after-attack to an even more thoroughly cautious "launch *only after* attack with *avoidance* of astronomical false alarms." This would require a very good understanding of the natural radioactive isotope content of different classes of asteroids and comets. Otherwise, these chemical elements, when vaporized within Earth's atmosphere, could contribute to false alarms of nuclear attack. This will be a practical, important application of *robotic and manned study of these objects* out in space, by governments and private corporations alike.

Conclusion: The Myriad Options for a Nuke First-Use Demand a Robust, Flexible Triad

Appendix 2 has elicited a number of different danger-inducing factors, inherent in the military-political and natural environments and topographies of the 21st century, which could motivate an adversary's first-use of nuclear weapons. Such factors include America's adversaries *recklessly* counting on international norms that might (or might not) help a limited nuclear war stay limited (such as discrimination and proportionality), and those adversaries *misguidedly* counting on American fears of nuclear winter and nuclear summer leading us to cave first.

The undeniable existence of Appendix 2's lengthy, varied menu of first-uses that offer (very vague, uncertain) flexibility as to objectives achievable, lethality, and likelihood of further escalation, all make effective nuclear deterrence a very hard job. Maintaining a right-sized and diversified, skillfully crewed and brilliantly commanded nuclear deterrence Triad is vital, but it is only part of that job. Fact-based messaging to adversaries, without cultural mirror-imaging blunders, is also critical. *Blind acts by Mother Nature* such as epidemics, population aging, and "deterrence challenged" terrains—such as ice caps, mid-ocean waters, islands, deserts, broken ground, invadable coastlines, and disputed land-border areas—plus *mid-sized asteroid impacts* that could imitate nuclear strikes, all mean that nuclear deterrence is a permanent life-preserving task for highly-trained, dedicated professionals.

APPENDIX 3

Some Metaphysics of SSBN Patrols

Executive Summary: Strategic Submarine Force Competition Is Inevitable and Necessary

It can be very enlightening to work through a metaphysical "plunge into the depths" of what nuclear-powered strategic deterrence submarines (SSBNs) are for, and are not for. As disarmament pundits vocally advocate reducing America's SSBN fleet down to dangerously small numbers, it is worthwhile to document rigorously some fundamental truths of *effective 21st-century survivable, undersea nuclear deterrence.*

Brilliantly crewed, superb-quality nuclear-powered strategic deterrent submarines (SSBNs), with their built-in stealth and their nuclear-armed sub-launched ballistic missiles (SLBMs), are the best and only choice to combine (1) undetectable invisibility, (2) capability for multiple and very prompt MIRVed strikes at very long ranges-to-target, (3) long-term at-sea independent cruising endurance, (4) rapid inter-ocean repositioning mobility—and thus for (5) *maximally credible* deterrence possessing *maximized immunity* from enemy interference, harassment, or (during wartime) destruction. In fact, a *sufficiently numerous* SSBN fleet is widely recognized as the *most survivable* leg of America's diversified, mutually supporting Triad (which now totals 14 Ohio-class SSBNs, 450 deployed non-MIRVed Minuteman-3 ICBMs, and several dozen B-52 and B-2 nuclear-capable strategic bombers.) For the U.S. Navy's new Columbia-class SSBNs—vitally needed to replace the venerable Ohios, now all approaching their 42-year maximum hull lives—the irreducible number in commission was determined in Department of Defense studies to be at least *twelve* vessels, each of which has sixteen SLBM missile tubes.

Alternative deterrent-sub cost/capability tradeoffs do exist, for those states with less money to spend and/or less technical prowess, or who have a smaller territory to protect or a smaller ocean area accessible in which to patrol. But these lesser designs for lesser nuclear powers compromise stealth and/or patrol endurance to save costs, and to avoid overreaching in the technological capabilities available to them. One tradeoff is to build or buy *diesel-powered* ballistic missile subs (type designation SSB), with nuclear-tipped SLBMs. Another is to build or buy modern *diesel/air-independent-propulsion* ballistic missile subs (SSBPs), or such subs but with nuclear-tipped cruise missiles (SLCMs), type designation SSGP. For instance, North Korea is reported to be working on a homegrown SSB; Israel is believed to deploy a seaborne nuclear deterrent on German-made SSGPs.

Indicative of the desirability of deterrent subs for any nuclear weapons-owning state (NWOS) is a fact that is part troubling, part reassuring. Some states that do or want to own nukes, terrorism-sponsoring *rogue states* which definitely shouldn't be allowed to have any (such as North Korea and Iran), are in some stage of building submarines capable of deploying and launching nuclear missiles. On the other hand, *responsible states,* that use their nukes only for deterring intractable adversaries, such as India (vs. Pakistan and China) and Israel (vs. Iran), are now either building their own initial fleet of SSBNs (India's Arihant-class) or are modernizing their imported SSBP fleet (Israel buying Dolphin-II's from Germany).

For the most robust possible strategic deterrence infrastructure, *other talking points* need to be added to the above issues and concepts, along with *important policy choices,* that are in play around the world regarding nuclear-deterrent submarine and other *submarine capabilities and modes of employment.* These various topics all affect proper *SSBN design, construction, force-protection tactics, and deterrence-mission strategy.* They are discussed in the rest of this Appendix 3.

ASW Drone Swarms Do Not Spell "the Doom of Doomsday Subs"

This "doom" premise is that a swarm of stealthy adversary unmanned undersea vehicle (UUV) anti-submarine warfare (ASW) drones would be able to wait for, and then surround, any friendly SSBNs departing a defender's naval bases to go on deterrent patrol. These UUVs, it is argued, even if unarmed, could damage the SSBN enough via ramming to force it to cancel its mission and return to base, or instead could trail it persistently and transmit position reports to an adversary's large, manned, heavily armed ASW forces including fast-attack subs (SSNs). In time of surprise attack or open war, *armed* UUVs might destroy the friendly SSBNs outright, using on-board explosive ordnance, by lurking and ambushing them as they come out of their home ports to steam to their forward patrol areas that are in range of assigned deterrence targets.

This is a valid concern. But what such pessimism doesn't consider is that the defender state, sending the SSBN out on patrol, will *also* deploy UUVs. The U.S. Navy is very active on R&D on this front. These *defender* UUVs can serve as *mini-escorts* and *"delousing" drones* for the Navy's SSBN fleet, *especially* in the restricted waters right outside SSBN home ports (Kings Bay, GA, and Kitsap, WA). There, the defender will have superiority of supporting undersea sensor installations, and better sea control and air superiority, relative to any intruder. The defender will enjoy other, decisive advantages as well.

The first will be *logistical.* Since the defender knows exactly where and when its SSBNs will sortie (or return), it can concentrate a superior number of freshly-topped-off UUVs at the decisive time and place. These have a much shorter distance to cover to deploy, act protectively, and return to port, or to rendezvous with a mother ship, for battery charge or fuel refill, maintenance, and weapons reloads, compared to the adversary's UUVs operating much farther from home in a forward-deployed aggressor role.

The defending drones can *divert* enemy UUVs away from the sortieing SSBN, by harassing or immobilizing them, and by deafening and blinding them. They could use decoys and noisemakers, non-acoustic detection measures, and foul their propulsors with snares and nets. They could even "safely" (for adversary personnel) destroy the hostile UUVs (using onboard weapons, or perhaps by "accidentally" ramming them) since the UUVs would all be unmanned.

A *defender's surface ships* could support its side's UUVs, using sturdy nets to capture enemy ASW drones, sweeping for them with paravanes, the way a minesweeper trawls for mines. Anti-submarine nets, familiar from old World War II movies, could make a comeback as drone barriers. Trained dolphins, and the sea lions used for harbor security by the U.S Navy, could patrol for enemy drones themselves, and guard against any attempts to cut holes in the anti-drone nets.

Other ruses, decoys, deceptions, and diversions can also help an SSBN elude drone pursuers, using *"undersea blockade-running"* tactics based on its *superior stealth.* Since SSBNs have *much more payload capacity* than a typical SSN, let alone a drone swarm, the SSBN can carry and deploy its own UUVs, more than an adversary SSN can, for additional protection as needed.

Once all these *friendly helpers* allow the SSBN to elude the waiting adversary UUVs, the SSBN can proceed to deep blue water and disappear on patrol, using its outstanding stealth and skillful evasive maneuvers—as U.S. Submarine Force SSBNs have always done, and as SSBN Gold and Blue crews practice constantly.

Another decisive advantage to the friendly SSBN over the enemy drones is the one of *sustained speed.* In this pursuit situation, i.e., drones vs. deterrent sub, only the quarry, the SSBN, is nuclear powered. It can outdistance drones whose cruising endurance and top speed will be limited. Drones that recharge their energy stores by harnessing wave- or tide power or oceanic temperature gradients—or by rendezvousing for a battery recharge with a mother ship—will not keep up with the SSBN's high ultraquiet knots capability, let alone the flank (maximum) speed it can easily sustain once detected.

The hostile SSN could try to keep up with the friendly SSBN. But the adversary drones will be left far behind. American next-generation *undersea superiority* would then allow success in what would fast become a modern version of the old, pre-UUV-era First Cold War contest, between "our" manned SSBNs and "their" manned SSNs.

A wealthy and technically sophisticated adversary might seek to develop and field nuclear-powered drones. While potentially having better speed and range than conventionally powered drones, their smaller size and lack of on-board human crewing will still cause major disadvantages.

Small size and lack of manning are not miracle cures to the harsh challenges of undersea warfare—they are *serious handicaps.* Larger undersea vessels can carry much larger and thus more powerful sonar arrays, better signal processing computers, and bigger power supplies to serve all this vital equipment. Humans are particularly important in the special science and art-form of being a seasoned Sonar Tech and Undersea Warrior.

Artificial intelligence, though potentially useful as a decision-support aid, in reality has a very long way to go to be of genuine utility to submarine tactics and strategy. It will always, at best, be a *mere adjunct* to the collective minds of highly trained and experienced submarine commanders and crews crews working in well-integrated teams. The inherently much better *real-time coordination* of personnel and equipment possible within one manned submarine control room, in an SSBN and/or SSN *deploying off-board drones of its own,* yields much better capabilities than a scattered network of small unmanned autonomous or remote-controlled undersea vehicles.

Where You Do or Don't Deploy Your SSBNs Really Does Matter

After assuring crew safety, and mechanical reliability of critical systems, the paramount characteristic of a survivable nuclear-deterrent sub is its *stealth*. Simply put, if it can be detected it can be targeted, and if it can be targeted it can be either (1) harassed and forced to surface and flee during peacetime—a terrible embarrassment for the crew, and the navy and the state that owns it—or, worse, (2) destroyed in time of war—which kills the crew, and denies the owning state the sub's remaining intra-war nuclear retaliation and peace-restoration (war-ending, armistice negotiation) assets.

Sending an SSBN (or other sub type as "poor man's boomer") too close to an adversary's shoreline exposes it to excessive risk of being detected and prosecuted (harassed, or depth charged/torpedoed). Any state's system of maritime domain awareness sensors, and related submarine, surface, and airborne ASW platforms, is *thickest and strongest* when closest to its own coastline, its own territorial waters, and its own homeland naval and air bases.

The generally most preferred areas for American deterrent submarine patrols are out in mid-ocean, where the seafloor well off any coastal continental shelves is very deep indeed (averaging 12,000 feet, with some places vastly deeper.) By exploiting undersea sound propagation, very deep water allows sub crews the *clearest, earliest sonar detection* of any approaching dangers. It also allows ample vertical *room to maneuver*, in order to confuse any nearby threat platforms, defeat surface-borne or airborne or seafloor detection technologies (whether permanent or disposable), and evade any anti-submarine weapons. Thus, as a rule, a nuclear deterrent sub would not go close to, say, an adversary's 200 nautical mile exclusive economic zone (EEZ), let alone its 12-mile territorial limit.

This raises an important flipside to the question of proper peacetime patrol areas. A state possessing strategic deterrence subs might *choose anyway* to deploy some, at certain times, within a relatively short distance of some adversary's coast, possibly then alluding to this incursion and daring the adversary to call the bluff.

The intention could be for:

1. aggressive military-political signaling; or
2. nuclear intimidation ("blackmail"); or

3. second-strike nuclear retaliation, with a very short tactical warning time to the victim leadership—less than five minutes; or
4. first-strike nuclear surprise attack, again with very little warning to the victim.

Item 4, a "bolt from the blue" surprise attack, could tempt a belligerent into making a decapitating nuclear strike against the victim head-of-state's ability to *order a retaliation*; the flip-side to such an egregiously aggressive move is that the victim state may then be rendered unable to undertake effective *peacemaking negotiations*.

These possibilities, especially during an international nuclear crisis (ala Cuba 1963), could panic a defender into making a preemptive nuclear strike, one that starts a nuclear war neither side wants—*inadvertent* Armageddon. This all, as was recognized during the Cold War, gets *very destabilizing* very quickly. It should be amply recognized by all strategists in all states that both deploying SSBNs too close to enemy shores, and counting on making a truly decapitating surprise nuclear strike against enemy leadership and strategic-weapons command and control, are absolutely *nuclear arms Worst Practices!*

SSBN Comms Infrastructure Best Practices Can Dissuade Preemptive-Decapitating Strikes

An effective way to dissuade well in advance any adversary even beginning to think about launching a preemptive and/or decapitating first nuclear strike is for the defending state to own, not just the SSBNs themselves, but also the *communication and environmental-monitoring equipment and procedures* needed to assure that a retaliatory second strike will *always occur when justified and necessary*.

A nation's commander-in-chief needs multiple, redundant ways to convey duly authorized launch orders to submerged SSBNs out on deterrent patrol. The U.S. dismantled its very-slow-baud-rate, extremely-low-frequency (ELF) antenna system after the First Cold War, in favor of more modern ways of implementing "submarine communications at speed and depth." These technologies use special antennas deployed by America's SSBNs to reliably receive very-low-frequency (VLF) comms, while running submerged to maintain stealth and tactical agility. Backing up ground-base commanders and transmitters are specialized aircraft, which can quickly take to the air and either relay—or if necessary, originate—comms to our SSBNs.

For even higher baud-rate comms, including high-definition color video, submarines have antennas that can receive data from special, dedicated military satellite constellations; this mode of tight-beam, jam-resistant secure communication requires the sub to come to periscope depth and raise a mast—modern masts have low-observable radar absorbing coatings that make them extremely stealthy.

In a worst case, some dastardly adversary might think they can get away with preemptively nuking America's top government officials in a "decapitating strike," so that no one is left alive to order the retaliatory strike. To cover even this extreme eventuality thoroughly, and thus plug any such imagined loophole in America's nuclear deterrence, U.S. Navy SSBNs that *somehow ever lose all contacts with higher headquarters* for a lengthy period can monitor regular commercial radio transmissions by different countries for signs of any nuclear attack on America, they can monitor their passive sonars for any signs of undersea nuclear blasts, and they can monitor the atmospheric environment above the surface for other such signs—including intense radioactive fallout off the U.S. Homeland land mass or elsewhere, and electromagnetic-pulse effects near the surface and in low-Earth orbit. (Details would be highly classified, for obvious reasons, but adversaries would presumably be made aware of the gist of these belt-and-suspenders capabilities.)

It should be recognized as international norms of Best Practice that all countries owning SSBNs should demonstrably conform with these infrastructure capabilities. (To *not* do so could imply that their nuclear-armed submarines are intended to be sent to sea with *pre-existing* launch orders, making them extremely destabilizing first-strike weapons.)

Some Small States Have No Choice But To Go In Close

States with good SSBNs and un-constricted access to deep oceans have a luxury of choice re selecting deterrent-sub patrol areas. States reliant on less capable SSBs or SSBPs with SLBMs of limited range, or SSGs or SSGPs with SLCMs (which have limited range by nature because of in-atmosphere aerodynamic drag), will in some cases have *little choice* about where they patrol. This is especially true if those states are also endowed with unfortunate geography, which constricts where their subs can go to remain undetected. One very instructive, illustrative example is Israel:

> The State of Israel, after officially being refused American nuclear-capable Tomahawk cruise missiles (TLAM-Ns) in the 1990s, sustains its submarine-based nuclear deterrence using German-made *Dolphin 1*- and *Dolphin 2*-class SSGPs. They are equipped with 100-KT warheads mounted on enlarged Popeye Turbo cruise missiles. These have a range of not quite 1,000 nautical miles.

Israel has a major port in the south, Eilat, on a rather short stretch of coastline on the Gulf of Aqaba (a northeastern extension of the Red Sea, which leads southward to the Indian Ocean); Eilat is sandwiched between Egypt and Jordan. Israel has a much longer coastline on the eastern Mediterranean Sea, with a major navy base at Haifa in the north of the country. Any Israeli submarines seeking to go from the Red Sea to the Mediterranean have a choice of either using the Suez Canal, with vulnerable surface running for several hours, or else, to maintain stealth, a sub has to circumnavigate the entire continent of Africa and enter the Med through the Strait of Gibraltar, then transit the whole Med from west to east to get back toward Israel and its neighbors. To leave Eilat through the Gulf of Aqaba, going south into the Red Sea, first requires passing through the Strait of Tiran, between Egypt and Saudi Arabia, which risks detection. For an Israeli sub to penetrate the Persian Gulf, which lies east of Israel through the Arabian Sea, in order to conduct a deterrent patrol that holds northern Iranian targets at risk, the narrow, traffic-choked Strait of Hormuz must be run.

Since most sub-launched cruise missile ranges tend to be restricted to a few hundred or at most one thousand miles—not the many thousands of miles of state-of-the-art SLBMs—Israel's SSGP deterrent patrols, even if performed in the more open and deep Mediterranean Sea, will need to remain quite close to shore to hold the Tehran area, say, within range. This brings them near Lebanon and Syria, which are hostile.

Israel has no choice but to deploy its deterrent subs in areas close to the coastlines of states that either are or have at times been dedicated to the Jewish State's utter destruction. Israel, faced with such existential threats, and with a culture of self-reliance for deterrence and defense, is unlikely to cease its nuclear deterrent submarine patrols, no matter how great the inducements from a friendly state (the U.S.) that could provide protection via its own SSBN fleet with an extended-deterrence nuclear umbrella deal.

What perhaps is the key to this situational puzzle is that Israel uses *subsonic* cruise missiles. If these SLCMs ever need to be launched, the actual transit time and thus the tactical warning time, over the effective ranges Israeli subs can achieve to their deterrent targets, would be comparable or even longer than the thirty minutes ICBMs provide over intercontinental ranges. This 30-minute interval has been accepted in international practice as an implicit norm of "adequate" warning time, since the height of the Cold War. In fact, a subsonic cruise missile would take about *two hours* to hit a target a thousand miles away. In the surreal context of nuclear war, this is almost an eternity.

(Of course, adequate warning time for national command authorities to *take cover and go to higher alert* is not the same at all as making the dreadful mistake of thinking said authorities need to respond right away by launching an immediate retaliatory nuclear second strike. The whole point of having a survivable undersea triad leg is to *obviate this overreaction* to what could easily be a *false alarm*, and allow the much safer and more responsible "launch after attack" ROEs—only hit back with your own nukes once an actual enemy nuclear detonation has been rigorously confirmed to have taken place on your own territory.)

Note however that Iran has discussed publicly its own solution to the constraints of Persian Gulf geography. Iran is working on SSGPs it would deploy in the land-locked Caspian Sea, to its north. (Surfaced passage to the Black Sea is possible along rivers and canals in Russian territory, and then into the Med through Turkish territory.) The Caspian Sea is bordered by states that were part of the USSR, and are mostly now friendly to Russia. (Russia recently launched conventional SLCMs from an SSGN in the Caspian Sea at targets in Syria.) Russia tends to support Iran's anti-U.S. regime. This seems to be just one more very good reason to make sure that Iran can *never* gain nuclear weapons.

After Your SSN Detects Their SSBN During Peacetime, Then What?

In such circumstances, as occurred a number of times in the First Cold War when American SSNs got "in trail" of Soviet SSBNs (following closely from behind), it will be vital to quickly and stealthily *establish the nationality* of the SSBN, SSB, SSBP, SSG, or SSGP. Nowadays, with global submarine proliferation, the unknown sub could easily be other than Russian. The specific identification of the contact designated "Sierra One" could get very tricky indeed in tomorrow's world: Some major sub-owning states either export, or license for foreign building, some of their best submarine designs, and have also leased their own subs to other states. It is essential to know in which state's navy the sub is actually commissioned—its true *citizenship*, not just its country of design or manufacture. Making this even more complicated is that for several manufacturers, a few different states each own essentially identical examples of their submarine product.

Submarines can be individually identified via passive (listening) sonar, by detecting and matching against exemplar (reference) *sound profile data* the *peculiarities* in that sub's *acoustic signature*. But this requires possessing a thorough, detailed individual sound-profile reference library *in advance*, via previous, successful submarine spying missions, and then to utilize such data for ID purposes it is necessary to get *very close* to the unidentified sub.

Assuming you are at peace with the state (and hopefully, with all states), you then have the opportunity (and duty) to trail that sub stealthily to *gather further espionage data* about its tactics, its acoustic profile, its crew skill levels, its external fittings and equipment, any weapons tests it performs, and so on.

It may also become part of the SSN's mission to send an *intimidating message of undersea superiority* over the adversary, via a *"sonar lashing"* or even, in very extreme cases, via a *harassing near collision.*

Eventually, practically speaking, you will need to *break off* the trail while *retaining or regaining own-sub stealth;* submerged SSNs can make their own air and drinking water virtually forever, but every submarine sooner or later, even with strict rationing, runs out of food for its crew.

Should Any SSBNs Be Sacrosanct, or Exceptional?

In a utopian world, nuclear powers would strive for maximum strategic stability by never even coming close to threatening another country's strategic deterrent SSBNs. But since the real world is more *anarchic* than utopian, wandering at times into the genuinely *dysphoric,* we need to think through some additional questions of "SSBN patrol metaphysics."

Should all strategic deterrent subs on patrol during peacetime be left alone? A radical alternative to the nuclear peacetime sub-on-sub trailing/spying/harassing options which prevailed during the First Cold War would be to deem other states' nuclear deterrence subs as "sacrosanct fortresses of nuclear peace," so as to foster the absolutely maximized survivability of everyone's undersea triad legs. If you detect one, your normative rule of engagement (ROE) would specify that you leave it alone, and quickly leave the area yourself.

The problem with this is that in the vast, harsh undersea environment, where top-quality submarines are very stealthy and they strive to maintain said stealth at all times and *remain undetected,* verification of such normative rules between different states would not be possible.

How could objective enforcement observers operate to assure that all states complied with this norm? Such referees would be needed, much like the UN's IAEA non-proliferation inspectors, due to the powerful incentives to cheat to gain competitive security advantages. The thought of basing them in *"referee neutral SSNs"* (let alone in referee neutral diesel subs)—like the undersea analog to a highway patrol that polices speeders—seems extremely impractical.

Suppose the norm's rules required, instead of either an honor system or a referee system, the filing, perhaps with the UN, of reports after any SSN-and-SSBN encounters, showing the other guy's SSBNs were duly avoided. Why should any state's claims in these reports, about its top-secret submarine operations, be believed? The *trust-but-verify* atmosphere behind mutual nuclear deterrence for states that are not friends with each other, empowered for instance by the on-site *inspection and overflight* provisions of the (endangered) New START and Open Skies treaties, means you can *never* just assume the other state is obeying such a norm: If you cannot verify, you should not trust.

Why not? The other guy or gal might always be trailing *your* SSBNs on patrol without you knowing it, perhaps thanks to superior SSNs with better-trained and better-led crews. To sustain your own effective deterrent-in-being, you must assume the other state is always doing its best to track your SSBNs—and you are thus forced to do your best to locate and track theirs, to maintain strategic balance. This is what actually went on in the First Cold War.

Of course, since the unprovoked shooting at another state's SSBNs during peacetime—an undersea *ambush*—is an act of war, it is (obviously) vital that during peace different states' subs never shoot at each other. It is equally vital that different SSBNs (or other nuclear missile subs), while on patrol (as opposed to in internationally-announced *training areas and test ranges*), not conduct such drastically realistic missile-launch drills as *opening their big SLBM hatches*, unless they really do intend to shoot some nuclear missiles—in which case it is the duty of a defending SSN in trail to immediately sink them. This would be to prevent, or at least blunt, a surprise nuclear attack on American vital interests, based upon the very credible on-the-spot indications (hatches opening) that such a bolt from the blue was starting. This, at least, was reportedly the procedure during the First Cold War.

In short, the compelling need for continual Indications and Warnings about any enemy surprise nuclear first strikes plays Hob with the idea of treating adversary SSBNs as sacrosanct, even if the (slightly less compelling) needs for "background intelligence" and "live sub-on-sub trailing practice" could somehow be held in abeyance.

Does an American exceptionalism apply to trailing of undemocratic-competitor SSBNs? The United States would certainly never act as aggressor, starting a nuclear war against another state via a surprise first-use nuclear strike. Use of such strikes for last-ditch self-defense, in case of an existential conventional or WMD attack by an aggressor, should not, according to our current nuclear posture, come as any "surprise," since the pre-existing serious enemy attack's provocation will be completely self-evident to all involved. On the other hand, use of a first nuclear strike for preventive or preemptive purposes, against a hostile state allegedly about to begin a strategic attack on American vital interests, is *severely problematic* due to the grave difficulty of avoiding a *false alarm*—which could trigger *inadvertent Armageddon.*

Our SSBNs, and those of other democracies that love both conventional peace and nuclear peace, are in this sense *special.* They would only be ordered to launch any nuclear SLBMs as a last resort, after another entity had begun such an overwhelming conventional or WMD assault and then refused to back off, or started a nuclear war via a nuclear first-use strike against the U.S., its nuclear-umbrella allies, and/or other U.S. vital interests. That being the case, the U.S. has the utmost duty to protect its SSBN fleet in every way possible.

On the other hand, it is not inconceivable that an adversary state that is belligerently expansionist and violently anti-democratic might try to use one or more of its SSBNs to help launch a surprise nuclear first-use against U.S. vital interests. *This is exactly the reason that we at all times require an effective, survivable nuclear deterrent in being.* If this first-use were to occur, that adversary state would have voluntarily and intentionally transformed its last-ditch survivable nuclear deterrence-by-retaliation subs into stealthy first-strike nuclear *offensive weapons.* If this ever happened, the U.S. would have the *absolute necessity*, and our Submariners the *utmost duty*, to immediately destroy all that enemy state's SSBNs (or their SSBs or SSBPs). Otherwise, they could launch *more* nuclear missiles, perhaps at American and allied cities. Even if the enemy intended for their initial nuclear surprise attack to remain limited—something which defenders can *never* be certain about—the war is too likely to escalate beyond anyone's control—in which case the enemy nuclear missiles *must* be put out of action *as soon as possible.*

It is the wide imbalance of relative trustworthiness and respect for human values, between freedom and tyranny, that ultimately impels U.S. Navy SSNs, and other American intelligence and ASW assets, to locate and trail opposition SSBNs at all times, with weaponry deployed that is adequate to stop those SSBNs from ever launching missiles, just in case. A corollary of this, inevitably, is that other states *including dictatorships* will also do their utmost to protect their own SSBNs, and to carefully track ours.

Thus, the idealistic notion that SSBNs of different states might ever somehow "peacefully coexist," without being diligently surveilled and trailed by each other's adversary's SSNs and other ASW forces, is a mere pacifist pipedream. At best it lies on that same slippery slope of delusional thinking that leads to the forlorn hope of total world nuclear disarmament.

Interestingly, while this whole metaphysical issue arises due to the *asymmetric* conflict between the U.S./NATO vs. Russia, China, North Korea, and Iran, regarding differing forms of government and differing attitudes toward human rights, the resultant is one of *symmetric* imperatives in undersea warfare for both sides. Tyrants have already publicly denounced any notion of American exceptionalism. That should tell American Submariners everything they need to know about the requirements for *forward presence and utmost readiness.*

Proliferating Submarines Mean Challenges and Opportunities

Continuing to try to get to the bottom of this important and "very deep" subject, we need to work our way through a few more challenging yet fascinating topics. A forward-leaning take on global *maritime domain awareness* is essential, and that is our main focus now.

SSBN Fleets Must Be Right-Sized to Be Truly Survivable as a Deterrence Team: It is, in an unfortunate but necessary *H-bomb bean-counting* sense, especially efficient for one country, during nuclear wartime, to sink another country's SSBNs. A single *Columbia*-class SSBN, for instance, will have aboard, due to the allowed-MIRVing norm and New START treaty limits, *sixty-four* separate nuclear warheads in total installed on its sixteen SLBMs in their launch tubes. This is a *very juicy, rewarding, tempting target* for an enemy to try to kill all at once with the *mere expenditure of a brace of torpedoes* aimed at the SSBN by one of that enemy's hunter-killer SSNs.

(The U.S. is now deploying a limited number of eight-kiloton *tactical* nuclear warheads on a few of its deployed SLBMs, for better deterrence via flexible, proportional response to any first-use of tactical nukes by an aggressor adversary.)

In comparison to this potent arsenal all *concentrated* aboard a *single* SSBN, it would be a forlorn hope indeed that anyone's "finite" Ballistic Missile Defense system could destroy all the sixteen SLBMs on even a single SSBN during their near-simultaneous boost phases—or even more impossible—that it could stop all of those separate sixty-four Reentry Vehicles once they simultaneously scatter in outer space in independent flight, reenter earth's atmosphere, and then plunge toward their separate targets. (The "trans-finite" magnitude of the superpower-level missile defense problem is in reality vastly more daunting than even this, since in many scenarios a nuclear strike will include many more delivery-platform launches, from land and sea, than just one SSBN's armaments. Finite missile shields are relevant and useful only against "the smallest" ICBM attacks—accidental or rogue/terrorist launches, or a "mere pin-prick" superpower launch, that start with only one or at most very few missiles.)

It is exceedingly unlikely that any adversaries could sink *all of several* U.S. SSBNs on patrol at any one time before our leadership would know—via incoming flash radio codes from our subs, emergency submarine message buoys, and SURTASS surface-ship surveillance sonars plus modern SOSUS-like seafloor-based surveillance sonar data—that nuclear hostilities had commenced, if this wasn't already evident by the *geopolitical/military situation "above the water"*—so that POTUS could react appropriately and order a counter-strike.

Besides this, and very importantly, enemy ASW warfare doesn't directly affect the deterring and retaliating nukes of *all the other U.S. Triad-leg* delivery systems. These would all to some unknown extent (but probably a lot greater than 0.000%) survive any surprise first-use nuclear attack by any enemy. All this reinforces for the properly equipped United States, as for any similar Triad-equipped defending state, the *total assurance* of a devastating (and fully justified) retaliatory second strike.

The whole issue of correlating (1) future missile-shield capability and capacity, against (2) defender vice attacker submarine fleet sizes and SSN-versus-SSBN tactical effectiveness, deserves more study and practical attention. In a *very dark future scenario*, it might be imagined that via using a mix of *non-finite BMD* (directed energy and particle beam weapons with rapid and essentially unlimited electric-power "ammo supplies"), very aggressive SSN-versus-SSBN tactics, along with close-to-target-shoreline, own-SSBN sorties, an aggressor might seek to deplete (blunt), disarm (perfectly interdict), or side-step altogether (out-psych by self-deterrence) a defender's entire nuclear-retaliation capability. But this idea is much more science fiction, even fantasy, than it is or could ever be science fact. Let's take a look at why:

> The ultimate vision of this comes back to President Reagan's old idea of a comprehensive "Star Wars" space-based missile shield. He thought that by sharing the technology with the USSR, nuclear weapons could be rendered truly obsolete. But POTUS Reagan was known later to be suffering from Alzheimer's disease, which degrades cognitive faculties for a decade before symptoms are overtly apparent. He did not vet the Star Wars dream concept with any of his advisers before springing it on the world. It was and still is hopelessly impractical for many technical reasons, and would be hopelessly expensive to implement even if all

> those tech problems could one day be solved. Also, the whole idea that it would be a panacea against nuclear war ignores the basic fact that there are *many and varied ways* to deliver nukes to their target that *don't go through or anywhere near outer space*. These include Russian president Vladimir Putin's infamous "Poseidon long-range nuke submarine-torpedo hybrid drones," different military or civilian types of aircraft, any number of surface vessels from cigarette boats through supertankers, narco submersibles, and numerous means of smuggling nukes by land.

Deterrent-Submarine Proliferation Demands Adequate SSN Fleet Size

Submarine proliferation necessitates SSN fleet growth: A greater number of submarines owned by a greater number of states around the globe creates more and more work for a defending state's SSN fleet. (Any state that owns SSBNs, SSBs, SSBPs, SSGs, and/or SSGPs armed with nuclear ballistic and/or cruise missiles intended for survivable second-strike capabilities is in this context a "defending state.") This is because *more areas* of the world need to be patrolled to monitor *more vessels* of interest, and known operational areas need to be surveilled *more intensely*, to gather intelligence, maintain forward presence, protect your own deterrent subs, assert undersea superiority, and be well prepared for anything. Modern SSNs afford a state excellent mission diversity and flexibility, well beyond just strategic and tactical ASW capabilities. But *capacity*, i.e. *the total number of SSNs in commission* in the defender's fleet, is just as important as *capability*, i.e., the *quality of each individual SSN* (e.g., SUBSAFE construction and operating procedures, superb crew training, state-of-the-art propulsion/sensor/weapon systems, and world-beating stealth).

If other states are obtaining more SSBNs, they too are very likely to also obtain more SSNs, to protect their own SSBNs, and for other missions that their leaders decide are required. China and Russia are both doing so. There is a clear and present danger here, of an arms race accelerating in submarine construction. To some degree, since SSNs perform active conventional missions all the time, and might someday even need to lethally engage adversary subs and surface ships and aircraft of many different types, a rising number of actual and potential peer competitor and adversary submarines puts upward pressure on any defender's submarine fleet size, especially on its SSN fleet size. To some degree, very high quality of defender SSNs and crews can make up for *some* shortfall in total numbers, but this cushion of quality can only go *so far*—it can't enable *any* SSN to be in two very different places at once.

How far can such a submarine arms race be allowed to go by the vying participants, before operational, national security, and maritime-safety problems are created for *all* undersea-going states?

Worldwide sub proliferation could go beyond modernization to a genuine arms race: For the U.S., given its essential leadership role in sustaining the open world order, global free trade, freedom of navigation, and maritime security, to allow itself by design or default to fall behind autocratic, expansionist global and/or regional naval powers in submarine-building numbers and quality would be a serious error. Nor can we afford to neglect the operational challenges to America's Silent Service of rogue states, such as North Korea or Iran, working on their own larger sub fleets, quite possibly in both states' cases, some day, with nuclear weapons. (North Korea is reported to be working on its first homegrown SSB.) National security and defense are by nature competitive endeavors between states.

During the Cold War, the U.S. had important advantages in the undersea realm, given the superior quieting, better sonar suites, and better trained and led volunteer crews of its nuclear subs, compared to the Soviet Union. But the competition continues apace, and the U.S. Submarine Force's leadership have stated publicly that in recent years, adversary sub operations have intensified and climbed the tech-and-tactics learning curve.

Russia and China are both catching up fast toward America's own high-and-always-going-higher standards in this essential arena of world peace or war. This is partly due to our near-peer adversaries' aggressive espionage over the years. But it is also due to their own undeniable talent, ingenuity, hard work, and ample funding. Had the relative competitive positions of the U.S. and USSR under the waves been reversed during the Cold War, would the Soviets perhaps have won and would America have gone Communist? Now, in the 21st century, the U.S. and our Allies, partners, and friends must work diligently to sustain world peace and international stability—via sustaining a totally viable and credible strategic nuclear deterrent Triad force. This *must* include a robust and numerous SSN fleet, for all the reasons given above, as in effect *the "fourth leg of America's Triad."*

Will there be undersea traffic jams? Unlike many military assets that, during peacetime, mostly remain on home turf or at foreign bases, submarines—like all navy ships—*need to be underway*. They need to get out of port continually, to train realistically and certify personnel preparedness, to verify mechanical readiness, and to maintain tip-top crew skills to complete their overseas missions and come home safe. As there become more and more subs at sea, *undersea traffic congestion* might become a real problem.

The world's oceans are truly vast, but submarines, by virtue of their need to move around to access militarily useful places, and to keep tabs on adversaries, tend to *congregate*. SSNs busy identifying numerous submerged sonar contacts that turn out to be friendly or harmless (neutral) *will be distracted from their main purposes*. The same might occur for deterrent subs, which generally need to *carefully avoid/evade any and all sonar contacts*.

Submarines coming and going submerged through *nautical choke points*, such as the Strait of Gibraltar or Strait of Malacca, with shallow but turbid depths and bad sonar conditions, could *collide with each other, or hit or be hit by a surface ship*, with terrible results; this has indeed sometimes happened. Collisions out in unconstricted waters seem more likely, too, as there are more and more deterrent subs and fast-attack subs *following each other around* at sometimes-very-close quarters. The impending population explosion of scientific, military, and even recreational manned and unmanned undersea vehicles and subs, of various sizes and capabilities, promises to make this whole underwater obstacle course even worse.

In wartime, diesel subs, even obsolete designs, can constitute dangerous *smart minefields*. As such, they are likely while on training missions, or operational patrols, to *concentrate at maritime choke points*. This would make any undersea traffic jams even more likely, and even more dangerous. Good modern navies have various, often highly classified methods to prevent friendly vessels from getting too close to each other. But there is no international system of *undersea traffic control for "de-conflicting,"* analogous to what exists for air traffic control.

When is an arms race not *an arms race?* If any state's targeted SSN fleet size (hull count) is based primarily on its own needs, rather than on keeping up with the Davey Joneses, and if projections indicate that its current submarine shipbuilding plan will, unless increased, lock in a shortfall against basic future numerical requirements, then that state acquiring a larger number of subs would constitute *needs-based acquisition*, and *not* a senseless, dangerous arms race. The replacement of worn-out subs by more modern classes, known as recapitalization, isn't an arms race either. It is a necessary replacement of vessels now past their safe and useful life expectancies.

For the U.S. Navy's Submarine Force, the number of SSNs now owned, and already locked-in by current building plans into the mid-2030s, *falls significantly short* of meeting projected national-security and peacekeeping needs. It is therefore probable that the Sub Force's original intention to acquire a total of thirty Virginia-class SSNs will need to be raised, and there is some talk that the eventual build-out might number forty-eight boats, with even more built of a developmental SSN(x) class. Again, this is *not* a "senseless arms race." It is an *essential recognition* of the fleet size needed to adequately cover priority operational needs while making due allowance for vessel maintenance and for crew leave and land-based refresher training.

Can and should SSBN and "poor-man's substitute" submarine proliferation be slowed or halted? There are some interrelated questions behind this basic question. Thinking back to the height of First Cold War tensions, would the U.S./NATO have preferred that the USSR *not have any* survivable triad submarine leg? How would this have affected mutual nuclear deterrence *stability* in that bygone, scary bipolar world—which has now officially returned in the form of an even more volatile, dangerous *three-player game* between the U.S., Russia, and China?

If, in today's world, a state is bound and determined to obtain its own nuclear deterrence assets, should it be *encouraged, or merely allowed, or discouraged, or actively prevented* from acquiring a survivable submarine triad leg? Which of these approaches would be better for *world nuclear stability*—which should itself be an *absolute priority* for *all* states?

Which approach would be better for America's already-stretched shipbuilding budgets, and already-grueling Silent Service operational tempos? Would it help to have fewer potential adversary submarines to need to keep track of? What happens, and what should be done, if only one side in a durable, long-term two-way dispute involving nukes—such as, say, India but not Pakistan—obtains SSBNs, SSBs, SSBPs, SSGs, or SSGPs?

If more and more nuclear powers seek deterrent subs, will there in the *early learning stages* of the newcomer activities be an accelerated rate of *lethal accidents* among these ships and their nuclear weapons? How will the loss of entire subs with their whole crews, as *did* tragically occur during the First Cold War to both sides, affect world stability? Would a sudden, inexplicable accident—perhaps with a nuclear detonation involved—risk starting an inadvertent nuclear war?

If a sub with nukes is disabled at depth while the crew remain alive, how might the presence of perhaps-damaged, perhaps-less-safe nukes on board affect the planning and execution of *rescue operations*? Since time would be of the essence, how best can the possibility of such an emergency ever occurring be prepared for in advance, by state navies and by international submarine rescue authorities? If the surviving crews themselves are not able to render safe their nuclear weapons, how best can *nuclear ordnance disposal* experts be gotten on scene ASAP as part of the rescue operations?

Could such disasters be prevented by *foreign technical/procedural assistance*, to new nuclear deterrent sub-owning states, from experienced submarine-owning states? Should such advisors be provided by the big nuclear powers (in competition for such nuclear-related *client lists*) as a form of *humanitarian foreign aid* and naval/nuclear *disaster prevention*? Or, should this assistance be *sold by commercial defense contractors* (including state-controlled ones in Russia and China) each bidding competitively on a for-profit basis? Might the U.S. be able to go after such business, or provide such foreign aid, for capitalist profits or for diplomatic influence (or both), without compromising military secrets?

These many open questions seem to be worthwhile topics for conferences and workshops on naval strategy and on global nuclear arms control. Answering them will not be easy or straightforward, but *asking the right questions* is a vital first step to *successful worldwide nuclear peacekeeping.*

What Global Norms and Bans About SSBNs, SSGPs, SSGs, SSBPs, and SSBs are Wise?

What international norms and agreements about nuclear deterrent subs are needed? We offer a few suggestions regarding survivable nuclear-deterrent submarine Best Practices and Best Perspectives, for further consideration by all interested parties:

- It is important to "sanitize" home waters of lurking adversary nuclear-missile subs, because their proximity suggests they might have aggressive intentions. While protection of one's own nuclear deterrent subs in *bastions* in one's own home waters is stabilizing and makes eminent sense, in contrast should deployments overly close to adversaries' coastlines be banned via an international norm? How can definitions of "overly close" be negotiated? What allowance is needed for states situated in constricted waters? During peacetime, enemy subs can be driven off by such tactics as Tom Clancy-style sonar lashings, or dropping non-lethal signal grenades. During wartime, lethal force is called for.
- No state's nuclear deterrence posture is survivable, reliable, and safe unless it includes high-quality strategic nuclear deterrence submarines, preferably SSBNs, or possibly SSGNs. Less

un-affordable SSGPs, SSGs, SSBPs, or even SSBs, might sometimes be used as less-capable substitutes, provided that the limitations of these subs and their weaponry are not inconsistent with local geography, and hydrography, of both the deterrer and the deterree(s).

- States that cannot afford the immense ongoing costs to acquire, base, and safely maintain highly capable deterrent subs and their nuclear missiles, and train and support elite crews, should *avoid acquiring nuclear weapons altogether.* Instead, they should look to obtain whatever nuclear deterrence protection they need by joining a major nuclear power's *protective extended-deterrence nuclear umbrella.*
- Trying to prevent proliferation of nuclear deterrent subs among states that do not now own them could be a useful way to *limit proliferation of nuclear weapons,* by a sort of back door. This approach splits into the questions of counter-proliferation for the submarine vessels (hulls) that play host to the nuclear weapons, counter-proliferation for the nuclear-capable missiles, and counter-proliferation for the nuclear warheads hosted on these subs' missiles. The most crucial juncture is denying the supply of nuclear warheads, since without them the vessels and delivery platforms become *conventional* weapons systems. On the other hand, if it were established as a *clear global norm* that every nuclear weapons state *required* a submarine-based nuclear deterrent triad leg, and it were somehow possible to *prevent* some states from ever obtaining the completed subs needed to establish such a deterrent leg, those states might be leveraged into not acquiring nukes. They could, instead, be encouraged and incentivized to enter into a nuclear umbrella treaty with an established nuclear power that owns a good triad. *Great caution* would be needed with this approach, since while *rogue states* might be *denuclearized* with the inducement/enticement of umbrella protection, their *inherent bad behavior* might exacerbate the problem of them *"chain ganging"* the superpower that protects them into an ill-conceived international crisis, one that risks escalating *horizontally* (more countries) and *vertically* (bigger weapons) into nuclear combat.
- Some of the problems of *insufficient warning time,* for nuclear-deterrent cruise missiles carried on an SSGP near an adversary's coast, might be avoided if there were a global ban

on hypersonic nuclear cruise missiles launched from nuclear deterrent subs. If the allowed airspeed of such special-purpose, nuclear-equipped cruise missiles were limited by treaty, to *subsonic or low-supersonic speeds* (Mach 1.2 maximum?), they could achieve their intended nuclear deterrence purpose, while giving sufficient warning time to inland strategic targets when launched from any patrol areas that are close to an adversary's coast due to restricted geography. (But note that SLBMs are by nature *already hypersonic*; when launched from close-in they can hit a target in *barely five minutes as it is*; introduction of modern hypersonic cruise missiles is *not* such a *great destabilizer* as some pundits claim.)

- There should be a global ban on *nuclear-armed drone mini-subs*. This should include the type recently publicized by Russia, the Poseidon, meant to sneak a nuclear weapon close to an adversary's targeted commercial harbor, naval base, or coastal city, for nuclear blackmail or nuclear attack. Such weapons should be deemed *terrorist devices*, designed to spread raw fear and kill vast numbers of innocent civilians. They are surprise first-use nuclear attack weapons, given their *stealthy ability to preposition for zero warning time*. They are especially *not* any sort of valid deterrent weapon. If they are ever actually deployed, superb multi-platform, multi-domain ASW would be the best defense against them, assuring they never reach friendly shores.

Conclusion: For the U.S. Navy's SSBN Fleet, Enough Is Not Too Much

Like the total number of nuclear warheads that a state needs, the number of SSBNs the state should have in commission is not just a function of the number of deterrent subs or nuclear warheads owned by that state's single biggest potential nuclear adversary, or by all such adversaries combined. The necessary SSBN fleet size, in order to maintain an effective nuclear deterrence system in being, is—just like their deterrent arsenal's total warhead count—a function of the quantity/magnitude of all strategic countervailing assets owned by all potential nuclear adversaries that the deterrer needs to hold at risk over decades.

And just as the total number of nuclear warheads on hand in a state must take account of a long and volatile future timeline, the total number of SSBNs in commission in the U.S. needs to make allowance for the possibility of operational and/or combat losses. Then, in a worst case, that depleted SSBN fleet would also need to cope with a possible, further off, second nuclear conflict beyond the first one.

Just as any First Nuclear World War would likely cost America its facilities for manufacturing new nuclear weapons, that same war would surely lead to the destruction of America's nuclear submarine construction facilities. Even with such facilities intact, and with all the expert workers alive and healthy, it takes seven (7) years or more to build a new, replacement nuclear sub from scratch, given the finalized design for it.

Also, such deterrence-platform-fleet sizes and their warhead numbers need to take account that *any* state might need to deter and defend itself against *more than one* well-equipped nuclear aggressors *simultaneously*. In years to come, as Russia builds a larger and very capable SSBN fleet, China's SSBN fleet will also grow in numbers and in modern capabilities. It may at times be very tempting for them to *team up* against America, in a prolonged contest where nuclear intimidation/blackmail and nuclear attack blend together most unpleasantly for America. For this reason, *three-way parity* in SSBN fleet sizes is as problematic, as potentially destabilizing, as is China attaining parity in *total nuclear arsenal warhead counts* with those of Russia and the U.S.

As Silent Service leadership has been emphasizing for some time now, the United States has determined after detailed modeling and analysis that one dozen (12) next-generation SSBNs are the *minimum needed* for America's 21st-century nuclear deterrence needs. There are several good reasons why the U.S. Navy needs to own at least twelve in order to assure that *at least four* are always in position, and a bevy of facts showing why at least four at once in position are always needed:

1. Some SSBNs will be transiting to and from their assigned patrol areas, and thus will be out of position due to the (top secret) relatively limited range of SLBMs compared to silo-based ICBMs.
2. Some SSBNs will be in homeport or a shipyard for maintenance and overhaul, and will be unable to launch missiles, or their missiles will be out of range of assigned targets. This downtime is inevitable, despite the Submarine Force's most diligent efforts at having two captains and crews for each SSBN (Blue and Gold), at conducting crew changeovers at forward operating basis, and at recently experimenting with underway replenishment.

3. The states that we need to deter are dispersed all across the vast Eurasian landmass, requiring some SSBNs to be in the Atlantic while others are in the Pacific, in order for their missiles to hold all strategic targets at risk all the time.
4. Allowance must be made for unforeseen mechanical casualties (breakdowns) and/or medical problems (e.g., COVID-19-like pandemics) aboard some patrolling SSBNs.
5. Allowance must be made, in the worst case, for some wartime combat attrition, as well as for operational losses via mishap (accidents).

Clearly, the whole subject of America's highly survivable SSBN nuclear deterrence fleet, and its recapitalization with the impending new Columbia class of an irreducible twelve vessels minimum, is quite essential to the future survival of democracy, and even of civilization, in a world that is more potentially dangerous than it has ever been before in human history.

GUIDE TO ACRONYMS

2-D Two-Dimensional

ABM Anti-Ballistic Missile
A-bomb Atomic [fission] bomb
ADM Admiral
AIDS Acquired Immune Deficiency Syndrome
ALCM Air-Launched Cruise Missile
AP Armor Piercing
ASAP As Soon As Possible
ASW Anti-Submarine Warfare

BCE Before the Common Era [i.e., B.C.]
BMD Ballistic Missile Defense
B-1 USAF strategic bomber, supersonic, not stealthy, no longer nuclear capable
B-2 USAF strategic bomber, subsonic, stealthy, DCA
B-21 USAF next-generation strategic bomber, subsonic, stealthy
B-52 USAF strategic bomber, subsonic, not stealthy, DCA

CIA Central Intelligence Agency
COMSTRATCOM Commander, U.S. Strategic Command
COVID-19 Coronavirus Disease 2019
CPA Certified Public Accountant
CSTO Collective Security Treaty Organization

CTBT Comprehensive Test Ban Treaty
C3 Command, Control, and Communications
C4I Command, Control, Communications, and Intelligence

DC District of Columbia
DCA Dual-Capable Aircraft
DOD Department of Defense
DOE Department of Energy
DPRK Democratic People's Republic of [North] Korea
DVD Digital Video Disk

EEZ Exclusive Economic Zone
ELF Extremely Low Frequency
EMP Electromagnetic Pulse
EMT Emergency Medical Technician
EU European Union

FSA Fellow of the Society of Actuaries

GBSD Ground-Based Strategic Deterrent
GP Ground Penetrating

HANE High-Altitude Nuclear Explosion
H-bomb Hydrogen [fusion] bomb
HD High Definition
HUMINT Human Intelligence

IAEA International Atomic Energy Agency
ICBM Intercontinental Ballistic Missile
INF Intermediate [range] Nuclear Forces
IRA Russia's Internet Resources Agency
IRBM Intermediate-Range Ballistic Missile
ISIS Islamic State of Iraq and Syria
ISR Intelligence, Surveillance, and Reconnaissance

JCPOA Joint Comprehensive Plan Of Action [No-nukes agreement with Iran]
JFK John Fitzgerald Kennedy

KGB Soviet-era version of CIA and FBI
KIA Killed In Action

KT Kiloton

LLC Limited Liability Corporation
LRSO Long-Range Stand Off

MARV Maneuverable Reentry Vehicles
MIA Missing in Action
MIRV Multiple Independently-targetable Reentry Vehicles
MIT Massachusetts Institute of Technology
MOAB Mother Of All Bombs [hyperbaric fuel-air explosive]
MRBM Medium-Range Ballistic Missile
MT Megaton

N Number of countries owning nukes
NASA National Aeronautics and Space Administration
NATO North Atlantic Treaty Organization
NCA Nuclear Capable Aircraft
NCA National Command Authorities
NC3 Nuclear Command, Control, and Communications
New START New Strategic Arms Reduction Treaty
NFZ Nuclear-Free Zone
NGO Non-Government Organization
NNPRR National Nuclear Posture Review Report
NPT Non-Proliferation Treaty
NSA National Security Agency

POTUS President Of The United States
POW Prisoner of War
PRC People's Republic of China
PTSD Post-Traumatic Stress Disorder

QED Quod Erat Demonstrondum [Latin for "what is to be proved"]

ROEs Rules Of Engagement
RV Reentry Vehicle
R&D Research and Development

SAC Strategic Air Command
SALT Strategic Arms Limitation Treaty
SEAL Sea, Air, Land [U.S. Navy special warfare commandos]

SLBM Submarine-Launched Ballistic Missile
SLCM Submarine-Launched Cruise Missile
SSB Diesel-powered ballistic missile sub
SSBN Nuclear-powered ballistic missile sub
SSBP Air-independent-powered ballistic missile sub
SSG Diesel-powered cruise missile sub
SSGN Nuclear-powered cruise missile sub
SSGP Air-independent-powered cruise missile sub
SSK Diesel-powered hunter-killer sub
SSN Nuclear-powered hunted-killer sub
SSN(X) U.S. Navy's next-generation SSN
SSP Air-independent-powered hunter-killer sub
SRBM Short-Range Ballistic Missile
STEM Science, Technology, Engineering, and Mathematics
STRATCOM U.S. Strategic Command
SUBSAFE U.S. Navy's submarine safety program
SURTASS Surveillance Towed Array Sensor System
Su-57 Russian stealth fighter
S-400 Russian mobile anti-aircraft missile system
S-500 Russian next-generation mobile anti-aircraft missile system

TLAM-N Tomahawk Land Attack Missile—Nuclear
TV Television

UK United Kingdom
UN United Nations
UNCLASS Unclassified
USAF United States Air Force
USN United States Navy
USSR Union of Soviet Socialist Republics
UUV Unmanned Undersea Vehicle
UV Ultraviolet

VE Day Victory-in-Europe Day
VLF Very Low Frequency
VPM Virginia Payload Module

WHO World Health Organization
WIA Wounded In Action
WMD Weapons of Mass Destruction

WWI World War One
WWII World War Two
WWIII World War Three

BIBLIOGRAPHY

The references listed below were studied in full during background research for this book. Additional sources included some relevant articles in the periodicals *Foreign Affairs, Foreign Policy, Scientific American, Undersea Warfare, The Submarine Review,* the U.S. Naval Institute *Proceedings, The Bulletin of the Atomic Scientists, Wired, The New York Times,* and *The Washington Post,* as well as news and commentary items excerpted within COMSUBLANT's e-digest *Undersea Warfare News,* plus some publications of the Submarine Industrial Base Council (to which I belong). Further readings included numerous on-line PDF texts and reports, especially various American Government .gov and .mil publications, pertaining to recent U.S., NATO, Chinese, and Russian defense strategies and nuclear deterrence postures. I also watched a number of website podcasts, and YouTube videos, presenting talks and interviews with various current and former government officials, military commanders, defense contractor executives, and university and think tank researchers, about strategic deterrence and national defense.

Clark C. Abt, *A Strategy for Terminating a Nuclear War* (Boulder: Westview, 1985).

Dmitry Adamsky, *Russian Nuclear Orthodoxy—Religion, Politics, and Strategy* (Stanford: Stanford University Press, 2019).

David Albright, with Stricker, Andrea, *Revisiting South Africa's Nuclear Weapons Program: Its History, Dismantlement, and Lessons for*

Today (Washington, DC: Institute for Science and International Security, 2016).

Graham Allison, *Nuclear Terrorism: The Ultimate Preventable Catastrophe* (New York: Henry Holt & Co., 2005).

Graham Allison; Cote', Owen R., Jr., Falkenrath, Richard A., and Miller, Steven E., Avoiding Nuclear Anarchy: Containing the Threat of Loose Russian Nuclear Weapons and Fissile Material (Cambridge: MIT Press, 1996).

Jeffrey A. Bader, *Obama and China's Rise: An Insider's Account of America's Asia Strategy* (Washington, DC: Brookings Institution Press, 2012).

Desmond Ball, and Richelson, Jeffrey, *Strategic Nuclear Targeting* (Ithaca: Cornell University Press, 1986).

Richard K. Betts, *Nuclear Blackmail and Nuclear Balance* (Washington, DC: Brookings Institution, 1987).

Hans Blix, *Why Nuclear Disarmament Matters* (Cambridge, MA: MIT Press, 2008).

Hans Blix, *Disarming Iraq* (New York: Pantheon Books, 2004).

David Bodansky, *Nuclear Energy: Principles, Practices, and Prospects* (Woodbury: American Institute of Physics, 1996).

Paul Bracken, *The Command and Control of Nuclear Forces* (New Haven: Yale University Press, 1983).

Paul Bracken, *The Second Nuclear Age: Strategy, Danger, and the New Power Politics* (New York: Times Books, 2012).

Bernard Brodie, *Escalation and the Nuclear Option* (Princeton: Princeton University Press, 1966).

Bernard Brodie, *A Guide to Naval Strategy: Newly Revised Edition* (New York: Praeger, 1965).

Bernard Brodie, *Strategy in the Missile Age* (Princeton: Princeton University Press, 1965).

Michael E. Brown; Cote', Owen R., Jr., Lynn-Jones, Sean M., and Miller, Steven E., *Going Nuclear: Nuclear Proliferation and International Security in the 21st Century* (Cambridge: MIT Press, 2010).

Alan Bullock, *Hitler: A Study in Tyranny* (New York: Harper & Brothers, 1952).

McGeorge Bundy; Crowe, William, Jr., and Drell, Sidney D., *Reducing Nuclear Danger: The Road Away from the Brink* (New York: Council on Foreign Relations Press, 1993).

Kurt M. Campbell, *The Pivot: The Future of American Statecraft in Asia* (New York: Hachette, 2016).

Glenn Alan Cheney, *Chernobyl: The Ongoing Story of the World's Deadliest Nuclear Disaster* (New York: Maxwell Macmillan International, 1993).
Bernard D. Cole, *Taiwan's Security: History and Prospects* (Abingdon, UK: Routledge, 2006).
The Committee for the Compilation of Materials on Damage Caused by the Atomic Bombs at Hiroshima and Nagasaki, *Hiroshima and Nagasaki: The Physical, Medical, and Social Effects of the Atomic Bombings* (New York: Basic Books, 1981).
John Pina Craven, *The Silent War: The Cold War Battle Beneath the Sea* (New York: Simon & Schuster, 2001).
Jacquelyn K. Davis, and Pfaltzgraff, James Jr., *Coalition Management and Escalation Control in a Multinuclear World* (Annapolis: Naval Institute Press, 2020).
Therese Delpech, *Nuclear Deterrence in the 21st Century* (Santa Monica: RAND Corporation, 2012).
J. J. Dicerto, *Missile Base Beneath the Sea: the Story of Polaris* (New York: St. Martin's Press, 1967).
Bradford Dismukes, and McConnell, James, eds., *Soviet Naval Diplomacy* (New York: Pergamon Press, 1979).
Paul R. Ehrlich; Sagan, Carl; Kennedy, Donald; and Roberts, Walter Orr, *The Cold and the Dark: The World After Nuclear War* (New York: Norton, 1984).
Mohamed ElBaradei, *The Age of Deception: Nuclear Diplomacy in Treacherous Times* (New York: Metropolitan Books, 2011).
Yair Evron, *Israel's Nuclear Dilemma* (Ithaca: Cornell University Press, 1994).
Harold P. Ford, and Winters, Francis X, S.J., *Ethics and Nuclear Strategy?* (Maryknoll: Orbis, 1977).
Norman Friedman, *The Cold War* (Seven Oaks: London, 2005).
John Lewis Gaddis, *The Cold War: a New History* (New York: Penguin, 2005).
Alexander L. George, and Simons, William E., eds., *The Limits of Coercive Diplomacy* (Boulder: Westview Press, 1994).
Alexander L. George, and Smoke, Richard, *Deterrence in American Foreign Policy: Theory and Practice* (New York: Columbia University Press, 1974).
Joseph Gerson, preface by Bello, Walden, *Empire and the Bomb: How the US Uses Nuclear Weapons to Dominate the World* (London: Pluto Press, 2007).

Avery Goldstein, *Deterrence and Security in the 21st Century: China, Britain, France, and the Enduring Legacy of the Nuclear Revolution* (Stamford: Stamford University Press, 2000).

Gerald S. Graham, *The Politics of Naval Supremacy: Studies in British Maritime Ascendancy* (London: Cambridge University Press, 1965).

Michihiko Hachiya, M.D., *Hiroshima Diary: The Journal of a Japanese Physician, August 6–September 30, 1945, Fifty Years Later* (Chapel Hill: University of North Carolina Press, 1995).

Devin T. Hagerty, *The Consequences of Nuclear Proliferation: Lessons from South Asia* (Cambridge: MIT Press, 1998).

Morton H. Halperin, *Limited War: An Essay on the Development of the Theory and an Annotated Bibliography* (Cambridge: Harvard University Press, 1962).

Wolfram F. Hanrieder, ed., *Technology, Strategy, and Arms Control* (Boulder: Westview Press, 1986).

Mark A. Harwell, *Nuclear Winter: The Human and Environmental Consequences of Nuclear War* (New York: Springer-Verlag, 1984).

John Hersey, *Hiroshima* (New York: Knopf, 1985).

William J. Holland, Jr., "Why a Triad?", *Proceedings*, October 2017, p. 20, (Annapolis: U.S. Naval Institute Press).

Ian Hughes, *Disordered Minds: How Dangerous Personalities Are Destroying Democracy* (Alresford, UK: Zero Books, 2018).

Fred Charles Iklé, *Every War Must End*, 2nd revised edition (New York: Columbia University Press, 2005).

Fred Charles Iklé, *How Nations Negotiate* (New York: Praeger, 1964).

Fred Charles Iklé, *The Social Impact of Bomb Destruction* (Norman: University of Oklahoma Press, 1958).

Irving L. Janis, *Air War and Emotional Stress* (Westport: Greenwood Press, 1951).

Robert Jervis, *The Illogic of American Nuclear Strategy* (Ithaca: Cornell University Press, 1984).

Robert Jervis; Lebow, Richard Ned and Stein, Janice Gross, *Psychology & Deterrence* (Baltimore: Johns Hopkins University Press, 1985).

Herman Kahn, *On Escalation: Metaphors and Scenarios* (New York: Praeger, 1965).

Herman Kahn, *Thinking About the Unthinkable* (New York: Avon, 1962).

Herman Kahn, *Thinking About the Unthinkable in the 1980s* (New York: Simon & Schuster, 1984).

Fred Kaplan, *The Wizards of Armageddon* (Stamford: Stamford University Press, 1983).

Fred Kaplan, *The Bomb—Presidents, Generals, and the Secret History of Nuclear War* (New York: Simon & Schuster, 2020).
Mark N. Katz, *Leaving Without Losing: The War on Terror After Iraq and Afghanistan* (Baltimore: Johns Hopkins University Press, 2012).
Paul Keckskemeti, *Strategic Surrender: The Politics of Victory and Defeat* (Stanford: Stanford University Press, 1968).
L. Douglas Keeney, *15 Minutes: General Curtis Lemay and the Count-down to Nuclear Annihilation* (New York: Saint Martin's Press, 2011).
Catherine McArdle Kelleher, *Germany & the Politics of Nuclear Weapons* (New York: Columbia Press, 1975).
George F. Kennan, *The Nuclear Delusion: Soviet-American Relations in the Atomic Age* (New York: Pantheon, 1982).
Feroz Hassan Khan, *Eating Grass: The Making of the Pakistani Bomb* (Stanford: Stanford University Press, 2012).
Henry A. Kissinger, *Nuclear Weapons and Foreign Policy: Abridged Edition* (New York: Norton, 1969).
Henry A. Kissinger, *World Order* (New York: Penguin, 2014).
Klaus Knorr, and Read, Thornton, eds., *Limited Strategic War* (New York: Praeger, 1962).
Andrew F. Krepinevich, *7 Deadly Scenarios: A Military Futurist Explores War in the 21st Century* (New York: Bantam, 2009).
William Langewiesche, *The Atomic Bazaar: The Rise of the Nuclear Poor* (New York: Farrar, Straus, and Girouh, 2007).
Jeffrey A. Larsen, and Kartchner, Kerry M., eds., *On Limited Nuclear War in the 21st Century* (Stanford: Stanford Security Studies, 2013).
Michael Levi, *On Nuclear Terrorism* (Cambridge: Harvard University Press, 2007).
Bobo Lo, *Axis of Convenience: Moscow, Beijing, and the New Geopolitics* (London: Chatham House, 2008).
Julius London, and White, Gilbert F., *The Environmental Effects of Nuclear War* (Boulder: Westview Press, 1984).
Edward N. Luttwak, *The Political Uses of Seapower* (Baltimore: Johns Hopkins University Press, 1974).
Michael Mandelbaum, *The Nuclear Future* (Ithaca: Cornell University Press, 1983).
John J. Mearsheimer, *Conventional Deterrence* (Ithaca: Cornell University Press, 1983).
Zhores Medvedev, *The Legacy of Chernobyl* (New York: Norton, 1990).
H. Peter Metzger, *The Atomic Establishment* (New York: Simon & Schuster, 1972).

Richard W. Mies, "Strategic Deterrence in the 21st Century," *Undersea Warfare*, Spring 2012, p.12 (Washington DC: U.S. Navy).
Steven E. Miller, and Van Evera, Stephen, eds., *The Star Wars Controversy* (Princeton: Princeton University Press, 1986).
Patrick M. Morgan, *Deterrence: A Conceptual Analysis* (Beverly Hills: Sage Publications, 1983).
Pervez Musharraf, *In the Line of Fire: A Memoir* (New York: Simon & Schuster, 2006).
Vipin Narang, *Nuclear Strategy in the Modern Era: Regional Powers and International Conflict* (Princeton: Princeton University Press, 2014).
Tom Nichols, Stuart, Douglas, and McCausland, Jeffrey D., eds., *Tactical Nuclear Weapons and NATO* (Carlisle, PA: U.S. Army War College, 2012).
Paul H. Nitze, *From Hiroshima to Glasnost: At the Center of Decision, A Memoir* (New York: Grove Weidenfeld, 1989).
Mahdi Obeidi, and Pitzer, Kurt, *The Bomb in My Garden: The Secrets of Saddam's Nuclear Mastermind* (New York: John Wiley & Sons, 2004).
Noel Perrin, *Giving up the Gun: Japan's Reversion to the Sword, 1543–1879* (Boston: David R. Godine, Publisher, 1979).
William J. Perry, *My Journey at the Nuclear Brink* (Stamford: Stamford University Press, 2015).
William J. Perry, and Schlesinger, James R., *America's Strategic Posture: The Final Report of the Congressional Commission on the Strategic Posture of the United States* (Washington, DC: U.S. Institute of Peace Press, 2009).
Barry R. Posen, *Inadvertent Escalation: Conventional War and Nuclear Risks* (Ithaca: Cornell University Press, 1991).
Charles L. Pritchard, *Failed Diplomacy: The Tragic Story of How North Korea Got the Bomb* (Washington, DC: Brookings Institution Press, 2007).
George H. Quester, *Nuclear Diplomacy: The First Twenty-five Years* (New York: Dunnelen Publishing Co., 1970).
George H. Quester, *Nuclear First Strike: Consequences of a Broken Taboo* (Baltimore: Johns Hopkins University Press, 2006).
Richard Rhodes, *Arsenals of Folly: The Making of the Nuclear Arms Race* (New York: Vintage Books, 2007).
Richard Rhodes, *Dark Sun: The Making of the Hydrogen Bomb* (New York: Simon & Schuster, 1996).
Richard Rhodes, *The Making of the Atomic Bomb* (New York: Simon & Schuster, 1986).

Richard Rhodes, *Nuclear Renewal: Common Sense About Energy* (New York: Penguin Press, 1993).
Richard Rhodes, *The Twilight of the Bombs: Recent Challenges, New Dangers, and the Prospects for a World Without Nuclear Weapons* (New York: Vintage, 2010).
Brad Roberts, *The Case for Nuclear Weapons in the 21st Century* (Stanford: Stanford Security Studies, 2016).
Scott D. Sagan, *The Limits of Safety: Organizations, Accidents, and Nuclear Weapons* (Princeton: Princeton University Press, 1993).
Scott D. Sagan, and Waltz, Kenneth N., *The Spread of Nuclear Weapons: A Debate* (New York: W. W. Norton & Co., 1995).
Thomas C. Schelling, *Arms and Influence* (New Haven: Yale University Press, 1966).
Thomas C. Schelling, *The Strategy of Conflict* (London: Oxford University Press, 1960).
Thomas C. Schelling, and Halperin, Morton H., *Strategy and Arms Control* (New York: Twentieth Century Fund, 1961).
Eric Schlosser, *Command and Control: Nuclear Weapons, the Damascus Accident, and the Illusion of Safety* (New York: Penguin Books, 2013).
Elaine Sciolino, *Persian Mirrors: The Elusive Face of Iran* (New York: Touchstone, 2000).
Glenn T. Seaborg with Loeb, Benjamin S., *Stemming the Tide: Arms Control in the Johnson Years* (Lexington: Heath & Co., 1987).
Anthony Sokol, *Sea Power in the Nuclear Age* (Washington, DC: Public Affairs Press, 1961).
Etel Solingen, *Nuclear Logics: Contrasting Paths in East Asia & The Middle East* (Princeton: Princeton University Press, 2007).
Etel Solingen, ed., *Sanctions, Statecraft, and Nuclear Proliferation* (Cambridge: Cambridge University Press, 2012).
Sherry Sontag, and Drew, Christopher, et. al., *Blind Man's Bluff: The Untold Story of American Submarine Espionage* (New York: Public Affairs, 1998).
Tom Stefanick, *Strategic Antisubmarine Warfare and Naval Strategy* (Lexington: D.C. Heath & Co., 1987).
Alix Strachey, *The Unconscious Motives of War: A Psycho-Analytic Contribution* (London: Unwin House, 1957).
Strobe Talbott, *Engaging India: Diplomacy, Democracy, and the Bomb* (Washington, DC: Brookings Institute Press, 2004).
The Weapons of Mass Destruction Commission, *Freeing the World of Nuclear, Chemical, and Biological Weapons* (Stockholm: Weapons of Mass Destruction Commission, 2006).

Jeffrey Till, ed., *Maritime Strategy and the Nuclear Age*, Second Edition (New York: St. Martins, 1984).

Al J. Venter, *Allah's Bomb: The Islamic Quest for Nuclear Weapons* (Guilford, CT: The Lyons Press, 2007).

Jerome B. Weisner, *Where Science and Politics Meet* (New York: McGraw-Hill, 1965).

Mason Willrich, ed., *International Safeguards and Nuclear Industry* (Baltimore: Johns Hopkins University Press, 1973).

Toshi Yoshihara, and Holmes, James R., *Strategy in the Second Nuclear Age: Power, Ambition, and the Ultimate Weapon* (Washington, DC: Georgetown University Press, 2012).

ACKNOWLEDGMENTS

U.S. Navy Submariners—both active duty and retired—are by nature rather reticent people, serving as they do in what, since early World War II, has been called (rightly, and accurately) the Silent Service. Accordingly, many of those folks who deserve acknowledgement here do prefer to remain anonymous. But they know who they are, and they have my sincerest thanks and admiration.

Over the years, many military people have helped my writing one way or another, including via informal encouragement, or by performing formal peer review and fact checking of my novels and my non-fiction, or by answering (at the UNCLASS level, of course) those technical and procedural questions that I couldn't find answers to for myself during my avid reading of the open literature. Many of these fine men and women made a beneficial contribution to shaping my work simply by welcoming me onto their bases and their ships—as nuclear subs are always called, not "boats"—and even into their social circles, letting me learn who they are as individuals, and what their very special cultures and traditions are all about.

I do want to call out for particular thanks the Naval Submarine League (of which I am a Life Member and Corporate Member), and especially current national executive director Tim Oliver, former *The Submarine Review* editor Jim Hay, former New London, CT Chapter president Ray Woolrich, and personal friend Jim Patton, Jr. Much thanks also go to the United States Submarine Veterans, Inc. (of which

I am an Associate Life Member), and to many of its members around the country including John "Gumba" Carciopollo, Steve Hallquist, Joe Campisi, Joe Shapona, and the late Bob Ondek. I also owe great appreciation to Peter Huessy, president of GeoStrategic Analysis, for so often putting me on the right track about the influences on American nuclear-deterrence posture of both domestic political factionalism, and foreign disinformation trolling.

Last and by no means at all least, I want to thank my wife of 35+ years, Sheila Buff, a successful non-fiction author, co-author, freelance editor, and book doctor, for her myriad well-informed inputs about writing and publishing, and for her immensely valuable professional encouragement and her devoted personal support.

INDEX

-B-

-D-

-N-

-O-

-T-

-U-

-V-

ABOUT THE AUTHOR

Joe Buff grew up in New York City. Winning a Westinghouse National Science Talent Search college scholarship at age 15 and later a National Science Foundation fellowship to grad school, he earned a BA in Math from NYU and an MS in algebraic topology from MIT. He became a Fellow of the Society of Actuaries (FSA) in 1980, spending twenty years working on quantitative modeling, risk-mitigation strategies, and process enhancement in the insurance industry, on Wall Street, and as a partner in a Top 10 global management consulting firm.

In 1997, Joe established Joe Buff, Inc., "An Independent Defense Think Tank of One." He penned six novels in the award winning, best-selling "Captain Jeffrey Fuller/USS Challenger" future submarine warfare series. Joe has also published hundreds of essays, op-eds, and articles for various military-related journals and websites. Five of his articles won Annual Literary Awards from the Naval Submarine League, of which Joe is a Life Member and a Corporate Member; his latest novel *Seas of Crisis* won the 2006 Admiral Nimitz Award for Outstanding Naval Fiction from the Military Writers Society of America. Joe Buff Inc. has been a member of the Submarine Industrial Base Council for a decade."

In early 2015, Joe began an ongoing project to research the theoretical and practical open questions and conundrums behind effective 21st-century nuclear deterrence Best Practices, and he is now writing a multi-volume book series about his conclusions and recommendations.

Joe and his wife of 35+ years, Sheila, live in New York State's scenic, rural Mid-Hudson Valley. Sheila is a NY Times bestselling author and co-author of books about health, wellness, nutrition, and medicine. Both Buffs are keen dog lovers, bird watchers, and avid gym-goers. (They got a home Bowflex during the COVID crisis.) Joe's leisure/hobby interests also include astronomy, history, and the workings of America's railroad industry.

Joe can be reached at readermail@joebuff.com. He welcomes your feedback!